D1572520

Mandarin Ducks and Butterflies

Mandarin Ducks

POPULAR FICTION IN EARLY

and Butterflies

TWENTIETH-CENTURY CHINESE CITIES

E. Perry Link, Jr.

University of California Press, Berkeley, Los Angeles, London

University of California Press
Berkeley and Los Angeles, California

University of California Press, Ltd.
London, England

© 1981
The Regents of the University of California
Printed in the United States of America

1 2 3 4 5 6 7 8 9

Library of Congress Cataloging in Publication Data

Link, Eugene Perry, 1944–
  Mandarin ducks and butterflies. Popular fiction in
early twentieth-century Chinese cities

  Bibliography: p.
  Includes index.
  1. Chinese fiction — 20th century — History and
criticism. I. Title.
PL2442.L5   895.1'35'09   80–15149
ISBN 0-520-04111-9

for Jean

Contents

Preface   ix
Abbreviations Used in Notes   xi

1   Introduction   1

2   The Love Stories of the 1910s   40
     1. Jade Pear Spirit   41
     2. The Love Story Wave   54
     3. The Romantic Route   64

3   The Rise of the Fiction Press   79
     1. The Early Growth of Modern Printing
       in Shanghai   80
     2. The Beginnings of the Modern Newspaper
       Press in Shanghai   95

4   From Nation-Building to Time-Killing to Profit:
     The Early Stages in Modern Entertainment Fiction   125
     1. Liang Ch'i-ch'ao's Advocacy of
       Modern Fiction   129
     2. Progenitors: Late-Ch'ing Fiction   133
     3. The Influence of "Idle Amusement" Invades
       the New Fiction   140
     4. The Discovery of Commercial Profit in
       "Idle Amusement" Journalism   149

5   Authors and Readers   156
     1. Life-styles   156
     2. Groups   164
     3. Outlook   170
     4. Art   179
     5. Readership   189

6   Fiction for Comfort   196

Afterword: Popular Fiction in China in 1979   236

Appendix: Magazines of the 1910s   249
Appendix: Photographs   261
Glossary   267
Bibliography   290
Index   301

Preface

Most of the research for this book was done during 1972–1973 with the support of a Fulbright-Hayes Dissertation Research Fellowship. I am also grateful for short-term grants at various stages of writing and revision from the East Asian Research Center at Harvard, the East Asian Institute at Columbia, the Program in East Asian Studies at Princeton, the American Council of Learned Societies, and the Academic Senate of UCLA. I have benefited from discussions with so many people that I cannot possibly list everyone here. I hope all those generous people can accept thanks in this blanket form.

Yet a few must be mentioned for unusual efforts. John K. Fairbank and Andrew J. Nathan lent their fine acuity to the criticism of an earlier version; both gave me many pages of those invaluable comments which are penetrating and practical at the same time. Cyril Birch, Eugene Eoyang, Patrick D. Hanan, Jeffrey C. Kinkley, Frederick W. Mote, and John S. Service have also read the manuscript and saved me from numerous errors and unclarities. Those which remain are my own, of course.

Ezra F. Vogel and Leo O. F. Lee helped me see the value of this research topic at an early stage, and have been unstinting in their support ever since. I wrote an overview of my initial findings for a conference on modern Chinese literature held at Dedham, Massachusetts in August 1974, and basically the same paper was presented to regional China seminars at Columbia (October 1975) and Berkeley (May 1978). I learned much at each of these meetings, especially from sensitive commentaries by C. T. Hsia and Cyril Birch. The overview essay appears in Merle Goldman, ed., *Modern Chinese Literature in the May Fourth Era* (1977), and I am grateful to Harvard University Press for permission to draw upon that essay in parts of chapter one of the present volume.

Since I feel my subject matter is of potential interest to the non-Sinologist who has comparative interests, and to the general reader as well, I have tried to present the material so that most of it can be followed with no knowledge of Chinese and not very much of China. My occasional plot summaries and excerpts of varying length and detail have been inserted to provide the non-specialist with a rudimentary access to the fiction (we have no translations) and, it is hoped, to lure those who read Chinese to try some of it.

P. L.

Guangzhou
January 1980

Abbreviations Used in Notes

CYLHIL   Pao T'ien-hsiao, *Ch'uan-ying-lou hui-i lu* (Hong Kong, 1971)

CYHIL:HP   Pao T'ien-hsiao, *Ch'uan-ying-lou hui-i lu hsü-pien* (Hong Kong, 1973)

YLH   Hsü Chen-ya, *Yü-li hun* (Shanghai, 1914)

YYHTP   Wei Shao-ch'ang, ed., *Yüan-yang hu-tieh p'ai yen-chiu tzu-liao* (Shanghai, 1962)

CHAPTER *1*

Introduction

On the eve of the Communist success in China, Mao Tse-tung told a group of newspapermen that "we have always maintained that the revolution must rely on the masses of the people, on everybody's taking a hand . . . ."[1] Here "we" means the Communist Party of China, but the spirit of Mao's message pervades a wide range of twentieth-century Chinese thought.

Hardly anything, in fact, differentiates Chinese political assumptions of this century from those of the last more clearly than the notion that everyone, all "the people," should participate actively in the processes of the modern nation. Full participation was felt to be vital to national strength. "Can nations be anything but strong," wondered K'ang Yu-wei in 1898, "when their rulers and the millions of their people are united in a single body?"[2] Four years later Liang Ch'i-ch'ao theorized on the "new citizens" *(hsin min)* who would comprise the great new unity; and, though Liang's ideas were challenged by later revolutionaries, his category called *min*, and the assumption of its fundamental importance, continued to find acceptance almost as a matter of course.[3] Attacks on Liang by anti-Manchu revolutionaries appeared in a newspaper significantly titled *The People's Journal (Min pao)*, which was published in Tokyo after 1905. A few years later in Shanghai the revolutionary journals of Yü Yu-jen appeared under names such as *The People Cry (Min hu)*, *The People Sigh (Min hsu)*, and *The People*

1. *Mao Tse-tung hsuan-chi*, 3:1317.
2. Andrew J. Nathan, *Peking Politics, 1918–1923* (Berkeley and Los Angeles, 1976), p. 4; and Richard C. Howard, "The Concept of Parliamentary Government in 19th Century China: A Preliminary Survey" (paper delivered to the University Seminar on Modern East Asia, Columbia University, New York, January 9, 1963), p. 21. The scholar K'ang Yu-wei (1858–1927) authored famous memorials to the throne in the 1890s calling for social and governmental reforms which were aimed at strengthening China. He is known as a "reformist" thinker in contrast to the anti-imperial revolutionaries of the 1900–1910 decade.
3. Liang Ch'i-ch'ao, scholar, editor, and bold advocate of reform, was the outstanding intellectual leader of China's modern generation during 1900–1910, the last Ch'ing decade. See chapter 4; also Hao Chang, *Liang Ch'i-ch'ao and Intellectual Transition in China*; Philip C. Huang, *Liang Ch'i-ch'ao and Modern Chinese Liberalism*; Joseph R. Levenson, *Liang Ch'i-ch'ao and the Mind of Modern China*.

Stand (Min li). "The people" became even more important after the revolution of 1911; a new "people's party" and "people's army"—the Kuomintang and its *min chün*—grew to prominence, acquired ideological support from Sun Yat-sen's "Three People's Principles" *(san-min chu-i),* and so on.

We should question whether *"min"* means literally all of the people in these contexts; the term seems often to have meant only a limited, politically active sector of the populace. With the May Fourth Movement in the late 1910s, a more radical generation of intellectuals, with some influences from Western populism, extended "the people" to include unequivocally everyone, including — often *especially* including—the lower classes. Creative writers produced stories about ricksha pullers, and activists ran night classes for janitors at Peking University.[4] As in the late Ch'ing period, the theoretical importance of the people, now sometimes called the "masses," was commonly assumed among people of widely differing political stance. Writers disposed to "art for art's sake" or "art for life's sake" both depicted the downtrodden with great sympathy; the Communist Party and the Y.M.C.A. alike called for "mass education."

In fact, of course, China's masses were overwhelmingly peasants, and eventually the tides of modern popular nationalism did reach the countryside. But the origins of these influences were urban; populism, if not the populace, came from the modern cities. Some aspects of China's modern popular nationalism have been studied in the form of student movements, labor unions, chambers of commerce, political parties, literary debates, and so on[5]—all primarily urban activities.

4. The ricksha puller may have been second only to the prostitute as a symbol of China's downtrodden masses in the May Fourth tradition. A theoretical recommendation of the ricksha puller topic was made by Hu Shih in April 1918 ("Chien-she ti wen-hsueh ko-ming lun"). Literary examples include short stories such as Lu Hsun, "I-chien hsiao shih" (1920) in *Na-han* (Hong Kong, 1972), pp. 38–40; Yü Ta-fu, "Po-tien" in *Ch'un-feng ch'en-tsui ti wan-shang* (Hong Kong, 1966), pp. 36–47; and Chang T'ien-i, "Tu-liang" in *Chang T'ien-i hsuan-chi* (Hong Kong, 1971), pp. 2–8. There were also poems such as Tsang K'o-chia, "Yang che fu" (1932) in *Sheng-ming ti chiao-han,* 2nd ed. (Hong Kong, 1962), p. 9; and Cheng Min, "The Ricksha Puller" (1942–47?), translated in K. Y. Hsü, *Twentieth-Century Chinese Poetry: An Anthology* (Ithaca, N.Y., 1970), pp. 233–234; and of course Lao She's masterful novel, *Lo-t'o hsiang-tzu* (1938).

5. On student movements see John Israel, *Student Nationalism in China, 1927–1937* (Stanford, 1966) and Tse-tsung Chow, *The May Fourth Movement.* On labor unions see Jean Chesneaux, *The Chinese Labor Movement, 1919–1927.* On chambers of commerce see James Sanford, "Chinese Commercial Organization and Behavior in Shanghai of the Late Nineteenth and Early Twentieth Centuries" (Ph.D. dissertation, Harvard University, 1976). On literary debates see Tsi-an Hsia, *The Gate of Darkness* (Seattle, 1968); Leo Lee, *The Romantic Generation of Modern Chinese Writers;* and Chün-jo Liu's annotated bibliography *Controversies in Modern Chinese Intellectual History: An Analytic Bibliography of Periodical Articles, Mainly on the May Fourth and Post-May Fourth Era* (Cambridge, 1964).

Not until the war against Japan in the 1930s and 1940s do we have an argument for significant "peasant" nationalism.[6] But even this is probably best viewed, if nationalism is to mean something different from native anti-foreignism, as an extension of the urban movement, brought to the countryside by politicized youth whose training and inspiration had originated in the cities. In many ways the gap between life in modern China's changing cities and her not-so-changing countryside grew wider in the early twentieth century. The urban-rural distinction in China may never have been larger than at mid-century.[7] The campaigns of the 1960s and early seventies to send urban youth to the countryside are evidence of the gap's persistence.[8] In short, our understanding of popular nationalism in modern China would seem to depend crucially on our view of its cities.

The study of nationalism, as of any "ism," is a study of ideas, in this case the idea of "loyalty to and the promotion of the culture and interests . . . of one nation" (*Webster's Third New International Dictionary*, 1969). For a society undergoing social change as rapidly as modern China's, the question of what "culture" a nationalist is to promote and be loyal to is complicated by a wide-ranging and oft-cited distinction between "new style" and "old style" life. To understand how people undergoing change felt about this distinction, whose simple formulations belie an extreme complexity, presents the historian of ideas with a considerable challenge.

One major problem is that of access. Aside from the several difficulties of "climbing back into" the mind of anyone anywhere, the problem has been compounded for historians of modern China by the inadequacy of sources. For some sectors of the intellectual and political elite, access has been made easier by the verbal record which has been left behind in speeches, essays, scholarship, autobiography, and creative literature. The value of these records has been amply demonstrated in a number of superior biographical studies of individuals; and some general studies, such as Tse-tsung Chow's *The May Fourth Movement*, Leo Lee's *The Romantic Generation of Modern Chinese Writers*, and Y.C. Wang's *Chinese Intellectuals and the West*, have been able to reach conclusions about the outlooks of certain elite groups as wholes.

6. Chalmers A. Johnson, *Peasant Nationalism and Communist Power, The Emergence of Revolutionary China, 1937–1945* (Stanford, 1962).

7. The argument that there is little evidence of a sharp distinction between urban and rural life in pre-modern China is made by F. W. Mote, "The City in Traditional Chinese Civilization," in James T. C. Liu and Wei-ming Tu, eds., *Traditional China* (Englewood Cliffs, N.J., 1970), pp. 42–49.

8. On the movement of urban youth to the countryside in the People's Republic of China, see Thomas Bernstein, *Up to the Mountains and Down to the Villages: The Transfer of Youth from Urban to Rural China* (New Haven, 1977).

Crucial as these accesses are, they give us the views of only a small portion of society. Members of the elite did, to be sure, frequently try to speak on behalf of everyone, expressing their views of what the masses' outlook appears to have been. But one should not assume these projections to coincide with the actual views of those who were spoken for. There is still a need, ideally speaking, for unmediated access to the views of the non-elite.

Who were the common people in modern Chinese cities? Generalizations must of course vary with the type of city in question, and in particular with the age and strength of its traditional functions versus the size and nature of its modern, Western-influenced activities.

As an example we might consider the cities of Soochow and Shanghai in the lower Yangtze Basin. Soochow, in the middle of the nineteenth century, was a provincial capital, the second largest city in China, and an important center of the civil service examinations and other aspects of cultural orthodoxy. Shanghai, on the other hand, was little more than a county seat and foreign outpost until refugees from the T'aip'ing Wars began to swell its population in the 1860s. After 1895, when the Treaty of Shimonoseki with Japan legalized foreign manufacturing in Shanghai, the city's population grew rapidly to nearly a million as textiles, flour, cigarettes and other industries supplemented its banking and commercial functions. When World War I curtailed Western competition in Chinese and Southeast Asian markets, Shanghai's economy received another impetus, attracted more immigration, and grew to more than a million and a half.[9]

Shanghai's growth and Soochow's decline should be viewed as parts of the same process. With the end of the civil service examinations in 1905 and the Republican revolution of 1911, Soochow increasingly came to be regarded as simply a pleasant residential area, a sort of backdrop for Shanghai's "new-style" leadership in commerce and industry, and eventually in politics and even art. Soochow parents who formerly forbade their children to go to Shanghai came to permit this more freely; merchants who had scorned Shanghai business increasingly allowed themselves its profits; intellectuals who had been devoted to the civil service exams now shifted their attention to the discussion societies and new journals of Shanghai. In Shanghai itself, many of the emerging professions, both new and old, came to be known as specialties of Soochow people: lawyers, druggists, silk merchants, pawnshop keepers, newspapermen, fiction writers, moneylenders and prostitutes in Shanghai were among vocations considered Soochow specialties.[10]

9. Rhoads Murphey, *Shanghai: Key to Modern China*, pp. 20–22 and 167–168.
10. See CYLHIL, pp. 216 and 317; also CYLHIL:HP, pp. 106–107.

how to define
小市民?

One can easily identify upper and lower classes in sorting out the various occupations in early twentieth-century Shanghai. Wealthy bankers, merchants, and industrialists—in the economic sphere—and politicians, some writers, intellectuals, and students—in the political-intellectual sphere—must be counted as a social elite. On the other hand, a lower class consisted of industrial workers, mostly from the lower Yangtze countryside, plus manual laborers such as servants, coolies, ricksha pullers, peddlers, and many others.

But it seems necessary to posit a third major class between these two. Contemporary Chinese descriptions of Shanghai often refer to *hsiao-shih-min* ("little city people") which *Han-yü tz'u-tien* explains as "the middle class or the petty bourgeoisie." The term is taken to include small merchants, various kinds of clerks and secretaries, high school students, housewives, and other modestly educated, marginally well off urbanites.

Except for the obvious differences between this group and the middle class of the modern West and Japan—a class peculiar in world history for its great affluence despite considerable distance from elite power or prestige—there might be no cause to apologize for use of the term "middle class." *Hsiao shih-min* were, without doubt, in the middle. Their literacy, which opened several occupational doors to them, clearly set them off from the urban laboring classes to whom these doors were closed. On the other hand, most of the new occupations did not bring the rapid wealth they seemed to promise, and *hsiao shih-min* were obliged to live well below the standards of the wealthy class. In intellectual terms they were also distinct from the generally more progressive elite, who advocated "new-style" ideas more readily than this urban middle class could comfortably tolerate. Many *hsiao shih-min* were from inland gentry backgrounds, knew little of the West, and apparently felt insecure in a modern, semi-Westernized city like Shanghai. Their basic tendency, in a Shanghai context, seems to have been conservative. While intellectual leaders often took them as the intended audience for urgent messages on reform and revolution, the fact that these attempts at leadership were so difficult is itself an important reason for distinguishing the two groups.

Returning to the question of access to "the mind" of urban China in the early twentieth century, we must now ask what is known, or knowable, about the ideas and attitudes of its two non-elite classes, the lower class and the *hsiao shih-min*.

The urban laboring classes have been studied by Jean Chesneaux and others.[11] Though Chesneaux does not focus primarily on ideas

11. Chesneaux, *Chinese Labor;* L. K. Tao, *The Standard of Living Among Chinese Workers;* Sung-ho Lin, *Factory Workers in Tungku.*

and attitudes (some attention is given to the ideas of labor organizers, usually not themselves from the laboring class), a certain amount may be surmised from his accounts of urban workers' histories and environments. Chesneaux is not to be faulted for stopping where he does, given the difficulty of reaching the realm of ideas for the people he studies.

The present work is an attempt to crack the problem in another way. It began as an attempt to understand popular ideas and attitudes in Chinese cities during the 1910s and 1920s through the study of the urban popular fiction which boomed during those decades. In the course of research I have become satisfied that the approach has great potential, but probably less for the working class than for the *hsiao shih-min* whom I have just called the urban "middle class." In the decade of the 1910s China's urban popular fiction was written primarily in a semi-classical language too difficult for the working class. Even more important is the fact that books in the 1910s cost much more than a worker could afford. The picture was somewhat different in the twenties, however, when popular fiction seems to have been enjoyed by a good portion of the working class in addition to the middle class. In the twenties almost all popular fiction was in vernacular style (influenced by, but not part of, the May Fourth Movement),[12] while new schools in cities like Shanghai had brought minimal literacy to more people, including some parts of the working class. The prices of books and magazines came down and popular fiction also began to appear in comic books, moving pictures, and radio storytelling, all of which were cheaper to enjoy than books as well as less demanding of literacy.

Establishing that a given audience enjoyed certain stories or kinds of story is, of course, only a first step in access to the "mind" of that audience. There are obviously many possibilities for the general relation between a work of fiction and the psychology of its reader. (To say nothing of influences on the readers' actual behavior, which is another knotty problem: everyone knows that most readers of murder stories are not themselves murderers.) I do make some conjectures on the fiction-and-popular-mind relation, especially in chapter six, and my arguments there may or may not be valid. In either case, however,

12. The term "May Fourth Movement" is used by scholars, and by the Chinese public, in two senses. Narrowly it refers to a student demonstration which was held in Peking on May 4, 1919, to protest the Chinese government's docility in accepting Japan's special rights in Shantung after World War I. More broadly, the term refers to the intellectual ferment associated with this demonstration and other activities of young modernizers and radicals both before and after 1919. See Chow, *May Fourth Movement;* on literature, see Merle Goldman, ed., *Modern Chinese Literature in the May Fourth Era* (Cambridge, 1977), and C. T. Hsia, *A History of Modern Chinese Fiction* (New Haven, 1971).

the basic working hypothesis I use, that there has to be *some* important connection between an especially popular work and the psychology of its audience, is, I feel, beyond serious doubt. Possible alternative explanations, for China in the early twentieth century, might attribute a story's popularity to deliberate commercial or political effort at its promotion, but these appear to have been minor factors except for a few, marginally popular works.

A second aim of the present work is to place China's popular fiction of the 1910s and 1920s in a context of literary history. Disparaged since the early twenties as the Mandarin Duck and Butterfly School (yuan-yang hu-tieh p'ai), this substantial corpus of fiction has remained largely untouched by literary historians. Existing accounts in Chinese, Japanese, and Western languages all tend to move from late Ch'ing[13] fiction to the May Fourth Movement, either skipping over the popular fiction of the 1910s or giving it brief treatment as a special category isolated from what came before and after. The present study will leave us short of definitive statements about the overall role of popular fiction in modern China, but the author will feel well rewarded if others are induced to take the question further.

A word is in order on the use of the label "Mandarin Duck and Butterfly School." It was first used in the late 1910s to refer disparagingly to the classical-style love stories of a small, but very widely read, group of authors who made liberal use of the traditional symbols of mandarin ducks and butterflies for pairs of lovers.[14] Originally the term was used narrowly and precisely to refer to this group, including Hsu Chen-ya, Li Ting-i, Wu Shuang-je and a few others, plus the group's imitators. But beginning in the early 1920s, the term was given a dramatically larger scope by ardent young writers of the May Fourth Movement. Cheng Chen-to, Mao Tun and many others began using the term to lead an attack on *all* kinds of popular old-style fiction. This included not only love stories but "social" novels, "knight-errant" novels, "scandal" novels, "detective" novels, "imagination" novels, "comic" novels and many other kinds. The consequent ambiguity in applying the term has persisted to the present day. Communist writings have meant it to include every kind of

13. The Ch'ing period is A.D. 1644–1911. I use "late Ch'ing" to refer to its final twenty years, or sometimes "last Ch'ing decade" for the final ten.

14. P'ing Chin-ya, a popular author in the 1910s, has written an account of the term "Mandarin Duck and Butterfly" in which he says it first came up in a word game at a Shanghai banquet in 1920. Following the publication of P'ing's account in 1962, it has been widely but uncritically repeated as the "origin" of the term. In fact, by 1920 the term had been in use for at least two years among detractors of popular fiction. The dinner party incident may have been the first time that popular writers themselves ironically accepted the term.

"old-style" fiction, while non-Communist writings generally use it to mean love stories only. A certain amount of confusion and even acrimony has attended the ambiguity. In the present work the broader definition (usually abbreviated to "Butterfly") is sometimes used, but only as a matter of convenience. It is intended that the reference be value-free, as the question of quality in "Butterfly" fiction should be determined on a case-by-case basis.

In addition to the context of Chinese tradition, it is important to view "Butterfly" fiction in an international context. Without overlooking its distinctively Chinese elements, one may easily recognize that various aspects of its historical setting, as well as some of its literary characteristics, are remarkably similar to those of urban popular fiction in other countries which have been part of the global spread of the Industrial Revolution. The extent to which modern life patterns are inherent consequences of industrialism may not be entirely clear; but modern-style entertainment fiction (or television, in recent decades) has, for one example, consistently appeared in tandem with industrialism around the world. From beginnings in eighteenth-century England this kind of fiction spread to Western Europe and America, in many cases through direct borrowing as stories were reprinted or translated across international boundaries.[15]

In East Asia, Japan was first to display the trend. In the 1870s and 1880s, primarily in Osaka and Tokyo, Japanese translated and imitated popular Western writers like Charles Dickens, H. Rider Haggard, and Jules Verne as a way of supplying the needs and curiosities of a new urban audience. Other items were not fiction but popular investigations of life and *mores* in the West, works which should be viewed as creative Japanese contributions to international entertainment litera-

15. England, the birthplace of modern popular fiction, was also first to study it critically. An article in *Contemporary Review* (London) in July 1881 (vol. 40, pp. 25–44) by Thomas Wright, "On a Possible Popular Culture," led in succeeding years to a number of similar articles such as "Penny Fiction" (J. H. Millar, *Blackwoods Magazine*, vol. 164, no. 998, December 1898, pp. 801–811) and "Cheap Literature" (Helen Bosanquet, *Contemporary Review*, vol. 79, 1901, pp. 671–681). Elegantly written for an elite audience, these pieces touch upon many interesting questions but achieve little analytical depth. Not until Queenie D. Leavis, *Fiction and the Reading Public*, do we have a serious account, though still perhaps too elitist, of forms and functions of English popular fiction. In 1957, with the appearance of Richard Altick's *The English Common Reader* and Richard Hoggart's *The Uses of Literacy*, the field advanced greatly in both depth and scope, although Hoggart's book is not about literature per se. Leo Lowenthal's *Literature, Popular Culture, and Society* (Englewood Cliffs, N.J., 1961) is also noteworthy. The American case is interestingly dealt with in Leslie Fiedler's *Love and Death in the American Novel* (New York, 1960) and in John G. Cawelti's *The Six-gun Mystique*. For references on Japan see note 16 below.

ture.[16] All these materials were printed ever more cheaply and abundantly on modern presses.

Beginning in the early twentieth century, Shanghai, the first Chinese city to undergo modern urbanization, also produced an outpouring of entertainment fiction. Most of the early examples, especially of fiction, came via Japanese translation, and China's pattern in modern entertainment fiction followed Japan's in its major outlines. On a trip to Japan in the 1910s, a leading Chinese writer-translator noted similarities between the modern press in Osaka and Shanghai, including its spread to the national centers at Tokyo and Peking respectively.[17] In the wake of its borrowings from Japan, Chinese writers looked increasingly to China's own vernacular tradition for models for their work.

Regardless of whether inspirations were native or foreign, fundamental themes were much the same. As in Europe, America, and Japan, the major types of modern popular fiction in China were: (1) love stories, (2) righteous-hero adventures, (3) scandal, or "muckraking" stories, and (4) detective stories. Each of these themes, however altered by modern circumstances, had strong roots in the Chinese vernacular tradition, i.e., (1) The love-story tradition of *ts'ai-tzu chia-jen* or "talent-meets-beauty" stories, plus, to a certain extent, *Dream of the Red Chamber;* (2) *The Water Margin, Tale of Heroic Young Lovers (Erh-nü ying-hsiung chuan)* and the whole "knight-errant" tradition; (3) *Forest of Scholars* and the late-Ch'ing "blame" novels; and (4) Ch'ing "public case" *(kung-an)* stories such as *The Cases of Judge Peng (P'eng kung-an).*

In terms of literary styles, modern popular fiction both East and West was distinct from elite fiction in ways which generally mark it as "popular." Stories often tell of strange, unusual events; their plots take unexpected turns; most of their leading characters are flatly all-good or all-bad; many are expressed in simple, direct language (though there are important exceptions to this); and most are filled with action, sparse with description.[18]

Since these same stylistic features were prominent in the vernacular tradition, and since themes likewise were similar, one might ask what sets "Butterfly" fiction off from its literary predecessors. Was it a matter of social role, as a wholesale supplier of urban entertainment? Cer-

16. See Senuma Shigeki, *Hon no hyakunen shi,* pp. 19–72; Shoji Sensui, *Nihon no shomotsu,* esp. pp. 93-133; and George Bailey Sansom, *The Western World and Japan.* For background on the Meiji periodical press see Nishida Taketoshi, *Meiji jidai no shimbun to zasshi.* Earl Kinmonth has made a study of the achievement ethic in Meiji popular literature in "The Self-Made Man in Meiji Japanese Thought."

17. CYLHIL, p. 438.

18. For the English case, see Leavis, *Fiction,* pp. 53, 58, 62, and Part III, chs. 1–2.

tainly popular entertainment was nothing new in Chinese cities, nor was fiction new as one of its more important modes. Yet in certain ways Butterfly fiction was distinctively a child of the early twentieth century. It was composed, published, distributed, and read (or listened to) differently from in the past. Instead of listening to storytellers at a marketplace or tea shop, increasingly people purchased books (or newspapers, where fiction was serialized), brought them home, and read in private. These changes were facilitated by a sixfold expansion of Shanghai's printing industry from the beginning of the century to the early thirties,[19] and by an apparent doubling or more of the urban literacy rate during the same years.[20] The move indoors to privacy would appear to be part of the general inward-turning tendency, well remarked by sociologists since Simmel, of residents of the modern city who develop a need to escape the onrush of stimuli in increasingly complex environments. The function of Butterfly fiction as a comfort in this circumstance is another feature which tends to set it off from its literary predecessors.

New schools with lofty aims were important in the spread of popular fiction, a fact as ironic in China as in parts of the West. In England, Sunday schools had pioneered the spread of literacy to increasing numbers of town and city youth; in China, the way was led by the reform movement "new schools" *(hsin hsueh-t'ang),* whose numbers appear to have increased from around 4,000 in 1905 to more than 120,000 by the late 1910s.[21] In neither case had it been foreseen that an ability to read about God or national self-strengthening would afford youngsters access to love and scandal stories as well.

Though Butterfly fiction eventually spread to most parts of China, Shanghai, from the 1910s on, was always its center. (In the 1920s and 1930s Tientsin became second most important.) Most of the major authors had come to Shanghai during the first decade of the century from gentry backgrounds in interior cities, primarily Soochow. Many had lost their fathers in childhood, and had also lost, in the collapse of the civil service examination system, their traditional route to success. In searching for alternatives they hit upon fiction writing partly because, around 1900, Shanghai publishers began paying for manuscripts. Politically, they stood on the fringes of the reform-and-

19. Chang Ching-lu, comp., *Chung-kuo ch'u-pan shih-liao pu-pien,* p. 279.
20. This approximation is based on: (1) the estimates of publishers of popular material in Shanghai during these years, specifically Pao T'ien-hsiao, Ch'en Ting-shan, and Ch'eng She-wo, in interviews with the author; and (2) evidence on primary school enrollment in H. T. Montagne Bell and H. G. W. Woodhead, *The China Year Book 1912* (London, 1912), p. 323, and H. G. W. Woodhead, *The China Year Book 1924* (Tientsin, 1925), p. 252.
21. Chow, *May Fourth Movement,* p. 379.

revolution ferment of their times; though firmly grounded in Confucian morality, they would stylishly adorn their stories with a few of the progressive "new-style" ideas of the day. In general they maintained lighthearted appearances, pretending detachment from the woes of the world and fashioning for themselves a variety of eccentric life-styles. They were generally friendly with one another and frequently came together for banquets, good cheer, and literary games.

There can be little doubt that their merrymaking covered feelings of bitterness and insecurity. Deprived of the traditional ladder of success, and handicapped in climbing the new one because of their conservative orientations, they had ample reason to feel cheated of proper outlets for their talent. Much of their playful fiction may be read as the message "life is but a game"; even their tragic themes, often cast in expansive Buddhist metaphors, served to provide comfort, the comfort of demonstrating that "some people, Dear Reader, are much worse off than you and I."

The fiction of modern cities in the West is known for a distinction of "elite" and "popular" levels. For Butterfly fiction in the 1910s such a distinction is difficult to support. This fiction generally represented the upper and middle classes together, while the masses, even the urban masses, had no modern fiction of any kind. With the 1920s, though, there came several important changes in this situation. First, the cultural revolution of the May Fourth Movement in the early 1920s brought to the fore a number of young writers—ardent, nationalistic, and comparatively Westernized—who displaced Butterfly writers from several prominent positions and challenged their leadership of the literary scene. The most important example of this changeover came in December 1920, when the Commercial Press relieved the Butterfly group of its control of a leading fiction magazine, *The Short Story Monthly (Hsiao-shuo yueh-pao),* and handed it over to May Fourth writers under the leadership of Mao Tun and Cheng Chen-to. The young writers of May Fourth proceeded to establish themselves among a better-educated, and more Westernized, but substantially smaller readership than that of Butterfly writers. For the decade of the 1910s it thus becomes easier to identify Butterfly fiction as "popular" and May Fourth literature as "elite" in the modern senses of these terms.

Another reason for calling Butterfly fiction popular in the twenties is its increased commercialization and use of new media. Before the twenties, nearly all Butterfly stories had been published in expensive fiction magazines, with the most popular works later appearing as books. Publishers in the 1910s normally operated with a target figure of only 3,000 copies for books and magazines, which was the minimum sales necessary to recover costs.[22] A circulation of more than 50,000 was rare. In the 1920s, however, when the most popular stories were also made into movies, comic strips, stage plays and even scripts for traditional-style drum-singing, "circulation" (including viewers and listeners as well as readers) reached well into the 100,000s, and perhaps over a million.[23]

The importance of the new media lay not only in their understandability by the barely literate and illiterate, but also in their lower cost. Instead of paying fifty cents (.5 yuan) for a book, about half a week's pay for many people, one could see a movie for two cents or less.[24] Comic books could be rented for even smaller amounts, or, if bought, could be traded and passed around among friends. Fiction magazines also lowered their prices and continued to flourish. Shanghai's leading commercial newspapers serialized some of the biggest hit novels of the twenties in daily fiction columns, the most important of which were *Hsin-wen pao*'s "Forest of Lightheartedness" ("K'uai-huo lin") and *Shen pao*'s "Unfettered Talk" ("Tzu-yu t'an").[25]

Newspaper serialization of fiction had important implications for publishers, authors and readers alike. For publishers it provided the chance to sell newspapers with more regularity by hooking readers on a story line. Especially popular novels not only maintained a newspaper's circulation but could substantially increase it. From a writer's point of view, a leading newspaper could establish one's reputation with a single novel. For readers, newspaper fiction was much less expensive than books. So at least it seemed to be, since the daily outlay was small and one got the news as well, making the fiction seem like a kind of bonus. Opportunity for exchange between readers and authors in newspaper letter columns increased the attraction to readers.

Much of the use of new commercialized media conforms to the general pattern of modern popular fiction in the West. In the 1830s the circulation of the *London Times* soared to 40,000 with the serialization of *The Pickwick Papers* in much the same way that the *Hsin-wen pao* reached a level of 150,000 shortly after its 1929–30 serialization of what was probably the most widely read Chinese novel in the first half of the twentieth century, Chang Hen-shui's *Fate in Tears and Laughter*

22. CYLHIL, p. 377.

23. See note 32 for a calculation of readership size.

24. William J. Reilly, "China Kicks in with a Champion," *Moving Picture World* (April 26, 1919), quoted in Jay Leyda, *Dianying: Electric Shadows. An Account of Films and the Film Audience in China* (Cambridge, 1972), p. 25.

25. In the present text the titles *Hsin-wen pao* and *Shen pao* are used throughout, in accordance with the Wade-Giles romanization system. The newspapers themselves, however, romanized their names as *Sin Wan Pao* and *Shun Pao*, respectively.

(T'i-hsiao yin-yuan).[26] This novel clearly establishes the "modern popular" character of twentieth-century urban fiction in China. The book, two movies, several stage plays and many comic book versions were all in circulation at once; a serialization in popular storytelling form was done for radio; the author was suing for his copyright; a leading actress in the movie was reported (falsely, as a commercial device to spur interest) to have committed suicide. The story's characters gained a kind of supra-fictional reality, as if "friends" of the public. Popular magazines referred to them as if they were real people. Sequels telling of their latest adventures issued from many quarters, and readers besieged the author with letters asking for more of the true story. Clearly, word-of-mouth had become an important new "medium" of the culture of popular fiction.[27]

The new media and the expanded market of the 1920s had a significant impact on the literary and personal styles of popular authors. Many of their stories in the 1910s had been translations, but in the twenties almost all were original. Most short stories had appeared in a kind of classical, or quasi-classical language; now, influenced by May Fourth, most were in vernacular style. Payment for manuscripts, which had been systematized during the period 1900 to 1910, was a supplementary and occasional source of income for writers in the 1910s; but during the twenties such payments were sufficient to nourish a new breed of commercial writers. Rates of pay, up from the 1910s standard of two yuan per thousand characters, now reached four or six yuan, sometimes higher. Leading authors could contract in more than one city to write serialized novels for as many as six or seven newspapers simultaneously; some newspapers hired fiction specialists on a permanent basis. Movie companies also paid handsomely. Writers used Buddhist metaphors less often and their topics became more "modern." Meanwhile the group spirit that writers had enjoyed in the 1910s diminished as individual enterprise grew. Between the traditional images of the lettered gentleman on the one hand and the street-corner storyteller on the other, a middle literary identity developed dramatically beyond what it had been before: this was the producer of mass commercial fiction, who wrote for the appetite of

26. On the Times of London see Altick, *Common Reader,* p. 279; on *Hsin-wen pao* see Lin Yutang, *A History of the Press and Public Opinion in China,* p. 145.

27. See P'ang Kuan-ch'ing, "T'i-hsiao yin-yuan Tien-ying shuang pao an," *Ta-jen,* 4:45–47; Fan Yen-ch'iao, "Min-kuo chiu-p'ai hsiao-shuo shih-lüeh," in YYHTP, p. 200; Yen Tu-ho, "T'i-hsiao yin-yüan, Yen Tu-ho hsü" (Shanghai: San-yu shu-she, 1930); Fan Chi-p'ing, " 'Wo ti t'ung-shih' Chang Hen-shui," *Ta-jen,* 16:60–62; interviews with Hu Tieh, July 24, 1973, and Ch'eng She-wo, July 23, 1973; Ch'en Tieh-i, " 'Li-pai liu p'ai' wen-hsien," No. 9, *Hsing-tao jih-pao,* October 26, 1973.

"average readers" he could not see and did not know, but to whom he could become a popular hero and in whose numbers he measured his success.[28]

Most authors remained reluctant to admit this new identity publicly. Some actually resisted it, despite its lucre and its glamor; those who pursued it unabashedly preferred to announce higher motives, such as nationalism or reformist zeal. For example, in a 1937 preface to his best-selling *Female Knight of the Wild Rivers (Huang-chiang nü-hsia)*, author Ku Ming-tao expounded upon the salubrious effects of knight-errant fiction. The Western countries and Japan, he explained, have regarded China as a "sick man" and a "sleeping lion." Yet in the Spring and Autumn Period (770–476 B.C.) China was once full of martial vigor. Today:

> . . . it's a pity indeed that this hundred-times refined steel has become soft enough to twist around your little finger. An effeminacy has obscured the martial spirit of our ancestors and a gloomy darkness has descended upon us until, today, we bow and scrape before foreign cavalries. Foreign insult is pervasive. The nation's plight is severe. China faces the worry of sinking. How excruciating! If we want to convert weakness to strength, and restore atrophied muscle, then we must promote militarist popular education and revive the gallantry of our ancient martial arts, spread their traditional techniques, train the people's physical spirit, and encourage nationalistic literature . . .

Naturally, Ku's kind of knight-errant fiction could help:

> . . . for all the above reasons, knight-errant novels are a very good kind of reading. It is no surprise that they have seen a wave of popularity in recent years. It's a pity that some distributors and authors, seeking selfish little profits, have produced a flood of crude works which, like fish eyes parading as pearls, contain extravagant descriptions and preposterous overstatement which borders on fantasy and insults the world. As a result, the value of knight-errant fiction has gradually declined. But how can we, just because we are choked with putrid fare, conclude that *all* knight-errant fiction is not worth reading? We still need it . . .[29]

Needed or not, knight-errant fiction has remained very popular to the present day.

Yet it was also in the 1930s that Butterfly fiction as a whole began to lose its predominant hold on China's urban readership. May Fourth

---

28. "His" may be taken literally here. Of hundreds of better-known Butterfly writers, not one was a woman. Even ostensible "women's magazines" were in fact dominated by men who used female pseudonyms. See Chapter 5.

29. Ku Ming-tao, *Huang-chiang nü-hsia*, pp. 7–9.

writers like Pa Chin, Mao Tun, and Ts'ao Yü by then were enjoying substantial readership among students and other "new-style" readers who in the 1910s might have read Butterfly stories exclusively. (By 1935 most urban readers no doubt read both kinds of literature, though in somewhat different moods.) Of at least equal importance in the relative decline of Butterfly fiction during the 1930s were the Japanese attacks on China and the consequent feeling of acute national emergency among the urban populace. Public opinion induced some of the leading popular writers, including Chang Hen-shui, Chou Shou-chüan, and Pao T'ien-hsiao, to step unequivocally into the political arena with calls for national unity and resistance of Japan. This move drew them closer to the May Fourth writers, who all along had been saying that literature should serve the modern nation.

At the same time, however, the crisis atmosphere occasioned by the Japanese threat increased the need for laughter and diversion, as the popularity of Lin Yü-t'ang's several humor magazines attests. The conflicting pressures of patriotism and the marketplace brought about a split among the popular authors. A "higher" level turned more towards May Fourth, though still adhering to traditional vernacular style; while a "lower" level, exemplified by Feng Yü-ch'i (who may, incidentally, be the most-published writer in Chinese history) reached new depths of hackneyed content. This "lower" level produced many hundreds of novels through the thirties and forties, a flow which was curtailed only with the Communist victory in 1949. Even then the traces of Butterfly fiction were not wholly eradicated. Stage performances of *Fate in Tears and Laughter* continued as late as 1962, and old books from the 1910s and 1920s could be found at bookstalls until the onset of the Cultural Revolution in 1966.[30] In Hong Kong and Taiwan the Butterfly tradition has remained very much alive, although sometimes in a more Westernized form.

It is probably impossible to achieve an accurate count of Butterfly fiction. The index of the only reference work in the field, Wei Shao-ch'ang's *Research Materials on the Mandarin Duck and Butterfly School* (Shanghai, 1962) lists a total of 2,215 novels, plus 113 magazines and 49 newspapers and tabloids which carried Butterfly fiction. The list of 2,215 does not include most of the serialized magazine and newspaper novels, nor does it include short stories (which easily outnumbered

---

30. On the stage performance of Butterfly stories after 1949, see (no author) "Yüan-yang hu-tieh p'ai tui hsi-chü ti ying-hsiang ho p'ing-lun chieh tui t'a ti p'ing-lun," *Hsin-hua yueh-pao,* January 1964, pp. 269–270. The availability of Butterfly fiction at bookstalls was demonstrated to me in 1972 by Pao T'ien-hsiao, who presented me in Hong Kong with a novel which he had written in the 1910s and which his friend (and fellow populist writer) Cheng I-mei had found for sale in Shanghai in early 1966.

the long novels), most translation novels (hundreds or more in the 1910s),[31] many sequels to the popular novels, or the many novels by unknown writers who, trying to sell, would pirate a famous writer's pen name. Including these considerations, it can be safely estimated that the volume of published popular fiction between 1912 and 1949 (including translations) must have reached the equivalent of five or ten thousand average-length novels. By "average length" I mean about 200 pages or 100,000 characters, though some stories were much longer. Li Shou-min's knight-errant story of the late twenties called *Swordsmen of the Szechwan Hills (Shu-shan chien-hsia)* runs to 357 chapters and about 3.7 million characters.

The question of readership size is equally difficult. Publication figures are rare, and those which exist were sometimes inflated for commercial purposes. In addition, copyrights were not observed, geographical distribution was seldom recorded, and most books in circulation had multiple readership. One can only guess at the numbers of people reached through media like movies or radio. Calculating roughly from what we do know, it would appear that in one form or another the most popular stories must have reached between four hundred thousand to a million people in Shanghai during the 1910s and 1920s, when that city's population is estimated to have grown from around 1.4 million to around 3.2 million.[32]

One reason Butterfly fiction has remained unstudied in China is that leading opinion has always disparaged it (a circumstance which

31. In studying the last Ch'ing decade, Ch'ien Hsing-ts'un has noted that around 400 titles appear in the *Han-fen-lou hsin-shu fen-lei mu-lu* and that his own estimate ranges to about three times that number (*Wan-ch'ing hsiao-shuo shih*, p. 1). Though there are no estimates of the number of translation novels and short stories in the 1910s, they would appear to be at least as many as in the late Ch'ing period.

32. This rough estimate is arrived at in the following way. Publishers and authors estimate that the very best-selling novels published in Shanghai during the 1910s and 1920s reached several hundred thousand, perhaps 300,000 to 400,000 or more. ("Very best-selling" refers to standouts like *Yü-li hun;* see Fan Yen-ch'iao, *Min-kuo chiu-p'ai hsiao-shuo shih-lueh* in YYHTP, p. 174.) The same types of informants estimate that perhaps a third to a half of the copies of these high-circulation novels were distributed in Shanghai, the rest being sent to other cities. On the question of multiple readership per volume, through borrowing or renting, Roswell Britton estimates that popular periodicals around 1910 would be shared by perhaps ten to twenty readers per copy (*The Chinese Periodical Press*, p. 129). Lin Yutang cites ten readers per copy as the "number usually given" for multiple readership of newspapers in the early thirties (*Press and Public Opinion*, pp. 148–149). For popular novels in book form, an average of four or five readers per copy would appear a safe, rough estimate, supported by the estimates of Butterfly personnel such as Ch'eng She-wo (interview, July 26, 1973), Pao T'ien-hsiao (Hong Kong, December 6, 1972), and Ch'en Hsiao-tieh (T'aichung, July 25, 1973). These inevitably rough figures yield the estimate of four hundred thousand to one million readers in Shanghai for the most popular novels. The figures on the population of Shanghai are from Murphey, *Shanghai*, pp. 20–22.

recalls parallel cases in the West). A strongly negative interpretation of Butterfly fiction was created in the early twenties by the young May Fourth writers, and this view has been widely accepted, usually uncritically, right to the present day. The May Fourth view does reflect some of the truth, but is quite inadequate to the complexity of the field it surveys.

May Fourth writers argued in the pages of *The Literary Thrice Monthly (Wen-hsueh hsun-k'an)* that since literature should serve social progress, Butterfly works were at best useless and at worst pernicious. Their authors thrived in Shanghai's festering "three-mile foreign mall" *(shih-li yang-ch'ang)* and were comparable, said Cheng Chen-to, to "intellectual bats."[33] They were motivated by unscrupulous greed: "literary prostitutes" in Cheng's phrase, "gold-worshippers" in Mao Tun's.[34] Perhaps worst of all, they monopolized the fiction market and poisoned the minds of youth—"stole the show," as Kuo Mo-jo saw it[35]—thereby depriving May Fourth of its audience. The issue was so urgent and clear-cut that all the early May Fourth groups, setting aside their own factional differences, enthusiastically joined in.

By the late twenties, however, factional strife among the May Fourth writers had diverted their attention from the persisting problem of Butterfly fiction. In 1931, Lu Hsun told the League of Left-Wing Writers:

> Last year and the year before, the scope of the literary war . . . really has been too small. None of the old-style literature and ideology has received notice from the new people. Quite the contrary: we have a situation where the new literature people are off in one corner fighting among themselves, leaving the old-style people free to stand comfortably by as spectators to the struggle.[36]

What fundamentally disturbed Lu Hsun was not, of course, that Butterfly writers were free to be spectators, but that they were free to continue spreading "feudal" ideas. Most of the urban readership continued to prefer traditional tales and Butterfly fiction, in all of their various new media. Of comic books in particular Mao Tun wrote:

> It goes without saying that the content of all comic strip fiction is poisonous, yet the strong influence of comics on the general

33. Cheng Chen-to, "Ssu-hsiang ti fan-liu," *Wen-hsueh hsün-kan,* no. 4 (June 10, 1921) in YYHTP, pp. 31–32.

34. Mao Tun, "Tzu-jan chu-i yü Chung-kuo hsien-tai hsiao-shuo," *Hsiao-shuo yueh-pao* 13.7 (July 1922) in YYHTP, p. 16.

35. Kuo Mo-jo, "Chih Cheng Hsi-ti hsien-sheng hsin," *Wen-hsüeh hsün-k'an,* no. 6 (June 30, 1921) in YYHTP, pp. 41–42.

36. Address at the inauguration of the League of Left-wing Writers, March 2, 1931, quoted in Ch'en Chi-ying, "San-shih nien-tai wen-t'an hui-ku yü Mao-kung p'o-hai tso-chia ti shih-shih," *Chuan-chi wen-hsueh* 22.5 (May 1963):27.

masses and on children is worthy of note. And we cannot deny that the form of comic strip fiction . . . is worthy of adoption. The comic strip portion not only can attract barely literate readers, but also can help the barely literate, by "self-cultivation," to read and understand the written portion.[37]

Ch'ü Ch'iu-pai observed:

> These things, at the bookstalls on alley corners, and so on . . . have they a certain, in fact a very great, influence? Of course they have . . . the literate masses read them day by day, and the illiterate masses often hear them spoken about in casual ways by others . . . and unconsciously absorb the "instruction" of the stuff.[38]

And:

> The working people's knowledge of their own existence, their view of social phenomena, in general their world view and life view, is practically all gained from this sort of reactionary popular literature.[39]

Ch'ü's tendency to exaggerate only underscores a frustration which was common among May Fourth writers at the continuing gap between them and "the masses."

Valuable though the May Fourth testimony is, it is also instructive to imagine the viewpoint of the popular audience. To them, May Fourth's "literary renaissance" surely appeared as a highly elite movement in many of its basic features. In the late 1910s and early twenties, the magazine *New Youth (Hsin ch'ing-nien)* was written and read primarily among a tiny number of China's most privileged young intellectuals, many of whom had studied in Japan or the West and spent their time in China clustered around leading universities. In a new and different way, they seemed as far removed from the mainstream of popular culture as the advocates of eight-legged essays whom they sought to overthrow. Even the same *Hsin ch'ing-nien* had elite overtones to the popular ear, since the term *ch'ing-nien* had traditionally been used only in reference to young males of upper-class households. To the ordinary person the name went half-way towards suggesting "new young gentlemen."

While May Fourth authors had studied abroad and were Western-oriented, the popular authors—to say nothing of their readership—had very limited experience outside China. Few of them studied abroad, and the exceptions only prove the rule that overseas study did not mix with Butterfly culture. Ch'en Shen-yen and Hsiang K'ai-jan

37. Chang Ching-lu, comp., *Chung-kuo ch'u-pan shih liao pu-pien*, p. 292.
38. *Ch'ü Ch'iu-pai wen-chi*, 2:898-899.
39. *Ch'ü Ch-iu-pai wen-chi*, 2:885.

explicitly repudiated their foreign study when they took up careers in popular fiction. In fact, Hsiang founded his writing career with the best-selling novel *Informal History of Overseas Study in Japan (Liu-tung wai-shih*, 1916) which bitterly satirized the profligate lives of Chinese students in Japan.

If the main barrier between early May Fourth fiction and the common reader was the issue of new Western ideas, an associated barrier, certainly, had to do with style. The popularity of the traditional vernacular style, well established over several centuries, if anything grew stronger, vis-à-vis classical style, under early influences from the West. Writers spoke of using the vernacular to "unify the people," and in 1915, more than three years before the appearance of May Fourth vernacular fiction, the "Butterfly" magazine *Fiction Pictorial* began a policy of publishing vernacular stories exclusively.[40]

The often heard assertion that May Fourth writers established the vernacular in modern literary use in China must, therefore, be further refined. Certainly one contribution of Hu Shih, Ch'en Tu-hsiu, and their colleagues was to establish the vernacular's respectability in the face of the traditional elite's scorn of anything nonclassical—a contribution not of creating the vernacular but of stooping to it. Their more positive contribution was, of course, the fashioning of a new *form* for the vernacular.

Perhaps still scorning the vernacular in its vulgar versions, they created a style which appeared to most readers as a strange new language strongly associated with the West and with the new Westernized elite. Missionaries had employed basically the same style for several decades,[41] but May Fourth writers were the first Chinese of any influence to adopt it, adding to it occasional bits of foreign vocabulary for purposes, depending on one's viewpoint, of either clarity or snobbery. In the early thirties, Ch'ü Ch'iu-pai reluctantly concluded that May Fourth writing amounted to "a new classical language,"[42] favored by the elite and impenetrable by the masses.

In its literary content, May Fourth writing did, of course, frequently portray lower class life and express great sympathy for the downtrodden. But the readership who found these portraits of the

40. CYLHIL, p. 380. The first story in the modern vernacular of May Fourth was Lu Hsun's "Diary of a Madman" (1918).

41. Missionary presses such as the Presbyterian Mission Press and the London Mission Society Press had been publishing in Westernized — often awkwardly Westernized — *pai-hua* since the mid-19th century. See Suzanne Barnett, "Silent Evangelism: Presbyterians and the Mission Press in China, 1807–1860," *Journal of Presbyterian History* 49.4 (Winter 1971): 298–300. These examples appear to have been imitated before May Fourth in the *Wu-hsi pai-hua pao* and similar journals which appeared around the turn of the century in the lower Yangtze area. See Chapter 3.

42. *Ch'ü Ch'iu-pai wen-chi*, 2:885ff.

lower classes appealing was not the lower classes themselves; it was, at least until the thirties, a highly educated minority. And the sympathetic feelings of privileged people toward the less privileged must be distinguished from the feelings of the less privileged themselves.

Judging from some of the most popular works of the 1910s and 1920s, Butterfly readers of the "middle class" certainly had ambivalent feelings about the May Fourth leadership and its advocacy of Western influence. On one level, they felt obliged to go along with the "new style" to some extent: they would carry a fountain pen, learn a few words of English, read novels about new-style dating, and maybe even try it out. But all this was superficial and largely a matter of stylishness. At a deeper level, traditional values were still dear to their hearts; in fact they preferred novels in which the homespun characters were shown, in the final analysis, to be more reliable than their new-style counterparts. At this deeper level, the May Fourth call for basic social reform aroused considerable suspicion.

This ambivalence toward Western influence, like other aspects of popular fiction, offered psychological comfort to the middle-class reader. From identification with pro-Western tendencies one could enjoy the stylishness associated with elite opinion and behavior, whereas (eating one's cake, too) rejection of the West at the deeper level reserved the security of tested and familiar life patterns. (From the May Fourth viewpoint, it is probably accurate to call this ambivalence "backward" or "reactionary.")

In addition to blunting the threat of Westernization, popular fiction could soothe a reader's worries about social status. Readers, like their authors, could easily feel bitter about the gap between their high expectations and their actual living conditions in the modern city. Originally attracted to the city by a promise of wealth and new-style advancement, most newcomers naturally felt disappointment at having to make-do with only a small share of the city's apparent abundance. Something as simple as window-shopping could give urban residents hundreds of ownership aspirations which would never have arisen in the hinterland but which few, in fact, could achieve in the city.

Certain kinds of fiction could comfort them. "Scandal fiction" *(hei-mu hsiao-shuo),* which unmasked corruption in high places, strongly suggested that the "haves" may have money, but they certainly lack virtue or happiness compared to us. "Knight-errant fiction" *(wu-hsia hsiao-shuo)* told tales of righteous heroes who topple evil powerholders and set things right, thus providing the enjoyment of vicarious victories where real-life victories were impossible. "Tragic love fiction" *(ai-ch'ing hsiao-shuo)* described beautiful people suffering great pain and injustice, thereby reminding the reader that suffering is

an affliction of the virtuous, and furthermore that, among the virtuous, some are in even worse condition than ourselves.

Besides comforting its readers, popular fiction could serve to introduce them to the "modernizing" environment, i.e., to the tendencies
toward nuclear families, "universalistic" public intercourse, general
education, and the rest of what sociologists call *Gesellschaft* culture. An
early characteristic of this shifting environment was the stream of new
scientific information which accompanied technological change and
demanded the attention of anyone who would thrive and advance in
the modern city. The forerunners of popular reading material in
China, Japan, and Western Europe alike were not novels, but journals
and magazines which offered self-taught science, practical know-how,
and whatever information was necessary to keep up with expanding
popular knowledge.

In Shanghai the strangeness of the new information, especially
information about foreign lands and technological devices (boats
with wings, etc.) soon made it clear that the new urban press could be
amusing as well as helpful. Articles on practical subjects became
interspersed with fantastic "science fiction" *(k'o-hsüeh hsiao-shuo)*
and "novels of imagination" *(li-hsiang hsiao-shuo)*. The readership's
thirst for amusement was intensified by the modern phenomenon
of a weekend day off—time which the new urban living seemed
to schedule for such things as fiction reading. Thus, just as the
nineteenth-century West saw weekend newspapers and magazines
swell with light fiction, jokes, and puzzles, Shanghai produced a welter of similar publications to help readers avoid the twin perils of
boredom and exertion. One of the best-known Shanghai magazines
was called, significantly, *Saturday (Li-pai-liu)*. It came out on Saturdays
because, its editor explained, from Monday through Friday "everyone
is busy with an occupation, and only on Saturday and Sunday has the
leisure to read fiction."[43]

The amusement function of popular stories could easily combine
with a testing function, as readers explored the "new style" of life
through a fictional medium. While generally keeping Westernization
at arm's length, readers could, in the security of their own homes,
identify with "new style" fictional characters to whatever extent they
wished, and without risking anything in real life. This "testing function" of popular fiction probably served both to ease the strains of
daily life and to facilitate longer-run social change by anticipating it.

As such change became more apparent, popular fiction clearly

43. Wang Tun-ken, "'Li-pai liu' ch'u-pan chui-yen," *Li-pai-liu*, no. 1 (June 6, 1914),
reprinted in YYHTP, p. 131 and in Ch'en Tieh-i, "Li-pai-liu p'ai ts'ang-sang shih,"
Ta-ch'eng, no. 11 (October 1974):67.

served as a forum for concerns about the security of the new Chinese nation. While modern communications made national news an increasingly important commodity, some authors, such as Keng Hsiao-ti in Peking, began to incorporate the day's news into the story lines of their serialized fiction; blind storytellers, the *hsia-tzu a-ping,* did the same. More significantly, the large issues underlying the news also came to be reflected in the popularity of certain themes in popular fiction.

Throughout the 1910s and twenties, this popularity arrived in waves, some large, some small, each based on a particular type of story. (A "wave" here means a sudden increase in both number of stories and number of readers; waves were only matters of degree, though, as every kind of story was circulating almost all the time.) The first of the major waves—the love stories of the early 1910s—explored the issue of free versus arranged marriages. Expectations that under the new regime of the republic young people would suddenly be free of the old family system were, however unrealistic, a key factor in the popularity of these stories.

The next major wave, which crested in the later 1910s, appears to have stemmed from the troubles with Yuan Shih-k'ai and general disillusionment with the new republic. It included three types of stories. First, there was an increase in the popularity of satirical "social novels" *(she-hui hsiao-shuo),* of which Li Han-ch'iu's *Tides of Yangchow (Kuangling ch'ao),* a multi-level portrait of Yangchow society, was the leading example. Second, the Western-style detective story was widely imitated, most successfully in a series by Ch'eng Hsiao-ch'ing under the general title *Cases Investigated by the Chinese Sherlock Holmes, Huo-sang (Chung-kuo Fu-erh-mo-ssu Huo-sang t'an-an).* Third, there was a great outpouring of "scandal fiction" which exposed corruption and depravity in officialdom, business, education, journalism, entertainment, diplomacy, religion and almost every other walk of urban life. Powerful people hired writers to attack their enemies by writing scandal fiction in single-sheet "mosquito" papers.

A third major wave, of "knight-errant" fiction, is well illustrated by Hsiang K'ai-jan's novel *Chronicle of the Strange Roving Knights (Chiang-hu ch'i-hsia chuan).* Though originally serialized in 1923–24, this lengthy hero-story and the many imitations which it inspired reached a peak of popularity during 1927–30. Significantly, these were also years when news reports of the Kuomintang's Northern Expedition against warlordism had a strong hold on the public imagination in cities.

Each of these three waves can be illustrated in Chang Hen-shui's supremely popular *Fate in Tears and Laughter,* which was serialized in

1929–30 and conveniently summarizes the appeal of much of the popular fiction of the first three decades of the century. Here we summarize this story, holding commentary to a minimum, in the belief that a relatively complete example may be the most effective introduction to the chapters which follow.

★   ★   ★

The story's protagonist is a nineteen-year-old student named Fan Chia-shu who has come to Peking from Hangchow in order to take university entrance examinations. His early background is unclear, except that it was comfortably upper-class and basically "old style." In Peking Fan Chia-shu lives in the home of his wealthy uncle, a consul general who spends most of his time overseas. The household is run by Chia-shu's cousin T'ao Po-ho and T'ao's wife, both of whom are a bit more tinged by the "new style" than is Chia-shu.

The story begins one day when Chia-shu is bored and goes to visit Peking's popular amusement area at the Bridge of Heaven (T'ien-ch'iao). Amid jugglers and storytellers, biscuit sellers and drum-singers, he happens across an old martial arts practitioner named Kuan Shou-feng, aged something over sixty, who amazes a crowd by lifting tremendous weights. Chia-shu and Kuan Shou-feng (who inevitably recalls his namesake, Lord Kuan Yü) develop an immediate sense of mutual trust despite their very different social stations.

The next day Chia-shu returns to the Bridge of Heaven to look for Shou-feng, and this time runs across a Peking drum-singer to whom he is immediately attracted. Shen Feng-hsi is fifteen or sixteen, poor, illiterate, and very pretty. She lives with her mother who is referred to only as Old Lady Shen (Shen ta-niang) and an evil uncle, Shen San-hsuan. Everyday San-hsuan and Feng-hsi go to the Bridge of Heaven where they perform together and earn a few coppers. Having listened to one performance, Chia-shu makes them a generous contribution but then withdraws, immediately embarrassed. He is, after all, an upper-class student, and has to guard against the public appearance of any connection with a singing girl.

Meanwhile, Chia-shu's cousins, the T'ao family, have been eagerly arranging a match for this handsome and successful young scholar. They have introduced him to Helena Ho (Ho Li-na), a daughter in the family of a wealthy bureaucrat. Helena, who is one year older than Chia-shu, is aggressive and very Westernized. In fact she likes to be referred to as "Mi-ssu Ho" and calls Chia-shu "Mi-ssu-t'o Fan."

The novel's love-story theme is dominated by the choice Chia-shu must make between Helena (willful, educated, Westernized) and Feng-hsi (passive, uneducated, untouched by the West). In the minds of the urban middle class, this choice readily symbolized the cultural choice between the whole "old" and "new" styles, and offered the chance to test one's feelings in the privacy of a fictional experience. Helena is strong and capable, yet unattractive in manner: pushy, coarse, superficial, un-Chinese. Feng-hsi is excessively weak of character, yet more gentle, approachable, and "like us." The author makes the contrast in character between the two young women all the purer by erasing physical differences: they look practically identical, in fact others in the story mistake them for one another.

How to conduct a modern-style "date" is one of the questions the novel allows its readers to test. Helena provides some negative examples. She invites Chia-shu out on her own initiative, picks him up in a car, orders two beers, downs hers at a gulp, and sits in a new-style dress which reveals the legs, while explaining that from "Western civilization" Chinese women derive "Western beauty."[44] She then chides Chia-shu for his inability to dance.

Yet Chia-shu's courting of Feng-hsi is hardly more comfortable. First, he must keep the whole matter absolutely secret from the T'ao family who take an adolescent delight in finding traces of lipstick on his cheeks, assuming, of course, that Helena put them there. Second, Chia-shu can never be comfortable with the class barrier which separates him and Feng-hsi. On his first visit to Feng-hsi's home he assuages his embarrassment by presenting Feng-hsi's mother with five yuan for a new pair of shoes. On later visits he brings much more money, and even pays for Feng-hsi to go to school. He feels unsure whether these hand-outs fit into the new style; but many neighbors, as well as Feng-hsi's uncle San-hsuan, are confident in their old-style view of the matter. They assume Chia-shu is purchasing her sexual services.

At one point T'ao Po-ho offers Chia-shu advice on the general topic of dating, which is that men must play their cards close to their chests. "If you want to know how to handle girls," he says, "I'm telling you that lying is the only requirement."[45]

Added to Chia-shu's pursuit of Feng-hsi and Helena's pursuit of Chia-shu, a third relationship develops between Chia-shu and the daughter of the old weight-lifter Kuan Shou-feng. The daughter, Kuan Hsiu-ku, is interesting counterpoint to both Helena and Feng-hsi. She combines their virtues in ideal forms: in life-style she is more solidly traditional than Feng-hsi (who does have a weakness for such things as wristwatches and tortoise-shell glasses); yet, like Helena,

44. Chang Hen-shui, *T'i-hsiao yin-yuan*, 1:34.
45. Ibid., 1:54.

Hsiu-ku is a strong, capable person. She and her father are, in fact, "knights-errant" *(hsia-k'e)*, though this fact is not immediately revealed. Hsiu-ku also falls in love with Chia-shu, and would seem the most fitting match for him. But alas, she is not as physically attractive as the other two.

The relationship between Chia-shu and the two Kuans develops solidly on the basis of mutual aid and respect. One day Chia-shu meets Hsiu-ku by chance and learns that her old father is gravely ill. Chia-shu races to the Kuan house and finds the old man about to die. He asks whether Shou-feng believes in Western medicine (another test of the new style) and, receiving the answer that "anything that works" is worth a try, brings Shou-feng to a modern hospital and pays the bill.[46] Shou-feng recovers, and he and Hsiu-ku feel profoundly grateful to Chia-shu.

Hsiu-ku begins to have dreams about Chia-shu, including a dream in which the two of them are strolling in a park together. Later in the story the dream comes true, thus raising the question of whether such things as dreams and omens in general deserve one's credence. Readers, knowing that modern elite opinion favored "science" and disparaged "superstition," felt pressure from this quarter to repudiate their "old beliefs." And it seems that most of them did, at least superficially.

But for most the basic question still went begging: are old beliefs *really* untrue? Later in the story Chia-shu reports a nightmare of his own to Hsiu-ku. He is afraid his dream might be saying something about Feng-hsi's fate. Hsiu-ku chides him: Does a "civilized" *(wenming*, a euphemism for "Westernized") person like yourself still believe that dreams come true? Chia-shu, allowing Westernization its due, concedes that such notions are unscientific. But he immediately objects that this particular dream is *persistent* and hence must be taken more seriously.[47] Events prove him right—the dream is true. In another aside, the generally new-style person T'ao Po-ho defends old beliefs on the grounds not that they are true but that they are harmless. For example, he says, China's myth of the Herd Boy and Weaving Girl (Niu-lang chih-nü) should inhibit science in China no more than does Santa Claus in the West.[48]

Chia-shu continues his suit of Feng-hsi by bringing her more and more presents. Eventually these include a gold ring which he ceremoniously explains to be an engagement ring, though his manner suggests that neither he nor Feng-hsi feels quite at home with this new-style custom. In any case, this is the highpoint of his relationship with Feng-hsi. Before he leaves for a short visit to his ill mother in

46. Ibid., 1:77.   47. Ibid., 3:6.   48. Ibid., 2:165.

Hangchow, he visits Feng-hsi's home and there are omens of trouble in their relationship: a string in Feng-hsi's yueh-ch'in snaps, a noodle bowl breaks.

More concretely, Feng-hsi's evil uncle San-hsuan, who has a quick eye for any profit, conceives a plan to sell Feng-hsi's good looks to a warlord named General Liu Te-chu. With his group of scoundrel friends, San-hsuan arranges a showing of Feng-hsi before the general. At the same time he begins the task of persuading Feng-hsi 's mother and other relatives that the relationship with Chia-shu cannot last: he is a rich young student who might be temporarily useful to them but that's all. Nor will Feng-hsi's own role as a new-style student last long: "How many of these girl students we see these days can get far enough in their studies to do big things like the young men? There's no way, as I see it. After three days at the books they're suddenly babbling about equality and freedom."[49] Eventually Feng-hsi's mother is won over to the scheme.

While the reader hopes that Feng-hsi will resist, there are indications she may not. Not only are the omens bad, but recently an unhealthy penchant for material wealth has emerged in her character. After only a few days of school she has asked Chia-shu for high-heeled shoes, a white silk muffler, a fountain pen, and other accoutrements of new-style vanity. Will she be able to resist the riches of a warlord? When a car with two private soldiers arrives to pick her up, she at first refuses to join them. The reader assumes she has perceived the perfidy of her uncle. But a moment later she reappears, without explanation, saying "I'll go."[50]

The general's mansion is as opulent "as in the pictures." He has a thick rug—how thick is hard to say—a phonograph, a radio set with short wave, and an electric fan. Servants are everywhere—holding doors, serving tea, thrusting spittoons before guests who seem about to clear their throats.[51] Feng-hsi is very impressed. She then is pressured into playing mah-jong, and the general arranges that she will have large winnings to bring home. Feng-hsi's mother, delighted with the money, decides to go into petty usury. A few days later the general asks Feng-hsi out to the theater and brings her home in his own car. He presses an expensive necklace and three hundred yuan into her hands as gifts, then proposes another date.

Meanwhile Chia-shu, still in Hangchow, is unaware of all this and continues to write Feng-hsi letters in which he stresses that their love is not based on money. (His presents to her are meant only to insure her independence.) With this thought in mind, Feng-hsi stiffens her resistance to the general. She gives his necklace and the three hundred

49. Ibid., 2:51.   50. Ibid., 2:62.   51. Ibid., 2:64, 65, 76.

yuan to her mother and persuades her mother to return them to the general with regrets. She resolves not to see him again.

But a general is not so easily stopped. Before long he sends a soldier to Feng-hsi's house on the pretext of taking a census. The evil uncle San-hsuan reports that he and Feng-hsi are drum-singers by profession, and a few days later some soldiers carrying revolvers return with the order that all drum-singers in Peking be brought to General Liu Te-chu's mansion to perform at a party.

At the party, the general publicly announces what has passed between him and Feng-hsi and says that his present purpose is to bring his colleagues and her colleagues together to determine whether she is worthy to join his household. Feng-hsi immediately faints, whereupon the general declares he will keep her at his house for treatment. He puts her in the private room of his former wife.

The general sends for Feng-hsi's mother to watch over the kidnapped maiden. Feigning sleep, Feng-hsi awaits the chance to whisper to her mother that Kuan Shou-feng, if anyone, can rescue her. The mother notifies Kuan, who has no trouble stealing his way to Feng-hsi's room using martial arts. (He extinguishes a streetlight with the toss of a coin, shatters a window blind by pinching it.)

But the general, too, has been at work, showering Feng-hsi with gifts and arranging to marry her. When Shou-feng peers into Feng-hsi's room, he sees the general kneeling before her holding great stacks of money, which Feng-hsi proceeds to accept. Shou-feng retreats in disgust, ready to abandon the whole rescue. He is shocked a second time when he goes to see Old Lady Shen and finds her talking in her sleep. The general has given us so much, she is saying, how can we have the face to refuse him?

This so angers Shou-feng that he has a monk write a letter (Shou-feng is illiterate) to Chia-shu telling him all. Chia-shu returns to Peking and goes straight to see Shou-feng. Initially, he defends Feng-hsi to Shou-feng. She is a poor, weak girl; how could she resist a general?

That afternoon, though, Chia-shu's sympathy turns to shock as he and the two Kuans are strolling in a park talking things over. They see an automobile pushing its way along a crowded promenade, forcing people to scatter before it. They comment on the injustice of the situation, then watch as the car pulls to a stop nearby. From inside, surrounded by armed guards, steps Feng-hsi. As soon as she sees Chia-shu she retreats quickly inside and the car speeds off.

With Shou-feng now thoroughly disgusted, and all Chia-shu's other friends and relatives still ignorant of the whole Feng-hsi matter, Chia-shu has only Hsiu-ku to talk with. He asks her about Buddhism, since he, like many despondent lovers in China's past, is considering withdrawal from the world. (Also like those lovers, he falls ill from excessive study and injury in love.) Hsiu-ku resolves to reach Feng-hsi and make one final effort to straighten things out.

One day on the street Hsiu-ku overhears a woman who works as an introducer of servant labor talking about General Liu's household. For an appropriate bribe the woman allows Hsiu-ku access to the mansion, and by a stroke of luck they meet the general personally. He takes an immediate liking to Hsiu-ku, and hires her to serve Feng-hsi. Within a few days Hsiu-ku is able to arrange a secret rendezvous between Chia-shu and Feng-hsi at a city park.

At this meeting Chia-shu does his best to persuade Feng-hsi to return to him. The effort includes a little speech on changing *mores*. In the old days when a girl "lost her body," it was as if a white cloth had been stained with indelible black ink. Now attitudes have changed, and so long as a man and woman really love each other, it doesn't matter at all if "one's body has suffered a little insult."[52] He, Chia-shu, can offer Feng-hsi real love, which the general never can.

Feng-hsi, though, is unmoved. She responds by offering to repay Chia-shu all the money he had given her. She takes out her checkbook and writes a check—a new-style skill of hers—for the entire amount. Chia-shu then tears the check to shreds and throws it to the wind, comparing it to ten or twenty little white butterflies dancing in the sunlight. With this Feng-hsi breaks down and cries pitifully, throwing to the ground the gold ring Chia-shu had given her. Chia-shu leaves the session in a burst of exaggerated laughter.

The worst is yet to come, though, as it turns out their secret meeting has not escaped the surveillance of the general's staff. When the general learns of the meeting he is livid with rage, and bellows at Feng-hsi that cuckoldry is the most fearsome thing a big general must endure. He whips her crazily, and desists only when Hsiu-ku restrains him. Although the general later makes a half-hearted apology, the damage has already been done: Feng-hsi loses her sanity. When Hsiu-ku reports these developments to Chia-shu, he simply says he doesn't care and introduces Hsiu-ku to Helena, who now is the object of Chia-shu's attentions. Helena treats Hsiu-ku snobbishly and pretends she and Chia-shu are engaged.

Only Shou-feng and Hsiu-ku still burn with righteous indignation. Taking advantage of the general's amorous advances toward Hsiu-ku, they carry out a plot to do away with him. Consenting to marry the general, Hsiu-ku proposes that they avoid the trouble of ceremony and banquets and simply retreat to the Western Hills outside Peking, then return a few days later with the declaration that they are married. The only requirement would be 1,400 yuan for Hsiu-ku's father to

52. Ibid., 3:23.

entertain his friends. The General loves this idea. Hsiu-ku then gives the 1,400 yuan to Shou-feng, who secretly distributes it among his friends and neighbors, advising them to leave town the next day. The reader can begin to guess the Kuans' motives.

Hsiu-ku and the general retire to an ancient temple in the Western Hills. The following day a monk at the temple becomes concerned when the nuptial couple does not emerge from their quarters. He investigates and finds the general dead in bed, Hsiu-ku gone, and a note smeared in blood on the chamber wall explaining that she killed him "to rid the nation and society of a great menace."[53]

The next day the police are searching everywhere for Shou-feng and Hsiu-ku. Chia-shu reads a newspaper report of the events and fears the police will come looking for him, too. He abruptly departs for Tientsin to visit relatives, explaining to the T'ao family that since he has just passed his entrance exams for university, he finally has the time to make a trip which he should have made long ago. (The reader is informed that Chia-shu studies hard, yet there is no description in the story of his spending time on anything but diversion and personal relations.)

To his and the reader's great surprise, Chia-shu is greeted in Tientsin with a round of teasing for what his relatives assume to be his engagement to Helena. The fact that Chia-shu has never proposed to Helena offers the reader another object lesson in the hazards of new-style romance. During Chia-shu's visit to Hangchow, it seems his mother had seen a photo of Feng-hsi whom Chia-shu owned to be his fiancée, and because of the close resemblance between Feng-hsi and Helena, the T'aos and everyone else (who still did not know about Feng-hsi) naturally assumed the photo to be of Helena. Helena herself considers this beyond question.

Chia-shu receives a phone call from Helena only hours after arriving in Tientsin. She has followed him there, and coyly asks why he is playing tricks on her, leaving Peking without telling her. Chia-shu asks her to meet him at a restaurant, where he explains the whole misunderstanding. Shattered, Helena takes the next train back to Peking. On board she dries her tears and orders a beer.

A few days later she throws a gala new-style party. There are swarms of photographers and much Western-style dancing. Helena does a hula dance—of "an uncivilized people"—and throws everyone a very stylish kiss at the end. Her parents, who pay for the party, say she is "Europeanized" and beyond their control.[54]

Part of the entertainment value of stories like *Fate in Tears and Laughter* lies in their frequent reversal of the reader's expectations. This happens once again when it turns out that Helena has not gone beserk,

53. Ibid., 3:85.   54. Ibid., 3:119–125.

but is preparing to devote her life to Buddhism. After her party she disappears, and everyone assumes she has gone to Europe. In fact, though, she has secretly withdrawn to the Western Hills, where she reads sutras and abstains from meat and wine. Her disappearance moves Chia-shu to his own reflections on the insubstantiality of things. Having been suddenly surrounded by three attractive young women, he now just as suddenly sees all three vanish.

The story's next turn is poorly integrated and is the only major flaw in an otherwise well-constructed plot. Chia-shu is suddenly kidnapped by mountain bandits. A 1932 review in the *Ta-kung pao* literary supplement offers the speculation that Chang Hen-shui included this episode only to show that his literary versatility extended to *wu-hsia* fiction as well.[55] A touch of "knight-errantry" has already appeared in Kuan Shou-feng's penetration of General Liu's mansion; here Shou-feng and Hsiu-ku reveal much more of their special skills in a dramatic rescue of Chia-shu.

When the rescue is over, the Kuans rejoin Chia-shu at a lower ontological level and they all catch a bus back to Peking. Chia-shu goes home but the two Kuans, as befits *hsia,* keep their own place of dwelling a mystery. Shou-feng gives Chia-shu an address where they can meet the next day, an address which turns out to be Feng-hsi's after she has left the general's mansion. Feng-hsi, still insane, barely recognizes Chia-shu. But she does have his picture on the wall. It is now pasted together having once been torn apart, an obvious symbol of her admitted mistake. Chia-shu arranges to have a doctor visit her, and the doctor advises that she be put in an asylum. A family council agrees to do this.

Chia-shu proposes that the two Kuans settle down near his school, where Shou-feng could be a martial arts instructor. Again he asks Shou-feng for their new address, and this time Shou-feng supplies one in the Western Hills. But when Chia-shu goes there, he finds it to be the country villa of Helena's father, where Helena herself has been hiding ever since her big party. The Kuans are there, but still decline to step back into the real world. They leave Helena and Chia-shu together at the villa, setting out for Shantung, they say, with two donkeys and a camel. Here the story ends.

★

Chang Hen-shui wrote *Fate in Tears and Laughter* in Nanking, and every week mailed one-chapter installments to Shanghai where they

---

55. Min Yu, "P'ing Chang Hen-shui 'T'i-hsiao yin-yuan'," *Ta-kung pao wen-hsueh fu-k'an,* January 4, 1932, p. 8.

were serialized on Fridays in the *Hsin-wen pao*'s "Forest of Light-heartedness" column edited by Yen Tu-ho. Within a year of the novel's completion in 1930, the publisher San-yu shu-she came out with a three-volume paper edition. While the story's circulation grew at a rate unprecedented in China, so did the readership's curiosity about the final resolution of its plot. Vernacular-style stories were not supposed to end until all important loose ends of the plot had been tied. But this author had left Fan Chia-shu's relationship with Helena Ho quite ambiguous, and there were also lingering questions about his feelings for Shen Feng-hsi and Kuan Hsiu-ku. Why didn't Chia-shu get married and settle the question? A great many letters with this and other questions poured in to Chang Hen-shui and his publisher.

Eventually Chang responded by publishing a little piece called "A General Reply to My Readers," in which he argued for the aesthetic value of *not* wrapping things up. "The universe is full of incompleteness," he wrote, and "to leave some incompleteness is the only way to leave a pleasant flavor in people's lingering thoughts, like the flavor of chewing olives. If you have to bring everything right down to its end, in one great festive occasion, it's like having a big, fat banquet: when it's over, it's over. The flavor is sure to be less appealing than that persisting olive aroma."[56]

But his readers, unmoved, continued to send in demands for a sequel, especially one with a happy ending. Chang again replied, this time in an essay called "Whether to Write a Sequel."[57] When the ancients traveled in the mountains, he wrote, didn't they deliberately leave a few mountains unvisited, as food for the imagination? It is the same with fiction. Do we have complete, happy endings for such great heroes as Kuan Yü, Chang Fei, and K'ung Ming in *Romance of the Three Kingdoms?* Was the tragic ending of *Dream of the Red Chamber* improved upon by the dozen or so happy-ending sequels later tacked on to that great novel? Besides, *Fate in Tears and Laughter* is a "childish work"; a sequel would be unworthy of the reader's respect. Thus, "I cannot, need not, and dare not write a sequel."[58]

He did write a sequel, though, after two years of continuing pressure from readers and his publisher. An important additional incentive arose from the fact that a number of inferior writers had already grabbed the opportunity to sell sequels of their own, some even daring to do so under Chang's name.[59] Chang explained his need to

56. Chang Hen-shui, *T'i-hsiao yin-yuan* (1948), 2:364.
57. Ibid., 2:364–365.
58. Ibid., 2:365.
59. Chang Hen-shui, "Wo-ti sheng-huo ho ch'uang-tso," *Ming Pao Monthly* 12:1 (January 1977):32.

answer their sequels. "I wrote the original work, so naturally know its characters more completely than anyone."[60]

The theme of the sequel departs markedly from the original work. One almost suspects Chang of a continuing effort to shelter the artistic effect of his original ending by issuing a sequel which gave only cursory attention to the questions which most interested his readers. The question which interested Chang himself was the Japanese threat to China.

Between the serialization of *Fate in Tears and Laughter* during 1929–30 and the appearance of the sequel in January 1933, the Japanese had occupied Manchuria (September 1931) and attacked Shanghai (January 1932). The Nanking government's policy of nonresistance became the subject of acute controversy in Shanghai and other cities. Writers in the May Fourth tradition who pressed for resistance to Japan had to dodge government censors. Influenced by these events, Chang Hen-shui joined May Fourth writers in public declarations for "national defense"; he also resolved that resisting Japan should be the theme of the sequel to *Fate in Tears and Laughter.*

★   ★   ★

An important new character in the sequel is Shen Kuo-ying, a young military officer who appears in the original story only as one of Helena's admirers at her big farewell party. In the sequel he approaches Helena's father with a marriage suit, but is turned down with the explanation that Helena has a new-style engagement with Mr. Fan Chia-shu. Thereupon Kuo-ying decides to seek out Feng-hsi, nurse her back from insanity, and marry her in order to show the world he can get a wife as pretty as Helena. He embarrasses Helena's family by inviting mutual friends to a banquet where he parades Feng-hsi dressed as Helena, announcing to all that this woman is his concubine. When Chia-shu hears of this escapade, the last traces of his love for Feng-hsi turn to shame and regret.

Meanwhile Chia-shu arranges to devote his career to national service. The T'ao family and Helena convince him that the study of engineering in Germany is the best route to this end, and that the Siberian railroad might be the best route back to China. Helena decides to accompany him, and their engagement notice appears in the newspaper just before they leave.

We are then told that four years have elapsed, which is also the length of time separating the writing of the novel from the writing of its sequel. This coincidence not only preserves the fiction, implicit from the beginning, that the story is a chronology of actual experience; it also makes possible the sequel's commentary on current

60. Chang Hen-shui, *T'i-hsiao yin-yuan* (1948) 2:368.

events. Because of censorship, the author feared to mention Manchuria or the Japanese directly. But how many readers missed the point when he wrote of heroes going "outside the pass" to "fight barbarians"?

After the four-year interlude, we find Shen Kuo-ying learning from a fellow soldier about a "righteous army" *(i-chün)* fighting a guerrilla war. The troops are ill-supplied. They get their food from the local population and their arms by capture from the enemy. Kuo-ying is eager to help, and a clandestine meeting is arranged with one of the deputy commanders.

From this valiant start towards a patriotic theme for his sequel, the author then feels obliged to integrate it with his original, and the combination is awkward to say the least. The deputy commander whom Shen Kuo-ying meets turns out to be Kuan Hsiu-ku. He agrees to join her effort and to bring a large donation of money with him. First, though, Hsiu-ku must do him a favor. Kuo-ying is still enamored of Feng-hsi, who is still insane. He believes that if he can recreate the scene which brought about her insanity she might "awaken" from it. Hsiu-ku, who witnessed General Liu's outburst, was needed to direct this reconstruction. She agrees, and it works.

Meanwhile Chia-shu and Helena have returned from Europe, where Chia-shu learned chemical engineering and prepared himself to make artificial fog in the war effort. Hsiu-ku knows of his return and goes to see him, but not at the railroad station, where secret agents would certainly be watching. Chia-shu and Helena both swear new relationships to Hsiu-ku as her younger siblings (thereby ending, incidentally, the competition to marry Chia-shu and neatly subordinating this whole question to that of the guerrilla effort). Hsiu-ku and Kuo-ying set out for Manchuria, and Chia-shu hosts a banquet to give them a hero's send off. Kuo-ying asks Chia-shu to look after Feng-hsi, and Chia-shu agrees, but Feng-hsi relapses and dies anyway.

At this point every young person in the story is contributing to the national defense effort. The rich variety of characters in the original story—new-style, old-style, student, soldier, knight-errant, Buddhist, etcetera—has collapsed almost entirely into the single identity of Japan-resister.

Helena asks her wealthy father for 800,000 yuan to build ten military hospitals in six cities, plus money for a military chemical plant for Chia-shu. When the father says "you're crazy," Helena dashes for a pistol and threatens suicide. He then gives in; only two weeks later one hospital and the chemical plant are ready. Chia-shu and Helena's father are praised in the newspapers.

Hsiu-ku, Shou-feng, and Kuo-ying all die in one glorious battle in Manchuria. When Chia-shu and Helena get the news, they go to

Feng-hsi's grave where they sprinkle wine, burn paper, and burn silk in commemoration of their friends. Despite the general solidarity in resisting Japan, it is obvious that fundamental social divisions are not questioned. The lower class dies on the battlefield while the upper class runs factories and hospitals. It never even occurs to Chia-shu or Helena that they might go to the front. After commemorating their last friends, Chia-shu and Helena (and two servants) climb into their automobile and drive away.

As if to show that the morality immanent in the natural order still rules in Chinese fiction, even in the twentieth century, a sudden whirlwind carries aloft the ashes from Chia-shu's and Helena's offerings, and petals fall from the wild peach tree above their heads. The sequel ends.

★

It must be said that by comparison with his "Butterfly" contemporaries Chang Hen-shui has put together a very tight plot in *Fate in Tears and Laughter.* The "loosely linked episode" style of popular tradition tended to be all the looser in the twentieth century with the beginning of newspaper serialization. Yet Chang's novel, serialized over thirty weeks, fits together as if by careful planning. Indeed, Chang tells us that the whole plot occurred to him in one burst of clairvoyance, and that the chapters naturally fell into place "like the scenes of a movie."[61] There are, of course, major flaws in the plot, such as the poor integration of the kidnapping incident and, if one counts it, the absurdly forced construction of the sequel. And some minor rough points, accountable to the tradition of loose plot construction, are the author's extraneous asides on Santa Claus as superstition, or on the unpopularity of May Fourth fiction.

Nevertheless it is clear that in *Fate in Tears and Laughter,* which is markedly different from Chang's earlier fiction,[62] plot is a major concern. (One suspects, although Chang nowhere admits it, that his interest in a somewhat Western-style plot was inspired by the example of May Fourth writers.) Whether consciously or not, Chang is ready to sacrifice the psychological credibility of his characters to interests of plot, as when Chia-shu calmly shrugs off the news of Feng-hsi's insanity in order to resume his relationship with Helena.

---

61. Ibid., 1:2.

62. Chang made his name in the mid-twenties on the serialization of *Ch'un-ming wai-shih*, later published in six-volume book form. The work can hardly be said to have a plot; it is a thinly-disguised account of interesting events in the lives of famous people, mostly in Peking.

But except for this interest in plot, and for a general wish to entertain and be paid for it, it is doubtful that Chang had any conscious purpose in writing *Fate* (minus the sequel, of course). Chang himself says as much.[63] Yet it has often been asserted that the story's lesson is to demonstrate the weakness of young Chinese women, particularly their weakness for gaudiness and wealth; rumor has it that Chang even chose his name "Hen-shui"—literally "hate water"—because of water's symbolic suggestion of *yin* or the female principle. The rumor appears to be untrue, however,[64] and the interpretation much too simple. It does not account for the differences among Helena, Feng-hsi, and Hsiu-ku, or for the important ways in which these three represent alternatives for modern China—new-style, old-style, or something in between—which Chia-shu and every reader must deliberate upon. The reader is offered dilemmas, not lessons.

Artistically speaking, Chang's strength appears in the fine texture of his words and sentences. His writing probably benefited from what he tells us was his wide reading of traditional vernacular fiction as a youth. (His formal education did not last through high school.) But whatever its origins, his style easily engages the reader's interest and makes a scene, even a very ordinary scene, seem to come alive. A good example from *Fate in Tears and Laughter* (although almost any page will do) is his description in chapter one of the bustle and flavor at Peking's Bridge of Heaven. Chia-shu is going there for the first time, in search of drum-singing at the Island Pavilion (Shui-hsin t'ing):

> When he arrived and the rickshaw came to a halt, the whole place was in a festive uproar. The sounds were of Shensi opera, two-stringed violins, gongs, drums, and all kinds of things. There lay before him a road crowded by three or four high buildings on wooden beams. On the fronts of these buildings hung a great many red paper signs sporting gold or black characters: "The Dogmeat Jug," "Child Actors," and so on, including things like "Little Peony and Daffodil in a Joint Performance of *Sawing the Clay Pot.*"
>
> He paid the rickshaw and walked over for a closer look. Next to the gate tower, a large number of peddlers' stalls were tightly strung together in rows. The one right in front of him was a monocycle with some big flat boards on top, and on the boards were a number of black lumps about the size of rice bowls. Great swarms of flies buzzed madly about. Two knives as white as snow rested among the black lumps. The man standing next to the monocycle would take a black lump, pick up a knife, and in a

63. Chang Hen-shui, *T'i-hsiao yin-yuan* (1930), 1:3–4.

64. Chang Hen-shui, "Wo-ti sheng-huo ho ch'uang-tso," *Ming Pao Monthly* 11.12 (December 1976):74.

frenzied burst of chopping slice off a number of thin brown strips. These he would place in a piece of filthy old newspaper and hold out to people. He was probably selling soy beef or cooked donkey meat.

Another stall consisted of a great iron kettle laid out on the flat ground and containing several very long strips of something pitch black. It looked just like dead snakes, their scales peeled, tangled to the top of the kettle. A bloody, foul stench leapt from the center of the mass. This turned out to be those boiled sheep intestines of which Northerners are fond.

Chia-shu frowned as he turned to look the other way. He now saw some dirt alleyways, both sides of which were lined with reed huts. The huts in the two alleys right in front of him, as far as one could see, had hung out all kinds of multi-colored clothing; this was probably the famous Second-hand Clothes Street. To one side was a little alley where people were coming and going in great numbers. At the head of the alley a pile of old shoes lay right on the grey earth. At several other points were stalls selling odds-and-ends; where the ground was covered with kerosene lanterns, porcelain-plated bowls, and items in iron and brass.

Chia-shu walked toward the little alley. On the south side were some reed-hut stores, and to the north was a big wide ditch. The ditch contained a mass of runny black mud with water that flowed blue. Its stench was overpowering. Chia-shu reminded himself that the Island Pavilion, with its beautiful trees and flowers, of course could not be here. So he turned around again and went toward the main street, where he asked a policeman. The policeman told him that the Island Pavilion was on the west of the street going south. (The whole city of Peking is a gathering of square shapes; all the streets and alleys run north to south or east to west. Peoples' houses are also the square-shaped "four-attached yards." So everybody there, young and old alike, knows the four directions, and in speaking refers not to up, down, left, or right but to north, south, east, or west.) Having listened to him, Chia-shu went straight on his way. . . .[65]

Chang Hen-shui loved Peking and knew it well, and his descriptions such as this are hardly less loving or colorful than those of that other literary master of Peking, Lao She.[66] Chang's dialogue, cast in delightfully natural Peking dialect, also suggests Lao She's, though Chang avoids the colloquial ostentation in Lao She's early works.

Occasionally Chang challenges himself to produce a vivid and realistic account of something which others might pass over. His hon-

65. Chang Hen-shui, *T'i-hsiao yin-yuan* (1948), 1:3–4.
66. Compare, for example, Lao She's descriptions in the final chapter of *Lo-to hsiang-tzu*.

est attempt to describe madness (Feng-hsi) is, for example, a rarity in modern Chinese literature.[67] T.A. Hsia, commenting that Chang Hen-shui "has ears, has eyes, and has imagination," rates him "a greater and better artist" than Wu Ching-tzu, author of *The Scholars*.[68]

Fate in Tears and Laughter is unique in modern popular Chinese fiction for its weaving together of three major types in that tradition—the love story, knight-errant story, and "social" novel. A basic characteristic of "social" fiction, as exemplified in paradigm cases such as Li Han-ch'iu's *Tides of Yangchow* or Chang's own *Informal History of Ch'un-ming*, is that it describes life at several layers of society, often through thinly disguised accounts of real people. Indeed, a story's main interest often lay in its revelation in fiction of what one dared not print as news. In the case of *Fate in Tears and Laughter*, the contemporary relevance of such underlying issues as the dilemma between the "old" and "new" styles was so broad that it actually matters not whether, as the author claims, the story is based on real events. What matters is that the characters represent an interesting range in society and are typical of people or trends familiar to the reader.

The particular branch of the social novel tradition best illustrated in *Fate in Tears and Laughter* is that of "scandal" novels or *hei-mu hsiao-shuo*. The spirit of these highly satirical stories, whose popularity boomed in the mid-1910s, is captured in General Liu's wanton abuse of wealth and power. His opulent surroundings, cruel treatment of servants, sexual abandon, and contempt for the public—as when his automobile barges its way through a crowded park—are all stock examples. Positive moral values also play a role in scandal fiction, indeed a crucial role, but only implicitly. The correct norms are powerfully upheld as author and reader tacitly agree on the egregiousness of their various infractions. (When positive values are explicitly stated, they usually come in the form of limited and concrete rules: one shouldn't believe in dreams, one shouldn't bind girls' feet, and so forth. Such rules are more reminiscent of the campaigns for new-style reform dating from the late-Ch'ing reform movement—and from missionary activity before that—than of the basic Chinese moral values whose implicit endorsement is the very heart of scandal fiction.)

As a kind of corollary to the satire of powerholders, a sympathetic view of the lower classes also appears in the social novels of the time, although such expressions actually are more characteristic of the knight-errant stories. The knight-errant usually comes from, and

---

67. Lu Hsun's "Diary of a Madman" (1918) is a better and much more serious story than *Fate in Tears and Laughter* – but not, of course, because of an interest in realistic description of madness.

68. C. T. Hsia, *Ai-ch'ing, she-hui, hsiao-shuo*, p. 226.

mingles with, the fringe elements of the lower class—beggars, bandits, entertainers—and it is typically his or her role to defend the downtrodden from bullying abuse. Shou-feng and Hsiu-ku are nearly pure examples, except for Hsiu-ku's tangential involvement in the question of the old and new styles.

Thus a basic assumption about the knight-errant, like assumptions about "the common man" in the West's Enlightenment, inverts orthodox notions about the source in society of truth and justice. Such virtues may not originate among the elite and filter down, as it were, but may originate among the downtrodden who occasionally force them upward. Chia-shu must keep his visits to the Bridge of Heaven secret because a household servant tells him it is full of scoundrels and crooks. But the Bridge of Heaven is where he meets the Kuans, the story's staunch defenders of righteousness. For principle alone Shou-feng sets out to save Feng-hsi, and for principle alone abandons his effort when Feng-hsi capitulates to the general's money. At the end of the story, when Shou-feng has completed his heroic rescue of Chia-shu, he takes his chance to reprimand the servant who had warned Chia-shu to avoid the Bridge of Heaven. "My friend! Your young master cousin didn't suffer too much, did he, from making friends with this old man? You can say the Bridge of Heaven is full of all kinds of shady characters, scrounging for a living, but there are also quite a few who make good friends. . . ."[69]

The more obvious marks of a knight-errant story are, of course, the knight-errant's extraordinary abilities and semi-mysterious manner. With unreal ease the knight-errant appears and disappears from view, as well as from the pale of normal human understanding. He or she has connections with higher principles which are perfectly real and exist everywhere, but are accessible only to those who attain a certain clarity of mind. This clarity helps them make brisk and correct judgments even in very confusing situations.

Their special abilities, both mental and physical, are a matter of occult training as well as inborn talent. We know Shou-feng's weight-lifting abilities have somehow been transmitted to Hsiu-ku when she rescues Chia-shu by carrying him on her back for miles. Shou-feng, meanwhile, fights off five bandits at once, catching flying spears between two fingers and hurling them whence they came. This pinching-in-mid-air skill, apparently a practiced one, he also uses for plain fun, as when he removes flies from the area of a dinner table by plucking them from mid-air with his chopsticks and killing them by breaking their wings—without dirtying his chopsticks. But even here Chang Hen-shui's interest in adjusting to the "new style" suddenly

69. Chang Hen-shui, *T'i-hsiao yin-yuan* (1948), 1:343.

pops forward. Shou-feng ends his fly-catching performance by commenting that China's martial arts are outdated: one cannot run onto a battlefield these days plucking bombs from the air.

The love story theme of *Fate in Tears and Laughter* must be seen in the tradition of the kind of popular love story which boomed in the 1910s, those called "Mandarin Duck and Butterfly" stories in the original and proper sense. We consider them in chapter two.

CHAPTER 2

The Love Stories of the 1910s

🦋 The more popular themes in China's modern urban fiction were always in evidence in Shanghai and elsewhere; what we refer to as popularity "waves" were matters of degree only. Major types (love stories, social stories, knight-errant stories, detective stories) developed major waves, and minor types ("imagination" stories, "morals" stories, "science" stories, and countless others) developed minor ones. A wave typically involved one or two pace-setting works followed by large numbers of imitators. Love stories, the first very large wave, boomed in Shanghai in the mid-1910s following the publication of Hsu Chen-ya's *Jade Pear Spirit (Yü-li hun)*. This story quickly became an item of avid discussion, especially among young people, and stimulated a more general interest in love stories as a type. Of all stories in the 1910s it was circulated and imitated most extensively, both numerically and geographically.

Popularity waves of basically the same type seem to have been common on the fiction markets of Chinese cities from late Ming times or earlier; but it is clear that in the early twentieth century they were more sudden than before and, at least in their written manifestations, larger as well.[1] The greater conveniences and lower cost of the media—books, magazines, comic books, and eventually movies—during these two decades made it possible for popularity to "snowball" much more rapidly than before, and to reach more readers in doing so. Readers could even be attracted to a certain story, or type of story, less because of an independent interest in its contents than because of a wish to participate in a new, often fleeting, popular style. In an important sense, a major cause of a popularity wave was often the news of the wave itself.[2]

1. See Wilt L. Idema, *Chinese Vernacular Fiction, the Formative Period* (Leiden, 1974) pp. xliv-lxiv for a brief discussion of the printing, marketing, and readership of fiction in Ming and Ch'ing times.
2. For interesting articles in the field of social psychology discussing fads and fashions, see Gardner Lindzey and Elliot Aronson, eds., *The Handbook of Social Psychology,* 2nd ed. (Reading, Mass., 1968), vol. 3.

Hsu Chen-ya wrote in an ornate classical style which later became famous as quintessential "Mandarin Duck and Butterfly" language. He had a small group of friends and colleagues who shared the style with him, exploited similar themes, and contributed to the same fiction magazines. Most important in this group were Ch'en Tieh-hsien, a senior figure whose *Teardrop Destiny (Lei-chu yuan)* was an important precedent for Hsu Chen-ya; Li Ting-i, whose novel *A Beauty's Blessings (Mei-jen fu)* was second only to Hsu's novels in popularity, and Wu Shuang-je, author of *Mirror of Evil Injustice (Nieh-yuan ching)*. Beyond this small circle of writers forms and styles varied somewhat, but the romantic theme epitomized in *Jade Pear Spirit* remained remarkably constant.

1. *Jade Pear Spirit*

Jade Pear Spirit tells of an extremely talented young man named Ho Meng-hsia, whose family has fallen into genteel poverty. Meng-hsia goes to serve as a tutor in the household of distant relatives named Ts'ui. The head of household, Patriarch Ts'ui, is a widower who lives with his 16-year-old daughter Yun-ch'ien and the 27-year-old widow of his deceased son. The young widow is called "Pear Mother," Li Niang, and has an adorable little son called P'eng-lang. Both of the young women are extremely attractive: the author likens Yun-ch'ien's beauty to the glamorous brilliance of the *hsin-i (magnolia liliflora),* while Li Niang's beauty, he tells us, is more like the gentle and delicate comeliness of pear blossoms. The metaphors are partly evaluative— pear blossoms being preferable—and take on added meaning as the story unfolds. During the first part of the novel, Yun-ch'ien is away at a "new style" school in the provincial capital, where she learns glamorous new ideas from the West. She returns home stridently proclaiming the arrival of the new day and disturbing the smooth workings of her father's Confucian household. Li Niang, by contrast, scarcely ventures from her inner chambers; she observes the codes of widow's chastity and traditional feminine grace.

We should note, in passing, a parallel between the magnolia and pear types of Hsu's novel and the contrast between Helena and Feng-hsi in Chang Hen-shui's *Fate in Tears and Laughter*. In fact, the symbolic opposition of the foreign or "new" style represented by a brilliant, aggressive woman, and the Chinese or "old" style represented by a comely, retiring one was common to a good number of love stories in the 1910s and 1920s, many of which were triangular affairs involving a male protagonist and these two female types. Tendencies toward this pattern can be found in the decade preceding the appearance of *Jade Pear Spirit,* as in the adventures in Tseng P'u's

Flower on a Sea of Evil (Nieh hai hua) of the glamorous Ts'ai-yun, courtesan *cum* ambassadorial spouse and inamorata of foreign men, who contrasts sharply with the ambassador's first wife Madame Chang, an exemplar of devotional virtues. Leo Lee has shown the importance of similar love triangles in Su Man-shu's *Tale of a Broken Hairpin (Sui-tsan chi)* and *The Lone Swan (Tuan hung ling yen chi),* both contemporary with *Jade Pear Spirit* but not written in imitation of it.[3] In *The Lone Swan,* the spirited "magnolia" type, Shizuko, actually is a foreigner (representing, as much as Japan itself, Japan as door to the West), while the Chinese girl Hsueh-mei, the "pear" type, quietly suffers and dies for virtue. Lee also points out Su Man-shu's heavy debt to *Dream of the Red Chamber.* Although a detailed comparison is beyond our present purposes, the basic triangle of sensitive hero, magnolia-type woman, and pear-type woman has clear applications in *Dream* and other premodern stories, though without, of course, the connotations of Western versus non-Western styles. Viewed in this context, the twentieth-century examples are interesting for their uniform association of the West with the "magnolia" side of the general dichotomy.

To return to the *Jade Pear Spirit* story, the young man Meng-hsia falls in love with the young widow Li Niang after a few weeks of tutoring her son P'eng-lang. Before the lovers have ever spoken face-to-face, he is tremendously impressed by her needlework and a few glimpses of her beauty. She, in turn, is impressed by his obvious genius (they pass letters and poems back and forth) and by the special love he lavishes upon her little boy. She bemoans his ill fate: possessing great talent, he lacks the opportunity to develop it through study in Japan, where all the other bright young men are. He, appropriately reciprocal, bemoans her lot: possessing great beauty, she must live as a widow. Their romance grows through secret missives, innocently delivered back and forth by P'eng-lang.

The love stories of the 1910s usually included some social "problem" currently on people's minds (though it is difficult to say whether the problems were considered seriously by readers or served primarily to divert nagging worries to harmless directions). The "problem" in *Jade Pear Spirit* shapes up when Li Niang decides that she can never marry Meng-hsia. Being a widow, she must be chaste. And by tying Meng-hsia down in a small Kiangsu village, she is hurting his future. She communicates her thoughts to Meng-hsia in a letter; and he re-

3. Lee, *Romantic Generation*, pp. 65–72. The precedents for the assertive "magnolia" type of woman may be as old as the Northern Dynasties (A.D. 386–581) and the famous story of Mu-lan, a young woman who fearlessly dressed as a man to replace her father and lead his troops into battle. "Mu-lan" is another name for the *Magnolia liliflora.*

sponds, with the spontaneity of the super-sensitive romantic he is, by vowing never to marry in this entire lifetime. Li Niang is determined that he should retract this oath, and falls seriously ill, thereby demonstrating both her grief and her sincerity. Meng-hsia responds by falling ill himself. But finally he accedes to the solution Li Niang presses upon him, which is that he should marry her young sister-in-law Yun-ch'ien.

Up to this point, the whole romance has been a closely guarded secret.[4] But now Meng-hsia confides in his very close friend Shih-ch'ih, a young man who has been doing very well in the world of "new studies." Shih-ch'ih feels the match with Yun-ch'ien to be the perfect solution and rushes to speak with Patriarch Ts'ui on Meng-hsia's behalf. Patriarch Ts'ui plaintively reports that he has little control over his "new-style" daughter—that she has already refused several times to hear of any matchmaking from him. Since this particular match seems so fine, however, he agrees to try having Li Niang approach Yun-ch'ien with the proposal. Li Niang, pretending the idea is new to her, succeeds in gaining Yun-ch'ien's acceptance, though Yun-ch'ien still regards it as an arranged, unfree marriage. Thus Meng-hsia, who still loves Li Niang, and Yun-ch'ien, who suddenly sheds her "new-style" veneer and accepts all Confucian rules, both agree to marry not for love but in order to please others. Yun-ch'ien still does not know of the secret love between Li Niang and Meng-hsia.

Seeking to free Meng-hsia completely from any responsibilities to her, Li Niang sends him a cut strand of her hair symbolizing a total severance of their relationship. When Meng-hsia resists this idea, Li Niang resolves to die. Only then will it be possible for Meng-hsia to forget her and transfer his affections to Yun-ch'ien. While Meng-hsia is away visiting his parents, she simply lies down on her bed, thinks of dying, refuses medicine, and dies. She is attended throughout her illness by a tearful Yun-ch'ien, who does not understand the secret cause of Li Niang's death until she reads a letter which Li Niang has left behind. The revelation shocks Yun-ch'ien, who then herself falls ill. In order to repay Li Niang's amazing purity and devotion, Yun-ch'ien also resolves to die, and does so.

. Meanwhile Meng-hsia has gone to study in Japan, to fulfill his potential and to serve the country as Li Niang would have wanted him to

---

4. Though closely guarded, the secret actually had been discovered by one outsider, identified only as So-and-so Li (Li mou). Li uses the secret to blackmail Li Niang. Taking advantage of Meng-hsia's absence for a few days, Li forges Meng-hsia's hand and writes an obscene poem to Li Niang. He then reveals to her that he knows of the obscene poem, and demands that he be given the same favors accorded Meng-hsia. The ruse causes considerable grief between the two lovers, but does not succeed.

do. At the same time he feels intensely that he must repay his love debt to Li Niang. He finds an opportunity to serve both ends simultaneously in 1911 at Wuchang, where he joins the revolutionary forces. Foolishly rushing out on the front lines, clutching his love poetry to his breast, he quickly achieves death-for-love and death-for-the-nation in one fell swoop.

At this point the narrator emerges as a character in the story to wrap things up. Playing the "detective" (and thus adding to the novel a touch of detective story interest, which was on the increase during the 1910s), the narrator goes back to discover the fate of the remainder of the Ts'ui household. Patriarch Ts'ui himself had died shortly after Li Niang and Yun-ch'ien. The little boy P'eng-lang had been taken away to live with distant relatives. In the courtyard, the pear tree and magnolia tree had died following the deaths of Li Niang and Yun-ch'ien, respectively. At the base of the dead pear tree lay little balls of hardened mud, which appeared to have been formed by the teardrops of a broken-hearted lover.

Little is known of Hsu Chen-ya's early life, except that he was born around 1876 in Ch'ang-shu, Kiangsu Province.[5] His given name was originally Chueh, and his several pen names included "The One Who Watches for the Wild Swan" *(wang hung lou)* and "Third Son of Tung-hai" *(Tung-hai san lang)*. (Tung-hai in northern Kiangsu was the home prefecture of the Hsu family, and Shanghai writers of the surname Hsu collectively preserved their identification with that area. In the twenties they founded a magazine called *Tung-hai* which carried only fiction written by authors named Hsu.)[6] Of Hsu Chen-ya's immediate family, we know only that he had an elder brother, Hsu T'ien-hsiao, though it appears likely he had an elder sister as well.[7] After his schooling, he spent several years in and around Ch'ang-shu as a family tutor. Said to be a morose youth, Hsu's best friends were his elder brother, who was very quiet, and Wu Shuang-je, the only one of the three who often laughed. These three friends swore an oath of brotherhood which lasted through the years in Shanghai when they wrote love stories together.[8]

Hsu was married, probably around 1910, to Ts'ai Jui-chu, and he moved to Shanghai about the same time. There his writing and editing career began almost immediately with a position at Chou Shao-heng's

---

5. The year of Hsu's birth is inferred from the fact that his first wife is reported to have died in 1924, when Hsu was about 50 *sui*. See Liu Wen-chao, *Chung-wen wen-chai,* 59:24; and Ch'en Ting-shan, *Ch'un shen chiu-wen,* pp. 155–156.

6. YYHTP, p. 343.

7. In what appears to be an autobiographical account in *Chronicle of the Great Tears of Bygone Days,* the character Ho Meng-hsia has an older sister as well as an older brother.

8. YYHTP, p. 491.

People's Rights Journal, where Hsu often contributed to the fiction page. Following the closing of the journal in 1914 (a forced closing for political reasons)[9] Hsu took a regular job at the Chung Hwa Book Company (Chung-hua shu-chü) working on textbooks and contributing to the company's fiction magazine, *The World of Chinese Fiction (Chung-hua hsiao-shuo chieh).* This job he was soon ready to quit, however, both because his moods did not suit the routine of daily desk work and because the editor of *The World of Chinese Fiction* insisted on altering his carefully-worded phrases. Hsu needed little persuading when his friend Liu T'ieh-leng, with whom he had worked on the *People's Rights Journal,* raised capital for a new fiction magazine and asked Hsu to be its editor. The new magazine was *Thicket of Fiction (Hsiao-shuo ts'ung-pao,* 1914–1919), and Hsu's salary was a comfortable three hundred yuan per month. Hsu later helped found a publishing and distributing company, the *Ch'ing-hua shu-chü,* and another major magazine, *Fiction Quarterly (Hsiao-shuo chi-pao,* 1918–1920). Altogether he published at least seventeen classical-style "mournful" *(ai-ch'ing)* love novels, *Jade Pear Spirit* being the first. All were reprinted many times. He also produced four volumes of miscellany under the title *The Wasted Ink of Chen-ya (Chen-ya lang-mo),* plus several volumes of letters and poems.[10]

During the 1910s Hsu apparently suffered the emotional strain of an unhappy family life, but details are unavailable. He is said to have worn a sour expression constantly. He often was in conflict with his fellow writers and editors, and even violated the generally convivial spirit among the Shanghai literary circles of the 1910s by engaging in public vituperation with his enemies. His brother T'ien-hsiao also had an unhappy family life, including the unexpected death of a wife and an infant daughter. The two brothers would spend time consoling one another, often sitting a whole afternoon in the offices of *Thicket of Fiction* sipping wine. Hsu Chen-ya especially enjoyed wine but drank very slowly, sometimes spending hours to the cup.[11]

In 1924 Hsu's wife Ts'ai Jui-chu died, and the events following her death came to provide Butterfly culture's dealers in anecdotes with one

9. See chapter 5 below for details.

10. Eleven novels by Hsu are listed in YYHTP, p. 520; ones which are not listed include *My Husband (Yü chih fu); The Heart and Soul of Mandarin Ducks (Yuan-yang tan-kan); Wicked Karma (Nieh pao); One Tear Per Word (I-tzu i-lei); Regrets of the Boudoir (Lan-kuei hen);* and *Thirty-six Mandarin Ducks (San-shih-liu yuan-yang).* It is possible that some of Hsu's stories were ghostwritten with his permission, a practice which became more common in the 1920s. There is no direct evidence for this, however.

11. YYHTP, pp. 294, 461–462, 478; Ch'en Tieh-i, "Hsü Chen-ya yü 'Yü-li hun'" (part 3), *Hsing-tao jih-pao,* November 1, 1973; interview with Ch'eng She-wo, July 26, 1973.

of their strangest and best-known stories. Chang Hen-shui was the first to record it in print, but in fictional disguise, in his late-1920s novel *This Person's Notes (Ssu-jen chi.)* The anecdote begins with Hsu's composition of an extremely sentimental, hundred-verse mourning poem (tao wang tz'u) for his deceased wife. He published it under the name "Weeper of pearls" (Ch'i chu sheng) and used this pen name for the rest of his life. ("Weeping pearls" was a mythical reference to a guest who felt so thankful to his host that he wept pearls instead of tears; but the character *chu*—pearl—was also the last character in Hsu's wife's name.) According to the story, the mourning poem reached the eyes of Liu Yuan-ying, daughter of Liu Ch'un-lin, who was the last *chuang-yuan* under the imperial examination system before it was abolished in 1905. Immensely moved by the poem, the daughter of the *chuang-yuan* sought out more works by the "Weeper of pearls." She pored over *Jade Pear Spirit*—so the anecdote goes—until she had grown literally sick with pity and grief. When her father inquired about her health, she could only hand him a copy of the book and weep. At the time already thirty years old and still unmarried, the daughter is said to have implored her father to arrange that she become Hsu's second wife. At first there was considerable difficulty with the idea that a *chuang-yuan's* daughter should marry a popular novelist. But the daughter persisted, it is said, and the *chuang-yuan,* who read *Jade Pear Spirit* himself, had to admit Hsu's "genius." He consented to make an initial enquiry about marriage. Hsu, for his part, was pleased at the prospect of the respectability such a match would bring him. For despite the immense popularity of his fiction, Hsu had recently been a major target in the attack by May Fourth writers on Butterfly fiction, and respectability from any source was most welcome.[12]

Accordingly, the match was made. On the marriage invitation cards, the customary *fu lu shou* ("fortune, happiness, long life") was replaced by *fu lu yuan-yang* ("fortune, happiness, mandarin ducks"). Apparently, though, Hsu's second marriage turned out no happier than his first. According to his friends Hsu's refined, over-sensitive temperament made him no match for the *chuang-yuan's* daughter, whose sentimentalism turned out to come in a spirited and aggressive form. On their wedding night she persistently interrogated Hsu regarding the real story of *Jade Pear Spirit*. Was Li Niang a real person? Where was she now? What had been Hsu's relationship with her? Hsu's answers only involved him deeper and deeper in details he could not satisfactorily explain. Ever after that time, according to the story, Hsu was henpecked. He continued to spend a good deal of time out-

12. Liu Wen-chao, "Hsü Chen-ya yü chuang-yüan ch'ien chin," *Chung-wen wen-chai,* 59:24; Ch'en Ting-shan, *Ch'un-shen chiu-wen,* pp. 154–156.

side his house, somberly sipping wine with close friends. Hsu had one son by Liu Yuan-ying; she, who became as depressed as Hsu himself, died a few years later. Afterwards Hsu retired to his family home in Ch'ang-shu, where he lived in poor health and genteel poverty until his death during the war with Japan.[13]

Whether or not Hsu's second wife badgered him about the real-life details of his involvement with Li Niang and Yun-ch'ien, suspicion that *Jade Pear Spirit* was autobiographical seems at least to have had some basis. It is known that Hsu held a position as tutor in the household of a family named Ts'ai in the town of Hsi-ts'ang near Wusih some time in the last Ch'ing decade.[14] To what extent this family resembled the Ts'ui family of *Jade Pear Spirit* is unclear, but the similarity of the surnames is suggestive. It is reported, furthermore, that on the occasion of the first stage performance of the story in Shanghai, Hsu wrote a poem in which he equated himself with Meng-hsia.[15]

Additional clues emerge from the text itself, where Hsu provides some glimpses of Meng-hsia's psychology in intimate and *ad hoc* terms which it is difficult to believe were concocted. Chapter 20, for example, tells of a nightmare Meng-hsia had in which he was trapped in a room by a seductive woman (trapped in engagement to the seductive Yun-ch'ien?), but escapes. Li Niang is his savior, and he can run when he sees her; otherwise his feet seem leaden. He and Li Niang sail off in a boat together, and Meng-hsia slips and falls into the water. He screams for help—then awakens in a bed of cold sweat.[16] The account reads like that of a real dream, almost in fact like the ones Freud taught himself to record carefully before interpreting. Certainly it does not resemble the obviously conjured type of dream, much more common in Chinese fiction, in which the future is forecast or messages received from the supernatural.[17]

Another indication is the content of the narrator's comments when he stands back from his story to offer philosophical observations or to pass moral judgment. His judgments on Meng-hsia are sometimes unusually quick to be negative, suggesting formulaic self-deprecation. He tells us Meng-hsia's letters to Li Niang hurt her needlessly;[18] and

13. Liu Wen-chao, p. 24; Ch'en Ting-shan, pp. 154–156; YYHTP, pp. 129, 461–462; Fan Tzu, *Hsing-tao jih-pao,* July 14, 1972, p. 10; Ma-wu hsien-sheng (pseud.), *K'uai-pao,* June 5, 1976, p. 6.

14. Fan Yen-ch'iao, in YYHTP, p. 172.

15. Fan Yen-ch'iao, in YYHTP, pp. 173–174; Ch'en Tieh-i, *Hsing-tao jih-pao,* January 28, 1974, p. 6.

16. YLH, p. 109.

17. Pao Yü's dream at the end of chapter 5 in *Dream of the Red Chamber* is another, more famous but still unusual, example of a dream which is notably realistic (and probably autobiographical).

18. YLH, p. 132.

that when Meng-hsia agrees to Li Niang's plan that he marry Yun-ch'ien, his private thoughts were only of himself and Li Niang, not of Yun-ch'ien.[19]

When the main part of the novel ends with Li Niang's death, the entire story seems to become much more fictionalized. Meng-hsia, who had always been sombre and inhibited, suddenly rushes off to Japan, then rushes back to die at Wuchang. It is clear that in real life Hsu rushed to neither place, but continued to live the sombre life. The author's oft-repeated concern to "report the facts" also changes subtly near the end as he seems to speculate with the reader about the advantages and disadvantages of the several ways he could have arranged to have Meng-hsia die.[20] It appears, in short, that Hsu recorded his own experiences during the years 1908–1909, years which are carefully identified in the novel, then added an imaginative ending to the story in an attempt to bring it to a close and perhaps to intensify its tragic theme.

Hsu also may have added a fictional ending in order to divert readers from the autobiographical trail. In particular he would not want readers to know that Meng-hsia had "in reality" married Yun-ch'ien, since this obviously would pull both characters from their noble pedestals. Yet it is precisely such a tie that the readership would naturally suspect from the apparent similarities between Ts'ui Yun-ch'ien and Hsu's wife Ts'ai Jui-chu. Hsu eventually decided to give in to his readers on this point. In 1924 his old friend Cheng Cheng-ch'iu produced a movie version of *Jade Pear Spirit* in which Meng-hsia and Yun-ch'ien do marry in the end. Hsu contributed a few stanzas of poetry as an introduction to the movie, tacitly confirming that the real-life Yun-ch'ien was indeed Ts'ai Jui-chu.[21]

In the novel, Hsu is obviously concerned to imply that autobiography is out of the question, a task which becomes somewhat thorny because of his simultaneous wish to insist that the story is true. He handles the dilemma by inserting himself into the story in the role of witness. Identifying the narrator as himself, he makes the narrator the "detective" who investigates events after Meng-hsia's death. The narrator also explicitly states that he has never met Meng-hsia: he has learned the whole story only through a mutual friend named Shih-ch'ih who sent a packet of materials which Meng-hsia had left behind in Japan.[22] The calamitous end of the story moves the narrator to tears, yet he repeats that the events "bear no relation" to himself.[23]

19. YLH, p. 112.
20. YLH, pp. 158–160.
21. Ch'eng Chi-hua, *Chung-kuo tien-ying fa-chan shih* 1:64; YYHTP, p. 407.
22. YLH, p. 156.
23. YLH, p. 165.

Hsu's efforts to preserve the semblance of truth are rhetorically important. Occasionally he provides details which seem unnecessary, even clumsy, but which do have the effect of seeming to lock into concrete fact a story which otherwise would be unbelievably ideal. For no particular reason, for example, we are told to the minute the time of Li Niang's death.[24] There are tangential vignettes on a lascivious blackmailer, on a peasant festival, on P'eng-lang the little boy, and on Meng-hsia's parents—all descriptions whose *ad hoc* quality suggests factual report. The sense of truth is especially important as the story nears its end where, in a fashion dating from Ming times, it takes on an ethereal, partly supernatural quality: its leading characters die for the highest principles, and nature itself responds as magnolias and pear trees wither. Good storytellers have always known that nothing adds to the enjoyment of such accounts more than the intimation that "I saw this with my own eyes."

Yet the author's literary embellishments are evident almost everywhere, even when the narrative seems closest to facts. Hsu surely labored over his manuscript, and tells us in the text itself that he expects the story to sell an extraordinary number of copies.[25] The story is in linked chapter format, comprising thirty chapters of about equal length. In the manner of Lin Shu's translations, most chapters begin with a few lines of parallel prose reviewing the previous chapter's ending (but without resolutions of artificially developed climaxes, as in traditional vernacular style). The flashback device, also quite fashionable since the late-Ch'ing decade, is prominently employed in the first chapter. In an airy midnight scene we see Meng-hsia burying flowers and weeping for Li Niang, and only later are we told how he came to be a tutor with the Ts'ui family in the first place. The whole narration is heavily laden with lyrical description, poetry and love letters. Its debt to *Dream of the Red Chamber* is obvious, and Hsu proudly displays this connection by frequently pointing out parallels.[26]

Yet *Jade Pear Spirit* is much more compact sentimentalism than *Dream of the Red Chamber*. Short and few indeed are the intervals between its intense moods. Meng-hsia and Li Niang abruptly fall in love, abruptly make sweeping vows, abruptly die. Relations between young people of the same sex—Li Niang and Yun-ch'ien, Meng-hsia and Shih-ch'ih—are almost equally sudden and effusive. (One has to imagine the readers of the 1910s, who made this story a bestseller, de-

24. YLH, p. 146.
25. YLH, p. 157.
26. In addition to the evident reference to *Dream of the Red Chamber* in Meng-hsia's burying of flowers in chapter one, see also the stated or implied references on pp. 9, 24, 126, 142, and 157 of YLH.

lighting in the quick alternations of intense emotion.) Though Hsu
generally does a good job of preserving the psychological credibility
of his major characters, he is also willing to exaggerate or distort for
the sake of magnifying sentiments. On several occasions the lovers
send one another letters which the reader can see very clearly will be
heartrending to the recipient.[27] Yet the letters are sent, the hearts rent,
and a celebration of emotion follows for several pages. If the author
were consistent about the supersensitive concern his lovers felt for one
another, the injuries inflicted by their letters would surely be antici-
pated and avoided. The sacrifice of consistency to sentimentalism
seems quite deliberate.

Several times in the text Hsu offers explanations, all rhetorical, of
his purposes in writing. He begins in chapter 5 with a standard dis-
claimer. In writing this novel, he says, he is not wasting precious ink to
offend his readers with simple stories of bodily desires—stories of
which there are thousands, all alike; no, he is writing of true and extraordinary love.[28] Near the end of the story he repeats this claim, not
merely *pro forma* but neatly woven into the drama of his final two
chapters. Chapters 29 and 30 impress a tragic picture upon the reader.
Everyone in the Ts'ui household dies except P'eng-lang, who is taken
far away. A lonely white flag is all that stirs at the desolate homestead.
This denouement, Hsu tells us, "can serve as a mirror for youth;"[29] it
can warn all future generations of young men and women about the
danger hidden in the character *ch'ing*. Hsu thereby extends the circle of
the story's tragedy to encompass potentially his readers as well. In a
second shocking enlargement of this circle, he reveals that he himself is
a victim of *ch'ing*. "I, too, am a brokenhearted person, writing this
brokenhearted tale," he tells us, four pages from the novel's end.[30]

The novel being entertainment fiction primarily, one cannot, of
course, take its warning about *ch'ing* at face value. The effect of the
warning could hardly have been to inspire a mass swearing-off of
romantic interest among young readers. On the contrary, it surely increased the readership's fascination with *ch'ing,* and with melancholy
and pathos, and surely whetted their appetites for more of the same. In
any case more of the same was on its way, from both Hsu and his
imitators.

Hsu was not as prolific as many other Shanghai love story writers,
but the several short novels he did write stand out from the crowd.

27. YLH, pp. 34ff, 62ff, 132ff and 139ff; pp. 148ff is another case in point, though
here the letter is from Li Niang to Yun-ch'ien.
28. YLH, pp. 25–26.
29. YLH, p. 157.
30. YLH, p. 165.

Though he always aimed at extreme sentimentalism, his relative success must be attributed to his ability to preserve verisimilitude. He obviously had an unusual sensitivity to human psychology. Having appreciated a certain person's feelings, he could embroider and enlarge them in fiction until he had shaped a gripping story. Most of his imitators, largely lacking these abilities, based their stories on a more speculative imagination or even on other fiction. Combined with extreme sentimentalism, this yielded a maudlin fare less moving than Hsu's because it seemed more removed. (This is not to say the imitators lacked readers, however.)

Besides Hsu's psychological sensitivity, it cannot be denied— despite his bad reputation ever since the May Fourth Movement—that he possessed a remarkable ability with words. His lyrical descriptions are sometimes extremely graceful, and fit well with the mood of his narrative. His numerous poems and parallel phrases, though not great art, are far from incompetent. They effectively draw out the sentimentalism implicit in his stories and, by encapsulating it, invest it with a heightened poignancy. Over several pages the poems and parallelisms can generate an intense, rarefied atmosphere which prose alone could not achieve (and which makes Hsu's art difficult either to translate or to excerpt). True, it is easy to fault his fiction, as the May Fourth critics did, as anti-progressive in content, old-fashioned in style, and oversentimental. But there is no doubt that a peculiar kind of genius was necessary to produce it. Certainly there was no lack of writers in the 1910s trying to duplicate his feats, yet none really succeeded.

The record of *Jade Pear Spirit*'s publication is as stormy as the novel's popularity was contagious. This record begins in 1912 when Hsu was hired on the regular staff of the *People's Rights Journal* and began writing *Jade Pear Spirit* for serialization on the entertainment page. In 1914, when the novel's great appeal had become obvious, the People's Rights Publishing Section (Min-ch'üan ch'u-pan pu), an affiliate of the newspaper, published it in book form. Within a few months it had gone through five printings and brought the publisher handsome profits. Hsu, though, received nothing. Ma Chih-ch'ien, the manager of People's Rights publishers, took the position that his press was merely reprinting material which had appeared earlier in its own newspaper, and for which the writer had been duly paid in the form of his salary at the time. Hsu, on the other hand, argued that he had been hired as a news editor only and that his fiction contributions had been voluntary; in such a case, that new, Western thing known as the "legal copyright" should remain with the author. The dispute grew increasingly antagonistic and eventually broke into the newspapers. Ma's and Hsu's public railings against one another (they took out advertisements for the purpose) only added to the frenzy of popular interest in the novel.[31]

Eventually the case went to court and was decided in Hsu's favor. In 1915 he and his brother T'ien-hsiao established the Ch'ing-hua shu-chü, which resumed publication of *Jade Pear Spirit*. By that time, though, the book was being widely pirated, and Hsu felt disgusted at the tremendous toll in nerves and energy which his struggle had already demanded. Out of spite for the whole business, and to strike back at the piraters, the moody genius conceived the idea of simply giving away Ch'ing-hua shu-chü's copies of *Jade Pear Spirit*. He ran an advertisement in the magazine he edited, *Thicket of Fiction,* which stated that he "deeply regrets ever having written this book" and announced his plans to distribute it free of charge.[32]

He was far from abandoning the profit motive, though. In an attempt to replace *Jade Pear Spirit* on the market, he completed his *Chronicle of the Great Tears of Bygone Days (Hsueh hung lei shih)* in February, 1915.[33] *Chronicle*'s story was the same as *Jade Pear Spirit*'s, but was told in the form of Meng-hsia's diary, each chapter corresponding to one month. Hsu tells us in the Introduction to *Chronicle* that he wrote it to "correct *Jade Pear Spirit*'s mistakes" and to make the writing correspond more nearly to actual fact.[34] We are given a much better introduction to the family backgrounds of the lovers. Meng-hsia's parents, older brother and older sister are all described in considerable detail. Assuming the writing is indeed autobiographical, these descriptions are the best account we have of Hsu's own family history. Li Niang's background, almost a total blank in *Jade Pear Spirit,* is also revealed: her parents died when she was young; then a sister died; her husband was extremely good to her, but also died. Recounting this background makes Li Niang appear a more realistic figure and a more completely tragic one. Yun-ch'ien is introduced early in the story, thus correcting what Hsu had regarded as the serious mistake of having her enter in the middle of the *Jade Pear Spirit* account.

31. Chang Ching-lu, *Chung-kuo chin-tai ch'u-pan shih-liao,* 2:433, and illustration caption opposite p. 317; YYHTP, pp. 172, 407–408; Chang Ching-lu, *Tsai ch'u-pan chieh erh-shih nien,* pp. 36-37.

32. YYHTP, pp. 407–408; Chang Ching-lu, *Chung-kuo chin-tai ch'u-pan shih-liao,* opposite p. 317; interview with Ch'eng She-wo, July 26, 1973.

33. As with many of Hsu Chen-ya's titles, *Hsueh hung lei shih* is ambiguous and difficult to translate. The meaning of *hsueh* as "snow" is suggested by the idiom *hsueh ni hung chua* meaning literally "tracks of the wild swan in the snow and mud" or figuratively "traces of bygone days," appropriately suggestive of the novel's sentimental theme. To further complicate the matter, Hsu sometimes wrote under the pen name *wang hung lou,* "The One Who Watches for the Wild Swan," which suggests that *hung* may have stood for one of his loves in life. See Ch'en Tieh-i, "Kuan-yü 'Hsueh-hung lei shih'," *Hsing-tao jih-pao,* November 1 and 2, 1973.

34. Hsu Chen-ya, *Hsueh-hung lei shih,* p. 6.

In general, the ethereal quality of *Jade Pear Spirit*'s romantic theme is diminished in *Chronicle* and replaced by a greater stress on Confucian relations and the tragedy of the family as a whole. The change in emphasis may have been due to the greater distance in time between Hsu and his personal experience of the romance. Meng-hsia is a less infatuated character in the 1915 writing. In the end he does not run blindly off to die for the country as in *Jade Pear Spirit,* but it is foreshadowed that he eventually will.

Chronicle of the Great Tears of Bygone Days is considerably longer than *Jade Pear Spirit,* includes more poetry, and is a better designed work. It was published first in *Thicket of Fiction* and then at the Ch'ing-hua shu-chü, where it was probably the company's most profitable book. Since Hsu and his friends owned that company, we may assume that *Chronicle* brought Hsu a measure of monetary as well as moral restitution after the *Jade Pear Spirit* affair. Yet there is no question that the total market for the story of Li Niang and Meng-hsia continued to extend far beyond the reach of his copyright. Though statistics are unavailable, both *Chronicle* and *Jade Pear Spirit* are generally estimated to have reached a total circulation somewhere in the hundred thousands, including large-scale reprintings in Hong Kong and Singapore.[35] Some have even estimated a total circulation of over a million, counting continued reprintings in the 1920s and later.[36] Hsu and his friends probably sold only a few tens of thousands.

Besides its magazine and book forms, the story received circulation in stage plays and movies. The Shanghai Min-hsing she was the first of many groups to produce a dramatization, which they began presenting shortly after the serialization of *Chronicle* was complete. In spite of the fact that they altered the story's ending to make it a happy one, they drew a tolerably favorable response from Hsu in the form of twenty-four lines of sentimental *chueh-chü.*[37] The first movie was directed by Cheng Cheng-ch'iu in 1924 at the Star Film Company (Ming-hsing ying-p'ien kung-ssu). The film's happy marriage between Yun-ch'ien and Meng-hsia, which was only part of a general de-emphasis of the story's pervasive pessimism, was surely due in part to May Fourth charges in the early twenties that the story was "useless" and "backward." Cheng Cheng-ch'iu, besides toning down the sentimentalism, accentuated the story's "social problem." It was advertised, in fact, as a "problem-of-widow-chastity" film, and Hsu

35. Interviews with Kao Chen-pai, November 14, 1972; Ch'eng She-wo, July 26, 1973; Ch'en Ting-shan, July 25, 1973. See also Fan Yen-ch'iao, in YYHTP, p. 174; YYHTP, pp. 297, 462; Ch'en Tieh-i, "Kuan-yü 'Hsueh hung lei shih'," *Hsing-tao jih-pao,* November 1 and 2, 1973.

36. Liu Wen-chao, p. 24.

37. Fan Yen-ch'iao, in YYHTP, pp. 173–174; Ch'en Tieh-i, "Hsu Chen-ya ti tzu-hua kung-chuang," *Hsing-tao jih-pao,* January 28, 1974, p. 6.

himself publicly concurred in the changes.[38] In later years at least two other film versions of the *Jade Pear Spirit* story were made in Shanghai and Hong Kong.[39]

2. The Love Story Wave

In literary terms, the love stories of the 1910s derived from precedents in the classical and vernacular traditions which are centuries, even a millenium, old; hence their general potential to "catch on" from time to time should hardly cause surprise. The particular wave of love story interest which crested in the mid-1910s had begun its swell some fifteen years earlier. Leo Lee has shown how Lin Shu's discovery of sentiment in *La Dame aux Camélias* set a trend in the romantic mood of Shanghai fiction.[40] The trend grew during the late-Ch'ing decade with more translations of Western romantic literature, with stories of the pleasure quarters such as Sun Chia-chen's *Magnificent Dreams in Shanghai (Hai-shang fan-hua meng)* and the closely related "writing of sentiment" novels *(hsieh-ch'ing hsiao-shuo)* of Wu Wo-yao and Chang Ch'un-fan. All these inspired similar works during 1906–1911 and led directly to the "Butterfly" stories of the 1910s.[41] By the time *Jade Pear Spirit* became a hit in the mid-1910s, there were quite a number of authors and author-translators ready to meet the crescendo in public demand for love stories. Several leading magazines cultivated their own groups of contributors, and literally thousands of short stories appeared.[42]

The stories grew more blatantly sentimental as their readership grew. Their literary quality suffered as most aspects of fiction, including plot, characterization, and moral lesson, were de-emphasized in comparison with the primary concern of evoking emotion. Authors would simply piece together one intense scene after another into a story line, seeking to evoke a range of emotions—love, anger, pity, sorrow—of maximum intensity in minimum space. Advertisements in contemporary magazines promised that novels would grip the reader's heart and call forth strong and true feelings.

Cultural historians of the modern West have often associated an interest in sentiment, especially the sentimental novel, with the

38. Ch'eng Chi-hua, *Chung-kuo tien-ying fa-chan shih,* 1: 64–65; YYHTP, p. 407.

39. T'u Kuang-ch'i directed two movies based on the *Jade Pear Spirit* story. The first, made in Shanghai, was called *Lung-feng hua chu* and starred Ch'en Yen-yen and Feng Che; the second, a Hong Kong product, was called *Nieh hai ch'ing-t'ien* and starred Li Li-hua, Lo Wei, and Lui Ch'i. See Lui Wen-chao, p. 24, and Ch'en Tieh-i, "Hsu Chen-ya ti tzu-hua kung-chuang," *Hsing-tao jih-pao,* January 28, 1974, p. 6.

40. Lee, *Romantic Generation,* pp. 44–46.

41. Ch'ien Hsing-ts'un, *Wan-ch'ing hsiao-shuo shih* (Hong Kong), p. 176.

42. See chapter 4 for information on the various groups of love-story authors.

emergence of an urban bourgeois class.[43] The growth of such a class has further been seen as a forerunner of industrialism and all the far-reaching economic and social changes which stem from it. New social patterns, in particular new roles for women, have been seen as causes for the expression, and psychological exploration through fiction, of the individual's changing relation to the social, and even cosmic, order.

The social background of bourgeois fiction in China has not been adequately studied in these terms. Marxist literary historians in China have used the word "bourgeois" without carefully examining its applicability. Passing reference is sometimes made to the emergence of Sung and Yuan urban storytelling as the artistic manifestation of a bourgeois or proto-bourgeois urban class; the urban circulation of Feng Meng-lung's collections of written stories in the late Ming has also been called a "bourgeois" development, but without detailed argument. In fact, it seems that neither of these cases is as close to the Western "bourgeois" experience as the social background of the sentimental stories of the 1910s. If we consider the original example of bourgeois sentimentalism in the West to have appeared in eighteenth-century England, where the novels of Samuel Richardson grew in popularity as the Industrial Revolution unfolded, nothing in China resembles the prototype quite so closely as Shanghai in the early twentieth century. (Shanghai's modernization is of course best viewed not as "similar to" Western modernization but as part of the single global process which happened to begin in England.) Chinese scholars since the May Fourth Movement who have referred to Butterfly love stories as "bourgeois" seem to have found firm ground for the application of the term to Chinese fiction and society.

Justification for using the term can be more than a general pointing out of the coincidence of industrialism and sentimental fiction. Specific similarities appear in how changing social patterns left the individual, especially among the young, with less support from traditional family and community ties; how the pattern of one's life was more in one's own hands than before; how a person's psychological security, which began with the basic ties of marriage and family, thus became cause for worry; how possibilities of new wealth in the city enticed people to try new social and economic roles; how fiction could help "socialize" the socially mobile into the class to which they aspired; how failure, or fear of failure, created a need for escape from present realities; and how these several changes required the formation of new behavioral norms

43. E.g., Arnold Hauser, *The Social History of Western Art* (New York, 1952) 2:558–559; Leavis, *Fiction*, pp. 154–157; Fiedler, *Love and Death in the American Novel*, pp. 20–89; Altick, *Common Reader*, pp. 45, 290; Lowenthal, *Literature, Popular Culture, and Society*, pp. 81, 83–85.

and their testing against the old, still domineering moralities of Christianity in Victorian England and Confucianism in the Shanghai of the 1910s. In both cases, there is little doubt that popular fiction served as a forum for the working out of new norms, as well as a source of comfort from the anxieties which attended the great search.

The importance of women in the rise of popular urban fiction in England, both as readers and as fictional protagonists, is often pointed out. Though there are notable differences in the Chinese case, the similarities are remarkable. In abbreviated form, the case is perhaps best illustrated in the female protagonists of two leading love stories, Li Niang of *Jade Pear Spirit* and Clarissa of Samuel Richardson's *Clarissa*. Both women are scrupulously virtuous, at least in their intentions: Li Niang is a chaste widow and Clarissa a virgin. Yet each is enticed, by circumstances and a handsome young lover, into what they and society agree to be the "fallen condition" of illicit love (sex in Clarissa's case, affection in Li Niang's). On trial before Morality, each resolves that suicide is the only solution and literally thinks herself to sickness and then to death. Both are presented sympathetically, as characters with whom young readers might wish to identify.

An attempt to account for these similarities can be intriguing. If one rules out coincidence, and the possibility that Hsu imitated Richardson—an almost unthinkable chance given the lack of any evidence and given *Jade Pear Spirit's* cultural authenticity—it is tempting to seek an explanation in the appetites of similarly conditioned readerships. The question becomes not "Why were the themes similar?" but "Why did novels with similar themes become popular?"

Discussions of emerging bourgeois readerships in the West usually assume that love stories answered a need which was primarily emotional. Richardson's novels helped, as it were, to release reservoirs of feeling which social change had generated. The particular anxieties of a female readership could be played out in the fictional world of female characters. It is here that one must notice some differences between Richardson and Hsu Chen-ya, and between their readerships. In Richardson's Clarissa much more than in Hsu's Li Niang, the reader gets an inner view of a young woman's mind. Clarissa's trials and her struggles in their full complexity are laid bare, and the reader is invited to become involved in her outlook. The handsome Lovelace is an objective force—an attraction, a threat, an enemy—in any case something whose management is part of Clarissa's trial. Our view of Li Niang, on the other hand, is primarily external. She, too, is on trial, but we have only an idealized version of her feelings. Fate, more than her lover, is her adversary. Meng-hsia's feelings are given to us much more fully and sympathetically than Lovelace's, while Li Niang's apotheosis as a chaste widow is presented to the reader from a point of view which, if not entirely "male," at least was sufficiently orthodox by late imperial times to deny much scope for ambiguous or complex feelings.

Thus, despite the similarities between Clarissa and Li Niang, the fact that Li Niang still upholds the rigid framework of Confucianism, and does not reveal the ramified and unsure psychology of a Clarissa, suggests that we must seek differences in the nature and tendencies of the two readerships. It does seem, first, that the Shanghai readership of the 1910s included a much smaller proportion of women than did Richardson's readership. That the best-selling stories were told mostly from a masculine viewpoint is, of course, an initial reason to suspect a predominantly male readership. More concrete evidence, insofar as it is available through interviews with publishers and authors, and through school enrollment figures, supports the hypothesis of a readership at least four-fifths male.[44]

More broadly, while there can be no doubt that Shanghai in the 1910s was beginning to undergo the general kind of social change which had accompanied industrialization in Western cities, the changes were clearly further from the cultural center (and therefore at once more ominous and more easily *called* irrelevant) than in the London and Manchester of Richardson's England. Shanghai differed from the English case in two fundamental ways: first, modern changes in Shanghai arrived together with an alien culture; and second, from a Chinese point of view, they arrived with astonishing rapidity, at least in their outward forms. In effect they presented an alternative life style whose contrast with existing forms was much more developed and explicit than the contrast between "new" and "old" had been in England or in other Western countries where industrialism was largely indigenous. While the new urban classes in England used novels to grapple with obscure "inner" upheavals (obscure *because* they were inner), readers of Shanghai love stories tended to deal in overly simple comparisons between two clearcut and outwardly-defined alternatives for life. In fictional form, "new-style" Western behavior patterns could be tried on and taken off as easily as a Western hat, whether for fun or as a serious experiment.

Many of the "experiments" concerned Western-style courtship and new social roles for women (as we saw reflected in *Fate in Tears and Laughter* in chapter 1). Beginning in the late Ch'ing decade there was little room for doubt among the Shanghai reading public that change in these matters was on its way. Old customs which held women back—footbinding, forced marriages, and the giving of child

44. See chapter 5 below.

brides—had all been denounced, while women's education in the new style was being advertised and promoted. Theoretical essays as well as works of fiction explored and advocated new social roles for women outside the household.[45] By the end of the decade, the first of the women's magazines specially devoted to these questions had appeared.

In the late Ch'ing decade, though, experimentation with new roles for women was almost entirely limited to the realm of thought. Reality lagged far behind, even in Shanghai. Women's schools received a great deal of public notice, but in reality were not numerous; the women's magazines which did appear were read mostly by men.[46] A few real-life heroines, such as the revolutionary Ch'iu Chin, received great public attention not because they were typical but precisely because they were so extraordinary.

The gap between ideas and reality is easily understandable, given the obvious need for due consideration before using anything too new or alien. But at the same time, reformist zeal demanded expression, and to some extent the difficulty of putting theory into practice was simplistically linked with the issue of removing the Manchu government. It was widely imagined among those who spoke of revolution that once the Manchus were out the new life would naturally spring forth on its own. Hence 1912 marked a high tide of anticipation: China would finally be free to reform herself as she wished.

Yet what, at a concrete level, was to be done? How were young women in the new day actually to behave? And how were young men to relate to them? In dealing implicitly with these questions, the love stories of the 1910s allowed their readers to try out their notions in a fictional context and "observe" the results. It is significant that most of the love stories were short stories, and even the ones of novel length were not very long.[47] Young readers wanted their lessons quickly, and wanted the latest views. The excitement of the times would hardly permit lengthy works. Magazines often promised that they would wind up serialized stories within two or three issues at most.

The literary forms and styles of the 1910s also illustrate the confusion and eclecticism of the times. Although there was less real experimentation with new literary and linguistic influences than during

45. Chapter 9 of Ch'ien Hsing-ts'un's *Wan-ch'ing hsiao-shuo shih* reviews important late Ch'ing fiction dealing with the liberation of women. The issue was pervasive among progressive circles in the treaty ports, and appeared with varying degrees of explicitness in a wide variety of works.

46. See chapter 5 below.

47. Some lengthy social novels were written and read during the 1910s, but were popular among somewhat older audiences.

the previous decade, authors did draw upon a variety of forms and styles, both Chinese and Western. Some stories were in traditional vernacular style, but many employed a mixture of styles—causing May Fourth detractors later to describe the standard mode as "half-classical-but-not-vernacular" *(pan wen pu pai)*. Allowing for some degree of intermixture, one can generally distinguish four styles, two classical and two vernacular.

Most common was a *ku-wen* style, in which stories were fashioned after T'ang *ch'uan-ch'i* or, more importantly, Lin Shu's elegant translations of *La Dame aux Camélias* and other Western fiction. In the 1910s stories in this style were short, had clearly shaped plots, made great use of standard clichés, and were often interlarded with seven-character *chueh-chü*.

A second important classical mode was the *p'ien-li* style which had developed in the Six Dynasties and was also called "four-six" style because it linked parallel lines of four and six characters. The style was not originally intended for fiction, and with one known exception in the T'ang period,[48] was not used for fiction until the 19th century, when a man named Ch'en Ch'iu wrote a novel called *Informal History of Yen Shan (Yen-shan wai-shih)*. Drawing his content from a Ming short story, Ch'en's aim was merely stylistic—to achieve the *tour de force* of completing an entire novel in "four-six" style. The author himself modestly described his effort as "presumptuous and absurd," and not something to be imitated;[49] but the appeal of his parallelism extended to the classical-style love stories of the 1910s a century later.[50] No author of the 1910s is known to have attempted a duplication of Ch'en Ch'iu's feat of doing a whole novel, or even a short story, in "four-six" style. But the style was widely used in the 1910s, especially in the opening lines of chapters.

When the fiery youth of May Fourth attacked popular love stories in the early 1920s, "four-six" parallelism was singled out as especially absurd. Its rigidity suited the technical show-off but not the serious literary artist. On the defensive, practitioners of "four-six" were obliged either to explain their interests or to conceal them. One reason they routinely cited *Dream of the Red Chamber* as a literary inspiration was that this novel was as beyond reproach as a Chinese literary prec-

48. This was *Travels to the Lodgings of Immortals (Yu-hsien k'u)* by Chang Cho, a book which was lost in China but preserved in Japan and rediscovered in the 20th century. See Lu Hsun, *Chung-kuo hsiao-shuo shih-lueh* (Shanghai, 1931), pp. 91–93.

49. Lu Hsun, *Chung-kuo hsiao-shuo shih-lueh*, p. 311.

50. Interviews with Ch'en Ting-shan, July 25, 1973, and Ch'eng She-wo, July 26, 1973; see also Chih Hsi in *Hsin Ch'ao* 1.1, (January 1919).

edent could be. Pressed in particular on the question of "four-six" style, Liu T'ieh-leng, a founder of *Thicket of Fiction* magazine in the 1910s, awkwardly attributed the use of "four-six" style to the unhappy political situation of the mid-1910s: "Under Yuan [Shih-k'ai]'s wanton abuse of power, one could hardly weep, and barely laugh, and so, beset by overwhelming depression, we used this [four-six] style to vent our rage."[51] Could he have afforded more candor, Liu might have observed that not only he and his friends, but tens of thousands of readers, found four-six genuinely appealing.

A minority of the love stories of the 1910s used traditional-style vernacular. *Dream of the Red Chamber* was widely imitated, but no 1910s stories were as long or as rich. Only diction had undergone significant changes from pre-modern vernacular style. In addition to the occasional Western term in transliteration, much more important was the addition of the modern, mostly two-character compounds (such as *fu-wu,* "service"; *ch'ang-ho,* "situation"; *wen-ming,* "civilization") which had been invented in Japan and introduced into Chinese literature during the late Ch'ing years when Western literary works in Japanese versions became frequent objects of translation into Chinese.[52] Stories about the brothel scene sometimes included dialogue in the Wu dialect, following the influence of late Ch'ing works like *Shanghai Flowers (Hai-shang hua), Magnificent Dreams in Shanghai,* and *Nine-tailed Turtles (Chiu-wei kuei).*

A second group of stories was fashioned after traditional storytelling in the Soochow style, it being no coincidence that Soochow was also the hometown of many Butterfly authors and a former center of popular fiction. The distinction in this storytelling between "great stories" and "small stories" *(ta shu, hsiao shu)* was still observed in the 1910s. "Great" originally meant "from the classics," but eventually came to signify any story about kings, generals, or heroes: for example, stories from *Romance of the Three Kingdoms* and *The Water Margin.* "Small" stories were love stories such as those from *Romance of the Western Chamber (Hsi hsiang chi), The Destiny of Three Smiles (San hsiao yin-yuan)* and *Jade Dragonfly (Yü ch'ing-t'ing).* These were performed as *t'an-tz'u,* a form in which vernacular narrative alternates with verse sung to the accompaniment of the stringed instruments called *san-hsien* or *p'i-p'a.*[53] Written forms of *t'an-tz'u* had been a standard vehicle for romantic stories in Ch'ing times, and in the 1910s Butterfly authors

51. YYHTP, p. 294.

52. More than 460 such terms are listed in Kao Ming-k'ai and Liu Cheng-t'an, *Hsien-tai Han-yü wai-lai-tz'u yen-chiu* (Peking, 1958), pp. 79–98; see also Paul Kratochvil, *The Chinese Language Today* (London, 1968), p. 67.

53. See CYLHIL, pp. 44–45. *Ta shu* were also called *yen-chiang* and *p'ing-hua.*

expanded upon this tradition. Magazines carried special sections for *t'an-tz'u,* clearly labeling which portions were to be sung and which read. The pieces were not intended for actual performance any more than their Ch'ing predecessors had been; nor is it likely that Shanghai readers often sang to themselves. Yet the rhythm of the lines in the sung portion certainly remained important in "bringing the story home" to readers who were familiar with the form and enjoyed its lilt.

Many love stories of the 1910s showed some degree of stylistic influence from Western fiction. An influence which the authors themselves were quick to claim was the use of psychological description, an "inner" view of the minds of fictional characters.[54] Their association of Western influence and psychological description stemmed from the early translations by Lin Shu and others who first brought Western psychological novels to the Shanghai literary scene. Yet this self-perceived influence may not have been as important as the authors claimed. One can, with Jaroslav Prusek, trace a tendency toward "subjectivism" in Chinese fiction to the middle Ch'ing or earlier,[55] and in such a context it is unclear that the love stories of the 1910s (excluding translations) were substantially more "psychological" than their Ch'ing predecessors. Moreover, though certainly emotional (perhaps "psychological" in that sense), the stories are not strong on "inner" descriptions; most description is of externally observable events.

Some authors claimed a Western influence in the use of flashbacks and of direct quotations in dialogue, unmediated by a narrator. An early example which became famous for both of these was Wu Wo-yao's *Fantastic Grievances of Nine Lives (Chiu-ming ch'i-yuan),* published in the fourth issue of Liang Ch'i-ch'ao's *New Fiction* (1902). The story begins:

> "Hey—partner—now we've had it. Look at the door—it's shut tight. How're we going to break in?"
> "Tch! Idiot! You think there's no way to knock open a couple of measly wooden doors like this? Come on! Come on!! Give me that iron hammer."

The dialogue continues with a total of thirty-seven direct quotations before the narrator finally breaks in saying:

> My goodness! Dear Reader, look how I have lost my head and so suddenly related this whole story of bandits at work . . . .

54. Interviews with Pao T'ien-hsiao, December 6, 1972; Kao Chen-pai, April 26, 1973; Ch'en Ting-shan, July 25, 1973; Yeh Ling-feng, April 28, 1973.
55. J. Prusek, "Subjectivism and Individualism in Modern Chinese Literature" *Archiv Orientalni* 25.2 (1957):261–283.

While this use of the flashback was startling in the context of tradition, it cannot be said that flashbacks were new in Chinese fiction. "*Ch'u . . .*" ("in the beginning . . .") had been standardly used to go back and fill the reader in on material which could explain a present circumstance. In this particular function it had been quite unobtrusive.

The coincidence of the "Western" flashback and its Chinese counterpart may explain why the device quickly became a frozen convention in the 1910s. For all its "newness" it did not inspire Butterfly writers toward creative experimentation with the use of time in fiction. After a beginning flashback, most stories proceeded in straight-line chronological order, one episode at a time (like a novice playing *go*, as Mao Tun once quipped).[56] The real reason for calling the flashback "new" and "Western" was stylishness. Like other things from the West, it was accepted by Butterfly culture as a gimmick, while deeper concerns of both writers and readers lay elsewhere.

By the mid-1910s the plots of most of the love stories converged into a few standard patterns. Two basic types emerged, the happy ending and the tragic ending, with tragic endings increasingly numerous. In both cases, the stories typically involved a struggle against some "social problem" such as widow chastity, child marriages, dowries, treacherous matchmakers, the difficulty of marriage between social unequals, and so on—all things which in one way or another put barriers between lovers. Besides dramatizing a story, the inclusion of such problems helped readers keep abreast, though still in a formulaic way, of "new" ideas about solutions to the problems. In happy-ending stories, the lovers naturally overcome their problems and blissfully unite. In the tragic endings, whose realism, as Lu Hsun acidly observed, "has to be regarded as a great step forward," the lovers are separated absolutely, usually by death.[57]

Readers could choose which type of ending they wished to read because of the way a story's title was labelled. Love stories generally, but especially the ones with happy endings, were called *yen-ch'ing hsiao-shuo* (usually the yen^2 meaning "words" but sometimes yen^4, "beauty"); the sad endings were called *ai-ch'ing* (ai^1, "lament") or *k'u-ch'ing* stories. The appropriate labels were given in small characters before a story's title in books, magazines, and newspapers alike. Even translations of Western works were categorized. Mark Twain's *The Californian's Tale*, which tells of a young man who waits in vain year after year for the return of his dead wife, was translated in 1915 as

56. Mao Tun, *Hsiao-shuo yüeh-pao* (July 1922), excerpted in YYHTP, p. 11.
57. Lu Hsün, "Shanghai wen-i chih i-tu," in *Erh-hsin chi*, reprinted in YYHTP, p. 176.

"Ch'i" ("Wife"). Chou Shou-chüan, the translator, duly categorizes and labels it an *"ai-ch'ing"* story.[58]

One must recognize the substantial truth of the charge brought by May Fourth writers, and those who have followed their lead, that the 1910s love stories were often unimaginative re-runs, "a thousand stories in the same mould." The charge referred to hackneyed themes and characters, a limited repertoire of "problems," tiresome use of poetry, and "frozen" use of flashbacks and standard plots.

But one must not infer from the stereotyped nature of the stories that they were dull to readers at the time: quite the contrary, they were hits. The standards of taste of Butterfly readers obviously differed significantly from those of the much more highly educated and widely read May Fourth literati. The common reader could find "sincere" and exciting works which literary scholars found unbearably sentimental. In this he matched popular fiction audiences elsewhere. The appeal of Samuel Richardson's sentimental novels has, for example, been explained by Arnold Hauser in terms of "the frankness of the self-exposure of their characters . . . however affected and forced the tone of these confessions seems to us today."[59] And like a Butterfly novel's hackneyed poems, the super-sentimental and woodenly rhymed messages of greeting cards in the West, as Richard Hoggart points out in *The Uses of Literacy,* are despised only by those who do not buy and treasure them. The English common people, says Hoggart, find sentimentalism "real."[60] The basic principle of "four-six" style must likewise be recognized as having very broad appeal. In the West, it has been known at least since the *Book of Psalms* that the human mind responds emotionally to verbal parallelism. Americans who remember John Kennedy's Inaugural Address in 1961 know the principle still works, even if superficially.

Thus the Butterfly stories of the 1910s, with the undeniable allure of both their style and their sentimental content, as well as their introduction of Western and reformist ideas and the excitement of popular "waves," offered much to compensate for clumsy or repetitive art.

For the social historian, the stories are, as we shall attempt to show in the next section, an invaluable access to popular conceptions and attitudes. These popular ideas may be discovered by examining stories for what the reader was obliged to think and feel in order to enjoy them, as we know many readers did. In practice this method is less difficult than it might seem. Almost all popular stories in Shanghai

58. Chou Shou-chüan, *Hsiao-shuo ta-kuan,* no. 1 (August 1915).
59. Hauser, *The Social History of Western Art,* 2:563.
60. Hoggart, *The Uses of Literacy,* p. 107.

(not just the love stories) led readers through the ins and outs of their narration along what might be called "lines of sympathy" which clearly indicated which characters were good and which bad and what behavior right and wrong. In addition, "new-style" and "old-style" behavior is clearly demarcated, frequently with evaluative connotations. It is extremely unlikely that a reader could enjoy a story if his own feelings differed substantially from the assumptions of its "line of sympathy." Without necessarily sharing the prescribed feelings, a modern reader can readily discover them by following "lines of sympathy" and imagining himself to concur in them. To a limited extent, it has been also possible to check results through interviews with readers from the time.

It should be pointed out that, for the purposes of this methodology, an author's intentions are of only secondary interest. One might object that the authors of popular fiction in the 1910s generally came from comfortable gentry backgrounds and hence could not speak for a "popular" level of urban residents. But we claim to be reaching the mind of the common reader not because the author so intended but simply because certain texts were, in fact, popular. If hundreds of thousands of readers found a story appealing, then we can infer something about "popular" attitudes from it, regardless of who wrote it or why.[61]

3. The Romantic Route

Young lovers are continually trapped by social custom, the hand of fate, and the treacheries of the love relationship, into hopeless predicaments whose consequences are worry, pain, remorse, sickness, and often death. The poignancy of all this is enhanced by the beauty, genius, sensitivity, innocence, and promise with which the young lovers began. In their most basic features, these love stories drew upon cultural myths of long-standing importance. *Dream of the Red Chamber* (in its form as an idealized love story myth) is continually in evidence in descriptions of supersensitive, crazily infatuated young lovers. The

61. The historian is on safest ground, of course, drawing conclusions from stories which he knows to have had large circulations. The observations in the following section, "The Romantic Route," are based on best sellers as well as a sampling of other love stories with more modest circulations. But the validity of an impression based on a story which circulated only in the thousands, let us say, does not decrease by a factor of one hundred from the validity of conclusions based on *Jade Pear Spirit* which circulated in the hundreds of thousands, because of the manifest high degree of similarity among the love stories of the 1910s. A small-circulation story can be assumed to reveal the feelings and attitudes of a large group of readers if we know that it belongs to a stereotype representing thousands of others. This assumption discounts only the absurd possibility that that one small group of readers was doing all the reading of thousands of similar stories.

Ch'ing period *ts'ai-tzu chia-jen* formula, according to which a poor but talented scholar finds solace with a beautiful woman who alone appreciates his genius, also plays a part, although these stories usually end in marital bliss. In the love stories of the 1910s written in basic imitation of *Jade Pear Spirit,* it is possible to descry a common pattern of important features which seems to have served authors and their reading public as a new composite myth. We might call this new composite myth the Romantic Route through life. The great number of stories which exemplified one or several parts of the Romantic Route not only reinforced its status as a paradigm but also gave it a completeness over the human life cycle, explaining everything from cradle to grave.

The Route may be analyzed in six stages: (1) Extraordinary Inborn Gifts, (2) Supersensitivity, (3) Falling in Love, (4) Cruel Fate, (5) Worry and Disease, and (6) Destruction. Although the six stages are roughly sequential in the actual telling of stories, they are never merely sequential. They are linked by an inescapable determinism; each stage bears within its whole conception either the recapitulation or the foreshadowing of every other. In fact they are better viewed as phases of a single experience than as separate experiences. Besides implying one another, the stages stand in a parallel complementarity whose suggestion of *yin* and *yang* is perhaps too obvious to need comment. The first, second, and third stages are positive; the fourth, fifth and sixth are negative. The first and fourth stages, a linked pair, both issue from the hand of fate, which never deals out one without the other. The second and fifth, which are the human reactions to the first and fourth, are also parallel and contrasting (and lavishly presented by novelists in bittersweet combination). The third and sixth stages are the inevitable ends of the positive and negative sub-cycles of the Route, yet, again in perfect reciprocity, are also the beginnings of change toward their opposites. Young people are attracted to love, yet love traps them in tragedy; normally they shun death, yet only death offers escape. We summarize below the character of each of the six stages of the Romantic Route.

Stage 1, Extraordinary Inborn Gifts, gives the reader that impression which is so important in popular, as opposed to elite, storytelling, namely, the impression that the author does not speak of ordinary persons and events. The young lovers of the story can, it is true, serve as examples for thousands of young lovers in the real world; but this is not because they are typical but because they are ideal. Right from childhood they exhibit remarkable talent, beauty, sentimentality, and sometimes willful independence. Their parents are surprised at them; neighbors marvel. In the absence of any normal, earthly way of explaining their extraordinary qualities, it is assumed by all that these are special gifts from heaven. And the gifts are more than just *from* heaven; they are part of the heavenly nature itself, a sharing in the human sphere of the purity of the cosmic order. The special gifts are the wherewithal from which true love of a special order will naturally spring, and only those born with the gifts will ever achieve that order of true love. Part of the struggle to which the specially gifted are destined will involve the search for partners of the opposite sex who are similarly endowed.

For men, the most important extraordinary characteristic is genius *(ts'ai)*. This is primarily literary genius, but not the ordinary kind of literary genius which brings official position and fortune. It is a highly independent, almost wizardly genius which obeys only its own standards. (This almost perverse element in its expression foreshadows the pain which lies in store for him who possesses it.) The reader is given to know a young man's genius through his brilliant poems and his great powers of understanding and sympathy, especially concerning the natural world. But ordinary society does not recognize the rare genius. He is isolated, and often impoverished. He rejects the normal world because he understands higher things; the normal world rejects him because it does not.

For women, beauty is the outstanding characteristic. But like a man's genius, beauty for the woman is not the normal type of beauty. Much of it does not appear on the surface. In purely physical terms, in fact, it is common that only a beautiful woman's face is described, in particular her eyes, which are windows to the spirit. (Beauties in magazine photographs of the 1910s are always heavily clothed from the neck down.)[62] The beauty's posture and movement are very important: a slim and graceful standing outline, the bending of a willowy waist, quick and agile fingers, smooth and silent footsteps. All these are only the external signs which bespeak an inner beauty—true beauty. True beauty is exciting. Cosmetic attractiveness is not; it is the province of entertainers and cheap women.

The extraordinarily gifted woman combines beauty with a soft, pliant nature and a great capacity for warm sympathy. (Some day she will be able to appreciate and love a moody genius whom others reject.) But her profuse emotion, like Lin Tai-yü's, issues from a frail frame. She is prone to weep, quick to fall ill. The delicacy of her beauty is also an omen of her destiny.

62. An interesting exception to this generalization are photographs of Western paintings and sculpture, usually famous art, whose subject is the naked female body. That such examples were Western seems to have been at least as important as their being art.

Although genius and beauty are predominantly tied to the male and female respectively, it is important to note that they are not strictly so tied. More than in Western popular romances, the men of the Romantic Route tend to display "female" characteristics and the women "male" ones. The specially gifted woman often possesses a measure of genius in addition to her beauty. Her genius evidences itself not only in women's skills, such as needlework, but also in the same way as the man's, through brilliant poetry. Similarly, the specially gifted man is usually almost as good-looking as the woman. Equally important, he shares her related qualities of "female" softness, including a less-than-robust physical constitution and great capacity for loving sympathy. He is young, callow, thin, beardless.[63] He will also fall sick, or burst into tears, at what seems a rather minor irritation. Often appearing indecisive and withdrawn, part of his appeal to women stems from his need to be mothered. He quite lacks "machismo."

This is not to say that the standard assumptions about sex-specific characteristics which were current in Chinese society, and which were certainly reflected in social novels and other popular fiction, were strangely and totally absent from the love stories. The author of *Jade Pear Spirit* at one point directly addresses his readers (direct address could be used to point out basic truths) to say that "the nerves of all women are weaker than those of men."[64] But the difference between ideal maleness and ideal femaleness in the Romantic Route is not great and rests on no hard-and-fast distinguishing marks. It is but a matter of emphasis.

If genius, beauty and sensitivity of a special order are what distinguish members of both sexes who will travel the Romantic Route, these are not the only important characteristics of such people. They also share with regular people—regular good people—a standard list of Confucian virtues including filial piety, benevolence, loyalty, continence, self-sacrifice and so on. All these may be regarded as necessary but insufficient criteria for joining the Romantic Route. They are learned virtues, whereas the requisite genius, beauty and sensitivity, which are part of Nature itself, are either inborn or lacking. Perhaps most important on the necessary-but-insufficient list is sincerity (including fidelity). For the woman, this specifically implies chastity, and is of the utmost importance. But sincerity is no less important for the man, and in a sense complements his lack of machismo. The domi-

63. The inference of beardlessness here is based on the notable contrast with contemporary "social" novels, where beards mark heroes and villains alike—but strong and gallant men all, not the young, supersensitive male of the Romantic Route.

64. YLH, p. 105.

nant, aggressive male, or the suave male, is rejected precisely because he may not mean well, or speak plainly.[65] The frail, worried male, who needs mothering, is always honest.

Stage 2 of the Romantic Route, the stage of Supersensitivity, probably occupies more pages than any other in the actual telling of stories. The quality of being *to-ch'ing,* or supersensitive, is, like beauty and genius, possessed in all its fullness only by a select group. It is probably celebrated in more words per story than any other aspect of the Romantic Route. It is, moreover, intimately related to all other stages of the Route. It follows naturally from extraordinary genius and beauty (stage 1); its sentimentality leads one to fall in love (stage 3); its fickleness contributes to tragedy (stage 4); its parallel relationship with sickness and worry (stage 5) is at the heart of the true lover's character; and the destruction (stage 6) of the supersensitive is always superpoignant.

He or she who is *to-ch'ing* (and neither sex seems to have the edge in this regard) has, first of all, a great supply of sincere emotion. Where normal people will slough over some potentially moving scene (flowers, the moon, a lonely person), the *to-ch'ing* person will always be drawn up short by it, appreciate it completely, and perhaps weep or produce a lengthy poem as others continue on their merry way.[66] Their preoccupation with sentiment isolates them, and they are immensely gratified ever to find another of their type.

What are the things the *to-ch'ing* person responds to? Certainly the feelings of other *to-ch'ing* people, especially their sad feelings, are paramount. When one feels that he or she has been the cause of the sad feelings in question, sensitivity turns to deep remorse. When two *to-ch'ing* persons worry about each other, which of course often happens in the love stories, remorse can easily spiral, and its pain eventually may far outweigh the pain of the original affront, if any, which set off the spiral.

The *to-ch'ing* person's response to the natural environment—a beautiful landscape, a thunderstorm, the change in seasons—often appears as a matter of passing involvement and momentary lyricism. But at a deeper level it is more than that. The *to-ch'ing* person's extraordinary inborn gifts are part of the natural cosmic order, and do not thrive when cut off from it. A grey room in a treeless courtyard can bring

65. Confirming the sense of his and other best-selling novels, Chang Hen-shui plainly states that the primary requirement for a girl to love a boy is that he be *chung-shih* (faithful, reliable); see "Tso-wan *T'i-hsiao yin-yuan* hou ti shuo-hua" in *T'i-hsiao Yin-yuan* (Shanghai, 1930), 3:178.

66. At the height of his *to-ch'ing* feeling, Ho Meng-hsia of *Yü-li hun* produces poems to the extent of an inch-high stack of manuscript in twenty days; see YLH, p. 107.

serious illness to a *to-ch'ing* person in a matter of weeks. In a larger sense, the physical environment is fundamentally continuous with the moral environment in the *to-ch'ing* person's outlook. The cardinal Confucian virtues are intrinsic parts of the natural universe, quite as "given" as landscapes. In the changing pattern of one's journey through life, there will be occasion for appropriate response to the moral aspects of one's environment as surely as to the physical. The *to-ch'ing* person gives total, unswerving loyalty to whatever moral duties become apparent. For chastity, a young widow like Li Niang will readily, even willingly, lay down her life. For filial piety, a young man will sever his own aorta to give blood to his father.[67]

At least as revealing of the nature of *to-ch'ing* people is what they do not respond to. Supersensitive to the natural (including cosmological and ethical) order, they respond much less than do regular people to the secular order. They reject the mainstream for the insular life, living in secluded rooms, or in remote areas, or even literally on islands. In one story, all the broken-hearted *to-ch'ing* lovers of the world (N.B.: the world! No distinction among human beings is as profound as that between the *to-ch'ing* and the non-*to-ch'ing*) flock to an "island of remorse" *(hen tao)* where, finally in like-minded company, they have a society of the extremely impractical and the intensely aware.[68]

The impracticality of the *to-ch'ing* temperament leads to its frequent description as *ch'ih,* a character which normally spans a range of meanings from "infatuated" to "silly" to "irrational" and even "idiotic," though usually the sense is benign. While definitely bearing connotations of this variety, *ch'ih* in the love stories is fundamentally favorable; one is "crazy," but supremely happy, when one is *ch'ih.*[69]

The word "infatuation" might best translate *ch'ih,* all things considered, but some specific components of its meaning are perhaps worth distinguishing. Fundamental is the idea of a sudden strong attachment—unreasonably sudden and strong as others see it—to a person or ideal. In the story of *Jade Pear Spirit,* for example, Menghsia's dramatic vow—that if he cannot marry Li Niang he will never marry at all—is a *ch'ih* vow. Why, the outsider wonders, must he be so drastic?

Besides sudden strong attachment, *ch'ih* includes a purblind quality. When fixed upon something, the *to-ch'ing* person simply will not see

67. Chou Shou-chüan, "Fu-tzu," *Li-pai-liu* 110 (May 21, 1921): 1–10.

68. Chou Shou-chüan, "Liu-sheng-chi p'ien," *Li-pai-liu* 108 (May 7, 1921): 1–12.

69. In his *Masks of Fiction in the Dream of the Red Chamber* (Tucson, 1975), Lucien Miller discusses some importantly related senses of *ch'ih,* in the cases of Pao Yü and others, as symbolic of the difficulty and peculiarity of a mortal seeking enlightenment. See pp. 82, 94–96.

many things he or she normally would see. Meng-hsia cares immensely for Li Niang, and is usually sensitive to the slightest signs of her mood; but in making his *ch'ih* vow he is strangely oblivious to the unmistakable likelihood that it will cause her great pain. In Li Niang's ultimate response to the vow—her decision to die—she is equally purblind to the devastating effects her *ch'ih* resolve will have on Meng-hsia and Yun-ch'ien.

Beyond a mere blind spot in one's sensitivities, *ch'ih* means stubbornness. When his or her blind spot is pointed out by others, the truly *ch'ih* person will not be swayed but will continue in his or her ways, marching to a more exalted drumbeat. At first Meng-hsia's vow appears impetuous, almost childlike. But he does not budge from it when his dear friend Shih-ch'ih begs him to relent, and reconsiders only after repeated entreaties from Li Niang. Stubbornness of this kind foreshadows the suffering and tragedy which will unfold in stages 5 and 6 of the Romantic Route. By insisting that one's own pain and death are small matters in comparison with high principle, the *ch'ih* person contributes in bringing about his or her own suffering. Thus *ch'ih* may also be said to include a fateful element.

The Romantic Route's *stage 3,* of Falling in Love, tells what naturally happens to people who are born with extraordinary beauty and talent and grow up to be *to-ch'ing*. It tells more than the story of the select few, though, since everyone recognizes that more regular people, including love story readers, also fall in love. The experience of *to-ch'ing* people is exemplary, but it is not unique, and in Stage 3 more than anywhere else, readers can, as it were, be "let in on" the Romantic Route. The "warnings" which narrators offer about the consequences of falling in love subtly invite the reader's vicarious participation in the Romantic Route as a whole. What reader, after all, is so far removed from the ideal *to-ch'ing* type? Like a Platonic form, the ideal Falling in Love always stands as a perfect idea for worldly fallings in love to emulate.

The English "falling" in love happens to be an apt metaphor for this phase of the Romantic Route, because here we have the sharp downward turning point in the fortunes of *to-ch'ing* lovers. In fact, Falling in Love may be viewed in two opposite yet thoroughly inseparable aspects, the ecstatic aspect and the tragic aspect.

The ecstatic aspect is the triumph of perfect love *(chih ch'ing)* between man and woman. The most important attribute of perfect love is probably its purity. All the love affairs of the world are based in some proportion on pure love *(ch'ing)* and its opposite number in this regard, bodily desire *(jou yü)*. Only perfect love, such as that between

Meng-hsia and Li Niang, is based wholly on *ch'ing*.[70] (An individual is disqualified from *to-ch'ing* status by any admixture of bodily desire.) Bodily desire has a superficial, transient quality about it, as when naughty boys gossip about the butcher's daughter.[71] Perfect love, in total contrast, has a deep, steady, somewhat occult nature. It flourishes on the subtlest of communication: poems, fleeting glimpses, coincident thoughts, shadows in the moonlight. Face-to-face meeting is almost too harsh for it. (Meng-hsia and Li Niang meet face-to-face only twice in their lives.)[72]

Much of the mystery and excitement surrounding "perfect love" comes from the fact that affairs must be kept secret. On the surface there are usually good reasons for this. Li Niang's being a widow of course requires extreme secrecy between her and Meng-hsia, and other problems separating lovers—class barriers, childhood engagements, astrological predictions, parental disapproval—press secrecy upon lovers in other stories. Secrecy is never, of course, a shield for immorality—only a precaution against the appearance of it in the view of those who are not *to-ch'ing* and would not understand. Even when external pressures for it are slight, secrecy is often preferred for reasons of shyness—that kind of attractive shyness which characterizes the specially gifted.

In addition to bringing "social problems" and the shyness of the noble into clear relief, the most important rhetorical purpose of secrecy is to magnify the excitement of whatever is secret. It is ever so delicious for the reader to learn that Li-Niang-the-lovely-widow has formed a secret alliance. The secrecy of her affair is a continual reminder of its hint of illicitness, and her purity—her perfect *to-ch'ing* purity—seems all the purer because of society's contrary view. Without secrecy, the thrill would be gone, and the precious purity with it. A widow's liaison would be merely gross, an object for satire rather than adulation by sincere youth.

Besides purity and secrecy, a third important element in the ecstatic aspect of perfect love is its bi-polar (two lovers) symmetry. The appeal of this symmetry is continuous with that of the parallel literary style which is so often used in the stories. Just as sounds, grammatical categories, and rhythms balance one another—now in agreement, now in contrast, pumping sentiment from the reader's heart—so also

70. See the explicit statement of *Yü-li hun*'s narrator on this matter, YLH, p. 25.

71. Li Han-ch'iu, *Kuang-ling ch'ao*, 1:127.

72. The purpose of their first meeting, after more than half the novel is over, is to try to save their relationship from the subterfuge of So-and-so Li, and the second meeting comes just before Li Niang begins her quest to die. See YLH, pp. 96 and 136.

do the parallel actions of the lovers which the phrases describe. A poem from one brings a poem from the other; a glance from the other, a smile from the one. Their thoughts of one another remain reciprocal during periods of separation. The characters *hsiang* ("mutual") and *tui* ("corresponding") get abundant use, as do metaphors of mirrors and reflection. The symmetry of perfect love is as natural as its purity. The lovers do not contrive their thoughts and actions to be parallel; they just happen that way, as naturally as the seasons change.[73]

The "ecstatic aspect" of perfect love stands to its "tragic aspect" primarily in the relation of cause to unforeseen but inevitable consequence. In the telling of stories, this relation is usually cast in terms of the thoroughly accepted Buddhist notion of *yin-kuo,* a principle which requires no argument, only illustration. The metaphor of a "love web" *(ch'ing wang)* is often used to convey, on the explicit level, notions of the delicacy, complexity, and symmetry of the love relationship. But on another level, the same character *wang* means "net" in the sense of "trap," an idea which is fundamental to the tragic side of perfect love.

The "love trap" depends on false illusion, which functions as bait does in other traps. The sad fact (but part of the ironic beauty of the Romantic Route) is that the final bliss which love promises to young people is not attainable. They pursue it only because they are *ch'ih.* The love net further resembles a trap, and a very good trap, in that once one is involved in it there can be no disengagement. In the moral summation of *Jade Pear Spirit* young readers are warned that the love trap is even more to be feared than isolation on a desert island, where at least there is a one-in-ten-thousand chance of escape.[74]

Thus love—the happiest thing on the Romantic Route—also turns out to be the most dangerous. It can embody the most fearsome of evils. Evil people exist, but people can be avoided or overcome; and there are "evil" customs like arranged marriages and foot-binding, but they, too, are conquerable and also turn out in many cases to have their good points as well as their bad. But the evil which lurks in the love net is pure evil itself. In her suicide note, Li Niang tells us she does not know whether she has hurt herself or whether others have hurt her. The question is immaterial. The real question is what debt of evil she could have incurred in an earlier life which would move the "love demon" *(ch'ing mo)* to trap her in the love net to die.[75] The love net appears to be the fault of no human, but a feature of the universe

73. Symmetry of the same kind, as well as great depth and purity, can attend nonhomosexual male-male relationships as well. See YLH, pp. 29–30 and 77.
74. YLH, p. 154.
75. YLH, p. 149.

which impinges from outside the human sphere. The danger of falling in love lies in *ch'ing* itself, which is the agent of fate. When fate is evil, it is evil at a higher order than anything else. It is the one intractable adversary.

This brings us to *stage 4* of the Romantic Route, the stage of Cruel Fate. In an important sense, this is parallel to stage 1, of Extraordinary Inborn Gifts. Just as one's genius and beauty are bestowed from beyond the sphere of human control, so it is that ill fate *(po ming)* arrives. It inevitably falls, moreover, upon the select few who were unusually blessed in the first place. Fate, the agent of cosmic nature, moves to take back from the human sphere that special beauty and talent which really had always been its own. Readers are repeatedly told: "Those rich in genius will meet threadbare days, those beautiful of face have a wicked destiny;" "If you have talent, Heaven offsets it with vexation;"[76] and so on. The first hint of ill fate is implicit right from stage 1 in the very selectivity fate shows in blessing its chosen few. Those blessed are *ipso facto* different from the crowd, and gradually grow separate from it; separate, they become unappreciated; unappreciated, they grow lonely, poverty-stricken, ill, and so on. "Evils never come alone," and eventually everything goes bad. A strong sense of waste accompanies the shift in the *to-ch'ing* person's fate, yet a considerable sense of tragic beauty attends it as well. The juxtaposition of sharply contrasting elements—talent and despair, beauty and suffering, love and death—was intended to, and obviously did, hold considerable appeal for readers.

Besides the aesthetic function in stage 4's appeal to readers, its linking of talent with talent's frustration seems clearly to have served a function of dispelling the self-doubt of young readers. Many of them had come to Shanghai with "new-style" success on their minds, as they would have travelled to take the exams at Soochow under the "old style." But the glitter of the new city, and the spirit of the revolution, seemed to extend the promise that talent could easily find good use and its possessor easily participate in the city's obvious wealth and adventure. When the harsh, or at best dull, realities of much of Shanghai life became apparent, individuals were often hard pressed to understand their own relative "failure." How could it be? It made little difference that many shared the same plight, for they needn't have realized this, and even if they had, the glaring gap between themselves and "success" still remained. Here stage 4 of the Romantic Route could provide a comforting explanation. In terms of measurable achievement and other surface appearances, there was, after all, little to distinguish the unappreciated genius of the Romantic Route from any

76. YLH, pp. 21, 24, and *passim.*

number of more-or-less "average" readers. Reading a story could allow almost anyone to view himself in the category of unappreciated genius, despite—or sometimes because of—whatever failures he may have encountered. Alternatively, the reader could withdraw from that identification and enjoy the comfort which comes from being able to pity someone who is even worse off than himself.[77]

Stage 5 of the Route, Worry and Disease, parallels stage 2, Supersensitivity, and follows from it as well. "Those with genius and talent are certain to be deep of feeling; those of much feeling will also have bitter worries."[78] A natural tendency towards worry and vexation (usually expressed by *ch'ou* and *hen*) is implicit in the *to-ch'ing* character, and the Cruelty of Fate in stage 4 only exacerbates this tendency. A great deal of the actual storytelling about the Romantic Route depends upon mixing the sweetness of *ch'ing* with the sourness of *ch'ou*.

In struggling with worry, it is standard for the *to-ch'ing* person to fall ill, typically with pneumonia or tuberculosis, and typically to the point of spitting blood, an act which symbolized strong emotion. To some extent, the parallel between *ch'ing* and *ch'ou* is extended by a parallel between *ch'ih*—the perverse and fateful affliction which grows from *ch'ing*—and *ping*, illness, which is a similarly perverse and fateful affliction which grows from *ch'ou*. (It is even slightly relevant that the "heart" radical of *ch'ing* and *ch'ou* parallels the "sickness" radical of *ch'ih* and *ping*.) One may feel that a non-parallelism between *ch'ih* and *ping* lies in the fact that *ch'ih* is a mental problem while sickness is a physical problem. For those who are *to-ch'ing*, though, this is not so. *To-ch'ing* lovers always show a very close, sensitive connection between mental and physical well-being, and though their symptoms include the physical, the causes of their disease are, more often than not, exclusively mental. It is for this reason that they usually will not respond to medicine, which is merely a physical treatment. Only the alleviation of their worry and regret can cure them.[79]

The inclusion of disease as part of the Romantic Route appears, as with ill fate in stage 4, to have served a comforting function for readers. Judging from "social" novels of the time, the awareness of illness and death was by no means limited to the rather unworldly, ideal sphere represented by the Romantic Route. Babies, grandmothers, tutors, neighbors—real and ordinary people of many kinds—die one after another with a frequency, perhaps astonishing by modern standards, that must be taken in stride as the sad side of the

77. See chapter 6 for examples and further discussion.

78. YLH, p. 9.

79. YLH, pp. 47, 85 and 138. Though the connection between worry and disease is particularly intense for *to-ch'ing* people, the connection is also felt to hold for regular people to a greater extent than is commonly believed in the modern West.

fabric of life. Tuberculosis, called in popular usage the "rich man's disease" *(fu-kuei ping)* because it tended to afflict mostly upper class people who labored little and stayed indoors, seems to have been especially common. The journalist and fiction writer Pao T'ien-hsiao recalls that during the years of his youth (ca. 1885–1905) a great number of young people in the Shanghai-Soochow area contracted tuberculosis, and that, in particular, it always seemed to be either urban youth or the wealthy sons of rural gentry who were stricken.[80] It may be no accident that these sectors of the populace—young, male, and either urban or wealthy rural—were the core of the 1910s love story readership. Like the reader who feels unappreciated, an ailing or dying young man, or his friends, could very well have found great solace in the Romantic Route's interpretation of disease: that it tends to befall geniuses, is caused by their high-minded concerns, and, if it results in death, does so because fate reaps the best youth for itself.

Tuberculosis may have been the worst of the diseases which reached epidemic proportions in the young city of Shanghai, but it was not the only one. In the late 1910s particularly, there was serious difficulty with scarlet fever, newly brought to Shanghai by Westerners, and a lung disease different from tuberculosis which may have been pneumonic tularemia.[81] The tularemia spread from Manchuria via Nanking, and at one point in 1917 reached such proportions that communications with Nanking were suspended.[82] It seems quite possible that the popularity boom of Romantic Route love stories in Shanghai in the 1910s was related to the city's actual experience with disease.

Stage 6, the stage of Destruction, ends the Romantic Route in several senses. Most obviously, it brings an end to the story lines of many a tale about the Route. Usually this happens through the death of one or both lovers, but sometimes it takes the form of such equally final partings as flight to monk- or nunhood, or banishment to a distant place. In any case it is, in these terms, always a tragic end.

Besides ending the story, stage 6 completes the symmetry of the Romantic Route's stages. Just as the supersensitivity of stage 2 leads to tight confinement in the "love net" of stage 3, so the worry and illness of stage 5 bring one to death in stage 6. (Here we use "death" as an abbreviation for "death and other less frequent modes of final parting.") And just as supersensitivity and worry coexist and nourish one

---

80. CYLHIL, p. 233; interview with Pao T'ien-hsiao, December 6, 1972.

81. F. L. Hawks Pott, *A Short History of Shanghai*, p. 224, refers to the disease as "pneumonic plague," which naturally suggests "bubonic plague," also a recent problem in Shanghai (see p. 182). Since pneumonic tularemia produces symptoms similar to those of the plague, including buboes in the armpit which grow from swollen lymph glands and discharge pus, we speculate that Pott's "pneumonic plague" was in fact tularemia.

82. Ibid., pp. 219 and 224.

another, so perfect love and final parting parallel and balance one another.

Death may also be considered the end of the Romantic Route in a teleological sense. It is in some way implicit in every other stage of the Route; no stage by itself can be completely conceived without the awareness of death in the offing. The sense of teleology is confirmed in stage 6 by what, despite "sad" endings, must be recognized as the uplifting aspects of this stage. First, the many-faceted completeness which stage 6 achieves for the Romantic Route as a whole is aesthetically satisfying. The human mind being what it is, completeness and symmetry convey the feeling of "naturalness," and hence rightness, about the Route, its tragedy notwithstanding. More positively, the "end" in stage 6 is an end of suffering in the Buddhist sense of release from worldly attachments which cause suffering. Death for Li Niang is the only possible escape from torment in the "love net," and even Yun-ch'ien, not so thoroughly caught, says she does not fear death nearly so much as the pain of the illness which precedes it.[83] The Romantic Route as a whole is a portrait of human suffering in the red dust; to the extent that that general outlook persuades the reader, to that extent does stage 6 of the Route appear as a welcome release.

In one interesting respect, the end of the Romantic Route mirrors its beginning, at least in the paradigm example of *Jade Pear Spirit*. Most of the way along the Route—in what we have called its four middle stages—it stresses the same type of experience for both men and women. Both sexes are supersensitive, fall in love, are stricken by fate, worry and grow sick in basically the same way and to similar degrees. But in stages 1 and 6 there is a noticeable separation of ideal experience by sex. In stage 1, beauty tends to be the primary female attribute and genius the primary male attribute (although, as explained above, there is also some overlap). In starting along the Romantic Route, beauty for females and genius for males have the same effect: they lead to supersensitivity and everything else. Only in stage 6 does there again appear a tendency to separate sex roles. When Li Niang dies, she dies "for love"; when Meng-hsia dies, he must find a way of dying "for the country."

The difference in stage 6 follows from the difference in stage 1. The main function of beauty is its service to the love relationship, hence it is fitting that beauties die for love; the main function of genius ideally is to serve China and pacify all under Heaven, and hence it is fitting that men of genius die for those goals. But as the example of *Jade Pear Spirit* so clearly shows, it was not always easy to weave a death-for-the-country ending smoothly into the fabric of a love story. For most of the Romantic Route, after all, the man of genius is a lonely figure,

83. YLH, pp. 137 and 162.

somewhat alienated from society, and dejected and sickly besides—hardly a hero for the public arena.

Yet, despite its element of incongruity, the male's death-for-the-country is more than a "tail" casually pinned onto the end of *Jade Pear Spirit* and certain other stories. In the 1910s at any rate, nationalistic order is an integral part of the genius's character, and is always present, albeit usually at a latent level. It is related to the purity of his original nature and the extraordinary quality of his sentiments about beauty and love. His heroic, or *ying-hsiung* passion parallels the passion of his romantic, or *erh-nü* attachments.[84] Both passions are of the finest order, standing at the high end of a spectrum whose lower portion includes food, drink, and sex.[85]

A young man's pure patriotic love and his pure love for a young woman are more than just similar. They are, in fact, two forms of what is fundamentally the same pure *ch'ing,* which a given individual will possess in one form if and only if he also possesses it in the other.[86] Blood is the "ingredient" which "produces" *ch'ing,* hence it follows that the truly *to-ch'ing* young man stands ready to spill his blood for woman or for country in equally unstinting measure. Those who are not *to-ch'ing* will spill it for neither.[87]

It is important to reflect upon the status of the Romantic Route. Of what is it a picture? It obviously does not describe the social reality of

84. The frequent mention of *erh-nü* and *ying-hsiung* in complementary parallelism in the fiction of the 1910s is indirectly attributable to the popularity of Wen K'ang's *Tale of Heroic Young Lovers (Erh-nü ying-hsiung chuan).*

85. Cf. YLH, p. 103; the degree of evil which indulgence in food, drink, and sex represents varies greatly according to one's station. It is not considered wrong at all that Ho Meng-hsia — young, male, unmarried — should drink himself sick (pp. 34–39).

86. See YLH, p. 133, for a relatively clear exposition of this idea. Other references suggest that *erh-nü* passions are necessary for the *ying-hsiung,* but not vice versa. For example a parallel couplet on p. 159 says: "Without a lover's passion, one will certainly not be a true hero / With a hero's spirit, one will be a good lover."

87. YLH, p. 133. The fact that the duty of patriotism, and its glory, falls to the man and not the woman in stories like *Jade Pear Spirit* may seem to be an endorsement of male superiority, something notably lacking in most of the Romantic Route. Actually there is no such endorsement. The reader's sympathy is led to appreciate the tragedy of the two sexes equally, with no preferential evaluation given the male for the "added" element of heroism.

The key to understanding this seeming paradox lies in distinguishing the nature of a person's *ch'ing* from the modality of its expression. The male channels his *ch'ing* partly into patriotic heroism not because his is more or better than the woman's but because that is the channel which is appropriate to a male. True, the common belief that patriotic heroism is a male more than a female function derives from a long tradition in whose development assumptions of male superiority played an essential role; and in modern knight-errant stories and military romances, heroic patriotism is, as it always had been, an overwhelmingly "male" virtue. (There are, of course, many female knights-errant in modern stories as in pre-modern ones, and this may seem on the face of the matter to contradict the generalization that the glory of knight-errant activity is "overwhelmingly the 1910s; and, despite a few comforting affinities to the reader's situation, it cannot have served as much of a practical model. (Most young people would not kill themselves for love, no matter how much they admired the fictional character who did.) Neither, however, are we discussing beliefs in a realm entirely apart from practical attitudes and behavior. Since the discoveries of Freud, it has become well-recognized that even one's "wildest" fantasies can be shown to stem from daily life concerns. Though we need not limit ourselves to the special categories of Freud, we should not doubt that popular fiction, however "fantastic," is linked to real life. The Romantic Route in particular comprises an important system of conceptions and attitudes to which more practical views of life and social change were inevitably related. It can be shown that within the relationship between "mythical" beliefs and the living of life, causality goes in both directions: real life concerns can generate a myth, and mythical beliefs can, in an indirect but sometimes profound way, affect daily life. Chapter 5 will consider some of these connections.

But before considering popular fiction's ties to its social context, we must understand more about its place in that context. Thus chapters 3 and 4 will treat publication conditions, readership, and the lives of authors, while the reader who so wishes may turn directly to chapter 5.

---

male." Upon analysis, however, it emerges that the female knight-errant is an intriguing and entertaining figure *precisely because* she is a female operating in what is distinctly a "male" province.) In Romantic Route love stories the male receives no *extra* credit, as it were, for his patriotic heroism. It is merely a vehicle for expressing *ch'ing*. He is judged not according to this vehicle, which is a given, but according to the purity and intensity of his sentiments. The woman is judged by the same standards. Oppressed to the limit by cruel fate, both sexes attempt a final demonstration of their special nature, and both insist on sacrificing themselves for others and for what is right. For a woman, the "others" are her love partner and her family; for a man, "others" includes the world at large. But the principle of action, "sacrifice for others," is the same.

The male's obligation to demonstrate patriotic heroism can even leave his final self-sacrifice appearing *less* pure and elegant than the woman's. After all, his heroism cannot achieve any concrete result to deflect the tragedy of the Romantic Route's end. This would require a victory over ill fate, which is quite impossible, since ill fate oppresses heroes and weaklings with equal ease. That being the case, an attempt at heroism can appear quixotic. It can demonstrate the sincerity of the hero's will, but at the same time distract from the impression of perfect self-contained purity and symmetry which characterizes his affections during all the rest of the Romantic Route. Meng-hsia's effort in *Jade Pear Spirit* to incorporate heroism into his self-sacrifice proves his superiority over regular men, but it gains him nothing in comparison with the pure and simple self-sacrifice of Li Niang. Li Niang faces death with firm, single-minded resolve; Meng-hsia, confused about how to execute his duty to his country, hesitates. One cannot even say that Meng-hsia possesses patriotic feelings which Li Niang lacks, because it is she who has continually urged him to study abroad and serve the nation.

CHAPTER 3

The Rise of the Fiction Press

The cultural dilemmas and anxieties which have afflicted residents of China's modernizing cities assuredly explain part of the boom in modern popular fiction, as we have argued in chapter two. Yet psychological needs have, after all, always been present; and storytelling as a response to them is probably as old as agriculture and the family. Hence, however accentuated in the early twentieth century, these needs cannot comprise a complete explanation for the modern boom in Chinese entertainment fiction. Part of the boom, obviously, had to do with technological change (new methods of printing and transportation), new commercial roles (the professional author, publisher, distributor, advertiser), and rising literacy rates. Collectively these changes allowed more people to get a message quickly, to hear a single author simultaneously, and to react to issues in a "timely" fashion. The public dimension of these changes was more obvious but hardly more profound than the private: the new possibility, through printed media, for reading and opinion-forming by oneself. We shall consider first some modern changes in the media.

In cultural terms, Shanghai served a kind of laboratory function by which institutions and technology of the West's Industrial Revolution—itself still unfolding—were tried in a Chinese context. That these introductions were made behind the strong arm of military force has understandably led Chinese patriots towards a dim view of the heterogeneous culture which resulted. In no way denying this aspect, we should also view the imported innovations as seeds of several aspects of social revolution in Chinese cities.

Within about four decades, Shanghai witnessed a great influx of modern hardware in the transportation and communications fields. This included Western shipbuilding and steam navigation inland (early 1860s), the Shanghai Local Post (1864), the telegraph (1865), daily Chinese-language newspapers (1872), the ricksha (1874, from Japan), the railroad (1875), telephones (1881), the Imperial Post Office (1896),

Connection between technological change + pop culture

79

automobiles (1902), and streetcars (1902).[1] Besides its obvious practical uses, the hardware had profound implications for society, including new media and readership groups, new uses of literacy, a widening geographical scope of concern for "the news", the rise of "public opinion" in a modern sense, and the roots of modern popular fiction. In the following two sections we consider, in outline form, the growth of Shanghai's printing industry during the late nineteenth and early twentieth centuries. This growth allowed the dissemination of reading material on an unprecedented scale, including modern books, magazines, and newspapers for an emerging readership of modern popular fiction.

1. The Early Growth of Modern Printing in Shanghai

If Chinese sensibilities were sometimes irritated in the late nineteenth century because modern technology had to be learned from imperialists, the irritation was compounded in cases like the printing industry where China's own credentials were ancient second to none. Paper had been an invention of the Eastern Han dynasty and wood-block printing of the Sui and T'ang. Movable type was developed during the Sung. Though copper plates and movable copper type were used during the Ch'ing,[2] wood-block printing remained the standard for book publishing until Western methods took root in the 20th century. In spite of the slowness of the carving process, woodblocks gave clearer impressions for larger numbers of copy than did other printing-block materials, including metal.[3] Ease in carving assured the continued use of certain less durable blocks, such as those made of beeswax-and-resin, for printings of small circulation or low cost.[4]

Missionary presses introduced the first "modern" printing methods for books in Chinese. Robert Morrison, a Scottish Presbyterian and the first Protestant missionary to China, urged the East India Company to bring to Macao in 1814 a British press, a Western type font, and equipment for making Chinese type.[5] This modest effort, made in spite of the Ch'ing court's ban on evangelism, produced only a Chinese dictionary compiled by Morrison before it folded. But the

1. Pott, *Short History,* pp. 103–106, 135, 144; Ying-wan Cheng, *Postal Communication in China and its Modernization* (Cambridge, 1970), p. 57; Kwang-ching Liu, *Anglo-American Steamship Rivalry, 1862–1874* (Cambridge, 1962), pp. 10–11.

2. Tseng Hsu-pai, *Chung-kuo hsin-wen shih,* p. 8; Chang Ching-lu, *Chung-kuo ch'u-pan shih liao pu-pien* (hereafter: *Pu-pien*), p. 274.

3. Roswell S. Britton, *The Chinese Periodical Press, 1800–1912,* pp. 83–84.

4. Britton, pp. 4–5.

5. Suzanne W. Barnett, "Silent Evangelism: Presbyterians and the Mission Press in China, 1807–1860," *Journal of Presbyterian History* 49.4 (Winter 1971):289.

printing equipment remained under missionary management, and within a decade presses for missionary materials in Chinese were founded in Malacca and Batavia (Djakarta), safely beyond the reach of Ch'ing authority. After the first Opium War (1839–1842) the mission presses returned to Macao and the China coast, most importantly Shanghai. An American, William Gamble, introduced electroplating for Chinese type matrices in 1860 at the Presbyterian Mission Press in Shanghai.[6] While electroplating did not spread quickly, the introduction of lithography by W. H. Medhurst at the London Mission Society Press in 1876 not only led to its adoption by many Shanghai printers but also became for about thirty years a "style of the times" *(feng-ch'i)* in Shanghai printing.

In lithographic printing, which is based on the incompatibility of grease and water, the characters to be printed were applied in an oily mixture, in mirror-image form, on a clean stone slab. Prior to each printing water was poured over the slab, wetting all but the oily parts, then a greasy ink was applied which adhered to the oily surface but not the wet one. When paper was pressed against the slab thus prepared, a clear, obverse image was obtained. The difficulty of having to produce a mirror-image copy in the first instance was avoided by writing the original copy, in the same oily mixture, on a special kind of grained paper which, when applied to a clean stone slab, immediately delivered the desired mirror image. To the publisher, the advantages of lithography were primarily the speed and lower cost with which a printing surface could be prepared. Instead of paying and waiting for an artisan to carve a block of wood or other material, one had only to hire a *hsiu-ts'ai* or professional copyist to make a neat transcription in oil on grained paper.[7] To the reader, lithography's appeal lay in the clarity and sharpness of the end result which, though printed, also suggested the grace of hand-copied style.

Following very shortly upon the initiative of Medhurst's press, the Shanghai *Shen pao,* through its book-publishing unit Tien-shih chai, sparked a considerable enthusiasm for lithography by using it to publish a pictorial called the *Hua pao.*[8] This magazine demonstrated that the new, refreshing sharpness of lithography could be effected in pictures as well as in script. Pictorial magazines came to enjoy their own wave of popularity close upon that of lithography itself. The T'ung-wen shu-chü, founded in 1881, was Shanghai's early leader in the use of lithograph and pictorial illustration.

6. Britton, p. 84; Barnett, p. 293.

7. Interview with Ch'en Ting-shan (Taichung, July 25, 1973); see also Chang Ching-lu, *Chung-kuo chin-tai ch'u-pan shih liao* (hereafter: *Chin-tai*), 2:357.

8. Chang Ching-lu, *Chin-tai,* 2:368 and 356ff.

At first all lithograph printing was in black and white. When colors were introduced, they first appeared in simple patches, both solid and primary, producing an effect which added excitement—but little realism—to the resulting illustration. This problem was alleviated beginning in 1894 when a press in Shanghai's French concession called the Fa-hsing shu-chü hired Japanese technicians to show how the lithographed surface of a stone block could be rubbed with metal files into a mesh-like texture which, during printing, produced shading effects.[9] Other presses were quick to follow suit and the quality of pictorials improved.

Aside from pictorials, the mainstay of lithography's popularity was books on traditional culture. During the last two decades of the nineteenth century, the classics and official histories found a new circulation in the attractive style of stone lithography, though wood-block printing of these texts by no means died out during these years.[10] Another staple of the lithography boom was lithographic reprints of seventeenth century anti-Manchu books; yet another, even larger, was books designed as direct aids in preparing for the civil service examinations. One type, called "works of the world's geniuses" *(t'ien-hsia ts'ai-tzu shu),* contained model eight-legged essays by famous scholars. Another type, called *ta-t'i wen-fu* and *hsiao-t'i wen-fu,* also contained copies of essays and poems from old examinations, but these were copied in the tiniest of characters — very clearly, thanks to lithography — and circulated in thin booklets which fit easily into the sleeves of examination gowns.[11] One veteran of their use, who took the exams in the early 1890s and in the next decade became a popular author, attributes many cases of severe near-sightedness, including his own, to reliance upon them as cribs.[12]

In the early 1900s, demand for these types of books declined somewhat, because of the phasing out of the civil service examination system. (Yet the decline was only relative; lithographed classics were widely sold even through the 1940s, especially in the book-hungry interior provinces during the war with Japan.) Meanwhile the stimulation of the late Ch'ing reform movement sparked a new interest in Western books, and demand for them, though small, rose steadily.

As the new demand grew, a major problem emerged in the use of lithography. How could one handle and store such large numbers of unwieldy stone slabs? Wood blocks posed the same problem. Yet

9. Chang Ching-lu, *Chin-tai,* 2:357.
10. Pao T'ien-hsiao, CYLHIL, p. 148.
11. CYLHIL, pp. 41–42.
12. CYLHIL, pp. 41–42.

economic sense dictated that all blocks and slabs be saved, in case the market for a book should survive through a second, third, or further impression. As a result, many Shanghai presses during 1900–1910 turned to primary use of metal type, especially white lead,[13] although some presses, including some of those which moved towards Butterfly publishing, continued into the 1910s and even the 1920s to use stone lithography because of its artistic and nostalgic appeal.[14] Lead printing was not done directly from the metal type but from a solid matrix produced by the use of paper molds: i.e., a workman would set a plate of type and then press a mixture of wet paper and asbestos against its surface to produce an indented mold; when the mold dried, molten lead could be poured into it to produce a replica of the original typeset. The replica was then used for printing while the original typeset could be dismantled and reemployed. After a book's first printing the paper molds—not the metal ones—were saved for future impressions; one paper mold normally could produce five or six lead replicas without significant loss of clarity in the printed result.[15]

Other important technical advances during 1900–1910 included new methods of pictorial reproduction. Lithography came to be replaced by copper and zinc photogravure (in which the inscription is indented into the printing plate), and by collotype (in which prints are made directly from a hardened gelatin).[16] The printing process itself became faster and more efficient as new revolving-cylinder *(kun-t'ung)* presses were installed, with British and Japanese technical advice, to replace the old flat-plate *(p'ing-pan)* machines.

No important publisher survived this technical revolution. The new books were printed by new enterprises with new machines. Either unwilling or unable to compete, the old publishers were obliged to choose between gradual extinction and reliance on the publication of novels.[17] Those who tried to survive on novels were confronted with commercial problems of a new severity, however.

First, the earlier, exam-oriented publications had sold for one or two yuan apiece[18] and, because of the importance of the exams, had never wanted buyers. But during 1900–1910 novels sold for only

13. Chang Ching-lu, *Chin-tai,* 2:357.

14. One example is the *Hsiao-shuo hua-pao* edited by Pao T'ien-hsiao in 1915 (see CYLHIL, p. 380). Many books of the Yu-cheng shu-chü continued through the 1910s printing in lithography.

15. Interview with Ch'en Ting-shan (Taichung, July 25, 1973).

16. Chang Ching-lu, *Pu-pien,* pp. 278 and 557ff; also Chang Ching-lu, *Chin-tai,* 2:368; and CYLHIL, pp. 359–360.

17. Chang Ching-lu, *Pu-pien,* p. 276.

18. Ibid., p. 275.

50 cents per volume at most, and there was no assurance of a captive patronage. Many such novels achieved circulations only in the hundreds.[19]

Second, there had arisen the new institution of paying for manuscripts. Before the twentieth century, when copy was taken from old examinations or from the histories and classics, a publisher needed only to hire a proofreader before printing a text.[20] When original manuscripts were offered for publication, the author normally submitted them not with profit in mind but with the more gentlemanly object of distribution among friends and acquaintances.[21] If the question of indebtedness arose at all, it was often the author who bore a debt to the publisher. But when the new presses of the late Ch'ing decade began to publish Western and Japanese books in translation, it was necessary to pay the translator. A large number of (mostly short-lived) translation houses sprang up to fill this demand.[22] The precedent of remuneration having been set, modern-style presses began to pay authors for original work as well. For a few years, the old publishers could and did avoid the new manuscript market by republishing the classics of China's vernacular tradition. Yet the public taste for translations and "new-style" works continued to increase until, after 1905, the purchase of manuscripts had become a near necessity for any publisher who would survive. By the 1910s, payment for manuscripts had become the greatest single expense of publishers.[23]

Third, the problem of distribution became a serious financial hazard within the new system of commercial publishing. New bookshops sprang up in Shanghai and nearby cities (Soochow, Hangchow, and Nanking in particular), while old shops were revitalized with the line of new materials. (Book shops throughout the Kiangsu-Chekiang area traditionally were run, and continued throughout this period to be run, by Shaohsing people who carefully cultivated the popular association of books and Shaohsing.) If a book was famous or popular, bookstores would purchase it wholesale and the publisher could rest at ease. The majority of books, however, were distributed by a "send-and-sell" method which placed all the risk with the publisher.[24] Under this system, the bookstore would remit payment only for those books

19. This is Hu Shih's estimate of the circulation of such relatively successful novels as the translations of Lin Shu. See Hu's "Introduction" to Chao Chia-pi, ed., *Chung-kuo hsin wen-hsueh ta-hsi* (Shanghai, 1935), 1:4.

20. Chang Ching-lu, *Pu-pien*, p. 276.

21. CYLHIL, p. 238.

22. Ibid., p. 220.

23. Interview with Ch'en Ting-shan (Taichung, July 25, 1973); with Tseng Hsu-pai, (Taipei, July 19, 1973); and with Ch'eng She-wo, (Mucha, July 26, 1973).

24. CYLHIL, p. 238.

it actually sold. If no payment arrived, the burden rested with the publisher to discover whether the bookstore had indeed made no sales. It often required a special trip to the bookstore to recover both money and unsold books, and when such trips involved inter-city travel the monetary harvest would scarcely cover traveling expenses. An additional shortcoming of the system was that the bookstore had little incentive to advertise or promote a book.

The combination of financial risks involved in the new publishing industry of 1900–1910 led to the demise not only of the old publishing houses but of many small, new publishers and book companies as well.[25] But the few among the new presses who survived laid the foundations of Shanghai's publishing industry for decades to come. They became known first for textbooks and Western learning, then for reference works and scholarly collectanea. No less significant financially, they also provided important media in the boom of Butterfly fiction in the 1910s, but they were less well known for this.

The Commercial Press, in several ways, was the most important of these modern presses. For one, most of the early twentieth century's technical innovations were due to its leadership. Founded in 1897 on a capital base of only about 3,000 yuan,[26] it was the first Chinese press to use paper molds (in 1900, having taken over a Japanese press in Shanghai)[27] and the first also to use photogravure (1903),[28] the modern revolving cylinder (1906)[29] and the collotype (1907).[30] During these early years it was known as a relatively small press with a distinctly foreign flavor—small in comparison with the established stone-lithograph and wood-block publishers such as Wu yun chi, and foreign-flavored because of its foreign machines and advisors, and because it was staffed exclusively by Chinese Christians.[31] Furthermore it published mostly religious books during its first five or six years, and then shifted to textbooks and books on commerce and Western thought.[32] Textbooks in particular were important in spreading the Press's name because of the immediate and widespread demand for modern textbooks following the education reforms ordered by the

25. CYLHIL, p. 239.

26. CYLHIL, p. 235; Chang Ching-lu, *Pu-pien*, p. 557.

27. Chang Ching-lu, *Chin-tai*, 2:427.

28. Chang Ching-lu, *Pu-pien*, p. 557.

29. Chang Ching-lu, *Chin-tai*, 2:431. Actually a simpler version of the revolving-cylinder machine was used as early as 1898; see Chang Ching-lu, *Chin-tai*, 2:427.

30. Chang Ching-lu, *Pu-pien*, p. 558. For an overview of the history of the Commercial Press, see Jean-Pierre Drège, "L'entreprise Privée d'Edition en Chine dans la Première Moitié du XXe Siècle: la Commercial Press de Shanghai (1897–1949)."

31. CYLHIL, p. 235

32. CYLHIL, pp. 221–222.

Ch'ing court in 1901. In that year the Press came out with China's first modern primary school textbook, the *Meng-hsueh k'e-pen* by Chu Shu-jen.[33] Some relatively big profits followed in the immediately succeeding years with the publication of texts for teaching English to Chinese children. The texts were adaptations of books originally published in London for use in India.[34]

From all this the Commercial Press gained distinction as the first Chinese-run press to flourish in commercial competition involving foreign technology. (The Press was, one might note, very appropriately named.) After six years, its office on Peking Road employed thirty editors, proofreaders and copyists—quite a large number for that day—most of whom had been hired away from the London Mission Society Press.[35] But in 1903 the Press's building caught fire and burned to the ground.[36] It is a tribute to Hsia Jui-fang, the Press's manager and guiding spirit through its early years, that a recovery from the fire was achieved with remarkable rapidity. Within a year, Hsia had accomplished publication of the very successful *Eastern Miscellany (Tung-fang tsa-chih)* and the inauguration of the Press's own translation department.[37] This rebuilding was done from the sale of stock shares, many to Japanese, who owned a large portion of the Press's capital until 1914, when all shares were repurchased by Chinese.[38]

Hsia Jui-fang was well known at the Press both for his industry and business acumen and for his disarming humility. Born and raised in Shanghai, he missed some years of schooling in his youth and was only semi-literate as an adult. His interest in publishing was said to have originated on his first job—that of a policeman in Shanghai's International Settlement—where he was assigned to a beat in front of the gates of the Hua-Ying (British-American) Publishing Co. The casual friends he made there advised him to try something new, emphasizing the fact that Chinese policemen received very low pay, even less than Sikhs.[39] Hsia took their advice and decided to try his hand at publishing, though he never returned to school to prepare himself. As a result it often happened, while he worked at the Commercial Press, that he came across a manuscript beyond his reading capabilities. In these situations he turned without embarrassment to one of his

33. Chang Ching-lu, *Pu-pien,* p. 276.
34. CYLHIL, pp. 159 and 221.
35. CYLHIL, p. 221.
36. CYLHIL, p. 312.
37. CYLHIL, pp. 312, 388, 389; and Chang Ching-lu, *Chin-tai,* 2:430.
38. Chang Ching-lu, *Pu-pien,* p. 559.
39. CYLHIL, p. 236.

better-educated assistants or friends for an appraisal: What did the manuscript say? Would it sell? Among what kind of reader? Practicality seems to have been the key to his humility. When the Press was busy, Hsia did not feel it beneath his dignity as manager to roll up his sleeves and get his hands dirty setting type.[40] His gift for managing people and his eye for business seem to have been crucial in setting the Commercial Press on its successful course at an early stage. Unfortunately, in 1914 he was murdered outside the door of the Press's new distribution center in Shanghai, apparently the victim of political assassination.[41]

Yet the Commercial Press continued to grow after his death, becoming larger and also more prestigious. Its technical innovations, purchased from Japanese, American, British, and German sources, included the automatic type-casting oven (1913), the colloid-plate printing machine (1915), tin-plate printing (1918), the Chinese typewriter (1919), and steel-engraved printing (1923).[42] The main room of the Press's editorial and translation office was impressively spacious. Its atmosphere was solemn in a manner more characteristic of a library than of the publishing offices in Shanghai at the time.[43] About forty or fifty desks were arranged in neat rows, with one especially large desk for Chief Editor Chang Chü-sheng standing at the head. There was a special reference library for staff use.[44] It was considered a privilege to work at the Commercial Press, and employment was normally attained only through personal connections. In fact, nearly the entire staff were Kiangsu people, and within Kiangsu the majority came from Changchow and secondly from Wusih.[45] While the Press offered some of Shanghai's highest rates of pay for manuscripts at the time (ca. three yuan per thousand characters), it could also, because of its prestige and its economic health, pay its authors, and even its staff, by offering Commercial Press stock at a hundred yuan per share. Many considered it a privilege to be paid in this fashion.[46]

In 1915 the Press completed its production of the modern dictionary *Tz'u Yuan,* a monumental work for its time, and had branched into the publication of collectanea on scholarly topics. Since 1910 it had also published the *Short Story Monthly (Hsiao-shuo yueh-pao),* which during those years was a leading organ of Butterfly literature. Yet the Press

40. CYLHIL, p. 236.
41. Ibid., p. 237. The identity and motivation of the assassins has remained unclear.
42. Chang Ching-lu, *Chin-tai,* 2:433–434; *Pu-pien,* pp. 560–561.
43. CYLHIL, pp. 390–391.
44. CYLHIL, p. 390.
45. CYLHIL, p. 391.
46. CYLHIL, p. 388.

never lost its basic emphasis on textbooks, and by the 1920s produced 60 percent of all new textbooks in China.[47] It was largely from the power to affect the content of so many textbooks that the chief editorship of the Commercial Press—a post which came to be filled by such luminaries as Wang Yun-wu, Shen Yen-ping (Mao Tun) and Cheng Chen-to—became a powerful position in the political arena as well as in publishing and education.

If the rise of the Commercial Press tells us approximately half the story of early publishing in Shanghai, most of the remaining half may be viewed as the rise and fall of its main competitors. The first of these were the Wen-ming shu-chü and the Kuang-chih shu-chü. Kuang-chih was run exclusively by Cantonese, who brought to their task the consciousness that Cantonese had had closer and longer contact with the West than any other Chinese. The original purpose of Kuang-chih's Shanghai branch was merely to sell in Shanghai books on Western learning which had been procured from Canton and Hong Kong. In 1903, however, Kuang-chih set up its own editorial and translation section which, with a staff of five or six persons, concentrated on translating new Japanese books on technical and scientific subjects, such as road engineering and sewerage systems.[48]

From its founding in 1902, the Wen-ming shu-chü placed its primary emphasis on textbooks, thereby benefiting, whether by luck or perspicacity, from the same early market potential that the Commercial Press had found in this line.[49] Like the Commercial Press being staffed by Kiangsu people, the Wen-ming shu-chü was run by Chekiangese, from Shaohsing in particular. But while Wen-ming survived Commercial's vigorous competition during the late Ch'ing decade, which several other small presses did not, it never seriously challenged Commercial's lead.

In 1911 a group of revolutionary educators led by Chang Chien and Chao Feng-ch'ang decided to create a new book company and publishing house, the Chung-hua shu-chü (Chung Hwa Book Co.), to serve and commemorate the new Republic of China. Officially founded January 1, 1912, Chung-hua was built upon the base of the Wen-ming shu-chü, officially listing Wen-ming as a subsidiary organ. Chung-hua followed Wen-ming's primary emphasis on textbooks,[50] but during the 1910s it gradually fell behind the Commercial Press in this department. In other categories of publishing, the competition between Chung-hua and Commercial was keen and explicit. To answer Com-

47. Chang Ching-lu, *Pu-pien*, p. 277.
48. CYLHIL, p. 245.
49. Chang Ching-lu, *Pu-pien*, pp. 276–277.
50. Chang Ching-lu, *Pu-pien*, pp. 277 and 565.

mercial's Butterfly magazine *Short Story Monthly,* for example, Chung-hua fashioned a competitor in 1914 called *The World of Chinese Fiction (Chung-hua hsiao-shuo chieh).* [51] But just as the Republic declined during the 1910s, so the Chung-hua shu-chü declined and, in 1917, nearly collapsed from financial difficulties. [52] In 1918 it moved to strengthen itself by formally incorporating the Wen-ming shu-chü. The head of Wen-ming in its adjunct status, however, was a willful Shaohsing man named Shen Chih-fang who left abruptly at this juncture to found his own World Book Company (Shih-chieh shu-chü), which he did by incorporating the Kuang-Chih shu-chü as well. [53] At the same time another group of Shaohsing book dealers banded together to form the Great Eastern Book Co. (Ta-tung shu-chü). [54] Around 1921 Chung-hua, with some assistance from Commercial in staving off the challenge from Shen Chih-fang, had nursed itself back into a competitive position, though it still could reach only about half of Commercial's volume through the twenties. [55] In basic outline, the Shanghai publishing scene had resolved itself into a quadrilateral balance: Commercial and Chung-hua stood as the first-echelon contenders, while Great Eastern and World vied at the second level. The main offices of all four presses during these years were located on Shanghai's Foochow Road between Shantung Road and Honan Road. Major newspaper offices were on the same block, which was known in the popular idiom as "Culture Boulevard." [56]

All four of these presses, plus many more, published magazines as well as books. Their short story magazines—weeklies, twice-monthlies, and monthlies—were the most important media for popular fiction in the 1910s. (A number of these magazines are reviewed in the appendix.) In the early 1910s these magazines carried mostly translations written in classical style, and shifted as the years went by towards original compositions and vernacular style. Short stories always outnumbered long novels by a wide margin, though serialized novels, used by newspapers to hold readers, were sometimes used for this purpose in magazines as well. Short stories, which seemed better to satisfy the needs for the quick explanation and gratification which the times demanded, remained the clear preference of both authors and readers.

---

51. YYHTP, p. 287.
52. Chang Ching-lu, *Pu-pien,* p. 277.
53. Liu Hsin-huang, *Hsien-tai Chung-kuo wen-hsueh shih hua,* p. 30.
54. CYLHIL, p. 382.
55. Chang Ching-lu, *Pu-pien,* pp. 277 and 279.
56. CYLHIL, p. 382. (The Commercial Press had first been located on Peking Road; see CYLHIL, p. 389.)

These pressures produced in the magazine press not only a great burgeoning of stories but of "types" of stories. The recognized types which had emerged from the late Ch'ing period ("love novels," "social novels," and so forth) were now joined by countless new "types," some of them seemingly made up on an *ad hoc* basis. The purpose of the "type" label became, in fact, less one of placing a story in context than of previewing its contents. Like a little headline, the "type" was printed before the titles in the tables of contents of magazines, making it easy for a reader to scan the fare at a glance. To take but one example, the first two issues of Pao T'ien-hsiao's *The Grand Magazine* (1915) list the following "types" of stories: "love" *(ai-ch'ing)*, "tragic" *(ai-ch'ing)*, "bitterness" *(k'u-ch'ing)*, "comic" *(hua-chi)*, "household" *(chia-t'ing)*, "social" *(she-hui)*, "youth" *(shao-nien)*, "realistic" *(hsieh-shih)*, "war" *(chan-cheng)*, "military spy" *(chün-t'an)*, "detective" *(chen-t'an)*, "political" *(cheng-chih)*, "revenge" *(fu-ch'ou)*, "marvelous" *(ch'i-ch'ing)*, "supernatural" *(shen-kuai)* and "science" *(k'o-hsueh)*.

One issue of a magazine would carry from five or six up to a dozen or more short stories or serializations of long stories, plus jokes, anecdotes, short essays, casual notes by famous people, and so on. Illustration sections at the front became ever more prominent, featuring photographs of Chinese and Western art, famous beauties, writers and painters, plus anything else strange or wonderful.

It was standard among the fiction magazines of Shanghai to operate with a minimum circulation target of 3,000 copies. Costs were such that circulation below this figure would likely mean a capital loss for the publisher, while anything above it would bring a profit.[57] The internal budgets of the magazines are not available, but something of their proportions may be inferred from known data. For example payment of authors, though a new institution which attracted much attention, does not appear to have been a major cost. One issue of the *Fiction Times (Hsiao-shuo shih pao),* which contained from 55,000 to 85,000 characters, would cost the publisher about 110–170 yuan in authors' fees at the standard rate of 2 yuan per thousand characters. Yet the magazine sold for 60 cents per copy, which at the break–even point of 3,000 copies would bring an income of 1,800 yuan. Similar calculation for the *Thicket of Fiction (Hsiao-shuo ts'ung-pao)* yields a cost of 145 yuan per issue for manuscripts and a minimum income around 1,200 yuan. For those magazines which were financially successful, therefore, authors' fees would appear, at a maximum, to range from ten to sixteen percent of costs. Typesetting labor amounted to only a small fraction of the per–character rate paid to authors, and editing was also

57. CYLHIL, p. 377; interview with Pao T'ien-hsiao, December 6, 1972; interview with Ch'en Ting-shan, July 25, 1975.

inexpensive—in fact editors were often paid little beyond the per-character rate for their own contributions.

It appears, in sum, that the ratio of per-copy costs—such as paper, ink, use of machinery and distribution—to per-issue costs (authoring, editing, typesetting) was high, probably higher than modern standards elsewhere. Consequently small-circulation publication could be more competitive than elsewhere, as Roswell Britton has pointed out.[58] The fiction market thus invited short-term speculation, and a great number of short-lived magazines came and went as the interests and fortunes of their publishers rose and fell. Serialization became a problem from the reader's viewpoint, as magazines could perish before a story concluded.

In 1921 and 1922, just when the May Fourth attack on Butterfly literature was at its height, there was a new efflorescence of fiction magazines in and around Shanghai. The new activity was not a direct response to the May Fourth attack; ironically, in fact, it was in part a result of the larger aspects of the May Fourth literary movement which asserted the patriotism, and respectability, of fiction writing. Most of the activity involved a rivalry between what I have called the two "second level" presses, the World Book Company and the Great Eastern Book Company. These two publishers in 1921 and 1922 procured for themselves two of the best editors in the popular fiction business, Chou Shou-chüan at Great Eastern and Yen Tu-ho at World. Chou was simultaneously editor of the fiction column of *Shen pao,* Shanghai's second largest newspaper; Yen was editor of the fiction column at *Hsin-wen pao,* the largest. At Great Eastern, Chou came out with five leading magazines in four years; at World Yen produced four in three years. The magazines answered one another with special issues, featured authors, and contests for readers. Since violets were popular, two of Great Eastern's magazines were called *Violets (Tzu lo-lan)* and *Fallen Violet Petals (Tzu-lan hua-p'ien).* Chou Shou-chüan also nicknamed his home "The Little House of Violets." Yen Tu-ho, on the other hand, capitalized on the color red, with its traditional connotations of luck and its contemporary associations with stylishness. Yen chose for his magazines the names *The Scarlet Magazine (Hung tsa-chih)* and *Red Roses (Hung mei-kuei).* He had the door of the World Book Company's main office painted with the two big characters *hung wu* ("red room").[59]

The competition between the Great Eastern and World companies was not marked by polarization among writers, who continued to be generally willing to send their stories to either place. But in the area of

58. Britton, p. 128.
59. See Appendix for references and more details.

CHART A: **Estimates of the Volume of Business in the Shanghai Book-Publishing Industry and Percentage Share of Leading Publishers**

Year	Total Volume	Commercial Press	Wen-ming shu-chü and two others*	Chung-hua shu-chü	Shih-chieh shu-chü	Others
	(million yuan)					
ca. 1910	4–5	33%	33%	–	–	33%
ca. 1915	10	30–40%	–	10–20%	–	40–60%
ca. 1930	30	30%	–	15%	5%	50%

Chung-kuo t'u-shu kung-szu and *Chi-ch'eng t'u-shu kung-szu.*

SOURCE: Lu Fei-k'uei, *Liu-shih nien lai Chung-kuo chih ch'u-pan yeh yü yin-shua yeh,* in Chang Ching-lu *Chung-kuo ch'u-pan shih liao pu-pien,* p. 279. It would appear that the later figures are somewhat more precise and reliable than the earlier ones.

readership, commercial competition was much keener than it had been in the 1910s and earlier. Almost all magazines by 1925 carried advertisements for their own companies and offered bonus gifts such as calendars or calligraphy to new subscribers.

Figures on the total number of magazines to have appeared can only be estimated. Postal figures are incomplete (because many of the less substantial magazines did not have mail-order subscriptions) and ambiguous (because fiction magazines were not explicitly distinguished from others). Lists of known titles, however, indicate at least 91 "old school" fiction magazines in the city of Shanghai in the 1910s and twenties.[60] A complete listing, including the smallest and shortest-lived, would undoubtedly reach well over one hundred.

The modern publishing business as a whole appears to have grown at least six-fold in Shanghai between 1910 and 1930. (See Chart A.) From its beginning level of 3,000 yuan in 1897, the capital of the Commercial Press grew to about 5 million yuan by the beginning of 1932, when Chung-hua's capital was about 2 million, World's about 0.7 million, and Great Eastern's about 0.3 million.[61] (January, 1932, is a crucial point in measuring the volume of Shanghai's publishing industry because the Japanese attack on Chapei late that month destroyed many of the large publishing warehouses.) Even more remarkable than the expansion of the major presses during the 1910s and 1920s was the

60. Seventy-nine are listed in YYHTP, pp. 280–365; in addition, there are at least the following titles not listed in Wei: *Hsiao-shuo ming-hua ta-kuan, Li-pai hua, Hsin Chung-hua hsiao-shuo chieh, Hsin nü-hsing, Ta shih-chieh pao, Hsiang-kuei hua-ying, Tung-hai, Hsin chia-t'ing tsa-chih, Ch'ang-ch'ing, Hsing pao, Hsing,* and *Yü-hsing tsa-chih.*
61. Chang Ching-lu, *Pu-pien,* p. 278.

concurrent appearance and growth of dozens of smaller presses. As Chart A indicates, despite the impressive growth of the major presses, their *share* of Shanghai's total publishing industry appears to have declined a bit during the 1910s and 1920s, the balance being taken up by the smaller presses. In addition to the growth indicated in Chart A, one must not overlook the numerous fly-by-night publishing ventures, involved in short-term speculation and pirating, whose output appears in no statistics. Considering these, a sixfold growth estimate for 1910–1930 is surely conservative.

The growth of the smaller presses is important for our purposes because it is a fairly good index of the growth of popular fiction. In general, the likelihood of a press's involvement in this line seems to have increased with diminishing size. Commercial, Wen-ming and Chung-hua published their Butterfly magazines as a kind of lucrative sidelight to their main effort in textbooks and serious works on science, politics, economics and philosophy. For World and Great Eastern, who published popular fiction in book form as well as in magazines, such publication was more nearly a mainstream activity. Many smaller presses were devoted wholly to Butterfly publishing. Some, like the Ch'ing-hua shu-chü, published exclusively the works of Hsu Chen-ya and his friends. Another, the Min-ch'üan ch'u-pan pu, was set up in 1914 by order of Yuan Shih-k'ai, who was consciously trying to assuage with love stories the readership of the revolutionary newspaper *Min-ch'üan pao* which he had closed for political offenses.[62] Other Butterfly publishers to arise in the 1910s were the Kuang-i Book Co., the Chin-chang Book Co., the Summer Star Society (Hsia-hsing she), the Chung-hua Library (Chung-hua t'u-shu-kuan), and the Continental Book Co. (Ta-lu t'u-shu kung-szu). The Chi-ch'eng Book Co. (Chi-ch'eng t'u-shu kung-szu) was founded in the late Ch'ing years and grew quickly in the 1910s on Butterfly fiction. Some of these companies did not survive the decade, but others sprang up in the twenties to replace them; a few, such as the San-yu shu-she, grew to healthy proportions.

One of the smaller publishing houses deserves special mention for its leadership role in the publishing of popular fiction. Called the Yu-cheng shu-chü, it was the book and magazine adjunct of *Shih pao (Eastern Times),* which began publication in Shanghai in 1904. Most of Yu-cheng's early publications were on politics, education, society and reform movement issues generally; but as the *Shih pao* itself began to experiment with fiction and poetry, Yu-cheng also moved in that direction and began publishing the prototypes of China's modern light

62. YYHTP, pp. 287–288; Fan Tzu, "Yüan-yang hu-tieh p'ai hsiao-shuo chia ch'ün-hsiang," *Hsing-tao chou-pao,* July 14, 1972, p. 10.

CHART B: **Cash Value of Output in the Chinese Paper Industry during the 1910s (includes paper of all types)**

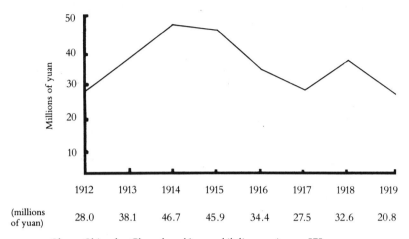

	1912	1913	1914	1915	1916	1917	1918	1919
(millions of yuan)	28.0	38.1	46.7	45.9	34.4	27.5	32.6	20.8

SOURCE: Chang Ching-lu, *Chung-kuo ch'u-pan shih liao pu-pien*, p. 575.

fiction magazines: *Hsiao-shuo shih-pao* (1909) and *Fu-nü shih-pao* (1912).[63] *Shih pao* was run in an experimental spirit and showed a perennial deficit which the Yu-cheng Book Co. was designed to recover. Yu-cheng's activity became better known and more lucrative after 1912, when Tseng Meng-p'u, author of the famous *Nieh-hai hua* and manager of the Hsiao-shuo lin she, went to serve in the Republican government, handing over his entire repertory of manuscripts to Yu-cheng for a modest rent. Yu-cheng used the manuscripts to good advantage (publishing, among others, the second impression of *Nieh-hai hua*) and for several years many creative innovations of the *Shih pao* continued to be possible as it depended on this wellspring of financial support.[64]

There was one problem which the revolution in printing technology in Shanghai during 1900–1920 never adequately solved: a cheap, reliable supply of new-style paper. Paper was, of course, a Chinese invention of more than two thousand years standing, but the new presses of Shanghai required a different kind of paper. The first Western-style paper factory was set up in Shanghai in 1891 by Li Hung-chang,[65] and by 1924 there were over twenty such factories in operation, most of them in the Kiangsu-Chekiang area. The largest produced about 7,500 tons per year.[66] Annual national production

63. YYHTP, pp. 280–284.   64. CYLHIL, pp. 427–428.
65. Chang Ching-lu, *Pu-pien*, p. 572.   66. Ibid., pp. 572–574.

seems to have peaked, however, during 1914–1915 (at a net value of around 45 million yuan), declining to less than half its peak volume by 1920. (See Chart B.)

A major reason for this decline appears to have been the growing demand during the 1910s for a new kind of imported newsprint which the most modern machines required. (When *Shen pao* once tried a domestic substitute, its machine clogged and there was no newspaper on the stands the next day.)[67] Before World War I, this paper was imported mostly from Sweden, Hong Kong, Japan, and Germany. After the war, Japan quickly pulled well ahead of the others.[68] Shanghai also began to produce the requisite product, but on a scale severely limited by the fact that wood pulp for the purpose was imported from Scandinavia and Canada.[69] In total, China's net imports of paper nearly doubled during the 1910s, reaching a monetary value by 1920 approximately two-thirds the worth of all modern domestic production,[70] and remaining a critical expense for the book and magazine press as well as for newspapers.

2. The Beginnings of the Modern Newspaper Press in Shanghai

Shanghai's modern newspapers got an earlier start than the new-style book and magazine press, but in many ways roughly paralleled the latter's development. Both began in imitation of foreign precedents in the late nineteenth century, underwent a technical revolution in the early 1900s, and grew rapidly during the 1910s. Like the book press, the new journalism was a key ingredient in the growth of modern popular fiction; the three Shanghai newspapers which led the way in reporting, circulation, and advertising also led the way in the serialization and popularization of fiction.

Two kinds of newspapers existed in Ch'ing China before the arrival of what we are calling the "modern" newspaper. One published official news (memorials, decrees and other public documents) of the court or a provincial capital for consumption by the scholar-official class. Though non-official enterprises, these gazettes were in the tradition of the official *ti-pao* which contained important reports for high officials during the Han and T'ang periods.[71] The second was a kind of handbill called *hsin-wen chih,* which were sporadically issued by printing shops when a particular story seemed salable. *Hsin-wen chih*

67. CYLHIL, p. 441.
68. Chang Ching-lu, *Pu-pien,* p. 577.
69. Ibid., p. 579.
70. Ibid., p. 578; see also Chart B.
71. Tseng Hsu-pai, p. 8ff; Ying-wan Cheng, p. 48.

were single-story operations; big stories were hastily carved into woodblocks in anticipation of extensive printing, while minor stories might be carved into the less durable clay or beeswax-and-resin blocks.[72]

The first newspapers in Shanghai to present readers with a varied fare on a daily basis were begun by Westerners. The English-language *North China Herald* began at mid-century, and the first Chinese-language newspaper in the new style, *Shen pao,* was begun in 1872 by the Englishman Ernest Major.[73] While the *North China Herald* continued for many years as an example—indeed a news source—for *Shen pao,* it was not *Shen pao*'s only important precedent. In 1858 a Chinese daily called *Chung-wai hsin pao* had been founded in Hong Kong on the model of English-language newspapers there, and by 1872 other Chinese dailies had appeared in Hong Kong, Canton, and elsewhere.[74] Of particular importance to *Shen pao* was *Hsun-huan jih-pao* (Hong Kong) edited by Wang T'ao, whose son-in-law Ch'ien Cheng became *Shen pao*'s first editor.[75] In 1884 Wang T'ao himself came to Shanghai and became a frequent contributor to the newspaper.[76]

From the start, these modern Chinese-language newspapers were printed with Western-style lead type. *Shen pao* at first used Chinese paper, but soon switched to imported paper.[77] During its early years it was issued every morning on a single sheet of glossy paper, printed on one side only.[78] At the top, after a routine listing of the newspaper's standards and regulations, was an editorial disquisition *(lun-shuo)* which formally expounded upon a prominent news item. Something of a cross between the Western idea of an editorial and a scholarly Chinese dissertation on moral order, it was not the liveliest portion of the paper. To readers it came to be known, in fact, as the "news office eight-legged essay" *(pao-kuan pa-ku).* [79] The next news category, moving down the page, consisted of imperial edicts, various court announcements both old and new, and other reportage in the style of old

72. Britton, p. 5.

73. Many sources list Frederick Major as the founder. Actually Frederick was Ernest's younger brother and also worked on the *Shen pao,* but Ernest was the founder.

74. Ying-wan Cheng, p. 48.

75. Tseng Hsu-pai, p. 11.

76. For a masterly account of Wang T'ao's contributions to modern history, see Paul A. Cohen, *Between Tradition and Modernity: Wang T'ao and Reform in Late Ch'ing China* (Cambridge, 1974).

77. Yuan Ch'ang-ch'ao, *Chung-kuo pao-yeh hsiao-shih,* pp. 77–78.

78. The newspaper was divided into eight sections *(chang)* which were not separate pages. See CYLHIL, p. 320 and Yuan Ch'ang-ch'ao, p. 77.

79. CYLHIL, p. 322.

capital gazettes. Below this were crowded together local, national, and occasionally some international news, together with a welter of advertisements and shipping schedules. Common items of advertisement were medical cures, foreign trading firms, and, a few years later, cigarettes. Occasionally *Shen pao* would attach a second sheet, called the *fu-chang,* which carried memorials to the throne by provincial governors and inspectors-general.[80]

Shen pao's opening editorial statement, apparently drafted by Ernest Major and his fellow Englishmen, expressed a populist sentiment much more characteristic of the post-Enlightenment West than of nineteenth-century China. The great aspiration of *Shen pao* was to: ". . . report current affairs concisely yet in sufficient detail that scholars and officials as well as farmers, artisans, traders and merchants can all understand."[81] The price of the newspaper was set at eight cash per copy, though it soon increased to ten. This was a rather high price— more than one-tenth, for example, of the daily wage of a skilled seamstress.[82] In order to reduce the burden of the purchase price, a policy was instituted of refunding six cash to anyone who returned an issue for resale on the same morning he bought it.[83] To encourage agency sales, anyone who took a bundle of one hundred copies was offered a twenty-five percent commission and a promise that *Shen pao* would buy back unsold copies.[84]

Yet the public response fell far short of the hopes of the newspaper's founders. In its early years, *Shen pao* printed scarcely six hundred copies per issue,[85] and these were read only among a narrow sector of Western-influenced treaty port society. Before long it became apparent that the best means of increasing circulation was to sacrifice the newspaper's other avowed goal, *viz.,* faithful and detailed reporting. The means was discovered by *Shen pao*'s chief editor Ch'ien Cheng, who discovered the principle, during China's 1874 conflict with Japan over the Ryukyus, that good news sells newspapers far better than bad: the best stimulant to circulation was to report Chinese naval victories. A second opportunity for such reporting arrived during the Sino-French War of 1884–1885, when naval reporting in *Shen pao* degenerated into a kind of heroic story-telling, based on fabricated incidents told in fantastic detail.[86] But *Shen pao*'s circulation grew from the hundreds

80. CYLHIL, p. 322.
81. As translated in Britton, p. 65.
82. CYLHIL, p. 124.
83. Britton, p. 68.
84. Ying-wan Cheng, p. 48.
85. Yuan Ch'ang-ch'ao, p. 78.
86. CYLHIL, p. 106; Ying-wan Cheng, pp. 48–49.

into the thousands.[87] It spread, moreover, to other Yangtze basin cities, including Soochow (where there were about 100 subscriptions in 1885),[88] Wusih, Changchow, Chinkiang, and Nanking. Even down the coast as far as Amoy, all the "good families" now read *Shen pao*.[89]

Circulation to these outlying cities was handled by private "letter agencies" *(hsin-chü)* who served as agents as well as transporters. They charged only about two cash for out-of-town delivery.[90] The salability of newspapers naturally depended upon speed of delivery, for which sailboats, the standard means, were less than ideal. They took, for example, three days and two nights to pass from Shanghai to Soochow.[91] In 1898 steamboats could make the same run in fifteen hours, and the railroad, built in 1903, could do it in three hours.[92] Before these innovations, the problem of swift delivery had been solved by use of a special kind of "hand-and-foot boat" *(chiao hua ch'uan)*. Light and streamlined, these could be rowed either by two persons using their arms or by one person using both arms and legs. They could cover the distance between Shanghai and Soochow as quickly as a steamboat, leaving Shanghai every night around ten or eleven o'clock and arriving in Soochow shortly after noon the next day.[93]

Following *Shen pao,* two smaller newspapers were founded in Shanghai, both of which were even more tightly bound to the treaty port culture than was *Shen pao*. In 1876 *Hsin pao* appeared, which was actually bi-lingual and aimed at influencing foreign opinion.[94] *Hu pao,* beginning in 1880, was a Chinese version of the *North China Herald*.[95] Both had very small circulations and were short-lived. During 1880–1900 newspapers sprang up in Hankow, Tientsin, Ningpo, Amoy, Canton and several other treaty port cities.[96] Many of these early efforts also collapsed under financial pressures, yet by 1900 most of the treaty ports and a few non-treaty ports had one or more successful newspapers. All, incidentally, were morning papers. China's first evening papers did not appear until the 1910s, and these totally lacked reporting networks; they were simply patchwork re-assemblages of

87. Britton, p. 68.
88. CYLHIL, p. 106.
89. Ying-wan Cheng, p. 49.
90. Ibid., p. 48.
91. CYLHIL, p. 49; Ying-wan Cheng, pp. 37–50.
92. CYLHIL, pp. 105–106, 275, 164.
93. Ibid., p. 106. It would seem reasonable to guess that the passage was undertaken at night in order to avoid strenuous exercise in the heat of the day.
94. Britton, p. 72.
95. Britton, p. 74, gives 1882 as the beginning date for the *Hu pao*; apparently closer to the material, Pott, in *Short History,* gives 1880 as the date (p. 179).
96. Britton, p. 76ff.

leading stories from various morning newspapers. The first evening papers with independent editorial and reporting staffs appeared in the 1920s.[97]

Shen pao's major competitor during most of its lifetime was *Hsin-wen pao*, founded in Shanghai in 1893. *Hsin-wen pao*'s original financing is obscure, though according to rumors of the time it may have received secret support from Sheng Hsuan-huai or Chang Chih-tung. The original aim of the newspaper was to undersell *Shen pao* by offering a similar newspaper—with the same single-glossy-sheet format, and the same editorial divisions—but selling for seven cash instead of ten. By 1895 *Hsin-wen pao* had reached a circulation of five thousand, or one-third of *Shen pao*'s.[98] Shortly thereafter it ran into serious financial difficulties and nearly collapsed, only to be bailed out in 1900 when a controlling interest was purchased by the American ex-missionary educator John C. Ferguson.[99] By the time Ferguson sold his shares to a group of Chinese bankers in 1929, *Hsin-wen pao* had increased its circulation to nearly 150,000.[100]

To the young progressive community which was developing in Shanghai, *Shen pao* and *Hsin-wen pao*—though printed in Chinese and intended for Chinese readers—were nevertheless indelibly tainted with certain non-Chinese associations. They had a "foreign flavor" *(yang wei)* about them. This was due in large measure to their close resemblance to foreign trading companies, or *yang hang*. Their buildings looked like trading company buildings. They were, moreover, owned by foreigners who hired Chinese managers to do the day-to-day work. (Chinese editors of *Shen pao* and *Hsin-wen pao* were referred to as "compradors" among the Chinese community.)[101] Their printing machines and the paper they used were entirely imported, and their many advertisements, which paraded English-language labels before the public, were uniformly for foreign firms and products.

Beginning in the late 1890s, a new sort of newspaper appeared in Shanghai which, except that they were still printed by imported machines on imported paper, managed to divest themselves of this "foreign flavor." These were China's first political newspapers, such

97. Interview with Tseng Hsu-pai, Taipei, July 19, 1973. (Tseng's own was one of the precursors.)

98. Britton, p. 74 and p. 68.

99. Ibid., p. 74.

100. While Britton, p. 74, says *Hsin-wen pao* was sold to bankers, Wei Shao-ch'ang, YYHTP, p. 402, says it was sold to Shih Liang-ts'ai of *Shen pao;* on the circulation figure of 150,000, see Tseng Hsu-pai, p. 355, and Lin Yutang, *The Press and Public Opinion*, p. 145.

101. CYLHIL, p. 229.

organs of the reform movement as *Ch'iang-hsueh pao* (1895) and *Shih-wu pao* (1896). Responding to the historical crisis brought by Japan's defeat of China in 1895 and the ensuing "scramble for concessions" among the imperialist powers, these newspapers scorned the commercial motives of *Shen pao* and *Hsin-wen pao.*[102] They were inspired, on the contrary, by ideas which Liang Ch'i-ch'ao expressed in an 1896 article called "On the Benefit to the Nation of Newspapers" (Lun pao-kuan yu-i yü kuo-shih). Liang there argues that newspapers, as the example of the Western countries clearly shows, are vital to the awakening and unifying of a nation. Ardent youth in Shanghai, Peking, and other major cities formed political and scientific study groups around such newspapers and other weekly, thrice monthly, and monthly publications.

Happily for the spread of this ferment, the railroad and the steamboat made inter-city transportation much easier during the decade of 1900–1910, especially in the Yangtze Basin. The changeover to rail and steam was facilitated through the new Imperial Post Office (I.P.O.), which was founded in 1896 by combining the foreign-run Customs Post (from 1878) with local posts which had sprung up in a number of Chinese cities in the early 1890s. Rather than competing with the private letter agencies *(hsin-chü),* the I.P.O. wisely sought to link up with them for better deliveries inland. The letter agencies were asked to register with the I.P.O., and only those which did were allowed to send mail by steamer.[103] In 1898 this new combined system offered special low rates for newspapers.

Shortly thereafter Shanghai publishing activities found imitators in near-by cities and towns. In Soochow a group inspired by the example of K'ang Yu-wei's *Ch'iang-hsueh pao* and its adjunct Ch'iang-hsueh hui founded its own Li-hsueh hui and *Li-hsueh i-pien.* The latter was a thirty-page monthly which introduced Western science, political ideas, and literature, taken almost entirely from contemporary Japanese publications. (The group of Soochow writers who ran the publication had hired a tutor from the Japanese consulate in Soochow to teach them Japanese for the purpose.) *Li-hsueh i-pien* cost two yuan a year, or twenty cents (more than the daily wage of a scribe) for any individual copy.[104] It achieved a circulation of 700-800, mostly around Soochow but reaching some inland cities as well. There being no lead-type printing press in Soochow, *Li-hsueh i-pien* was perhaps one of the few magazines in history to be printed using engraved wood blocks.[105]

102. CYLHIL, p. 229.
103. Ying-wan Cheng, pp. 58, 100.
104. CYLHIL, pp. 123, 166–167.
105. CYLHIL, pp. 166–167.

One important consequence of the new reform journals was the appearance of *pai-hua* newspapers in China. Though Western missionaries had published didactic stories and the Bible in *pai-hua* before this time, they had not done journalism. The first person to attempt *pai hua* journalism seems to have been *Shen pao*'s founder Ernest Major, who in 1876 introduced a *pai-hua* supplement to *Shen pao*. Called *Min pao,* it was designed to reach new types of readers among the less-than-classically literate.[106] In reality, though, *Min pao* could not have had more than a handful of such readers and the experiment was probably just as much an expression of Major's Western populism as it was a harbinger of China's *pai-hua* movement. With the arrival of the turn-of-the-century reform movement, however, *pai-hua* journalism developed steadily from several more indigenous sources. Curiously, first appearances were made not in Shanghai but in those epicenters of late Ch'ing ferment scattered through the lower Yangtze basin. The first example was the *Wu-hsi pai-hua pao,* founded in 1898. Its imitators followed, like bamboo shoots after rain, totaling more than fourteen within a few years.[107] Prominent examples were *Hang-chou pai-hua pao,* begun in June, 1901 by a group which included the well-known translator Lin Shu, and *Su-chou pai-hua pao,* begun in October of the same year by the translator and editor Pao T'ien-hsiao and a number of his friends.[108]

These *pai-hua* newspapers were published every ten days, cost around twenty coppers, and ran to eight pages per issue. They carried local, national, and even international stories, plus their own editorial opinions in the form of *lun-shuo* borrowed from the pattern of *Shen pao* and *Hsin-wen pao.* Editorial decisions were dominated by the contemporary issues of social concern which emanated mostly from Shanghai: anti-opium, anti-footbinding, and anti-superstition, for example. Consistently oriented towards progressive Shanghai culture, most of these newspapers were also printed there. The comparative ease of transportation to and from Shanghai seems, in fact, to have inhibited for many years the development of modern presses in lower Yangtze urban centers.[109]

In December of 1903, the largest of the early *pai-hua pao,* called *Chung-kuo pai-hua pao,* was founded in Shanghai. Managed by Lin Pai-shui, *Chung-kuo pai-hua pao* ran to eighty pages per issue and was

106. Yuan Ch'ang-ch'ao, p. 78.
107. T'an Pi-an, *Wan-Ch'ing ti pai-hua wen yun-tung,* pp. 12–13; also Ko Kung-chen, *Chung-kuo pao-hsueh shih,* pp. 113–119.
108. Britton, p. 115; CYLHIL, pp. 168–170.
109. Hangchow was one prominent exception to this rule, as the *Hang-chou pai-hua pao* was printed by a local press. CYLHIL, p. 169.

bound like a Western-style book. It agitated for social reform and divided its contents according to essays, history, biography, theory, education, industry, current events, science, fiction, drama, songs, and miscellaneous.[110]

Among the social doctrines of the *pai-hua pao* was precisely the campaign to publish in *pai-hua,* and this twenty years in advance of the May Fourth Movement. Their primary aim was to bring the issues of the day to the largest possible readership. In addition to reaching as far down the literacy scale as possible, managers of these early newspapers consistently directed their efforts at distribution toward outlying towns and villages. *Su-chou pai-hua pao* at one point considered waiving its purchase price as a spur to circulation, yet decided against this course fearing that their newspaper might then be mistaken for one of two other kinds of free handouts, viz., the "moral tracts" *(shan-shu)* occasionally distributed by the Confucian gentry, and the religious pamphlets of Western missionaries. To the editors, the great danger of such misidentification was that the recipients of these free handouts habitually did not read them. People needed to pay for the newspaper, they reasoned, since "if they pay for it, they will make a point to take a look at it."[111]

In the wake of the reform periodicals there arose in Shanghai another group of more seriously political newspapers which came to be known as "revolutionary" because they dared to advocate the overthrow of Manchu rule. *Su pao,* which became the most famous of these, was founded in 1896 in the International Settlement, where it received Japanese financial aid and was officially registered with the Japanese consulate as a foreign property under the name of the Japanese wife of its first manager, Hu Chang. It was a tiny establishment. Located in the downstairs of a house on Chessboard Street, behind two glass doors with "Su Pao Kuan" written vertically in red characters, its premises consisted of a single room divided down the middle by a glass partition: in front were two editor's desks, and in back were shelves of lead type and a photogravure printer.[112] The newspaper's fame did not arrive until 1903 when six of its editors and contributors were arrested for publishing inflammatory essays which the Ch'ing court saw as "slandering the emperor."[113] *Su pao* was not alone, however, and closing down the newspaper by no means ended its cause. Among several new "revolutionary" newspapers which con-

110. Yü Ping-ch'üan, Li Yu-ning and Chang Yü-fa, comps., *Ch'ing-chi ko-ming yun-tung ch'i-k'an hsu-mu hsuan-chi* (Washington, D.C., 1970), p. xiii.
111. CYLHIL, p. 169.
112. CYLHIL, p. 182.
113. Tseng Hsu-pai, pp. 211–213.

sciously took up its task were Chang Shih-chao's *Kuo-min jih jih-pao* (1906) and Yü Yu-jen's *Shen-chou jih-pao* (1907).[114]

The rise of these political newspapers in Shanghai had several consequences of profound importance for the development of the modern Chinese press generally. One was the institutionalization of the principle that newspapers in the foreign concessions could, within certain limits, express dissenting political opinion beyond the reach of the Chinese government. Though the notion of the treaty port as a haven was at least as old as the T'aip'ing wars, when hundreds of thousands of refugees crowded Shanghai's foreign settlement,[115] the question of whether the foreign powers would positively intervene in order to protect dissident Chinese from the Chinese authorities had remained untested until the *Su pao* case.

Protection turned out to be a matter of degree. The governor of Kiangsu had little trouble persuading the foreigners to arrest the *Su pao* editors. But he failed in numerous attempts to have them extradited, a step which the foreigners felt would violate their extraterritorial rights. (The extraterritorial issue was made the weightier in the foreigners' view by the fact of *Su pao*'s official registration with the Japanese. This aspect of the *Su pao* precedent led later newspapers to pad their protection by similar means of foreign association or registry.)[116] After much negotiation, the final decision to try the *Su pao* editors in Shanghai, with both a Chinese and a British judge presiding, led to sentences which undoubtedly were much lighter than they would have been in Kiangsu. Yet sentences there were, and the young martyr Tsou Jung died in jail. The principle of treaty port protection thus appeared as a qualified one: anti-government expression was assuredly less risky in the foreign concessions, but it could not be ventured with impunity. In the ensuing years the situation gradually worsened. As anti-foreign and anti-imperialist journalism developed, the foreigners, originally protectors, discovered that they too would have occasion to attempt repression of certain views.[117]

A second important influence of *Su pao* and the other "revolutionary" newspapers was their diversifying effect upon the commercial newspapers already in existence. *Shen pao* and *Hsin-wen pao,* which in the past had stood aside from political controversy, became increasingly embarrassed during 1900–1910 by their "foreign flavor" and

114. Ibid., p. 213.

115. Pott, *Short History,* pp. 37, 51, 64 and 79. (Pott's estimates of Chinese in the foreign settlements during the war run as high as 1.5 million.)

116. Tseng Hsu-pai, p. 210; CYLHIL, p. 181; Britton, p. 124.

117. Pott, pp. 179–180; Harold R. Isaacs, Introduction to *Straw Sandals: Chinese Short Stories, 1918–1933* (Cambridge, 1974) pp. xxxii–xxxiii.

began to accommodate their editorial policies to the reformist-nationalist temper of the times.[118] The *Su pao* court proceedings provided the occasion for a new political audacity in their editorials.

With this qualified shift in the nature of *Shen pao* and *Hsin-wen pao,* we may mark the end of the early era of purely commercial newspapers and the beginning of a period when leading papers were multi-functional. Instead of turning to separate newspapers and magazines for political, commercial, and entertainment interests, readers began to expect a good newspaper like *Shen pao* or *Hsin-wen pao* to provide all three. *Su pao* itself, whose role has appeared so "political" to posterity, was in fact an example of this new diversity, its back pages carrying both advertisements and literary games.[119]

A third and most important consequence of the political journalism after 1900 was its stimulation of a whole new breed of newspapers. In addition to being multi-functional, these newspapers contributed many lasting innovations to Chinese journalism in the areas of editorial style, reporting and distribution, and the use of advertisement and entertainment columns. They were also the first newspapers of relatively large circulation to be owned and run entirely by Chinese.

The original example was *Chung-wai jih-pao,* founded in 1902 under the editorship of Wang I-nien.[120] *Chung-wai jih-pao* expanded its news coverage by hiring on a permanent basis two specialists in the translation of foreign news sources, one for Japanese and one for English. Following the example of foreign newspapers, it also completely overhauled the old top-to-bottom editorial format established by *Shen pao* and adopted a system of free arrangement of news stories whose headlines and relative importance might be grasped at a glance. In place of the glossy paper used by every other Chinese newspaper until this time, *Chung-wai jih-pao* substituted fresh-looking white newsprint and—also a first—printed it on both sides.[121] For all these reasons, *Chung-wai jih-pao* caught the eye of the reading public in Shanghai and thereby established an example which no newspaper after it could ignore.

More significant than *Chung-wai jih-pao* in journalistic innovation was *Shih pao* or *Eastern Times,* founded in 1904 by Ti Ch'u-ch'ing. Ti was an activist of the reform movement generation, a student of K'ang

118. Britton, p. 114.

119. CYLHIL, pp. 181–182.

120. Pao T'ien-hsiao maintains that while the management of *Chung-wai jih-pao* has often been attributed to Wang K'ang-nien, actually it was this man's younger brother, Wang I-nien, who was in charge. CYLHIL, pp. 214 and 230.

121. CYLHIL, pp. 166 and 214.

Yu-wei's, and a signatory of K'ang's famous "Ten Thousand Word Memorial" which urged the Ch'ing court to continue the war against Japan in 1895 and to make great reforms to strengthen China.[122] Ti Ch'u-ch'ing was party as well to fund raising for the revolutionary putschism of T'ang Ts'ai-ch'ang which failed at Wuhan in 1900, after which Ti fled to Japan and assumed a pseudonym. In Japan he became close friends with Liang Ch'i-ch'ao and fell under the strong influence of Liang's views on the importance to China's salvation of an active and effective press.[123] When Ti returned to Shanghai to found *Shih pao*, he came equipped both with inspiration from Liang and, apparently, with a certain amount of capital left over from his fund-raising for T'ang Ts'ai-ch'ang.[124]

Although Ti himself was unambiguously associated with the "reformists" *(wei-hsin p'ai)*, he gathered around him at *Shih pao* a staff whose variety of interests reflected the new diversity in Shanghai journalism. As assistant editor he hired Ch'en Ching-han, a vociferous anti-monarchist who brought a revolutionary element to the paper's editorial make-up. A second assistant editor was Pao T'ien-hsiao, former manager of *Su-chou pai-hua pao,* whose growing interest in entertainment fiction blended another strain into *Shih pao.* The newspaper's peculiarly multifaceted nature has confused many who have looked back at this period with classificatory interests; it has been labeled everything from "monarchist" to "revolutionary" to "Butterfly."[125] Yet it may have been precisely the paper's diversity and innovation which led to its rapid growth. Quickly outstripping its smaller competitors, *Shih pao* soon rivaled the twin pillars *Shen pao* and *Hsin-wen pao* as the third major newspaper in Shanghai, though it never exceeded them in circulation.

Building upon the revised format established by *Chung-wai jih-pao, Shih pao* boldly located its heading at the right hand side of the paper instead of at the top and organized its news coverage into new clear-cut categories.[126] (Throughout these years *Shen pao* and *Hsin-wen pao* continued to resist such changes, fearing that any radical changes might frighten off their advertisers.)[127] The first news category was called "important news" *(yao wen)* from Peking, for which *Shih pao*

122. Ibid., p. 421.
123. Ibid., p. 318.
124. Ibid., p. 421; Tseng Hsu-pai, p. 227. According to Tseng, Ti finished his studies in Japan before cooperating with T'ang Ts'ai-ch'ang in 1900.
125. Chang Ching-lu, *Chin-tai,* 2:430; Britton, p. 115; YYHTP, pp. 404–406.
126. CYLHIL, p. 319.
127. Ibid., p. 424.

was the first newspaper to hire a special correspondent who sent daily telegraphic reports to Shanghai.[128] *Shen pao* and *Hsin-wen pao* had had Peking correspondents before that time, but on a much more casual and intermittent, and nontelegraphic, basis.[129] Second was news from other cities *(wai-pu hsin-wen)* which primarily meant lower Yangtze cities such as Nanking, Wusih, Soochow and Hangchow, where *Shih pao* went beyond the practice of engaging roving correspondents and established the first permanent branch offices of any Shanghai newspaper. The third category was local news from Shanghai *(pen-pu hsin-wen)*.[130]

In the matter of editorials, *Shih pao* gradually replaced the lengthy, tiresome "news dissertations" *(lun-shuo)* of the *Shen pao* and *Hsin-wen pao* style with brief, pungent editorial commentaries. Three of these were supplied every day to accompany each of the three news categories. The little essays were called *shih p'ing*, a pun suggesting "timely remarks" and "commentary by *Shih pao*."[131] In the estimation of the editors, the *shih p'ing* and the telegraphic "important news" from Peking were the main drawing cards in *Shih pao*'s rapid growth in circulation. The regional and local news were considerably less vital.[132]

Following close upon its innovations in news reporting and editorials, *Shih pao* turned its efforts towards special interest columns. Their columns elicited an increasingly enthusiastic reader response, until, during the 1910s, they were publishing regular supplements on literature, education, industry, women, children, English, drawing and art[133] (a list which, incidentally, roughly indicates the concerns and stylish interests of the progressive Shanghai readership of those years). Accumulated output from these supplements often led to the publication of books by *Shih pao*'s own publisher, the Yu-cheng shu-chü.

Special columns on literature, including both poetry and serialized fiction, were among the first to develop. *Shih pao*'s assistant editor Ch'en Ching-han, writing under the pen name of *leng-hsüeh* ("cold blood") proved to be not only an articulate revolutionary but a skillful fashioner of mystery thrillers as well.[134] Pao T'ien-hsiao, who alter-

128. CYLHIL: HP, p. 148.
129. CYLHIL, pp. 320 and 348.
130. CYLHIL, pp. 319–320.
131. CYLHIL, pp. 319–320.
132. CYLHIL, p. 322, and interview with Pao T'ien-hsiao in Hong Kong, December 6, 1972.
133. Tseng Hsu-pai, p. 271; YYHTP, p. 404.
134. CYLHIL, pp. 313 and 318.

nated days with Ch'en, wrote in a lighter vein, basing his stories primarily upon Western fiction in Japanese translation. Together they also ran a column on poetry called the "Equality Chamber" *(p'ing-teng ko)*, so named in order to encourage all readers to exercise their "equal" opportunity in creating poetry, and gradually gained a reputation as a center of the new poetry movement of the late Ch'ing and early Republican periods.[135] They also began a fiction column called "Surplus Spirit" *(Yü hsing)*, which was the prototype for all the fiction columns which were so important in the spread of modern popular fiction in the 1910s and twenties.

Shih pao's supplement on women built on an interest which had had its beginnings in the early (1895–1905) developmental stages of the late Ch'ing reform culture in Shanghai. Though social realities lagged behind, the notion of women playing new and prominent roles in outside society captured public imagination in these years; the idea was savored and experimented with in fiction and in increased attention to a few actual living examples. Part of the excitement of the first *pai-hua pao* to appear (Wusih, 1898) was that its editor was a woman.[136] A few years later, in 1902, Ch'en Hsieh-fen, the daughter of *Su pao* editor Ch'en Meng-p'o, carried public fascination further along the same lines by editing her own newspaper for women called *Nü pao*. Sent out gratis to the subscriber list of *Su pao,* its special aim was to promote women's rights, especially education. In 1905 a newspaper appeared in Peking which was edited and published exclusively by women, and in 1906 *Chung-kuo nü pao* appeared, founded by the famous woman revolutionary Ch'iu Chin.[137] In addition to venturing beyond *Shen pao* and *Hsin-wen pao* by publishing special columns and supplements on women's issues—and (another bold departure!) being the first newspaper office in Shanghai to allow women on its premises—[138] *Shih pao* added in 1912 a special women's magazine called *Fu-nü shih-pao,* which continued for several years to specialize in stories about the new-style woman's image.[139]

Shih pao also gained an early reputation for interest in education. In the years prior to the 1911 revolution they ran a kind of club for activist intellectuals called the "Resting Place" *(hsi-lou)*. Every afternoon, on the second floor above *Shih pao*'s main office on Foochow Road, the "Resting Place" served as a center where members could sip tea and

135. Britton, p. 115.
136. Ibid., pp. 97–98.
137. Ibid., p. 116; CYLHIL, p. 182.
138. CYLHIL, p. 419.
139. YYHTP, pp. 283–284; see also Appendix.

debate the issues of the day. The membership included leaders in new-style education in the Kiangsu-Chekiang region,[140] and their intellectual interchange produced material for many of the *Shih pao*'s special columns and supplements, especially those on education.

The newspaper's association with education was strengthened by its advertising policy. Eschewing the examples of *Shen pao* and *Hsin-wen pao,* which relied on the advertising revenue available from foreign firms, cigarettes, and quack medicines, *Shih pao* sought advertisements from book and magazine publishers. They devised a special arrangement with the Commercial Press, for example, whereby the press selected two books each month it wished to promote and, for a fee of two thousand yuan per month, had these advertised daily in a special side-top corner of *Shih pao.* As a consequence of this educational emphasis, most of the new-style schools in Shanghai and other cities within the circulation area of *Shih pao* used it to advertise their entrance examinations.[141] Gradually the paper became the standard fare for the intellectual community of the lower Yangtze and to a certain degree held that reputation throughout its lifetime. Hu Shih recalls scarcely missing an issue of *Shih pao*'s first six years.[142] While it never approached *Shen pao* and *Hsin-wen pao* in circulation within Shanghai, in outlying cities, where the proportion of readers not from the intellectual classes was smaller, *Shih pao* became the leader.

The appearance of the multifunctional newspapers like *Chung-wai jih-pao* and *Shih pao* during 1902–1912 was accompanied by a revolution in the news gathering systems of Shanghai newspapers. In particular *Shih pao*'s employment of a full-time professional reporter in Peking set an example which spread through the industry. Before 1910, out-of-city reporters were nothing more than casual correspondents whose main source of livelihood lay elsewhere; paid by piece-work or not paid at all, they would send in occasional essays in the manner of travelogues or light-interest columns. Only in the most extraordinary of circumstances would they send a telegraphic report.[143] But *Shih pao*'s original Peking reporter was a very different type. He worked at news gathering on a full time basis, despatched a telegram daily, and was paid the very high salary, for a newsman of that time, of two hundred yuan per month. When other newspapers established their own special reporters, salaries were driven higher still, and soon, fol-

---

140. These included Shen En-fu, Yuan Hsi-t'ao, Huang Yen-p'ei, Kung Chieh, Lin Tsu-chin, Shih Liang-ts'ai, Wu Huai-chiu, Chu Shao-p'ing and Yang Pai-min; CYLHIL, pp. 329–330. For characters, see glossary.
141. CYLHIL, p. 424.
142. Hu Shih, "Shih-ch'i nien ti hui-ku," in Ko Kung-chen, p. 142.
143. CYLHIL, p. 320.

lowing the example of the Tientsin *Ta kung pao,* included expense accounts as well.[144]

High pay was a requisite for early professional reporters because their work was unusually troublesome, even dangerous. Fundamentally, the new-style reporter's role simply did not rest well with Chinese social values: how could one consider it at all honorable for an outsider to pry into someone's affairs, make them public, and receive money for doing so? Early reporters were typically adventuresome personalities who took up their new profession in the face of the opposition of family and friends.[145] They pursued their day-to-day work running the continual risk of antagonism from all quarters of society. Furthermore, since formal news releases and interviews were few and unproductive, it was precisely from among a reporter's social contacts that he had to develop news sources. He was obliged to tread the delicate line of appearing as inoffensive as possible to as wide a range of persons as possible within a society whose strong predilection was to scorn him. In the case of Peking reporters, a source of government news was an absolute necessity, and official outlets were far from adequate. Especially before 1912, good material could be garnered only by secret arrangement with a willing bureaucrat. Such an arrangement was always difficult and tenuous, however, because the news-smuggling bureaucrat stood to lose, if discovered, very much more than he stood to gain.[146] The difficulty of getting news of the imperial court before 1912 was so great that very often foreign newspapers could get better court news through their legations than any Chinese newspaper could get by other means. This left the Chinese press in the embarrassing position of having to print news of their own government a day late, translating it from foreign newspaper reports. The practice appears to have decreased, but not to have ended, after 1912.

One of the most effective of the early Peking reporters was Shao P'iao-p'ing, who served during the 1910s as Peking correspondent for several Shanghai newspapers, including both *Shen pao* and *Shih pao.* In 1920 he set up his own local newspaper, *Ching pao,* and soon thereafter established a general agency for out-of-town newspapers. Shao carefully cultivated a wide network of contacts—a network which constantly shifted as his work required him to cross and double-cross those who trusted him. In 1913, after a brief imprisonment at the hands of Yuan Shih-k'ai, Shao exiled himself briefly to Japan. But he returned to Peking in 1916 and continued his unabashed pursuit of the

144. CYLHIL, p. 349.

145. See for example the cases of Pi I-hung and Shao P'iao-p'ing in CYLHIL:HP, pp. 42–78.

146. CYLHIL, p. 347.

news with such energy that even the Shanghai newspapers which depended on his reports began calling him an "adventurer" who sought
to "monopolize" the news. He was frequently accused of offering the
editorial support of his *Ching pao* for sale. Both court cases and unofficial rumors against him piled up until, in 1926, he was executed on the
apparently groundless suspicion that he had political connections with
the Soviet embassy.[147]

Other early newsmen met similar unfortunate ends. Huang Yuan-
yung, who was the original Peking telegraphic correspondent for *Shih
pao* and *Shen pao,* left Peking in the mid-1910s and fled all the way to
America out of fear of Yuan Shih-k'ai's wrath. Yuan's agents followed
him there and carried out the assassination anyway.[148]

Yet despite its dangers, Peking news reporting grew as a feature of
Shanghai newspapers. By the middle 1910s at least half a dozen Shanghai newspapers hired special correspondents on a regular basis.[149]
There ensued among them a lively competition which centered not
only around news-gathering but, inevitably, around the technical
problem of telegraphic transmission as well. Before 1912, telegraphic
news reports cost ten cents per character, which was the standard rate
for all telegrams to Shanghai. After 1912 the new government, in order
to encourage modern journalism, instituted a special rate for news
reports of only three cents per character. The drawback of this arrangement was that news telegrams took lowest priority among four
telegraphic categories: government telegrams, express telegrams, and
regular commercial telegrams all had to be despatched, in that order,
before news telegrams were handled. As a result news despatches seldom reached Shanghai until the wee hours of the morning, earlier or
later according to traffic. The message arrived, moreover, in numerical
telegraphic code which had to be deciphered in greatest haste if it was
to appear in morning editions. Most newspapers hired an expert at the
telegraphic code who, for the majority of common characters, could
decipher their numbers at a glance. Yet difficulties remained because of
the large number of mistakes included in these late-night, low-priority
telegrams. A single mistaken digit would cause a piece of nonsense,
and messages often had to be studied and interpreted even after they
were deciphered. If a telegram were particularly late in arriving, newspapers would often set the type for the whole morning edition except
for a blank area on the front page of what they guessed to be adequate

147. CYLHIL, p. 349; Howard L. Boorman et al., *Biographical Dictionary of Republican China* (New York, 1968), 3:93–94.
148. CYLHIL, p. 320.
149. These were *Shen pao, Hsin-wen pao, Shih pao, Hsin shen pao, Shen-chou jih pao,
Min-kuo jih pao, Chung-hua hsin pao,* and *Shih-shih hsin pao.*

size for the awaited telegraphic report from Peking. (It was impossible to consider omitting the Peking report, since one's competitors might not do so.) Sometimes the very worst happened and the Peking report never arrived. In such cases, the front-page blank itself became a problem, the solution for which, inevitably, was the faking of the Peking report. The party newspaper of the young Kuomintang, *Min-kuo jih-pao,* could not afford a reliable Peking correspondent and managed to receive telegraphic reports only on an intermittent basis. Eager to stay within the circle of major newspapers with Peking reports, *Min-kuo jih-pao* kept on its staff in Shanghai a pundit who, it was said, could guess the Peking news about as accurately as others could report it.[150]

For Shanghai newspapers, the glamor surrounding the institution of telegraphic reports from the capital dwarfed all other advances in news gathering during the early 1910s. The reporting from other Chinese cities became somewhat more frequent as more and more branch offices were opened, but the reports themselves remained irregular and anecdotal.[151]

Prior to the 1910s, the local news in Shanghai newspapers was also reported in a quite superficial manner. With infrequent exceptions, it consisted entirely of reports on law cases being tried in the International and French settlements. Reporting being a simple matter, it was paid at the humble rate of only ten yuan per month. Yet reporters could survive on this salary by maintaining themselves on the payrolls of several newspapers simultaneously and by collecting privately from parties involved in law cases who preferred that their involvement go unreported. For the convenience of everyone, the lawsuit reporters met daily in a teahouse across the street from the courthouse of the International Settlement on North Chekiang Road. This group withered away during the 1910s, when local news coverage turned (though by no means completely) in the direction of political and social issues, while the role of the reporter became increasingly competitive and professional.[152]

Though local, regional, and national (i.e., Peking) news grew to be standard categories of reportage during the first two decades of the twentieth century, international news was seldom considered a category worthy of regular treatment. Foreign reporting consisted of travelogue or light-interest stories which occasionally were contributed on a voluntary, nonpaid basis by overseas Chinese students or consulate personnel who had friendly ties with a given newspaper.[153]

150. CYLHIL, pp. 347–348 and 415ff.
151. CYLHIL, p. 320 and *passim.*
152. CYLHIL, p. 320.
153. CYLHIL, p. 348.

A major reason for the slow development of foreign reporting appears to have been that demand for this type of news had from the outset been remarkably low. Aside from the curiosity of the travelogue, public interest in foreign affairs seems to have been limited to those events which impinged directly upon the fate of China, such as the Boxer suppression, the American exclusion act, or the Twenty-one Demands. (In the case of the Boxer incident, for example, Shanghai newspapers reported events quite casually until the rumor spread that the eight foreign armies had decided to come next to Shanghai, whereupon reporting suddenly became much more earnest.)[154] When serious coverage of foreign events did seem necessary, the usual practice was to translate stories published in foreign-language newspapers, and major Chinese newspapers hired translators-in-residence for this purpose.[155]

The alternative to this hand-me-down source of news was the foreign wire services. *Reuters* was the first wire service in Shanghai, having arrived in 1872 and remaining without competition for many years.[156] The *Reuters* service was designed for foreign newspapers, however, and to the Chinese press seemed a bit haughty. For many years *Reuters* would not sell to Chinese newspapers; when they did, their fees were exorbitant by the standards of the Chinese press and had to be paid in English pounds. Then, of course, the reports still had to be translated.[157] For these reasons and because of the low demand for foreign news, *Reuters* was seldom used by the Chinese-language newspapers. French, American, German, and Russian wire services arrived during the first two decades of the twentieth century, but likewise were infrequently used. The first international wire service to achieve significant popularity with the Chinese press was the Japanese *Tōhō tsūshin sha,* whose reports in Japanese were less expensive and easier for Shanghai newsmen to read.[158]

The revolution in news reporting during the 1910s made a few newspapers stronger than ever, while others declined or perished. Estimates of the total number of newspapers in China show an abrupt decline for the years immediately following 1911, flanked by periods of steady increase before and after.[159] Chang Ching-lu and Roswell Britton have pointed to the heavy hand of Yuan Shih-k'ai and others in closing down some newspapers during these years and instilling a

154. Cf. CYLHIL, pp. 183–184.
155. CYLHIL, pp. 230, 319 and 429.
156. Graham Storey, *Reuters: The Story of a Century of News Gathering,* p. 69.
157. CYLHIL, pp. 319, 328, 428–429.
158. CYLHIL, p. 429.
159. Chang Ching-lu, *Chin-tai,* 2:304.

paralyzing fear in others.[160] In Shanghai, with its qualified protection from censorship, a further explanation would appear to be that after 1912 many of the "revolutionary" papers had lost their leading issue. The 1911 revolution in many ways took China by surprise, as Mary Wright has pointed out,[161] and in the newspaper world in Shanghai it appears that few people in 1912 were prepared to argue Republican politics with the same deep commitment which had sustained their pre-revolutionary anti-Manchu campaigns. They expected that, since the revolution had arrived, their political ideas could leave the pages of the newspapers and be quite easily put into practice. It was not until the mid-1910s, when disillusionment with the Yuan regime became widespread, that this expectation was seen to be naive. Only two of Shanghai's outspoken political newspapers of the late Ch'ing period, *Shih-shih hsin pao* and *Shen-chou jih-pao,* continued publishing through the early 1910s.[162] And even these gradually changed in nature, *Shih-shih hsin pao* turning more intellectual, while *Shen-chou jih-pao*'s biting political commentary degenerated towards scurrilous gossip about the private lives of prominent citizens.[163]

Shen pao and *Hsin-wen pao* both grew remarkably in circulation during the 1910s. *Shen pao*'s fortunes skyrocketed in 1912 when the political and educational elite of the Kiangsu-Chekiang area, led by Chang Chien and Chao Feng-ch'ang, moved to create in Shanghai the substantial organs of public communication which they felt a "republic" must possess. In book publishing, they oversaw the founding on January 1, 1912, of the Chung-hua shu-chü. Similarly in journalism, they concerted their efforts to make *Shen pao* the newspaper of the new republic.[164]

Had matters been only slightly different, their choice might have been to support *Shih pao,* which in 1911 seemed the most forward-looking newspaper in Shanghai. Because of the past association of *Shih pao* manager Ti Ch'u-ch'ing with the K'ang-Liang reformists, however, that newspaper had come to be thought of as "monarchist" among a considerable portion of the reading public and no protestation to the contrary could erase the label after 1911. The strategy of the Kiangsu-Chekiang leaders therefore became one of supporting *Shen pao* while attempting to transfer to it the important innovations of

160. Britton, p. 124; Chang Ching-lu, *Chin-tai,* 2:304.
161. Mary C. Wright, Introduction to *China in Revolution: The First Phase, 1900–1913,* esp. pp. 53–54.
162. Britton, p. 124; CYLHIL, p. 394.
163. Notable among these was the *Ching pao* attached to *Shen-chou jih pao.* See CYLHIL, pp. 444–451, and YYHTP, pp. 409–421.
164. CYLHIL, pp. 413–414.

Shih pao and other newspapers. As a first step, personnel were hired away from *Shih pao* to staff the renovated *Shen pao*. These included several of the leading journalists and educators associated with *Shih pao*'s intellectual club, the "Resting Place." Notable among them was the energetic young educator and minor salt official Shih Liang-ts'ai, who became chief editor of *Shen pao* and handled that position with extraordinary skill until his assassination by government agents in 1934.[165] Of nearly equal importance to *Shen pao,* and a much sharper blow to the fortunes of *Shih pao,* was the hiring away of Ch'en Ching-han, assistant editor at *Shih pao* for six years and responsible for many of that newspaper's stimulating innovations, including his own mystery stories.[166] A third key person taken from *Shih pao* was Huang Yuan-yung, the famous Peking correspondent, who now assumed the same position for *Shen pao.*

Shen pao's new regime gained it both new readers and a more elevated social standing than it had enjoyed before.[167] Increased respectability brought more advertisements from publishers and bookstores, an area which only a few years previously had been the special province of *Shih pao.*[168] As a kind of badge of its progressive new status, *Shen pao* purchased in 1918 China's first revolving-cylinder printing machine for newspapers and placed it in its front window for passersby to observe.[169]

Until 1911, the three-way rivalry of *Shen pao, Hsin-wen pao,* and *Shih pao* had effectively pressured each to keep up with the progress of the other two. When one opened a new branch office or stationed a reporter in another city, the others always tried to do likewise; as soon as the general manager of *Shen pao* began to ride to work in an automobile, his counterparts at *Hsin-wen pao* and *Shih pao* did so as well.[170] But the rise of *Shen pao* under its new patronage after 1911 led to several readjustments in the mutual status of the leading three newspapers. First, a splinter effort developed when Hsi Yü-fu, who had been editor at *Shen pao* before Shih Liang-ts'ai and the other new people displaced him, left in a pique to found *Hsin shen pao (New shen pao).*[171] The maneuver did not succeed in carrying the prestige of the old *Shen pao* with it, however. While *Shen pao* was becoming preemi-

165. CYLHIL, p. 330; Boorman et al., 3:128.

166. CYLHIL, p. 426; Ho Ta (pseud. Ning Yuan), *Hsiao-shuo hsin hua,* pp. 100–101.

167. Tseng Hsu-pai, pp. 12 and 269.

168. CYLHIL, p. 426.

169. CYLHIL, p. 439; Tseng Hsu-pai, p. 269.

170. CYLHIL, p. 427.

171. Chang Ching-lu, *Chin-tai,* 2:431; Tseng Hsu-pai, p. 269. Pao T'ien-hsiao uses Hsi's *hao,* which is *tzu-p'ei* (CYLHIL, p. 427).

nent politically and intellectually, *Hsin shen pao* was left to compete in the standard commercial way with *Hsin-wen pao*. This switch in its competition greatly aided the fortunes of *Hsin-wen pao*. While commerce and industry, and with them advertising revenues, grew rapidly in Shanghai during the 1910s, the redirection of *Shen pao*'s major interests and the relatively much weaker competition of *Hsin shen pao* allowed *Hsin-wen pao* to achieve a remarkable expansion along its traditional lines. By the 1930s it probably exceeded *Shen pao* in total circulation, advertising, and size of reporting network.[172]

While both *Shen pao* and *Hsin-wen pao* benefited from the postrevolutionary situation, *Shih pao* suffered seriously. *Shen pao*'s raid upon the human resources of *Shih pao* hurt the latter even more than it helped the former. *Shih pao*'s intellectual leadership was all but destroyed when the "Resting Place" disbanded, its journalists and educators going to work in politics or at *Shen pao*.[173] In losing Ch'en Ching-han, *Shih pao* lost not only a skilled editor, commentator, and novelist but also its major symbol of revolutionary respectability. Ch'en had always been the most radical among *Shih pao*'s otherwise "reformist" editors—the only one, for example, to dress in the Western style and cut off his queue.[174] In 1912, with Ch'en gone and the failure of monarchical reform a plain fact, *Shih pao* had to face the reading public with a tainted image, in much the same way that *Shen pao* and *Hsin-wen pao* a decade earlier had suffered from their "foreign flavor." During the early 1910s *Shih pao* suffered declines in both circulation and advertising;[175] in literature and education, formerly its strongholds, it lost ground to *Shen pao* and to *Shih-shih hsin pao*.[176] In 1915–1916 it regained a measure of its former creative energy with the arrival of Pi I-hung, a skilled novelist and news editor, and Ko Kung-chen, a hard-working and vastly ambitious young journalist who came to *Shih pao* as a proofreader and rose to become chief editor. Ko also lectured on journalism at several Shanghai colleges and in 1927 published his detailed and well-respected *History of the Press in China (Chung-kuo pao-hsueh shih)*.[177] During the May Fourth Movement, Ko created *Shih pao*'s popular *Illustrated Weekly (T'u-hua chou-k'an)*, China's first pictorial to achieve the high-quality color reproductions made possible by modern copper plates.[178] *Shih pao* under Ko's de-

172. Tseng Hsu-pai, p. 355; Lin Yutang, p. 145.
173. CYLHIL, pp. 408 and 426.
174. CYLHIL, p. 408.
175. Tseng Hsu-pai, p. 336; CYLHIL, pp. 408ff.
176. Tseng Hsu-pai, p. 355.
177. CYLHIL, pp. 418–419; Boorman et al., 2:238–239.
178. Tseng Hsu-pai, p. 336; CYLHIL, p. 420.

CHART C: **The Circulation of** *Shen pao*

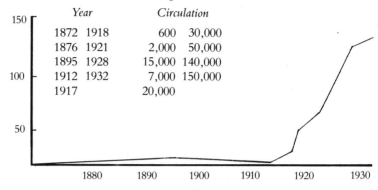

Year		Circulation	
1872	1918	600	30,000
1876	1921	2,000	50,000
1895	1928	15,000	140,000
1912	1932	7,000	150,000
1917		20,000	

SOURCES: Yüan Ch'ang-ch'ao, p. 78; R. S. Britton, p. 68; Boorman et al., 3:127; Tseng Hsu-pai, p. 355; Lin Yü-t'ang, p. 145.

termined leadership began to regain some of its former standing among educational and professional circles, and might have continued on that course had the energies of founder and manager Ti Ch'u ch'ing remained sufficient to the effort. In times when a younger generation had seized leadership of the revolution, Ti Ch'u-ch'ing, aged 51 in 1924, developed a sudden passion for Buddhism, decided to retire, and sold *Shih pao* to an American-returned student named Huang Po-hui for forty thousand yuan. Huang, with an eye to profit, turned the newspaper toward social scandal and a political association with the Research Clique.[179] In 1929 the newspaper was reorganized with the help of an editor from the *Shen pao,* divested itself of partisan politics, and pursued a more purely commercial route. In the next few years it reclaimed some of its original status alongside *Shen pao* and *Hsin-wen pao* as a leading Shanghai newspaper.[180]

While the fortunes of *Shih pao* rose and fell, the other two of the leading triumvirate—and Shanghai newspaper circulation in general—grew steadily from the 1910s through the 1930s. *Shen pao*'s circulation appears to have increased sevenfold from 1912–1921 alone, reaching a level of 50,000 at the end of that period.[181] (See Chart C.) Though fewer estimates are available for *Hsin-wen pao,* it has com-

179. Tseng Hsu-pai, pp. 336– 337. The "Research Clique", short for the Association for Constitutional Research, was a political group organized in 1916 after Yuan Shih-k'ai's abortive attempt to restore a monarchy. Originally devoted to constitutional government as a means to strengthen and unify China, it became involved in factionalism and warlord politics. See Andrew J. Nathan, *Peking Politics*.

180. Tseng Hsu-pai, pp. 325 and 355.

181. Boorman et al., 3:127.

monly been estimated that, from the 1910s on, *Hsin-wen pao*'s circulation exceeded *Shen pao*'s in varying amounts. In the early 1930s, the *Shen pao Yearbook* put the daily circulation of both at 150,000—a figure which, though perhaps inflated, has been widely accepted.[182] At the same time the circulation of *Shih pao* was around 35,000.[183]

With the dramatic increase in circulation of these Shanghai newspapers, their special fiction columns began to overshadow the magazine press as leading organs of popular fiction. Writers would give their best works to *Shen pao* and *Hsin-wen pao,* knowing stories published there had the best chance of becoming hits. By the early 1930s, the publication in *Hsin-wen pao* of such supremely successful popular stories as Chang Hen-shui's *Fate in Tears and Laughter* and Ku Ming-tao's *Female Knight of the Wild Rivers* had established the primacy of newspapers in popular fiction.

Shih pao had instituted newspaper fiction columns in the late Ch'ing decade with its "Surplus Spirit" and had followed that in the 1910s with "Comical Chatter" (Hua-chi yü t'an) and "The Little Times" (Hsiao shih-pao). Pao T'ien-hsiao edited all three columns, with the help of Ch'en Ching-han on the first and of Pi I-hung on the other two. In the late 1910s, when Pao T'ien-hsiao devoted himself entirely to magazine editing, *Shih pao* attempted to bolster its fiction columns by hiring a succession of new editors—Liu Hsiang-t'ing, Li Han-ch'iu, K'uang K'uei-sheng, Chang Pi-wu and Wen Kung-ta. None was successful, however, at preventing the columns from continuing to decline in comparison to the fiction columns of *Shen pao* and *Hsin-wen pao.*

"Unfettered Talk" (Tzu-yu t'an) in *Shen pao* was begun in August, 1911 and edited, successively, by Wang Tun-ken (during 1911-14), who later founded *Saturday;* Wu Chueh-mi (1914-1916), who, on the theory that the public needed stimulation of its martial spirit, particularly sought the poetry of Ho Hai-ming and other military officer-litterateurs; Yao Yuan-ch'u (1916), who relied heavily upon his Southern Society friends for manuscripts; Ch'en Tieh-hsien (1916-1917), one of the volume's steady contributors from the start who left only when his tooth powder business became an overriding concern (see chapter 5); Ch'en Ching-han (1917-1920), Pao T'ien-hsiao's partner at *Shih pao* before 1912; and, beginning in April, 1920, Chou Shou-chüan. Chou edited the column through the height of its influence in the 1920s, and handed it over in December, 1932, to Li Lieh-wen, a strong advocate of the "new-school" fiction of the May Fourth tradition. Li maintained

182. Tseng Hsu-pai, p. 355; Lin Yutang, p. 145.
183. Tseng Hsu-pai, p. 355.

the column until it closed in October, 1935. The transition to May Fourth writing had been made in response to rising public sentiment for patriotic fiction to resist Japan. The attraction of "old-school" fiction still remained, however, so when "Unfettered Talk" passed from his hands, Chou Shou-chüan immediately established another column called "Spring and Autumn" (Ch'un ch'iu) for old-school fiction. "Spring and Autumn" continued into and through the period of the Japanese occupation, when the occupiers installed their own editors in an attempt to use fiction to pacify and assuage public opinion.[184]

The "Forest of Happiness" (K'uai-huo lin) fiction column at *Hsin-wen pao* appeared intermittently in the 1910s as *Hsin-wen pao*'s attempt to match "Unfettered Talk." Edited throughout by Yen Tu-ho, "Forest of Happiness" flourished in the 1920s and probably surpassed "Unfettered Talk" in popularity by 1930. After the Japanese attack on Shanghai in January, 1932, Yen Tu-ho changed the title of the column to "New Spring Forest" (Hsin ch'un lin), explaining that the old title, since it contained the word "happiness," was no longer appropriate in such unhappy times.[185]

The serialized fiction in columns of this kind was always accompanied by several other entertainment items, the most important of which were the daily comments of the entertainment editors, especially Chou Shou-chüan, Yen Tu-ho, and Pao T'ien-hsiao, who cultivated a terse and witty style which attracted readers as much as fiction did. It was also the custom to publish in the entertainment column small items of gossip which were infectiously interesting, and usually true, but not quite fit for publication in the newspaper proper. These bits of gossip were the beginnings of the new press's gossip columns; the first example as a separate column was *Shih pao*'s "Special Little Wire" (Hsiao chuan tien), so called because it was delivered over the telephone by a gossip reporter.[186] As the gossip columns grew, they began to be published and sold separately, forming what was known in English as the "mosquito" press and in Chinese as *"hsiao pao."* Those who ran the mosquito press were among the first in Shanghai to discover that public opinion could be manipulated by newspapers. Individual mosquito papers zeroed in on each other in extended verbal feuds. Before long political figures became targets, as mosquito newspapers made themselves available to subornation for the purpose of factional struggle. But their principal fare continued to be gossip, anecdotes, and fiction, and most of the "old-school" authors of the 1910s became heavily involved as contributors. The early mosquito

184. YYHTP, pp. 399–401; interview with Kao Chen-pai, April 26, 1973.
185. YYHTP, pp. 401–404.
186. CYLHIL, p. 350.

newspapers did not carry advertisements, and even in the 1920s and 1930s had many fewer than the big newspapers. Aside from an occasional extortion, they supported themselves only through sales, and hence cost more per unit size than the major newspapers. They were usually single-sheet papers, and about half the dimensions of the big newspapers.[187]

Since data on the mosquito press is even more elusive than on the magazine press, no formal count of their numbers or circulation is feasible. They appear to have numbered roughly one-half to two-thirds as many as the popular fiction magazines. Shanghai was their center, though a few did appear in Tientsin, Peking, Canton and elsewhere. Like the fiction supplements in the major newspapers, the mosquito press was taken over by the Japanese during their occupation in an attempt to pacify the public. In occupied Peking they were known as the "square papers" *(fang-hsing k'an-wu)* because of their distinctive shape.[188]

By the 1930s, the term "mosquito press" had come to include a wide range of levels and varieties. From the gossip sheets, which might be called the mosquito press proper, they ranged upward in quality to include what were actually regular newspapers in tabloid form. Some of these existed as evening papers which would copy news from the regular morning papers and offer it at a reduced price. Others, in the tradition of the late Ch'ing political tabloids such as *Ch'ün-ch'iang pao,* offered serious and responsible commentary on current events.[189] Within the context of the whole periodical press, the mosquito papers grew to assume a role which was complementary to the major newspapers. If, for example, a complete reader in 1930 referred to *Shen pao* for commercial news, *Ta-kung pao* for political news, and *Chung-yang jih-pao* for the government's viewpoint, he would certainly refer to *Ching pao,* a leading mosquito paper, for morsels the others would not print. Hawkers on the streets of Shanghai knew this, and would alternate cries of "Buy the big *Shen pao!*" with "Buy the little *Ching pao!*"[190]

Ching pao, whose name might be translated as *Three-day Crystal,*[191] was the premier example of the mosquito press for two decades. It

187. CYLHIL, pp. 445–446; interview with Ch'eng She-wo, July 26, 1973; Ōtsuka Reizō, "Shanghai no shōhō ni kansuru ichi kōsatsu," *Mantetsu Shina gesshi,* 6.3 (June 1929): 63–73.

188. Fan Yen-ch'iao, in YYHTP, p. 273.

189. Interview with Ch'eng She-wo, July 26, 1973; Britton, p. 127.

190. CYLHIL, p. 451.

191. The Chinese character for "crystal" (also meaning "bright and clear") is formed of three ideographs for "sun," thus also suggesting three-day periodicity. (It is also possible that the name was inspired by the London boys' weekly called *Gem.*)

began in 1919 as a supplement to *Shen-chou jih-pao,* which had been an outspoken revolutionary paper when it was founded by Yü Yu-jen in 1907. But *Shen-chou jih-pao* was never a great success. Its premises burned down two months after it opened, and in the ensuing years editorship changed hands many times while circulation steadily dwindled. In the winter of 1917, when the newspaper was passed into the hands of Yü Ta-hsiung, its circulation had fallen below a thousand. It was then that Yü conceived the idea of *Crystal* to spur interest and circulation. He devoted full time to editing *Crystal,* which appeared every third day, and handed the rest of *Shen-chou jih-pao* to Wu Tuan-shu, who served as its eighth editor and entire staff. *Crystal* was a great success as a supplement, and *Shen-chou jih-pao* enjoyed fast improvement in circulation—but only every third day. Yü therefore decided to liberate *Crystal* from its mother organ and allowed it to be sold separately while continuing also as a supplement to *Shen-chou jih-pao.* Separate subscriptions cost two yuan a year or twenty cents a month. *Crystal*'s circulation quickly rose above ten thousand while *Shen-chou jih-pao* continued to lag far behind. In 1926, when *Shen-chou jih-pao* was transferred to Chiang Yü-ch'üan, its separation from *Crystal* was complete. A few years later *Crystal*'s fame and influence reached the point where Shih Liang-ts'ai, editor of *Shen pao,* made a bid to purchase it. Negotiations failed, however, when Shih offered a maximum of 10,000 yuan and Yü Ta-hsiung demanded a minimum of 40,000.[192]

Besides Yü Ta-hsiung, *Crystal* was edited by Chang Tan-fu, an eccentric poet from Yangchow and member of the Southern Society. Yuan Han-yün, the second son of Yuan Shih-k'ai, was also a steady contributor and came to be known, together with Chang, as "the two heroes" *(erh-chieh)* of *Crystal.* In addition to serialized fiction and irregular news, *Crystal* carried poetry and poetry games, a song and dance column, drama review, letters, a column called "clever talk," calligraphy, and advertisements. One section contained autobiographical sketches of well-known persons pieced together from their personal letters to friends.[193]

Yü Ta-hsiung stuck to three principles in the publication policy of *Crystal.* He would print: (1) what other newspapers did not dare print, for fear of reprisals, (2) what other newspapers found awkward to print, in consideration of someone's face, and (3) what other newspapers found unworthy to print, in spite of obvious interest, such as morsels of gossip essentially unrelated to major events. Yet, however scandalous the content, Yü took great care to be sure that it was true,

192. Tseng Hsu-pai, pp. 272–273; CYLHIL, pp. 429, 446, 447 and 451; YYHTP, pp. 409–410; Cheng I-mei, "Hui-i 'Ching pao'," *Ta-jen* no. 21 (January 1972), p. 88.
193. YYHTP, pp. 411 and 415; CYLHIL, p. 447.

as the continuing credence of his readership depended on this. His policies sometimes brought him to court or put him under threat from hired hooligans. On one occasion he was forced to apologize to the underworld leader Huang Chin-jung, whose pursuit of a certain dance-hall hostess he had exposed; but neither then nor at any other time was he known to have abridged his three criteria of publishability.[194]

Yü employed two methods of gathering his news and manuscripts. First, he cultivated a wide circle of friends among writers, reporters, doctors, lawyers (the latter two were especially important contacts), "foreign mall geniuses" *(yang-ch'ang ts'ai-tzu)*, bureaucrats, and wealthy retirees. He constantly made the rounds to ferret out stories, and in fact became known as "the foot editor" *(chiao pien-chi)*. But he lost friends along the way, since he would not let a person rest when he wanted a manuscript. Second, he made the office of *Crystal* into a kind of club for his circle of friends, somewhat in the fashion of *Shih pao*'s "Resting Place" before 1911. He picked up many leads by listening to the general chatter. Sometimes friends would come to him volunteering stories. *Crystal* paid nothing for manuscripts, so if someone volunteered, it was because he desired the satisfaction of seeing his story in print. The source of this satisfaction was obvious in cases when the story was partisan. But even when it was not, many writers, including fiction specialists, liked to publish in *Crystal* because they knew that there their creations would receive an immediate and relatively large readership. Furthermore, Yü followed a strict policy of not tampering with authors' manuscripts, as other editors habitually did, and writers could have their words exactly as they wished them.[195]

Of all the quarrels instigated by reporting in *Crystal*, perhaps the best known in Shanghai society was the case of the "Notes on the Sage's Palace" *(Sheng tien chi)*. Writing in 1949, Pao T'ien-hsiao recalls the several facets of the incident in a way which nicely reveals the place of the mosquito press in Shanghai:

> The "Notes on the Sage's Palace" had to do with a German doctor named Schmidt who came to Shanghai to practice medicine. He wasn't an ordinary doctor, but a practitioner of "the technique of return to the vigor of youth," as people in Shanghai used to say. When he arrived he undertook a great advertising campaign to tell how it was that he could restore one's sexual vigor: with one needle he could change the sexually exhausted into the likes of prancing dragons and flexing tigers, never again to decline. At the time, given what Shanghai society was, this kind of thing really could catch on. Schmidt published notices in

194. CYLHIL, pp. 447 and 449.
195. CYLHIL, p. 448.

all the major papers, and at the same time sought out famous people to try the method for no charge. He listed five names as having tried the shot, and one of them was K'ang Yu-wei. It then happened that two young doctors in the "German school" of returned students (medical practice in Shanghai at the time was divided between two groups, the "English-American school" and the "German-Japanese school"), who were named Huang Sheng-pai and P'ang Ching-chou, took to their pens. They produced "Notes on the Sage's Palace," and submitted it to *Crystal*.

And how did it come to be called "Notes on the Sage's Palace?" The "sage" part was said in reference to K'ang Yu-wei, who, ever since the appearance of his work "Examination of Confucius' Reforms" had occasionally been referred to as "K'ang the Sage." Then what about "palace"? Well, it turns out that in ancient style *tien* meaning "palace" could stand for *t'un* meaning "buttocks" . . . so what it all signified was a needle being inserted into the rear end of K'ang the Sage. The piece was extremely funny, and included its share of satire. K'ang, gentleman and great person that he was, felt it best simply to ignore the gibes of mosquito papers, and paid no attention. But who would have guessed that the great German Doctor Schmidt would be infuriated? He had come to Shanghai all set to unfold his mammoth design, and hardly could imagine that someone would throw cold water on it and make his luck turn sour. So he engaged one of Shanghai's big famous lawyers to bring suit against *Crystal,* charging its editors with libel, and demanding restitution of damages.

Could *Crystal* afford such damages? Its head was certainly in the lion's mouth, and all of Yü Ta-hsiung's friends advised him that, since Chinese always get the short end of the deal in lawsuits with foreigners in this treaty port of ours, he would do best to come to some understanding with that lawyer, to make an apology and get it over with. Schmidt was only doing this to display his bravado and to promote his quack medical practice. All that we needed was to say some nice things about him in our newspapers, give him a bit of free advertising, and that would be that. But Yü Ta-hsiung was the intransigent type. *Crystal* may be small, he said, but we've always claimed to fear no intimidation, and many of our readers like us for just this reason. Now we have a foreign quack doctor, who relies on the power of the foreign concession, trying to threaten my little paper, and I am determined to give him a fight. What's more, that article of ours was only a little joke on K'ang Yu-wei, and had nothing to do with any kind of libel against Schmidt. And K'ang, after all, did not take offense, so who is this Schmidt?

Thanks to Yü Ta-hsiung's obstinacy, the case was won. On the day of the adjudication, it was the turn of the English consular official to preside—whether or not the Chinese judge was in attendance I cannot now remember. The verdict: "Defendant Yü Ta-hsiung is ordered to pay Plaintiff Schmidt restitution in the amount of one yuan." Pay damages of one yuan?! Was this not a bit of satire from the bench? How could this represent "victory" for the plaintiff and "defeat" for the defendant? Besides, what Schmidt had demanded was restitution of damage to his reputation. And the value of his reputation had been assessed at one yuan? So after the decision Schmidt went storming out, roaring vilifications, and *Crystal* people found themselves in high spirits. It was said later that the granting of trivial damages had precedent in English law, a discovery owed to those who had researched the subject. Yet, formally speaking, it was still true that the white man had won the case. Before long, Schmidt quietly slipped out of Shanghai, and *Crystal,* because of this lawsuit, saw its circulation increase by a thousand copies.[196]

Crystal continued publishing according to form until the Japanese attack on Shanghai on January 28, 1932. During the seven weeks after that event, they set aside all fiction and other entertainment items to publish a half-page sheet of war news. Later in the year, the paper's old interest gradually reemerged, and beginning in October, 1932, it appeared daily. But many contributors had already left Shanghai, or left journalism, and *Crystal*'s contents fell far short of the standards of former times. Editor Yü Ta-hsiung, who began cooperating with the Japanese, was killed in an ambush, and editorship was passed to Ch'ien Chieh-ch'en, then to Wu Nung-hua. When the Japanese military took control of the International Settlement, *Crystal* was strictly censored and so lost, naturally, the essence of its appeal and gradually died out.[197]

Second to *Crystal,* probably the best-known mosquito paper was a rival of *Crystal*'s called *The Diamond (Chin kang tsuan),* a name evidently intended to suggest superiority to *Crystal*. Besides being more valuable than crystals, diamonds, it was claimed, would "cut anything." *The Diamond* was founded in October, 1923 by a group of ten writers of whom Yen Tu-ho and Shih Chi-ch'ün were the best known. All ten founders had been attacked or satirized in *Crystal*. Pursuing revenge, each donated ten yuan from his own pocket (little capital was needed to begin a mosquito newspaper) and *The Diamond* grew rapidly. No chief editor was officially appointed, though

196. CYLHIL, pp. 450–451.

197. YYHTP, pp. 411 and 420. *Crystal* had left a strong and generally favorable imprint in the memories of many contributors and readers. More than thirty years after its demise, when Pao T'ien-hsiao decided to publish his recollections of Shanghai in a Hong Kong newspaper, he chose the *Hong Kong Crystal (Hsiang-kang ching pao)* for this purpose, even though it was unrelated to the original *Three-day Crystal.*

Lu T'an-an (the detective story specialist) and Chu Ta-k'o contributed the bulk of the writing and editing. In at least one case, the lack of an official editor saved *The Diamond* from being pinned down in court. After several years of growth, however, it became obvious that a regular manager (still not called an "editor") was needed, and Shih Chi-ch'ün assumed that post. Cheng I-mei took it over in 1932, and the paper closed down on the eve of the Japanese war. In its prime, it carried fiction from such leading popular writers as Chang Hen-shui and Ku Ming-tao, and also featured a number of "crazy-quilt" novels with many well-known names participating.[198]

The mid-1930s saw a reform trend among mosquito newspapers, as many de-emphasized fiction and interest pieces in favor of the serious reporting of war news and other issues. *Li pao,* founded in March, 1935, by Ch'eng She-wo, was the best known of this new breed. It was similar to the mosquito press in matters of form (terse reporting, convenient size, reduced cost), but resembled the large newspapers in content.[199] In the mosquito press as in other Shanghai media, the January 28 Incident and the onset of the war mood gradually depressed the market for popular fiction.

198. YYHTP, pp. 430–433.
199. Tseng Hsu-pai, pp. 366–367; CYLHIL:HP, pp. 34ff.

CHAPTER 4

From Nation-Building to Time-Killing to Profit

THE EARLY STAGES IN MODERN ENTERTAINMENT FICTION

If the material base of China's modern popular fiction consisted in the rapid growth of journalism and modern printing, its human inspiration is best traced—ironically, it may seem—to the birth of nationalist feeling in the "reform" years after 1895. Following the successive shocks of the defeat by Japan, the crushing of the 1898 reforms, and the Boxer affair, a progressive elite in Shanghai looked outward with great urgency for any way to save China. They studied foreign things, published magazines, and organized new schools and discussion groups. They were among China's earliest modern radicals, willing to turn from compromise with Western methods towards wholesale adoption of them. Their numbers included those who were to become the first authors, and first readers, of Butterfly fiction.

To many in this group Japan seemed the best source for China's renovation, not only because Japan had demonstrated a mastery of Western military techniques after 1895, but also because Japan was closer to China geographically as well as culturally and linguistically. Chinese students in Japan, whose numbers increased rapidly after 1895 to reach 8,000 or more by 1905,[1] discovered voluminous materials about science and the West in Japanese. These they excitedly translated and sent back to China in "study journals" *(hsueh-pao),* often named after their home provinces. The *Szechwan Study Journal, Hunan Study Journal,* and so on bespoke a sense of provincial affiliation among the students who organized them. Yet that provincial sense, coming from students who were overseas, just as clearly implied a more basic sense

---

1. Sanetō Keishū, *Chūgokujin nihon ryūgaku shi,* pp. 55–58; also Philip C. Huang, *Liang Ch'i-ch'ao and Modern Chinese Liberalism,* pp. 37, 41, and 175.

of nationalism: the provinces were coordinate sections of a new larger unit, the nation of China.[2]

The "study journals" from Japan helped sustain the spread of reform ideology in Shanghai, the lower Yangtze region, and major provincial centers in China. K'ang Yu-wei's *Ch'iang hsueh pao* ("strength" study journal) and its adjunct study society, the Ch'iang hsueh hui, elicited echoes in the form of journals on Western sciences like the *T'ung hsueh pao* ("know-how" studies), the *Hsin hsueh pao* ("new" studies), the *Shih hsueh pao* (studies of "fact"), the various *pai-hua pao* (vernacular journals, see chapter 3), and many others.

At least as important as the journals and study societies was "new-style" education. In the last decade of the nineteenth century, and especially after the 1898 reforms, there developed a great urge in progressive circles to set up schools called "new schools" *(hsin hsueh t'ang)* or, more colloquially, "foreign-style schools" *(yang hsueh-t'ang)*. These were often organized on the model of the old "academies" *(shu-yuan)*.[3] Teachers were taken, where possible, from among those young masters of the "new learning," the returned scholars from Japan; and the students, both young and old, included almost anyone who felt the impulse to keep up with the times. The wish to stay abreast of developments from overseas was a radically new wish in nineteenth century Chinese society, yet very urgent among those who held it. Pao T'ien-hsiao, later to become a leading popular novelist, tells of there being no "new-style" school in Soochow when he and a handful of young friends first felt a great urge to study English. Initially they thought of going to Shanghai, but their elders were not yet ready to permit them this risk; so they hired instead one of Soochow's leading English tutors, a Chinese employee of the telegraph service who knew English well enough to "converse directly with Westerners."[4] The great aim of these inspired youth was to go to Shanghai and take the entrance examination for the Nanyang Academy (Nanyang kung-hsueh). If one tested well there were scholarships to be had, or, even better, a chance to study abroad.[5]

These youth are appropriately called "radical" because they accepted some of the subversive implications the "new learning" had for

2. On the relationship between the provinces and the nation in the late Ch'ing period, see John Fincher, "Political Provincialism and the National Revolution" in Wright, *China in Revolution,* pp. 185–226; and Joseph R. Levenson, "The Province, the Nation, and the World: The Problem of Chinese Identity" in Albert Feuerwerker, Rhoads Murphey and Mary C. Wright, eds., *Approaches to Modern Chinese History* (Berkeley and Los Angeles, 1967), pp. 268–288.

3. CYLHIL, p. 203.

4. CYLHIL, pp. 158–159.

5. CYLHIL, pp. 179–180.

established institutions. According to Pao, for example, some of the earliest reports on the new learning to reach Soochow claimed that all Western knowledge was based on arithmetic. This news surprised him greatly because in China, scholars did not calculate. Merchants calculated, using an abacus, and teahouse waiters calculated very efficiently in their heads. But a scholar did not use an abacus, and certainly would feel uncomfortable calculating with ink and brush. (Pencils had not yet arrived in Soochow.) The notion that learning should be based on arithmetic upset many people, and young Pao and the others who pursued Western studies did so with the feeling they were taking a major, and perhaps irrevocable, step.[6]

The publicly proclaimed ideology of the "new study" may be summarized in a few basic principles. Its clarion call was to save and strengthen China. Metaphors of "awakening" China from her "dreams" or her "intoxication" abounded in the journals. After awakening, China would require the purgation of various scourges new and old: opium, superstition, footbinding, Manchus. Awakened and cleansed, the nation was to be revitalized, and to achieve wealth and power on the basis of practical science from the West. It is significant that two of Shanghai's leading "study journals" after 1895—ones which were most widely imitated—were *Agricultural Studies (Nung-hsueh pao)* and *Industrial and Commercial Studies (Kung-shang hsueh pao)*.[7] Other journals ranged widely across the physical and social sciences, geography, Western history and foreign languages. Yen Fu's translations of Thomas Huxley and Herbert Spencer in the early 1900s fueled the feeling that China must catch up, compete, and survive. Though all of this Shanghai-based ferment remained limited to a tiny portion of the Chinese populace, its final goal, at least as stated, was very different. The "Western tides" might involve, directly or indirectly, every area and every social level of the new nation-to-be. The early *pai-hua* newspapers sought to convey "deep" meaning in "shallow" phrases, that is, to write serious messages in simple language for the broadest possible audience.[8] The well-being of the new China would have to depend upon the well-being of all its constituents.

While rebuilding China was the avowed purpose of the new learning, from the viewpoint of the individual reader one can analyze other of its uses. Studies of literacy during the Industrial Revolution in England have revealed that one of the functions of early popular periodical literature was that of orientation to a changing environment.[9]

6. CYLHIL, p. 156.
7. Chang Ching-lu, *Chin-tai,* 2:429; Britton, p. 95.
8. CYLHIL, p. 169.
9. See Leavis, *Fiction,* esp. pp. 176–177; Altick, *Common Reader,* esp. pp. 97ff; Lowenthal, *Literature, Popular Culture and Society,* esp. p. 97.

Common readers in London and Manchester found in popular science magazines their best route to interpreting the Industrial Revolution. In Meiji Japan, where similar changes arrived much more rapidly, urban youth were infatuated with the "self-help" ethic expressed in numerous translations of Samuel Smiles.[10] The same phenomenon is clearly present in the early reform journals in Shanghai, which presented readers with knowledge one needed in order to thrive in a rapidly "modernizing" environment: the principles of household electricity, how a modern bank works, streetcar routes, lessons in foreign languages, and so on.

The presumption of the social function we are here calling "orientation" is that information which readers absorbed could actually be used in their daily lives. For many readers, though, the reform journals presented material which reached far beyond any foreseeable practical use. In these cases the function served was simply to satisfy readers' curiosity about all the strange things Western contacts had brought. In explaining the appeal of the reform press, Liang Ch'i-ch'ao wrote in 1902 that:

> It is in the nature of human beings that they often cannot content themselves with the stimulations of their own environment, and the environment which can be reached and absorbed through the clumsy shell of one's body is terribly narrow and limited. Therefore one often wishes to have, in addition to what one directly reaches and experiences, something indirectly reached and experienced—what might be called a body outside the body, a world outside the world.[11]

The range of topics covered in this spirit of discovery was remarkable. Magazines would interlard their translations of Western literature with short reports on "New Affairs and New Things": reports on the habits of cannibals, an American underground political party, new asbestos suiting for fire-fighters, and veterinary methods for curing the tongue disease of a lion.[12] Topics were not exclusively foreign: many pieces introduced special characteristics of localities across China. Nor were they limited to reports of true circumstance. *Shen pao*'s *Tien-shih-chai hua pao* began as early as the late 1880s to report developments in Western aerodynamics, describing not only manned balloons but something called a "flying vessel" *(fei-t'ing)*, equipped with sails, oars, a rudder and two wings. An illustration accompanied the report.[13]

10. See Earl Kinmonth, "The Self-Made Man in Meiji Japanese Thought."
11. Liang Ch'i-ch'ao, in Chang Ching-lu, *Pu-pien*, p. 106.
12. *Hsiao-shuo shih pao*, no. 1 (September 1909).
13. CYLHIL, p. 113

1. Liang Ch'i-ch'ao's Advocacy of Modern Fiction

One of the many discoveries of the Shanghai reform culture was Western literature. In the 1880s *Shen pao* published some fragments of Western fiction in translation which were probably the first to appear in Shanghai. First to have a significant impact, though, were the magazines of Liang Ch'i-ch'ao. In 1896 his string-bound, ten-day periodical *Shih-wu pao* appeared, each issue of which included at least one trenchant essay by Liang himself on the necessity of political reform. But among its other items on current affairs, political problems, the lives of famous men, etc., was a section near the back called "Translations from English Newspapers." There Liang introduced Western detective stories in translation, including *The Adventures of Sherlock Holmes,* which became famous in the ensuing decades and served as a model for a great number of Chinese creations of the same type.

Other reform journals took up the translation of fiction. One of these, the Tientsin *Kuo-wen pao,* undertook in 1897 what Liang had not yet done, i.e., to justify the inclusion of fiction as part of the total reform effort. In a lengthy article entitled "An Exposition of the Reasons Why the Present Newspaper is Printing Fiction Supplements" (Pen-kuan fu-yin shuo-pu yuan-ch'i), it was argued that a strong connection exists between fiction, the public ethic, and national strength.[14] The piece did not attract a great deal of attention in reform circles, however. It was left to Liang Ch'i-ch'ao to pick up the challenge, restate the issues, and achieve a broader impact.

Liang's advocacy of fiction was effective not only because of the vigor of his style but also because of his sudden rise to fame in the reform movement. In 1895, at age 22, he was a member of K'ang Yu-wei's Ch'iang hsueh hui and had already memorialized the throne. His essays in *Shih-wu pao* were like required reading among reform-minded youth, who found he had a gift for expressing in clear and forceful terms exactly what they felt in their own minds.[15] They listened when Liang passionately declared, in "Preface to the Publication of Political Fiction in Translation" (I-yin cheng-chih hsiao-shuo hsu, 1898), that fiction was vital in the success of a modern state—a conclusion which is perhaps less puzzling when one considers how Liang reached it. We know that Liang was impressed with the energy and seeming unity of the modern nation states of the West and their quick

14. *Kuo-wen pao,* November 15, 1897; reprinted in Chang Ching-lu, *Pu-pien,* pp. 91–104. The article was unsigned, but Ch'ien Hsing-ts'un attributes authorship to Yen Fu and Hsia Sui-ch'ing. (See A Ying, *Wan-Ch'ing hsiao-shuo shih* [Hong Kong, 1973], p. 2.)

15. CYLHIL, p. 150; Joseph R. Levenson, *Liang Ch'i-ch'ao and the Mind of Modern China,* pp. 18–22.

pupil, Japan. How was such strength and unity possible? In Japan, he knew, a kind of *seiji shōsetsu*, or "political novel," had grown increasingly popular through the 1880s and 1890s. These political novels strengthened a nation in two ways. First, they caused modern political ideas to spread among all the people, binding them together for unified action. Second, their instruction came from political leaders, the heads of the bodies politic. This could easily be shown for both Europe and Japan.[16]

It is clear that Liang must have reasoned from the strength of the West to the efficacy of novels and not the other way around. The foreign fiction with which he began could not, by itself, have suggested massive national rejuvenation. Although his choice of *Sherlock Holmes* for the *Shih-wu pao* may have predated his theory of the political role of fiction, it is worth noting that, when he did construct the theory, Sherlock did not appear to him as a counter-example. If it worked for England it can work for us. The point is even clearer in his translation around 1900 of a Japanese novel by Shiba Shirō called *The Strange Encounters of Beauties (Kajin no kigu)*, which he serialized in his own *Ch'ing-i pao*. (The latter magazine, and *Hsin-min ts'ung pao*, were published by Liang in Yokohama, where he fled after the failure of the 1898 summer of reforms.) *Kajin no kigu* tells about a sort of wandering Bohemian who, while gazing at the Liberty Bell in Philadelphia, meets two beauties who have strong credentials in nationalist spirit. One is the daughter of a Spanish constitutionalist, the other of an Irish patriot who died in jail. This romantic threesome then travels together all over the world meeting stalwarts of many national movements including a Chinese butler who had been exiled for opposing the Manchus. *Kajin no kigu*'s themes—of romanticized nationalism, of Bohemian lifestyle, and of a wide-eyed exploration of the great outside world—were all ones which were to become popular in Shanghai over the next twenty years (1900–1920), just as they had been popular in Japan over the past twenty. But Liang's assumption that such superficial treatment of political ideas could set a whole nation in motion can only have rested on a theory of extreme efficacy of any message in fictional form. In 1902, with the publication of his journal *New Fiction (Hsin hsiao-shuo)*, Liang expounded just such a theory. His lead article in *New Fiction*'s first issue was called "On the Relation between Fiction and Popular Sovereignty" (Lun hsiao-shuo yü ch'ün-chih chih kuan-hsi).[17]

16. Chang Ching-lu, *Pu-pien*, pp. 104–105; Liang Ch'i-ch'ao, *Yin-ping shih ho chi: chuan chi* 2:41–42. For an illuminating discussion of Liang Ch'i-ch'ao's concept of the political novel, see C. T. Hsia, "Yen Fu and Liang Ch'i-ch'ao as Advocates of New Fiction," *Journal of Oriental Studies*, 14.2 (July 1976): 133–149.

17. *Hsin hsiao-shuo*, no. 1; reprinted in Chang Ching-lu, *Pu-pien*, pp. 106–110.

The appeal of fiction, according to Liang, lies in its extension of the reader's experience. Vicarious experience of a wider world is, in the first place, enjoyable for its own sake. Beyond that, one may discover more about one's own life by using fiction as a foil: as one reads fiction and appreciates in it emotions such as anger, delight, or jealousy, one can better understand these feelings as they occur in oneself. In this process of resonance between fictional feelings and real feelings, a story attains access to a person's inner self; and with this access, it can magnify one's normal emotions. Those who read *Dream of the Red Chamber* are certain to feel the emotions of pining attachment *(lien)* and woe *(pei)* more strongly than otherwise, as *Water Margin* readers will feel lightheartedness *(k'uai)* or rage *(nu)*.

Beyond simply magnifying feelings, fiction can change ideas and attitudes, or even create them from nothing. Their cumulative influence can reshape one's world-view. Liang asks:

> Where does the Chinese idea of brilliant officials and prime ministers come from? . . . Where does the Chinese idea of geniuses and beauties come from? . . . Where does the Chinese idea of the itinerant bandit come from? . . . Where does the Chinese idea of phantom wizards and fox fairies come from?

In each case, Liang answers, "from fiction." Then, in the final step of his analysis, Liang holds that ideas and attitudes derived from fiction affect a person's behavior in real life.[18] In the Chinese case, this effect on behavior has in the past been almost entirely bad: it accounts for the presence in society of geomancy, divination, and "all kinds" of superstition; for the "worshipping" of the examination system and the willingness to bribe for office; for the tendency of young people to be frail and temperamental like Pao Yü and Lin Tai-yü in *Dream of the Red Chamber;* for the existence of rough behavior and secret societies after the fashion of the *Water Margin* heroes.

And what kind of person is susceptible to the influence of these traditional stories? Everyone, according to Liang, from "great men and teachers" at the top to "butchers, cooks, vendors and soldiers" at the bottom. "If we wish today to improve order among the masses," Liang concludes, "we must begin with a revolution in the realm of fiction." Upon the base of "new fiction" all else might be accomplished: new citizenship, new morality, new religion, new govern-

18. Although the connection between attitudes absorbed from fiction and a reader's behavior has been widely assumed, especially in Chinese tradition, the assumption is not beyond question. See Thomas Wright, "On a Possible Popular Culture," *Contemporary Review,* 40 (July 1881):35; and Herbert J. Gans, *Popular Culture and High Culture,* ch. 1.

ment, new customs, new art and new personal character. So moving was Liang's whole argument that a host of theoretical pieces by others followed after 1902, all making essentially the same points.

In fact theoretical statements outnumbered actual literary works for a time. But Liang, hoping that "political novels" like those in Japan would appear all over China, himself began this effort with a few creative works, the best-known of which was a four-chapter "novel of ideals," an apology for constitutional monarchism called *An Account of the Future of the New China (Hsin Chung-kuo wei-lai chi)*. This work, filled with records of laws, documents, and political disquisitions, was scarcely readable as fiction—a fact which Liang himself recognized.[19] His readers at the time were left to assume that his fictional ideal might be more closely approached by the other novels he chose for publication in *New Fiction*. Most prominent among these, serialized from 1902, was Wu Wo-yao's *Strange Phenomena Viewed Over Twenty Years (Erh-shih nien mu-tu chih kuai hsien-chuang)*. In this loosely-structured expose in the tradition of *The Scholars (Ju-lin wai-shih)*, Wu satirizes with delight almost all kinds of powerholders: officialdom, the business world, literary and scholarly circles, the clergy, and the military. Except by negative example, he has very little comment on how to build a new nation. In considerable degree his work is entertainment fiction—a direction which he developed more thoroughly in later stories like *Sea of Resentment (Hen hai)*, a prototype for the popular love stories of the 1910s, and *Annals of Sorrow (T'ung shih)*, a patriotic account of the fall of the Sung to the Mongols. Other items in *New Fiction* included translations of Western historical novels and science fiction, and Chinese short stories which, while stressing reformist themes, also drew upon traditional storytelling about the supernatural. In addition there was a sprinkling of curious anecdotes and even jokes.

Looking at this odd melange from the perspective of seventy-five years, it is perhaps difficult to see *New Fiction* and the writing it inspired as a bold and serious departure. Yet at the time, the distinction between "new" and "old" fiction was, for those who attended to it, as sharp and exciting as ever it was during the May Fourth Movement. The distinction lay not only in matters of form and content, however large or small those differences may have been; it lay also in the sudden respectability of the "new" fiction. At least among the reform generation, the "new" fiction was completely different from the "idle books" of the past—those "old" novels which were aimed at entertainment and were forbidden to children. Liang Ch'i-ch'ao had proclaimed the new fiction a means for serving the highest of purposes, and had buttressed this proclamation with his own prestige by writing fiction himself. Ironically, the mantle of respectability Liang created

19. Ch'ien Hsing-ts'un, *Wan-Ch'ing hsiao-shuo shih* (Hong Kong), p. 76.

was sturdy enough to protect for many years even those types of fiction which he most strenuously opposed. On June 15, 1915 (to take but one example) a leading love story magazine which paid only the most superficial lip service to Liang's social ideals announced in a "Note to Advertisers" that "the beneficial effects of fiction on society are by now publicly recognized in the world."[20] Liang was painfully aware of such misuses of his ideas. It was also in 1915 that he issued "An Appeal to Novelists,"[21] denouncing recent corruptions of fiction's role and acknowledging, it seemed, some guilt feelings.

2. Progenitors: Late Ch'ing Fiction

The young city of Shanghai was fertile ground for the growth of the "new fiction" of Liang's, and indeed, of many other varieties. Besides leading China in modern printing, Shanghai had accumulated a reservoir of literate talent which, in several senses, lay on the fringes of Chinese society, ready for a new calling. Some of the first of these were refugees of the T'aip'ing wars from the lower Yangtze region. The abandonment of the Grand Canal in subsequent years obliged travelling officials to pass through Shanghai on their way to and from Peking, thereby making Shanghai a crossroads for domestic travel as well as for contact with the West. Finally, an elite corps of scholars and reformers had descended upon Shanghai following the debacle of the 1898 reforms and the Western occupation of Peking in 1900. Soon more than a crossroads, the city became a base to which Chang Ping-lin, Wu Chih-hui and other leaders attracted young advocates of new learning and political change.[22]

Yet, in weighing Shanghai's importance in the context of the larger Chinese society, it is important to recall that, as seen from inland towns and cities, the foreign concessions were themselves a half-step into the curious outside world, almost as extraterrestrial as extraterritorial. Though some young men moved from Soochow to Shanghai to become students of the new learning, most visitors from Soochow to Shanghai came only temporarily and as spectators. Pao T'ien-hsiao records that two of the main attractions for such visitors were to eat in a Western restaurant and to ride a horse carriage. (On his first visit as a child, Pao was denied the restaurant visit by his grandmother, who was sure he would cut his mouth eating with a knife and fork.)[23] Shanghai's rickshas, whose popular name "Japanese carts" *(tung-yang ch'e),* was a constant reminder of their foreign origin, were another

20. *Li-pai-liu,* June 15, 1915.
21. "Kao hsiao-shuo-chia," *Yin-ping-shih ho chi:wen chi,* 12:67–68.
22. CYLHIL, pp. 224 and 226; Pott, *Short History,* pp. 37, 51, 67 and 79; Cohen, *Between Tradition and Modernity,* p. 34.
23. CYLHIL, p. 31.

remarkable spectacle. Their pullers wore distinctive tall hats which looked like inverted trumpets and blue uniforms with numbers on the back. The large iron wheels (rubber wheels came with the twentieth century) impressed one for their appearance as well as for the great convenience they afforded in comparison with the sedan chairs of the hinterland.[24] Western cultural institutions in general were labeled with the characters *wen-ming,* the modern compound invented in Japan to translate "civilization." By investigating the by-ways of Shanghai one could savor impressions of *wen-ming* clothing fashions, a *wen-ming* marriage, or *wen-ming* theatre. The spirit was voyeuristic rather than practical; to the bulk of those who had any experience with it, Shanghai and its reformist ferment appeared as little more than an interesting experiment.

It may be a cliché to remark that "disaffected" or "marginal" intellectuals in Chinese history have often been the source of unorthodox or antiestablishment activity such as leadership of rebellion, calls for reform, or (not too far down the same spectrum) the writing of fiction. But true to the cliché in most respects, the reform culture in Shanghai was as ready to include fiction in its program as it was to support political change itself. In the decade following the appearance of Liang's *New Fiction* in 1902, at least a dozen important fiction magazines answered the call in Shanghai. Three of these were run by men who came to be recognized, along with Liu O, author of *The Travels of Lao Ts'an (Lao-ts'an yu chi),* as leading writers of the decade. They were Li Po-yuan's *Illustrated Stories (Hsiu-hsiang hsiao-shuo,* 1903); Wu Wo-yao's *Monthly Fiction (Yueh-yueh hsiao-shuo,* 1906); and Tseng P'u's *Forest of Fiction (Hsiao-shuo lin,* 1907).[25] Though assuredly part of the overall "reform" culture in Shanghai, most of the authors and editors of these magazines were less steely-minded than Liang Ch'i-ch'ao in pursuit of political and social reform. Some, availing themselves of the comforts of teahouses, female entertainment, and opium, consciously assumed the image which May Fourth later deplored, that of "literary wizard of the foreign mall" (yang-ch'ang ts'ai-tzu, see chapter 5). Such *ts'ai-tzu* became the dominant type at Tseng P'u's *Forest of Fiction* and at the *Fiction Times (Hsiao-shuo shih pao,* 1909), published by *Shih pao,* and the *Short Story Monthly (Hsiao-shuo yueh-pao,* 1910), published by the Commercial Press. These three magazines should, in fact, be viewed as vehicles of a gradual transition from late Ch'ing fiction to the Butterfly fiction of the 1910s.[26]

24. CYLHIL, p. 30.
25. CYLHIL, p. 357; Ch'ien Hsing-ts'un, *Wan Ch'ing hsiao-shuo shih* (Hong Kong), p. 2.
26. YYHTP, pp. 280 and 282.

Ch'ien Hsing-ts'un has estimated in his authoritative *History of Late Ch'ing Fiction* that at least fifteen hundred separate pieces of fiction appeared during the last Ch'ing decade.[27] Though we can hardly attempt even a summary analysis of this corpus, which in itself would require a lengthy book, it is essential that we consider briefly its origins and general types. For it is easily shown that these types included the direct ancestors of the popular fiction of the 1910s and 1920s.

A clear majority of late Ch'ing works, probably about two-thirds, were translations of Western stories, most of them English and French. Interest in translations grew rapidly during 1902–1905 in Shanghai, and a number of "translation centers" *(i-shu ch'u)* sprang up to meet the demand.[28] The emphasis on translation must be seen as part of the outward-looking orientation of the reform culture generally, as part of its insatiable interest in new things from the West. The plots and themes of European novels were viewed as an exciting storehouse of new and different material. Fidelity to originals was not nearly as important as the stimulation they could provide, and Chinese author-translators freely embroidered stories with their own details, dialogue, and moral observations. It was, therefore, immaterial whether Western writers were, within Western tradition, regarded as good or bad, popular or refined; stock for story-making was drawn with equal ease from Shakespeare, Dickens, A. Conan Doyle and H. Rider Haggard.[29]

Late Ch'ing writers developed two distinct methods of translation-interpretation. The first, which is usually associated with (but by no means limited to) Lin Shu, was the tandem arrangement whereby one person who could read a Western language would report a story to another, who would render it into appealing Chinese. The original example of such cooperation was set by Lin Shu (who did the Chinese) and his friend Wang Tzu-jen, who knew French, in their 1895 rendi-

27. Ch'ien Hsing-ts'un, *Wan-Ch'ing hsiao-shuo shih,* p. 1; a discrepancy exists between two editions of Ch'ien's book regarding the number given as his total estimate of the number of late Ch'ing novels. The Jen-jen wen-k'u edition (Taipei, 1968) gives 1,500 as the number, while the Hong Kong edition (1973) gives 1,000. In view of the internal arithmetic of the paragraph in question, the Taipei version makes better sense. Ch'ien states that "almost 400" titles of translation novels and "about 120" original novels appear in the *Han-fen-lou hsin-shu fen-lei mu-lu.* He then states that his own estimate is "about three times" what appears in this index.

28. CYLHIL, pp. 218–224, 241, 242–250, and 312.

29. Lee, *Romantic Generation,* ch. 3; CYLHIL, pp. 171–172, 343. In the early years of the decade Yen Fu had established the three criteria —*hsin* (fidelity), *ta* (lucidity), and *ya* (elegance)— for translations from the West. (See "*I-li yen*" in Yen Fu, trans., *T'ien-yen lun.*) In fiction translations, lucidity and elegance meant a good deal to Lin Shu and others, but the fidelity criterion was not an object.

tion of Dumas fils' *La Dame aux Camélias (Ch'a-hua nü).*[30] So well-known was this work, and so moving and elegant Lin's classical Chinese in his 172 translations, that a stylistic standard was set from which variations were extremely rare right up to the May Fourth Movement: nearly all fiction translations, in other words, were in *wen-yen.*[31] Lin's style of *wen-yen* was based in the tradition of the T'ung-ch'eng school which had grown prominent in the late nineteenth century as the preferred style of Tseng Kuo-fan and others. Lin's use of marginal circles in his texts served as a kind of punctuation which made his stories understandable to a larger group than could otherwise have read them.[32] He set another example by writing prefaces to his translations which set forth salient moral points for the reader to bear in mind.

The second method of translation to emerge from the late Ch'ing years was associated with Pao T'ien-hsiao and Chou Shou-chüan, and it came to be more widely used than the tandem method.[33] It consisted of using Japanese translations of Western works for re-translation into Chinese, again classical. Users of this method frequently knew no Western language, and, just as often, knew little or no Japanese. As in the tandem method, all that was sought was a gleaning of the essential plot of a story as a basis for telling one's own. For such purposes, a perusal of the *kanji* (Chinese characters) used in Japanese writing could suffice. With the help of friends in Japan, Pao T'ien-hsiao made special efforts to procure works in Japanese which used *kanji* copiously and well, while using a minimum of *kana* and colloquial Japanese. The translations by Morita Shiken and Kuroiwa Ruikō were especially desirable by these criteria.[34] Pao T'ien-hsiao's story "Orchid in an Empty Vale" *(K'ung ku lan),* of which Pao was very proud, was based on a story from the pen of Kuroiwa Ruikō called "The Wild

30. Lee, *Romantic Generation,* pp. 42–44. There has been some uncertainty over whether Lin's translation of *La Dame* was done in 1895 or sometime during 1897–1899. Chang Ching-lu, *Chin-tai,* 2:425; CYLHIL, pp. 171–172; and Lee, pp. 42–44, all indicate the earlier date. Fan Yen-ch'iao, *Min-kuo chiu-p'ai hsiao-shuo shih lueh* in YYHTP, p. 227; and Leo Lee, "Lin Shu and His Translations: Western Fiction in Chinese Perspective," *Papers on China,* 19:163, indicate the latter alternative. It seems likely that the translation was done in 1895, and that the famous publication occurred in 1899.

31. Fan Yen-ch'iao in YYHTP, p. 227; CYLHIL, p. 312.

32. Hu Shih, "Introduction" to Chao Chia-pi, ed., *Chung-kuo hsin wen-hsueh ta-hsi,* vol 1.

33. We overlook here, because of its rarity in fiction, a third method of translation employed during the late Ch'ing years, i.e., that of direct translation into Chinese by a single person who read a Western language. Chou Shu-jen (i.e., Lu Hsun) and Chou Tso-jen used this method in translating their *Ch'eng-wai hsiao-shuo chi;* but seem to have achieved a circulation of only about 21. See Hu Shih, "Introduction," p. 4.

34. CYLHIL, pp. 173–174.

Flower" *(No no hana)* which was serialized in 1900 in the Tokyo newspaper *Yorozu Chōhō*. Kuroiwa's story was, in turn, a creative translation of a story which appeared in a popular British magazine as "The Mother's Heart" by Lady Mary Duffus Hardy, wife of Sir Thomas Duffus Hardy, Deputy Keeper of Her Majesty's Records.[35] Changes made in the cultural adaptation of stories such as this one constitute an intriguing area which has yet to be adequately studied.

During the 1910s, Japanese translations of Western fiction became easier to procure, as a number of Japanese bookstores established themselves in the Hongkew section of Shanghai. But at the same time the Chinese method of translation-by- *kanji* declined because of shifts in the way Japanese translators did their work. They now transformed Western stories entirely into a Japanese context, using Japanese personal and geographical names, dialogue and usage, and even customs and social structure. Moreover, they used fewer *kanji*. In the 1910s Pao T'ien-hsiao found it difficult to locate a good book to translate.[36]

The premium which late Ch'ing translators placed upon *kanji*-intensive Japanese not only determined their selection of Western works for translation; it was also part of what deterred them from translating Japanese literature, which generally used fewer *kanji* than the translations did. But the lack of Japanese literary influence on late Ch'ing fiction is too striking to be explained by this language factor alone. Chinese writers, still beholden at some level to the traditional view of Japan as a subsidiary culture in the Confucian world, seem to have overlooked Japan as they peered West. Japan was certainly admired, together with the West, in technological and developmental spheres; she was the host of thousands of progressive Chinese students and an important base for the writing and publishing of late Ch'ing fiction. Yet, in cultural terms, Chinese writers viewed modern Japanese writers and translators primarily as assistants in their own program of discovery.[37]

While turning toward the West, late Ch'ing writers stood well behind the front line who embraced the West. (This point is important in the trend toward Butterfly fiction.) They were vocal in their opposi-

35. CYLHIL:HP, p. 96; Pao T'ien-hsiao, *K'ung ku lan* (Shanghai, n.d.); *Kindai bungaku Kenkyū sōsho* (Tokyo, 1956–1978) 19:431, 432; Helen C. Black, *Notable Women Authors of the Day* (London, 1906) pp. 198–204. I am indebted to Martin C. Collcutt for tracking down the Japanese version of the story.

36. CYLHIL, p. 174.

37. Sanetō Keishū points out that about 60% of books translated from Japanese to Chinese during 1896–1905 were Japanese originals and not translations from Western works. This does not imply that Chinese were mostly interested in Japan itself, however; it means only that they acknowledged Japan to have been quicker to understand the West.

tion to Western military incursions; in fact the critique of officialdom in leading novels such as Li Po-yuan's *Panorama of Officialdom (Kuan-ch'ang hsien-hsing chi)* or Wu Wo-yao's *Strange Phenomena Viewed Over Twenty Years* frequently based itself on the failure of Chinese officials, military and civilian, to resist the West effectively. In the sphere of cultural influence, though they seemed eager to spread the "new" Western currents of science, antisuperstition, women's rights and so on, their basic preferences clearly drew upon Chinese far more than Western tradition. While devoting the prime of his life to the translation of Western novels, Lin Shu, for example, was also able to introduce them with such words as: " . . . the bad customs of the people in the time of semi-civilized England are here clearly revealed under our very eyes."[38] And Liu O, who begins *The Travels of Lao Ts'an* with an elaborate metaphor about the sad condition of the modern Chinese ship of state, leads his readers in the end toward soothing escape into Taoism.

The cultural orientation of late Ch'ing writers and translators can be further illustrated by the general character of their themes. The selection of works for translation which appears so random from a Western viewpoint can also appear, in terms of the translators' own moorings within Chinese tradition, as an entirely natural one. Leo Lee has astutely analyzed three major strands in Lin Shu's interest in Dumas, Dickens, and Haggard, respectively, as "the world of sentiment," "the world of ethics" and "the world of heroism."[39] It may be too much to equate these with the "worlds" in Chinese popular tradition of (1) *Dream of the Red Chamber* and other love stories, (2) *The Scholars* and its late Ch'ing scions, and (3) *Water Margin* and "knight-errant" *(wu-hsia)* tales, but the resemblance certainly is not accidental. The popularity of Sherlock Holmes during the early 20th century also draws upon the Ch'ing tradition of "public case" *(kung-an)* fiction such as *The Cases of Judge Shih (Shih kung-an)* and *The Cases of Judge P'eng (P'eng kung-an)*.

After the peak in demand for Western translations during the early years of the late Ch'ing decade, translators turned increasingly to writing their own fiction.[40] From the mixture of Chinese and Western traditions, a number of "types" of story emerged and set a pattern for the fiction of the 1910s both as thematic models and as a system for labeling stories in a context of cultural confusion. In the late Ch'ing decade the most important fiction type was what Lu Hsun later called "castigatory novels" *(ch'ien-tse hsiao-shuo)* in his *Outline History of*

38. Preface to *David Copperfield*, quoted in and translated by Leo Lee, "Lin Shu and His Translations," p. 171.
39. Lee, *Romantic Generation*, pp. 44–56.
40. CYLHIL, pp. 175, 312 and 357–358.

Chinese Literature (1931). Lu Hsun lists as leading examples the four novels which have been regarded as the most important of the decade, *viz.* Li Po-Yuan's *Panorama of Officialdom* (1901), Wu Wo-yao's *Strange Phenomena* (1902), Liu O's *The Travels of Lao Ts'an* (1906) and finally Tseng P'u's *Flower on a Sea of Evil* (*Nieh hai hua*, 1905),[41] a spicy chronicle of the romance, adventure and international intrigue surrounding the life of Sai-chin-hua and her husband, the *chuang-yuan* and Ch'ing ambassador Hung Chün.

Prior to the widespread adoption of Lu Hsun's label, these novels were known under the category of "social novels" *(she-hui hsiao-shuo)*. Besides being most numerous and widely read in the last Ch'ing decade, social novels were also most far-ranging in scope, their subjects extending beyond the satire of officialdom to include social portraits of shopkeepers, students, monks, laborers, bullies, loiterers, and anyone else in the panorama of life. A number of social novels, paramount among them a work of undetermined authorship called *The Bitter Society* (*K'u she-hui*, 1905), detail the suffering of overseas Chinese in California and their anguish at the American Exclusion Act.[42]

While social novels usually described the sorry state of the world, a type called "novels of ideals" *(li-hsiang hsiao-shuo)* told how things ought to be. These often concentrated on progressive issues from the reform movement such as "opposing superstition" and "freedom and equality" for women. Leading examples of these two themes which appeared in 1905, under undeciphered pseudonyms, were, respectively, *The Superstition Broom* (*Sao-mi chou*) and *Huang Hsiu-ch'iu*.[43] "Novels of ideals" often carried an air of not-quite-feasibility about them, the point being to ponder their content rather than to practice it. In this respect their interest converged with that of another type, the "science novels" *(k'o-hsueh hsiao shuo)*, whose program, like the Western science fiction it partially imitated, was to extol the potentials of modern science. A novel called *The Electric World* (*Tien shih-chieh*, 1909) describes a society in which all menial work is done by electric robots.[44]

China's love story tradition re-blossomed during the late Ch'ing years, though it sometimes showed the influence of the predominant social novels of the time. Wu Wo-yao's *Sea of Resentment* (1902), called a "writing of sentiment" novel *(hsieh-ch'ing hsiao-shuo)* and a paradigm

41. The dates given are those of the publication of the first installments of the novels.

42. Ho Ta (pseud. Ning Yuan), *Hsiao-shuo hsin-hua*, pp. 72–74; Ch'ien Hsing-ts'un, *Wan-Ch'ing hsiao-shuo shih*, ch. 5. The Bitter Society was reprinted in August 1959 in Shanghai by the Chung-hua shu-chü.

43. Ch'ien Hsing-ts'un, *Wan-Ch'ing hsiao-shuo shih* (Hong Kong), pp. 105–106 and 116–118.

44. *Hsiao-shuo shih pao*, no. 1 (September 1909).

for late Ch'ing romantic love stories, sets its background with a store of social gossip surrounding the Boxer incident. Romance and social commentary were also combined in the novels about the lives of prostitutes which followed *Shanghai Flowers* and *Magnificent Dreams in Shanghai*. There were, in addition, a good number of "history" novels *(li-shih hsiao-shuo)* about both Chinese and Western history written in the historical romance *(yen-i)* style, "detective" novels *(chen-t'an hsiao-shuo)*, and several other types, though labels had not proliferated to the point where they were made up to suit particular works, as often happened in the 1910s.

Though Shanghai was unquestionably the center of late Ch'ing fiction, the ferment concentrated there had some spillover in other major coastal cities. Little noticed in accounts of late Ch'ing fiction, for example, are the novels of Huang Shih-chung published in Canton and Hong Kong.[45] Obviously inspired by the Shanghai novels, Huang produced *Magnificent Dreams of Twenty Years (Erh-shih tsai fan-hua meng,* 1907), an exposé of official corruption in Canton, especially of alleged embezzlement by the Kwangtung governor Chou Jung-yao, who eventually makes it to Peking and purchases China's ambassadorship to Belgium;[46] *Ta ma pien,* a political novel supporting K'ang Yu-wei's reforms and opposing Ch'ing rule; and *Rise and Fall in the Sea of Officialdom (Huan-hai sheng-ch'en lu)*, a tract on the life of Yuan Shih-k'ai published in 1909—before Yuan became a villain—which therefore provides an unusual picture of Yuan cast in a favorable light.

Late Ch'ing fiction observed rules of "type" in certain matters of form as well as of content. Following the precedents of Lin Shu, almost all translations, of both short stories and full-length novels, used Lin's style of classical language. Creations, on the other hand, were with few exceptions written in classical language if they were short stories and in traditional vernacular style if they were long novels.

3. The Influence of "Idle Amusement" Invades the New Fiction

Prior to the twentieth century, vernacular fiction in China had been viewed as anything but the agent for serious political and social change which Liang Ch'i-ch'ao and others wished to make it. Fiction had been generally viewed—along with teahouses, theatre and other

45. Ch'ien Hsing-ts'un, *Wan-Ch'ing hsiao-shuo shih* (Hong Kong), pp. 135–138, discusses one of Huang's novels under Huang's alternate name Hsiao-p'ei.

46. In the novel Chou Jung-yao is presented under the similar sounding Chou Yung-yu. The author, who was also called Huang Hsiao-p'ei, was executed in the 1920s by the revolutionary-turned-warlord Ch'en Chiung-ming.

entertainment—as nothing more than a way, and not always a salubrious way, of amusing oneself. Phrases such as "whiling away the time" *(hsiao-hsien)* which remains "after tea when food is done" *(ch'a-yü fan-hou)* were often used to describe the pursuit of fiction's "interest" *(ch'ü-wei* or *hsing-ch'ü)*. No one needed to stand up on a barrel to proclaim these ideas when the sudden new capacity for printing and circulating fiction appeared on the scene in Shanghai. Despite the idealistic calls of the reformers, the undertow of traditional conceptions of fiction wrought a gradual but inexorable influence on the "new fiction" and led, after a decade, to the phenomenon of Butterfly fiction.

The influence was felt in Shanghai's periodical press from its very beginnings, decades before the appearance of the reform fiction. Chinese attitudes were in certain ways reinforced by the custom in British journalism, from which the Shanghai press took its early cues, of publishing games, puzzles, and interest pieces to amuse readers and increase circulation.[47] The first editor of Shanghai's *Shen pao* in 1872 planned to make that newspaper a miscellany of fiction, verse, and light essays and was deterred from this course only through the efforts of a colleague who had worked with Wang T'ao in Hong Kong. Yet even Wang T'ao, often credited as a founder of modern Chinese journalism, was himself not immune from the lure of amusement. After moving to Shanghai in 1884, Wang published a number of little books with whimsical titles like *Surplus Chatter from a Tiny Window (Weng-yü yü-t'an)* which simultaneously introduced Western science and entertained readers with humor and strange stories, many based on Wang's own travels in the West.[48]

Because of the political significance of the reform press after 1895, it is easy to overlook the fact that the general efflorescence included entertainment as much as politics. Side-by-side with the "study journals," there appeared during 1897–1898 a series of entertainment sheets whose names are a good indication of their content: *Laughter (Hsiao pao), Pastime (Hsiao-hsien pao), The Wide, Wide World (Shih-chieh fan-hua pao), Pleasure Quarters Gazette (Ch'ing-lou pao)* and *Chamber of the Flying Clouds (Fei-yun ko)*, among others.[49] Most important of the lot was *Recreation (Yu-hsi pao,* 1897–1910), whose circulation grew as fast as the fame of its editor, the fiction specialist Li Po-yuan.[50] The follow-

47. Altick, *Common Reader*, p. 87.

48. Hung Shen, "Wang T'ao k'ao-cheng," *Wen-hsüeh* 2.6:1024 (1934); Britton, p. 67.

49. Ch'ien Hsing-ts'un, *Wan-Ch'ing wen-i pao-k'an shu-lueh*, pp. 53ff; Britton, p. 96; Hsu Hsiao-t'ien, *Chung-kuo wen-hsueh shih*, p. 451.

50. Ch'ien Hsing-ts'un, *Wan-Ch'ing wen-i pao-k'an shu-lueh*, pp. 58–62; and CYLHIL, p. 445.

ing description of these papers by Pao T'ien-hsiao reflects a mild bias accountable to fifty years of hindsight:

> And what was the content of these entertainment papers like? Fun, of course, was their core. Their first principle was not to speak of politics; they would hear nothing of "the great affairs of the nation" and things like that. What they carried was only gossip and rumor, anecdotes and overheard secrets—nothing that amounted to much. All the writers were those so-called "foreign mall geniuses" of the time, who would play around with poetry games and whatnot, which many readers did indeed enjoy. Later on they got increasingly worse, writing exclusively about the affairs of prostitutes and actors. Sometimes they even confronted the brothels with a show of force, groundlessly extorting payoffs from them. For example: the high-class brothels of Shanghai collected their bills for banquet entertainment three times a year. If the entertainment papers had some reason to quarrel with a certain institution, they would start a rumor to the effect that such-and-such a courtesan was soon to be married. When this happened all of the male customers who had been showing up because of their special feelings for that lady would "float their accounts" ("floating an account" was professional jargon for failing a debt). Or take the way they treated actors. They also had drama reviews (at that time none of the major newspapers had drama reviews), and if a famous actor had come from Peking, they would go barging in the door to watch the play for free— Shanghai theatres did not yet use the ticket-buying system—and if you didn't let them go in, the next day a drama review would appear scolding the daylights out of you. All the theatre managers hated them with a passion, but there was nothing they could do.[51]

Drastic as the distinction may appear between this entertainment fiction and the serious program for fiction of Liang Ch'i-ch'ao *et al.*—and drastically as the distinction has been drawn in historiography both Chinese and Western[52]—the two elements were very

---

51. CYLHIL, p. 445. Pao calls these entertainment sheets *hsiao pao,* the same term used to refer to the "mosquito" papers like *Ching pao.* This usage is unusual, and lumping the two together may be a failing of Pao's retrospective view.

52. Roswell Britton introduces the amusement magazines with the following words: "Alongside these [reform press] high-minded and idealistic magazines which advocated and undertook to inform and educate the spreading progressive sentiments, there arose at Shanghai in 1897–1898 some half dozen pictorial periodicals of more or less obscene character." Ch'ien Hsing-ts'un's comments may be taken as representative of the standard view in Communist Chinese historiography: "This type of small newspaper was born from the combination of life in a semi-colonial city and feudal-landlord life . . . [and] reflects some of the degenerate life patterns of the comprador class, the "foreign mall geniuses," the urbanites, and the bureaucratic landlords" *(Wen-i pao-k'an shu-lüeh,* p. 50).

closely intertwined in publications throughout the late Ch'ing period, becoming more clearly stratified only in the 1910s. It was *Recreation* magazine, for example, which began serialization in 1901 of the first of the famous late Ch'ing "castigatory novels," Li Po-yuan's *Panorama of Officialdom*.[53] Conversely, it was Liang Ch'i-ch'ao's very serious reform journal *Shih-wu pao* which introduced Sherlock Holmes and his *New Fiction* which, in addition to progressive essays and fiction, published joke-and-anecdote columns called "Notes on New Curios" (hsin ku-tung lu), "New Jokes on the Examinations" (k'ao-shih hsin hsiao-hua) and many others. Except for Liang's own novels, the fiction published in *New Fiction* (as well as in *Illustrated Stories, Monthly Fiction, Forest of Fiction* and the other "new-style" fiction journals) generally does not fall easily into categories of either purely reformist or purely amusement interest.

Even the "revolutionary" *Su pao,* famous for the anti-Manchu agitation which sent six of its editors to prison in 1903, ran a column on its back page for the amusement of idle talent. On certain days, *Su pao* would announce a topic and invite its readership to join a contest aimed at producing the best parallel couplet *(tui-lien)* to express the topic's essence. On other days, two characters would be announced which seemed to have totally unrelated meanings; a contest was then undertaken to see who could write the most harmonious poem using both the characters. The column appeared daily, winning solutions were published and prizes awarded.[54]

Riddles, jokes, "random notes" *(sui-pi)* by well-known people, anecdotes and gossip were almost universally present in the periodical press during 1900–1920. And reader response was increasingly important. Contests would ask readers to attempt essays on topics sometimes serious—"the importance of women's education"—and sometimes frivolous—"the new style in Western hats." Other times an editor would collect and publish answers to an announced question which was no contest at all but a playful "survey" of the public's experience, e.g., "What was the first thing you said to your bride on the wedding night?"[55] Prying into the private lives of public figures was the specialty of the "mosquito press" (see chapter 3), whose skirmishes in court or with hired hoodlums in the streets became themselves items of journalistic interest.[56] Photographs were another popular drawing card as the techniques of color lithography, copper

53. Chang Ching-lu, *Chin-tai,* 2:428; CYLHIL, p. 445.

54. CYLHIL, pp. 181 – 182.

55. Peking University, Department of Chinese, Class of 1955, "Hsin-hai ko-ming hou hsiao-shuo ti fan-tung," in YYHTP, p. 98.

56. CYLHIL, 447– 450 and CYLHIL:HP, p. 84.

photogravure, and the collotype successively improved the quality of reproductions during the late Ch'ing years.[57] Common subjects included famous scenic spots in China, female beauty, paintings and sculpture from the West, plus any kind of curious item which had to be seen to be believed.

These "light interest" items, if they were not used as filler pieces, were normally concentrated in a special part of a newspaper or magazine which remained fixed from issue to issue. In magazines, photographs were printed one after another right at the beginning, whether or not they were mutually related or related to anything else in the issue. In newspapers, the contests, jokes, and anecdotes normally were clustered on a part of the back page which came to be known as the "newspaper's rump" *(pao p'i-ku).*[58]

Yet it is important in understanding the genesis of modern popular fiction to see that the relation between light interest material and the serious news and reform literature which it accompanied was much more than that of strange admixture. During a period of discovery of new things—things at once curious and potentially useful—there was great room for individual writers and editors to emphasize either the amusing or the serious aspects of whatever appeared over the horizon. There were no sharp breaks along a spectrum of seriousness which extended from Liang Ch'i-ch'ao at one pole to the "newspaper's rump" at the other. Articles about the automobiles which Englishmen brought to Shanghai could be part of a solemn approach to new science. Articles about the racing dogs they brought were a matter of derivative interest—"background" to major events as well as food for the curious. When a piece appeared explaining dog-racing from *the dog's point of view,* with illustration, the same line of interest had moved into the realm of pure and fanciful entertainment.[59]

The tendency to view the same thing both seriously and satirically seems to have come from its value as a defense. A serious but unpleasant topic, such as how to accommodate Western ways, could be treated humorously, and therefore with less pain, without at the same time denying the necessity for considering it. Take for example a piece which appeared in *The Fiction Times* in 1909 called "The Lawyer-like Attitude of Washington" (Lü-shih t'ai-tu chih Hua-sheng-tun). Readers were probably aware that George Washington was a modern Western hero of the kind Liang Ch'i-ch'ao's "political fiction" might tell. At the same time, everyone knew that certain things from the West could be offensive and difficult to understand — things like law-

57. See chapter 3 above.
58. CYLHIL, p. 350.
59. *Hsiao-shuo shih pao,* no. 1, September 1909.

yers. How could anyone consider it honorable to make a profession of profiting from others' fights? Besides, lawyers defended Westerners, or Westernized Chinese, against the rest of us, and they did it through specious reasoning and nit-picking. The piece in *The Fiction Times* begins thus:

> One day the father of Washington, with a distraught look on his face, and barely managing to control his rage, interrogated his son.
> "George, you know that someone has chopped down my beloved cherry tree. Do you know who did it?"
> The young Washington fixed his eyes directly at his father and replied with the most serious of expressions: "Your son, sir, is very well known for honesty. If I knew, why would I be evasive, and prevent the truth being known to you? But I have another question for you, sir. Does the fact that you interrogate me, and not others, mean that you suspect me, sir? May I please know upon what evidence it is that you base your suspicion and interrogation of me?"
> Washington's father lost his temper and raged at his son: "I know you have an axe! There's nothing you can't chop down with that axe! Especially my beloved cherry tree!"
> Washington smiled and said, "Father, you are speaking illogically. According to you, anyone at all who owns an axe is capable of having chopped down your cherry tree. Our neighbor to the west is a carpenter, and our neighbor to the east a woodcutter. Both of these workmen have axes. Why is it that you do not suspect them, sir? But let us leave this question for a moment. Just now you referred to 'my beloved cherry tree.' Does the ownership right to the cherry tree really reside with you, sir?"
> "Of course it does!" said the father.
> "Upon what evidence is it that you base this claim? . . ."[60]

Part of the interest to readers of this passage was, without doubt, the serious issue which lay in the background: George Washington was the founder of a constitutional republic, which some were advocating for China, and lawyers were also part of the "new style." The reader could therefore test out the idea of George Washington, and of lawyers, but at the same time avoid any commitments by retreating to satire.

Increasingly, though, the popular press came out with jokes which bore no real relation to serious reform issues but simply claimed one as a shield against disrepute. The following joke, which may be taken as typical of many, makes use of the "castigatory novel" tradition as if to

60. Ibid.

· "expose" the irresponsibility of a certain bad teacher. On the first day of classes the teacher asks his students, "Do you know what I'm going to talk about today?" The students say no, and the teacher replies, "If you're all as stupid as that, there is no use in teaching. Today's class is over." The second day the teacher begins with the same question and the students say they do know; the teacher says, "Then there is no need for me to lecture. Today's lesson is over." The third day the students say half of them know and half do not, and the teacher rejoins, "Then let those who know inform those who don't" and once more leaves.[61] The invocation of the "castigatory" tradition had come to be nothing but a stylish gesture.

A more insidious misuse of the reform ethic grew out of the possibility of confusing the women's rights movement with interest in sex. Magazines such as *Women's Times (Fu-nü shih-pao*, 1912) and *Women's World (Nü-tzu shih-chieh*, 1914) billed themselves as magazines written primarily by and for women, and about the women's movement. In fact, however, they pandered increasingly to the interests of men, and kept the reader's sympathy at arm's length from any woman who really carried through with the "new" style. The pictures of women from the entertainment quarter which adorned these magazines are further evidence of their purpose. (Because photography was a new fad, women from the entertainment quarter could be induced to pose for no reimbursement beyond the promise of a copy of the photograph for themselves.)[62] The extremes of duplicity are exemplified by a minor publisher who, daring to call itself "The Shanghai Progressive Book Co." (Shang-hai chin-pu shu-chü), came out with a series of books called *The Secrets of a Girl Student (Nü hsueh-sheng chih mi-mi chi), The Malicious Adulteress (Yin tu fu), Mandarin Duck Dreams (Yuan-yang meng)* and *A Beauty's Disaster (Mei-jen chieh).*[63]

With novels such as these, which grew plentiful during the 1910s, the ambiguous combination of reform and entertainment in fiction resolved itself into a clearer distinction between the two. Liang Ch'i-ch'ao's "new fiction" appeared to be an interlude which had now dwindled to almost nothing. Though the "reform" rubrics continued to be used, even the pretense of believing them was dropped. Advertisements for novels unabashedly spoke of "unbeatable pastime reading" *(wu-shang hsiao-hsien p'in),* ideal for "after-dinner amusement" or to carry in the pocket while travelling.[64]

61. Hsu Cho-tai, "San k'o," in *Hsing kuang,* no. 1, 1923.
62. CYLHIL, p. 360.
63. *Hsiao-shuo ta-kuan,* no. 1 (August 1915), advertisement for the Shanghai Progressive Book Co.
64. Hsu Chen-ya, *Yü-li hun* (Shanghai, 1914, fifth printing), advertisement on the back cover for the novels of Wu Shuang-je.

It is difficult to point out milestones in the gradual degeneration of the new fiction between, say, 1905 and 1915. Like a change in the weather, each moment resembles the next yet the end points are very different. Some of the important factors at work were sociological: the rise of new groups of readers and authors, and new commercial publishing arrangements. These we will treat in the next section and the next chapter. In terms of literary influences originating in the late Ch'ing years, we might here single out three factors which help to explain the shift and which appear more important than others.

First is the great importance of detective stories—that Pandora's box opened in Liang Ch'i-ch'ao's *Shih-wu pao* in the late 1890s. In a survey of novels published in Shanghai during the year of 1907, including both translations and creations, detective stories outnumbered all other kinds.[65] While seeming to readers part of the "new fiction," their actual support of reform issues was scant indeed. Continuing into the 1910s as popular items for translation, they soon gave rise to imitation by Chinese writers. Ch'eng Hsiao-ch'ing's *Cases Investigated by the Chinese Sherlock Holmes, Huo Sang (Chung-kuo Fu-erh-mo-ssu Huo-sang t'an-an)* was a staple of popular fiction in the 1910s.[66]

Second is an important transitory role played by one of the late Ch'ing period's most prolific writers, Wu Wo-yao. Wu began his career quite within the aegis of Liang Ch'i-ch'ao. His widely acclaimed *Strange Phenomena Witnessed Over Twenty Years* was published in the first issue of *New Fiction,* and *Fantastic Grievances of Nine Lives* followed it there. *Monthly Fiction,* which Wu edited, fell within the reformist train of *New Fiction* and Li Po-yuan's *Illustrated Stories.* Wu's own interests were remarkably diverse, however, and it is doubtful that any literary or political school could have contained him for long. The themes of his novels include commerce in Shanghai, the lives of coolies in America, unofficial histories of Yunnan and the Eastern and Western Chin dynasties, support for the late Ch'ing constitutionalist and antisuperstition movements, and his own social philosophy and philosophy of history. He had, in addition, a severe weakness for romantic love stories, as exemplified in *Sea of Resentment, Ashes of Disaster (Chieh yü hui)* and *New Story of the Stone (Hsin shih-t'ou chi).* In these novels Wu claimed to be "writing of sentiment" *(hsieh-ch'ing),* which he said was not sexual desire but "the inborn nature planted in the heart" of every human being.[67] Nevertheless, the theme of love between the sexes was sufficiently predominant in these stories to exert a strong influence in the transition to the entertainment fiction of

65. Chang Ching-lu, *Chin-tai,* 2: 275.
66. Fan Yen-ch'iao in YYHTP, pp. 240–245.
67. Ch'ien Hsing-ts'un, *Wan-Ch'ing hsiao-shuo shih* (Hong Kong), p. 173.

the 1910s. Ch'ien Hsing-ts'un feels "no doubt at all" that Wu's sentimental novels were the immediate progenitors of Butterfly love
stories.[68]

Third, one must return to the innovative role of the *Shih pao* (see
chapter 3). *Shih pao*'s late Ch'ing literary supplement called "Surplus
Spirit," which included a balanced fare of stories, poems, and essays,
elicited an enthusiastic response from the reform generation youth
who formed the base of *Shih pao*'s readership.[69] After 1911, when *Shih
pao*'s political role was seriously curtailed, its role in entertainment
grew correspondingly. "Surplus Spirit" grew into the columns called
"Comical Chatter" and "The Little Times." These were the models
for *Shen pao*'s "Unfettered Talk" and *Hsin-wen pao*'s "Forest of
Light-heartedness"—which, beginning in the 1920s, became major
organs of modern popular fiction.[70]

A further seminal aspect of *Shih pao*'s fiction supplements was the
bringing together of a group of writers who became leaders in popular
fiction, including Pi I-hung, Fan Yen-ch'iao, Chou Shou-chüan and
the leading editor throughout, Pao T'ien-hsiao. It is interesting to note
that Pao's successive pen names seem to encapsulate the gradual shift
in the interests of this group of writers from the late Ch'ing period to
the 1910s. Through a combination of happenstance, Pao's given name
as a child was Ch'ing-chu, suggesting "pillar of the Ch'ing."[71] With
his participation in the reform movement, Pao naturally felt embarrassed by this name and changed it to Kung-i to suggest "public-
minded and persistent." It was not until he began editing light-interest
columns that he changed his name to T'ien-hsiao—"sky" and
"laugh"—and finally, for short, to Hsiao.[72]

Again we face the irony that the three elements here singled out as
causing the drift toward amusement fiction originated from the most
progressive of quarters. Detective stories, love stories, and amusement
columns derived, respectively, from an experiment of Liang Ch'i-
ch'ao, the cosmopolitan interests of Wu Wo-yao, and the progressive
bent of *Shih pao*. In a period of transition as creative and uncertain
as the last Ch'ing decade, innovation could hardly foresee its own

68. Ibid., p. 176.
69. CYLHIL, pp. 349–350.
70. Ibid., p. 350; YYHTP, p. 405.
71. According to the Pao family's "family record" *(chia-p'u)*, Pao was destined to
have the *ch'ing* character in his name. Since his *pa-tzu* also lacked "wood," it was felt the
second character of his name should employ the wood radical. Since one could not
choose lightly among characters which would be combined with the name of the current dynasty, Pao's family settled on the "pillar" character, *ch'ing-chu*.
72. CYLHIL, pp. 188–192.

consequences. But, literary influences alone are inadequate to explain Shanghai fiction's drift towards entertainment.

4. The Discovery of Commercial Profit in "Idle Amusement" Journalism

In the last Ch'ing decade, despite the prevalence of fiction and games in the periodical press, readers probably did not doubt that amusement was second in importance to history, politics, "new studies," or current affairs. The few magazines which were devoted to pure play were viewed as insalubrious. But in the years just before and after the 1911 revolution, when the urban readership emerged and the facility of rapid printing became clear, publishers began to see fiction in a new light. It could now shed its secondary role, move to the main stage, sell magazines on its own, create fads, and garner profits.

The proof of this notion lay, naturally enough, in circulation figures. Translations by Lin Shu circulated only in hundreds of copies when they were first published around the turn of the century.[73] A decade later publishers were using their break-even target of three thousand copies for an initial printing, while widely-selling novels, such as Tseng P'u's *Flower on a Sea of Evil,* were approaching a figure of fifty thousand through fifteen successive printings.[74] With the arrival of the *Jade Pear Spirit* frenzy in the 1910s, commercialization of fiction escalated from supplying public demand to creating, stimulating, and coaxing it. Advertisements filled with extravagant praise for particular works appeared in magazines, newspapers and the backs of books. Publishers devised catchy names for magazines—*Glamorous Trifles (hsiang-yen hsiao-p'in), Eyebrow Signals (mei yü),* etc.—and used attractive pictures for their covers. They also made the most of well-known names. The manuscript of a third-rate or unknown writer would, for example, be published behind a cover carrying the conspicuous announcement "Revised by so-and-so" (a leading name).[75] Sometimes famous names would simply be pirated, or imitated closely enough that the ring of a big name would be suggested to the ear (Liu T'ieh-leng suggested Liu T'ieh-yun and T'ien-hsiao Sheng suggested Pao T'ien-hsiao, etc.). In addition to a famous name, the fact of large circulation itself, or merely the claim to such circulation, became a selling point for novels among high school students and others

73. Hu Shih, "Introduction" (see note 32 above), p. 4. Interviews with Yeh Ling-feng, April 28, 1973; and Ch'en Ting-shan, July 25, 1973.

74. Ho Ta, p. 63; Ch'en Shou-yi, *An Introduction to Chinese Literature* (Taipei, 1971), p. 620.

75. *Hsiao-shuo ta-kuan,* no. 1, August 1915.

to whom group participation was important. Advertisements made great claims about novels whose multitudinous printings "have caused the price of paper to rise in Loyang" and whose authors "are known by nine people in ten."[76] At the same time novels whose selling potential was a matter of record were widely published, re-advertised, and re-published. Copyrights existed but were unenforceable.

The various ways of achieving circulation for novels frequently had little to do with authors. It was the work, rather, of those in another of the new professional roles emerging in Shanghai society, i.e., the modern commercial publisher. Authors protected the distinction between themselves and this group, and in fact did not always see eye-to-eye with them. Pao T'ien-hsiao tells of disagreeing with his publisher over a name for his *pai-hua* fiction magazine which was published in 1915:

> There was nothing I could do but accommodate myself to his advice. By that time I knew how important the distribution of a publication was, and that there was a great deal of skill involved in achieving circulation. I could not deny the existence of "an eye for business," as they call it in the commercial world, and this man had a good grasp of the matter of distribution. We [authors] had no choice but to believe him and rely on what he told us.[77]

The publisher had decided to call a new magazine of Pao's the *Hsiao-shuo ta-kuan* (literally something like "panorama of fiction," although the official title in English was *The Grand Magazine*). Pao and his contributors had felt this name was trite—all kinds of magazines were calling themselves this or that *ta-kuan*. But they finally accepted their publisher's view when he told them circulation would suffer were they to use any of their own, more elegant ideas.

Not long after the commercial potential of fiction magazines and books emerged, it also became clear that fiction could be used to sell daily newspapers. The practice originated in *Shih pao*, not, ironically, with sales as the motive but as part of a serious effort to participate in the reform movement. Ti Ch'u-ch'ing, associate of Liang Ch'i-ch'ao and general manager of *Shih pao*, had published in *New Fiction* his own detailed defense of Liang's thesis of a connection between political fiction and good government.[78] But writers at *Shih pao* were not entirely in tune with their manager's theory, at least not in practice. Their growing indulgence during the last Ch'ing decade in humor and adventure stories was, as in the example of George Washington and the

76. Hsu Chen-ya, *Yü-li hun* (Shanghai, 1914, 5th printing), advertisement on back cover.
77. CYLHIL, p. 376.
78. CYLHIL, pp. 313 and 317.

cherry tree, part of a defense against the "new learning" by making it seem more ambiguous and allowing a wider range of psychological response. Almost inadvertently, it was discovered that fiction and *Shih pao's* increasing circulation were related. When this was noticed other newspapers, especially the semi-respectable "mosquito press," were quick to adopt fiction as a sales device.[79] In 1911, with the appearance of *Shen pao's* famous "Unfettered Talk" column, fiction became an established feature of the modern Chinese press, and remains so to the present day.

The key role of newspaper fiction in the development of both newspapers and popular fiction cannot be separated from the fact of its serialization. In fiction magazines of the late Ch'ing, serialization had been practiced simply as an expedient for publishing novels too lengthy to appear in a single issue. But when newspapers began serializing fiction, the device took on an economic logic for both readers and publishers. For readers, newspapers were—or at least seemed to be—a less expensive source of fiction than books or magazines. Newspapers cost four cents at most, which meant one could buy a newspaper every day for two or three months for the price of a single novel in book form. If that were the length of time required to serialize one volume—which roughly it was—the total cost would not be different but the *feeling* of affordability would be present because each daily outlay seemed unimportantly small. And since there were, of course, many other good reasons for buying a newspaper, getting to read a novel could be viewed as a kind of bonus. Some newspapers even printed their fiction installments in a form ready to be stitched between homemade book covers.[80] Beyond these economies, newspaper fiction could often be read at no cost at all. It is estimated that Shanghai newspapers had as many as ten readers per copy, a result of their being posted on bulletin boards, supplied in common to offices, and passed around among family and friends.[81] If all else failed, one could pick up a discarded day-old newspaper. Its news value might have tapered off after twenty-four hours, but not so its fiction value.

The utility of serialization from the viewpoint of a newspaper publisher lay in the ability to "hook" readers on a story, thereby ensuring not only that they stick with the same newspaper but also that they avoid missing an issue. The "tension-and-curtain" format, which left readers at the end of each day's episode with maximum curiosity for the next day's continuation, had been widely employed in the newspaper fiction of nineteenth century England. In Shanghai, the example

79. Tseng Hsu-pai, interview, July 19, 1973; CYLHIL, p. 318.
80. Britton, pp. 122–123.
81. Britton, p. 129; Lin Yutang, pp. 148–149.

of English-language newspapers was very readily adopted by the Chinese press because of the basic congruence of its principle with the tradition in China's vernacular literature of writing in "linked chapters" *(chang-hui)*. (If it is true, as commonly assumed, that the "linked chapter" format itself originated with Sung storytellers passing the hat at opportune moments, then the same commercial motive emerges as the determinant of a popular form in both China and the West.) The only real adjustment which had to be made when "linked chapters" were put into modern newspapers in Shanghai was to shorten the intervals between mini-climaxes, since a chapter of traditional length would be enough for two or three days' serialization.[82]

The program of selling fiction to readers comprised but one side of the new commercial role of Shanghai publishers. The other side was the commercialization of their relations with authors. In the modern revolution in popular fiction, the payment of authors became more common, open, and clearly articulated than ever before. Though writers in earlier centuries did sell fiction manuscripts, which publishers also printed and sold, such were considered casual, even shady affairs to be handled in semi-secrecy. The practices in twentieth-century Shanghai of openly soliciting manuscripts, of advertising rates of remuneration in carefully distinguished categories, of honoring well-known writers with extra high rates, and so on, required a significant turnabout from earlier attitudes about the printed word.

Some of the first writers actually to sell their work in Shanghai, such as Lin Shu and Pao T'ien-hsiao, began not with the intention of realizing a profit but with the more traditional and gentlemanly goals of expression and enjoyment for themselves and their friends. The discovery that a living wage could be had from the modern presses of Shanghai came somewhat as an unexpected boon, yet one whose allure was undeniable. Pao recalls his feelings upon receiving a hundred yuan from the Civilization Book Co. (Wen-ming shu-chü) for the manuscript of his first translation, that of H. Rider Haggard's *Joan Haste:*

> From that time on my fascination with translating fiction steadily increased. It was a delightfully free and unencumbered job, and my thoughts of earning stipends from the academies came to be replaced by thoughts of selling translations. The one hundred *yuan* I had received from the Civilization Book Company, for example, was enough for the family to live on for several months,

82. Leavis, pp. 152–154; Ssu-ma Hsiao, "Wo ti t'ung-shih Chang Hen-shui" in *Ta-jen* 16 (August 1971): 60–62; interview with Fan Chi-p'ing (pseud. Ssu-ma Hsiao), June 30, 1973.

not counting my travelling expenses to Shanghai. What could possibly keep me from pursuing this?[83]

The commercial route in fiction was at first very narrow. In the early 1900s only a few publishers offered pay, and then only for fiction. (While it was common for essays and informal reportage to be contributed to a newspaper or magazine by outside persons, publication was on a courtesy basis and without remuneration.) Toward the end of the first decade, though, and throughout the 1910s, fiction manuscripts were not only paid for but actively solicited, especially by magazines. Solicitation was done in two ways. The most important, from which the great majority of actual publications resulted, was to approach well-known, successful writers directly and urge them to contribute. But in addition, notices were regularly published in magazines announcing what kind of fiction a magazine sought (whether novels or short stories, original compositions or translations, and so on) and what rates of pay they offered. The public at large was invited to submit manuscripts.

The earliest manuscripts purchased by Shanghai publishers were paid for according to length, but only roughly, without any careful measurement or fixed rules.[84] By the 1910s commercialization had advanced to a point where payment was calculated with precision according to a fixed rate per thousand characters. Magazines advertised rate scales, typically including rates of one, two, or three yuan per thousand characters, depending on quality. In practice, two yuan per thousand characters was a standard rate from about 1907 through the 1910s. The use of other rates, either higher or lower, required special justification. Inferior manuscripts—ones which had potential but needed substantial editorial revision—would be paid for at one yuan, one-half yuan, or even as little as twenty cents per thousand characters.[85] Rates higher than two yuan per thousand characters were reserved for writers of established reputation and were offered only by the major publishers. The Commercial Press allowed Pao T'ien-hsiao three yuan per thousand characters for his "education novels" (chiao-yü hsiao-shuo), which were used as school textbooks. For Lin Shu's translation novels, Commercial Press paid the special rate of five yuan per thousand, and later six. Part of the justification for the high rate

---

83. CYLHIL, p. 174. Pao's translation of *Joan Haste,* done in 1898, was an incomplete version, as he could find only the second volume of a two-volume set in the old bookstores of Soochow. Later Lin Shu did a complete translation of the entire novel.

84. CYLHIL, p. 173.

85. Ibid., p. 324; written interview with Pao, May 1973, reply to question 24; interview with Ch'en Ting-shan, July 25, 1973.

was that Lin needed to divide his income with his collaborators.[86] Higher than Lin's pay stood only such extraordinary cases as Liang Ch'i-ch'ao writing on scholarly subjects. Though Liang's rate was never publicly divulged—for fear, some said, that others might claim equally astronomical rates—it was commonly believed to have been ten yuan or more per thousand characters.[87]

Though most fiction was bought and sold in yuan-per-thousand-characters, there did exist alternative modes of remuneration. In its early years, *Shih pao* offered its contributors coupons redeemable in books published by their adjunct book company, the Yu-cheng shu-chü; and the Commercial Press sometimes encouraged authors to accept their pay in stock in the Commercial Press Company.[88] Throughout the development of all these scales and devices of payment, there continued to be a category of writers who published for pleasure and scorned the profit motive. For them, it was a custom to write the three characters "will not receive compensation" *(pu shou ch'ou)* at the head of their manuscripts.

Most important of the new kinds of pay for fiction was the fixed salary. Fiction specialists, both writers and editors, could secure positions on the regular staff of newspapers or magazines and be paid by the month. The salaries grew rapidly during the first two decades of the century. A young editor at the *Shen pao* named Sun Tung-wu, for example, began with a salary of 28 yuan per month in 1904. In 1907 Pao T'ien-hsiao put together a monthly income of 120 yuan by working three hours in the morning at Tseng P'u's *Forest of Fiction* for 40 yuan, and taking 80 yuan for his afternoons and evenings at *Shih pao*. Only a few years later a writer could get 300 yuan per month, this being Hsu Chen-ya's salary at *Thicket of Fiction* in 1914 and Ch'en Ting-shan's at *Shen pao* in 1916.[89]

The advent of salaries such as these in the fiction business had important consequences for publishers and authors alike. Publishers now had to reckon the considerable cost of manuscripts, whether in salaries or piecework, along with other publication expenses in labor, paper, machinery, and distribution. For authors and would-be authors, the new salaries were a clear demonstration that one not only could live from fiction but could live very well from it. While Pao T'ien-hsiao was drawing his 120 yuan per month salary, he could rent a pleasant

---

86. CYLHIL, p. 325; interview with Kao Chen-pai, April 26, 1973 (Hong Kong).

87. Interviews with Kao Chen-pai (see note 86 above), and Ch'en Ting-shan (see note 85 above).

88. YYHTP, p. 405; CYLHIL, pp. 325 and 350.

89. CYLHIL, pp. 124, 317; Ch'en Tieh-i "Hsu Chen-ya yü *Yü-li hun* (3), *Hsing-tao jih-pao,* November 1, 1973.

house in Shanghai for only 7 yuan and cover all household expenses for 50–60 yuan at most.[90] Salaried writers generally made more than those paid by piecework, but even the latter could live comfortably so long as their manuscripts sold. An individual's average output might be one or two thousand characters a day—five thousand or more when pressing oneself.[91] At the standard rate of two yuan per thousand characters, this would mean that even a comparatively small output could render a superior living wage. Writers with a name for themselves could, moreover, "moonlight" by holding salaried positions and selling piecework on the side.[92] Some became entrepreneurs on their own, founding magazines to compete with those of the publishing houses.[93]

The financially successful authors in the 1910s were a small minority, but they had established an attractive and reasonably well regarded new profession. To literate young people in Shanghai, the life-style they exemplified seemed easier than a school teacher's, freer than an office-worker's, and more romantic than a news reporter's. With a bit of luck, it could also pay better than any of these. The number of aspiring professional writers soared in the 1920s, as, alas, did the number of frustrated failures.

90. CYLHIL, pp 317 and 324. According to Kao Chen-pai (pseud. Po-yü), a writer in Shanghai in the twenties could support a family of eight on 100 yuan per month, "Chi tsui lao ti tso-chia Pao T'ien-hsiao hsien-sheng," in *Ta-ch'eng*, no. 2 (January 1, 1974), p. 37.

91. Kao Chen-pai, "Chi tsui lao ti tso-chia," p. 37; CYLHIL, pp. 317 and 376; interview with Ch'en Ting-shan (note 85 above); interview with Cheng I-mei, May 9, 1973.

92. Pao T'ien-hsiao often wrote as much for piecework outside his salaried jobs as he did in his salaried jobs. His *Shih pao* salary required about 1,000 characters per day during a time when he was producing as much as 4,000–5,000 characters per day (CYLHIL, p. 376). When he edited the *Fiction Times (Hsiao-shuo shih pao)*, which was a *Shih pao* publication, he drew no salary as its editor but took fees for his own contributions of fiction (CYLHIL, p. 324).

93. These included Li Ting-i's *Hsiao-shuo hsin pao (New Fiction Journal)*, Hsu Hsiao-t'ien's *Mei-yü (Eyebrow Signals)*, and Yao Yuan-ch'u's *Ch'un sheng (Spring Voices)*.

CHAPTER *5*

Authors and Readers

Of the many young people attracted to the new profession of fiction writing in Shanghai, about fifty can be said to have achieved the status of well-known author. Shanghai's "literary scene" *(wen-t'an)* in which they participated was an informal association of three or four distinct but mutually amiable subgroups. Although considerable variety obtained among the writers (in fact they enjoyed cultivating their individual characters), the commonalities of their background and of their experience on the 1910s "literary scene" are sufficient to permit certain generalizations about the group as a whole.

1. Life-styles

Most of the Shanghai writers in the 1910s were migrants from towns and cities of the Yangtze Basin, especially Soochow. They were part of the larger social transition in which Shanghai, its population constantly swelling, gradually replaced the commercial, industrial, political, and even artistic functions of its older neighboring cities. Like many other educated youth, the early fiction writers had spent some time groping for directions within this larger transition. Usually from well-to-do backgrounds, where they had begun on the examination route towards success, they rather suddenly found no clear road ahead for them. A remarkably large proportion of them also had lost their fathers while very young, a circumstance which perhaps contributed to their footloose quality. Shanghai drew them because of its romantic "new thought," its new-style possibilities for wealth and fame, and the freedom it offered to explore new occupational alternatives. The young writers did not repudiate their provincial homes, but regarded them as a kind of background from which to launch Shanghai adventures.[1]

From the viewpoint of the older generation, they were rebels in several ways. They would leave wives and children at home in the provinces while forming extra attachments within the glitter and

---

1. CYLHIL, p. 275; and CYLHIL:HP, pp. 49ff and 57ff.

foreign atmosphere of the city. It was, moreover, unclear in the hinterland that their new pursuits were of the slightest use. Journalism and
the writing of "castigatory" fiction were viewed as risky at best, reckless at worst. A stroke of one's pen could endanger another person's
entire reputation, and hence there were also reprisals to be feared. Ever
since the *Su pao* case, Shanghai journalism appeared to the conservative countryside as a first step towards jail. Family heads pleaded with
their youth to give up such adventurism and return home. The father
of one young journalist-author, Pi I-hung, made a special trip to
Shanghai from home in Hangchow in a vain attempt to bring back his
son; in addition to fear for young Pi's safety, and concern for his bride
back in Hangchow, the father was apprehensive that his son would
write something to offend the Hangchow warlords, who were known
to have a sharp distaste for Shanghai journalists.[2]

But if the writers were black sheep in their families' view, they
could reach positions of considerable eminence according to the terms
and standards of the new city. Some even reached the pinnacle of
the fiction world from relatively disadvantaged backgrounds. Chou
Shou-chüan, whose father was a boatman and mother a seamstress,
grew up from poverty to become the editor of *Shen pao*'s "Unfettered
Talk," one of the most powerful positions in the Shanghai fiction business. Chang Hen-shui never finished high school, but led the field of
popular writers in the 1930s and eventually made a fortune from writing. Most of the successful writers managed their climb to the top not
exclusively through fiction but together with one or another second
profession. Chou Shou-chüan was also a teacher and journalist (the
two commonest of the combined roles), and Chang Hen-shui began in
drama.[3] There were no conventional limits to the range of what else
one might try one's hand at, as the following examples illustrate.

Lu Shih-o studied Chinese medicine with a famous traditional herbalist in his hometown of Ch'ing-p'u in Kiangsu. When his father died
he moved to Shanghai and tried medicine, but as a callow youth in his
early twenties could not be credible in that line. Searching around for
an alternative, he noticed a great amount of fiction being read all
around him, and decided to go into the book-renting business. Risking
most of his accumulated savings to purchase a large number of novels,
he rented them at low rates and personally delivered copies back and
forth. This business succeeded, and in the bargain he got to read the
novels himself. Eventually he tried his own hand at writing and discovered he had no trouble selling manuscripts. His modest reputation

2. CYLHIL, p. 322; CYLHIL:HP, pp. 52–53.
3. YYHTP, pp. 90, 457, and 515–516.

then found its way to the ears of Sun Chia-chen, the well-known late Ch'ing author of *Magnificent Dreams in Shanghai* and proprietor of a book company called Shanghai Library (Shang-hai t'u-shu-kuan). Sun sought out Lu and discovered his erstwhile interest in medicine. He encouraged Lu to reopen practice at his (Sun's) own Shanghai Library and at the same time to publish popular works on medicine. Lu accepted the idea and began writing "medicine" columns in newspapers. Before long he was widely known as the "doctor-writer," though his novels were always clearly more successful than his medicine. He was most famous for his dozens of knight-errant stories, such as *The Three Swordsmen (San chien-k'o)* and *White Knights (Pai hsia)*. In his later years he enjoyed a very handsome standard of living.[4]

Hsu Cho-tai, from Soochow, lost his father at age seven. Always fond of physical exercise, dancing, and games, he was one of the first Chinese students in modern Japan to major in physical education. When he returned to Shanghai he set up the city's first physical education school, served as its principal, and through his students developed a substantial following in the physical education departments of the "new-style" schools of the area. During the 1910s his interest turned to drama, and he authored the earliest articles in *Shih pao* calling for modern reform in theater. (In the early twenties, under the name Hsu Pan-mei, he joined the Masses Drama Society (Min-chung hsi she), a May Fourth group whose members included Cheng Chen-to, Mao Tun, Chang Ching-lu and Hsiung Fo-hsi.) His writing of fiction also began at *Shih pao,* where Pao T'ien-hsiao noticed his gift with words and his knack for humor. Hsu's specialty became "comic stories" *(hua-chi hsiao-shuo)* which drew heavily upon the device of abrupt surprise, every page turning the reader's expectations upside down. (Ch'ien Hsing-ts'un rates Hsu's literary skill high among the popular writers, above Chang Hen-shui's or Ku Ming-tao's.)[5] With financial success from fiction and education behind him, Hsu and his wife, T'ang Chien-wo, who was known in her own right as a promoter of physical education and a calligrapher, ran a factory which produced artificial soy sauce.[6]

Ch'en Tieh-hsien (T'ien-hsu wo sheng), also from Soochow, authored love stories with titles such as *Teardrop Destiny (Lei chu yuan)* and *Gossamer Love-net (Ch'ing-wang chu-ssu)* and some detective stories

4. YYHTP, pp. 494–495; interview with Ch'en Ting-shan, July 25, 1973.

5. Ch'ien Hsing-ts'un, "Shanghai shih-pien yü yuan-yang hu-tieh p'ai wen-i"; in YYHTP, pp. 55 and 61.

6. YYHTP, pp. 460–461; interview with Ch'en Ting-shan, July 25, 1973; Li Hui-ying, "Hsu Pan-mei ti hui-i lu" *Hsing-tao wan-pao,* July 9, 1973, p. 8; Mou Hsien-sheng, "Hsu Cho-tai yü Wang Hsiao-i," *Chen pao* (Hong Kong), July 15, 1973, p. 3.

fashioned after *Sherlock Holmes*. He was an early contributor to *Shen pao's* "Unfettered Talk" starting in 1911, became its editor in 1916, and from there became, in the manner of Pao T'ien-hsiao at *Shih pao,* an important entrepreneurial figure on the "literary scene" of the 1910s.

Before writing fiction, though, he had been employed in a prison as an overseer of handicrafts. There he developed an interest in, and detailed knowledge of, various crafts and household products such as soaps, waxes, and drain repair. When he went to *Shen pao* he introduced a special column called "common knowledge" *(ch'ang shih)* which became a great favorite with readers. Later the contents of the column were published as a book entitled *Household Common Knowledge (Chia-t'ing ch'ang shih)* which, in fact, outsold most of his fiction. Ch'en's expertise along these lines allowed him to take advantage of a rare opportunity in the late 1910s. Toothpowder was one of the "new-style" attractions in Shanghai, where the market had been dominated by two brands, Diamond Toothpowder (Chin-kang-shih ya-fen) and Lion Toothpowder (Shih-tzu ya-fen). Both brands were Japanese. Following Japan's Twenty-one Demands on China in 1915, when an effective anti-Japanese boycott in Shanghai cut off the market for Diamond and Lion toothpowder, Ch'en saw the chance for an industrial use of his reputation for household common sense. His Peerless Facial and Tooth Powder (Wu-ti p'ai ts'a-mien ya-fen) — two uses for the same powder — was a great success. Shortly thereafter he went into the manufacture of hand cream, soap, and eventually cement. He gave up writing. When he died he was the owner of forty-two factories and a very wealthy man.[7]

Success on the literary scene brought writers not only fame and fortune but contact with the social elite as well. Pao T'ien-hsiao, a central figure among the popular authors of the 1910s, got an early start in building such contacts when he helped to run *Shih pao's* social club the "Resting Place" in the years immediately preceding 1911. The "Resting Place" was frequented by a group of reformists and revolutionaries whose abilities spanned journalism, education, finance, industry and transportation. After 1911 many of them assumed high government posts in these areas. For years they maintained their friendships with Pao and other fiction writers. They included, for example, Shih Liang-ts'ai of *Shen pao;* Lin K'ang-hou, principal of the

---

7. YYHTP, pp. 177, 399 – 400, 479 – 480; interview with Ch'en Ting-shan, July 25, 1973. Ch'en Ting-shan reports that his father's pen name "T'ien hsu wo sheng" is an allusion to the seventh line of Li Po's poem "Chiang chin chiu" which reads "t'ien sheng wo ts'ai pi yu yung" (roughly, "since Heaven has given me life, it must be put to use"); in this case Ch'en's pen name was self-effacing, meaning something like "the one whom Heaven produced in vain."

Nan-yang Kung-hsueh's primary school and later manager of the Shanghai-Hangchow Railroad; Kung Tzu-ying, a leading Shanghai gold merchant, editor of the late Ch'ing magazine *New New Fiction (Hsin hsin hsiao-shuo)* and, after the revolution, Finance Agency head for Kiangsu Province; Wu Huai-chiu, Shanghai's most energetic and effective proponent of girls' schools during the early Republic; and Chu Shao-p'ing, educator, veteran of the T'ung-meng hui, founder of the "International Chinese Students' Association" (Huan-ch'iu Chung-kuo t'ung-hsueh hui) which helped worthy students finance overseas study, manager of the literary "Southern Society" (Nan she) and later Vice Consul in the Chinese Embassy to the Philippines.[8]

In 1912 the political leadership in Shanghai publishing shifted to *Shen pao* and away from *Shih pao* and its "Resting Place." But Pao T'ien-hsiao, who stayed at *Shih pao* and worked with young writers, continued to maintain his friendships in elite circles and to introduce others into them. Because of the popularity of "scandal novels," officials and financiers had reason to stay on good terms with popular writers. They found various ways to do this. For example when Pao T'ien-hsiao wrote his "education novels" at the Commercial Press, Yuan Kuan-lan, another old friend from the "Resting Place" and currently Deputy Minister of Education in the Republican government, was instrumental in recommending government prizes for Pao.[9]

In some cases the presence of fiction writers in leading circles encouraged highly-placed persons themselves to turn to fiction. Ho Hai-ming, for example, was a revolutionary journalist and soldier before 1911. He had worked under Yü Yu-jen on the anti-Manchu newspapers *Min hu pao* and *Min li pao,* and for these efforts had been jailed for three months. In 1913 he was sent to Nanking as the city's top military officer. There he participated in Huang Hsing's "Second Revolution" against Yuan Shih-k'ai, and fled with Huang to Japan when the effort was crushed. Upon returning from Japan he retired from politics and the military to devote himself to writing amusement fiction, especially stories about prostitutes. He published primarily in the love-story magazine *Elements of People's Rights,* where political figures such as Tai Chi-t'ao also contributed. Ho's major works, very well regarded by his peers, were *The Old Lute Player (Lao ch'in-shih)* and *Record of Marrying Out of the Pleasure Quarters (Ch'ang-men sung-chia lu).*[10]

8. CYLHIL, pp. 329–331.
9. CYLHIL, p. 329.
10. YYHTP, pp. 456–457; interviews with Ch'en Ting-shan (note 4 above), and with Kao Chen-pai, April 26, 1973.

Yeh Ch'u-ts'ang is well known as an anti-Manchu revolutionary, an editor of the *Min-kuo jih-pao,* Director of the Kuomintang Propaganda Department, and KMT Party Secretary. But under the name Yeh Hsiao-feng, he was also widely known in the 1910s as a fiction writer who contributed regularly to *Saturday, Grand Magazine* and other entertainment magazines. He wrote mostly "social novels" with a humorous bent; one of the best-known was *A History of the Alleyways (Lung-t'ang hsiao-shih),* which is said to be an hilarious description of Shanghai society from a cobbler's point of view.[11]

Writers who had achieved social recognition, whether through fiction or other means, typically scorned those who wrote purely for money. Some almost routinely included disclaimers of a commercial motive in the opening chapters of their stories. They cast aspersions, without mentioning names, on writers who would "casually whip together some junk" in order to "live off the pen." In all of this they closely followed traditional attitudes towards writing, claiming for themselves the unsullied status of "literary man" *(wen-jen).*

This image of the "literary man" took several interesting forms among writers of the 1910s. The basic pose, which many a writer carefully cultivated, was that of the "genius of the foreign mall" *(yang-ch'ang ts'ai-tzu):* an ailing, grief-stricken young man, who lived a solitary life in the possession of inexpressibly profound talents, but who was appreciated only by one or two beautiful courtesans. Newspapers encouraged such role-playing by claiming to draw "wizardly abilities" from mysterious litterateurs, and by running advertisements to study fiction-writing with one or another "great literary genius."[12]

Though the notion of the *ts'ai-tzu* is centuries old in China, its peculiar fascination for writers in the 1910s stemmed from the examples of certain well-known late Ch'ing writers. Wu Wo-yao, famous for his "sentiment" novels, was one of these, as was Sun Chia-chen chronicler of the brothel scene. From a different angle, Yen Fu undoubtedly contributed to the image. Yen's temperamental disposition lent him the air of genius in the eyes of many who found his Western learning beyond the pale of comprehension. One wonders, in fact, whether Yen did not consciously work on his image. Through the late Ch'ing years, he wore gold wire-rimmed glasses, broken on one side and bound up with black thread. His manuscripts were meticulously neat—in black ink, with the traditional bright red for amendments. He talked in slow, measured tones with a perfectly clear Peking accent,

11. YYHTP, pp. 512–513; letter to the author from Ch'en Ting-shan, August 11, 1973.
12. YYHTP, p. 71.

even though he was a native of Fukien. His manner, in Pao T'ien-hsiao's phrase, was "Bohemian" *(ming-shih p'ai).* [13]

But the most important late Ch'ing model of the "foreign mall genius" was probably Tseng P'u. Tseng wrote under the pen name "The Invalid of East Asia" *(Tung-ya ping-fu)* with a double meaning — as a comment on China's plight and as a description of his own health. He lived separate from his family in the upstairs portion of his *Forest of Fiction* office, where he labored over his masterpiece *Flower on a Sea of Evil* and other manuscripts. A regular opium smoker, his work-style was to revise and re-revise, working late into the night and sometimes until dawn. When he did retire he often slept until three or four in the afternoon, and upon arising needed opium in order to retrieve an adequate mental state for meeting people, conducting business, or beginning to write again. [14]

Though the "genius of the foreign mall" was a kind of general model for young popular authors, there certainly were no rules about particulars. Indeed, a certain non-conformity was valued, and writers often cast themselves as one or another kind of eccentric. The life-style of Hsiang K'ai-jan, whose knight-errant novel *Chronicle of the Strange Roving Knights* was the most widely-circulated novel of the 1920s, is a good example. Hsiang made his name in the 1910s (his pen name was *P'ing-chiang pu-hsiao sheng,* the "Unworthy Son of P'ing-chiang") with his exposé of the decadence of Chinese students in Japan entitled *An Unofficial History of Overseas Study in Japan.* Though this novel quickly became famous, Hsiang had been unknown before its publication and had had difficulty selling the manuscript. His highest bid had been only 50 cents per thousand characters. He sold the manuscript at that rate but afterwards, as if miffed, disappeared. Though it was suspected he had returned to Hunan, one day a fellow writer, Chang Ming-fei, discovered him living in a tiny second floor apartment on a back street in Shanghai called "Elegance Alley" (Ssu-wen li). He shared the apartment with his mistress, a dog, and a monkey. Hsiang appeared to have a very happy, bantering relationship with his mistress, but complained that he lost too much time in settling fights between the dog and the monkey. True to the rule for geniuses of the foreign mall, he smoked opium and slept late. After Chang Ming-fei's visit, he made it known that other writers could visit him, but only in the late afternoon. When they came, he was a very warm host. Before long he was persuaded to return to the fold of writing fiction, this time at standard and proper rates of pay. His first two pieces upon returning were a

13. CYLHIL, pp. 219, 222, and 228.
14. CYLHIL, p. 326.

sequel to *An Unofficial History of Overseas Study in Japan* plus a novel called *Incidental Notes of a Hunter (Lieh-jen ou chi)* which was based on his experience tiger-hunting in Hunan and which established him in yet another way as an inimitable addition to the literary scene. Hsiang wrote his manuscripts on extra long paper and in tiny characters. While most writers wrote 400–500 characters per page, Hsiang typically totaled 150 or more per *line,* each line perfectly straight and vertical.[15]

Often a writer's personal image would fit the nature of his fiction. Indeed, as viewed by the community of writers, there was no sharp distinction between a writer's life and work. Each was an extension of the other. The childlike playfulness of Hsu Cho-tai, for example, was as much in his life-style as in his stories: he encouraged the reputation that, at age 43, he actually looked only 33, wrote stories which seemed written by a 23-year-old, joked with the lightheartedness of someone 13, and, if he really tried, could make himself up and effectively imitate the speech and laughter of a 3-year-old.[16] Li Han-ch'iu, on the other hand, developed an image which might be called "genius country bumpkin." His very popular, ten-volume social novel *Tides of Yangchow (Kuang-ling ch'ao)* was a social portrait of the Yangchow society Li grew up in. But unlike other popular writers, Li did not move to Shanghai and was largely unfamiliar with treaty port culture or, for that matter, with anything outside of Yangchow. When he made his first trip to Shanghai in the late 1910s, his pen was already famous enough that people peered and pointed from a distance at the tall, slender genius from the hinterland. But when shown to his hotel, Li stayed in character by pretending not to know what an elevator was, complaining upon entering that he could not accept such a small room.[17]

Writers always had several pen names. Originally the purpose of a pen name had been, at least in part, to protect a writer from society's scorn. In the 1910s, however, the function of pen names for the new professional writers became almost entirely one of projecting individual images. Names such as "House of the Bracelet Shadow" *(ch'uan ying lou),* "Ink-chewing Hut" *(chueh mo lu)* and "Residence of Red Ice and Green Blood" *(hung-ping pi-hsueh kuan)* were intended not only to attract notice but also to indicate something the writer felt to be significant in his character.[18]

---

15. CYLHIL, p. 383; YYHTP, pp. 505–506.
16. YYHTP, p. 461.
17. CYLHIL:HP, p. 60.
18. Cheng I-mei, in YYHTP, pp. 144–147; CYLHIL, pp. 193–197. "Green blood," in the last example given, is a well-known symbol for patriotism or loyalty, and perhaps would be better translated that way.

2. Groups

While the aim of all this fashioning of character was individualism and distinctiveness, it was an individualism whose value depended upon group participation. The people for whose scrutiny and enjoyment writers presented their images were, at least in the 1910s, other writers as much as the reading public. Almost all the writers knew each other and participated in formal and informal associations. They would meet to share one another's company in teahouses, banquet halls, wineshops, and theaters.

The main groups of writers were gathered around major publishing organs and under the patronage of leading figures. Pao T'ien-hsiao at *Shih pao,* Ch'en Tieh-hsien at *Shen pao,* and Wang Tun-ken, first at *Shen pao* and then at *Saturday,* were senior figures around whom the rest centered. Unlike the literary factions of May Fourth, these groups in the 1910s were not antagonistic toward one another. Perhaps they had little to disagree about; they managed to share manuscripts, banquets, and fun. We review the main groupings below.

Pao T'ien-hsiao's following was built upon what remained of *Shih pao* after most of that newspaper's best personnel, including novelist Ch'en Ching-han, moved to *Shen pao* in 1921. Pao's "Surplus Spirit" *(yü-hsing)* column attracted a number of young writers, mostly ten to twenty years Pao's junior, and from these Pao picked his regular contributors. His highest praise went to Pi I-hung who wrote social novels like *Hell on Earth (Jen-chien ti-yü),* a portrait of Shanghai society. Pi was hired on *Shih pao*'s regular staff. Other, less regular contributors included: humorist Hsu Cho-tai; Chang I-han, who co-authored several works with Pao; Chiang Hung-chiao, a love-story specialist who could effectively imitate the tone of *Dream of the Red Chamber;* Chou Shou-chüan, who began by translating from the Japanese and grew to become an influential fiction editor at *Shen pao* in the twenties; and Fan Yen-ch'iao, a successful teacher and administrator in the "new-style" schools of Soochow, who left education to be a Shanghai writer, literary historian, and important entrepreneur in popular fiction.[19]

It was true of most groups of popular writers, but perhaps especially of this following of Pao's, that personal relationships cemented professional ones. Chiang Hung-chiao was a cousin of Pao's wife, and Pao was best man at Chou Shou-chüan's wedding.[20] When Pi I-hung met an untimely death in his early thirties, Pao immediately adopted

19. Yao Min-ai, in YYHTP, pp. 148–149; CYLHIL, p. 359; CYLHIL:HP, pp. 42–64; interview with Wu Hsing-tsai, June 23, 1973.
20. CYLHIL, p. 381; CYLHIL:HP, p. 54.

one of his eight children and saw to the proper care of the others.[21] Pao
had met Chang I-han's mother before meeting Chang. She was an
educated widow who supported her small family by translating English novels, and Pao published some of the translations. I-han, as a
twelve-year-old son, would deliver the manuscripts back and forth.
Since he also knew English, he began translating, and then writing his
own fiction, which Pao helped him edit and rewrite.[22] It is hardly
stretching a point to say that Pao was a kind of surrogate father for
most of his group, as most had lost their natural fathers early: Chang
in infancy, Chou at age five, Hsu at six, and Chiang at nine. Pao's own
father died when Pao was sixteen. All but two of the group were from
Soochow. Pi was from Hangchow, and Chang, the infant orphan, was
Cantonese from Shanghai.[23]

Pao's patronage grew beyond the *Shih pao* circle when he stepped
outside it to edit *Grand Magazine* (*Hsiao-shuo ta-kuan*, 1915–1921) and
Weekly (*Hsing-ch'i*, 1922–1923). His regular contributors to these magazines included, in addition to the *Shih pao* group: Yeh Hsiao-feng (i.e.,
Yeh Ch'u-ts'ang, the KMT politician); Yao Yuan-ch'u, who wrote historical novels and later became a Kiangsu provincial secretary; and Yao
Su-feng, who began by writing miscellaneous filler pieces and in the
1930s became a well-known movie producer.[24]

A second group formed around the "Unfettered Talk" fiction column at *Shen pao*. The column was created in 1911 by Wang Tun-ken,
an old friend from Soochow of *Shen pao* editor Hsi Yü-fu. After a few
months Wang collected his own contributions to the column and tried
publishing them separately as two issues of *Unfettered Talk Magazine*
(*Tzu-yu tsa-chih*). The reader response to this effort was so encouraging that Wang decided to spend most of his time planning magazines
and enlisting younger talent. He began *Recreation Magazine* (*Yu-hsi
tsa-chih*) in 1913 and *Saturday* (*Li-pai-liu*) in 1914. His group of young
writers grew to the point where it divided, in basically a friendly way,
into what may be considered two or three subgroups. Wang resigned
from *Shen pao* to become the first editor of *Saturday*, while the "Unfettered Talk" column continued to be run by Wang's friends and pro-
tégés, most importantly Ch'en Tieh-hsien, who became its editor in
1916. Ch'en, the "Butterfly Immortal," continued to build the *Shen pao*
following by hiring one of his sons, Ch'en Hsiao-tieh ("Little But-

21. CYLHIL:HP, pp. 62–64.

22. CYLHIL, p. 359; and in YYHTP, pp. 126–127.

23. CYLHIL, p. 117; YYHTP, pp. 126, 455, 457, 460 and 464.

24. CYLHIL, pp. 377 and 382; YYHTP, pp. 477–478; interview with Liu Chieh,
April 23, 1973.

terfly"), on the regular staff. He also accepted contributions from a second son, Ch'en Tz'u-tieh ("Next Butterfly").[25]

Meanwhile, *Saturday* under Wang Tun-ken became very popular with both readers and writers. It attracted a varied and loyal group of talent, authors of love stories, social novels, detective novels, and many other types, who became famous as the "Saturday School" *(Li-pai-liu p'ai)*. These included Chou Shou-chüan, who by the mid-1910s had ventured from under the wing of his mentor Pao T'ien-hsiao to become a most active figure in the "Saturday School"; Hu Chi-ch'en, an Anhwei native well educated in classical literature, who taught poetry at three Shanghai colleges and wrote social novels and humor stories which often carried an other-worldly flavor of Taoism or Zen;[26] and Yeh Sheng-t'ao, who became famous after May Fourth for his *Schoolmaster Ni Huan-chih* and other stories about the lives of "new-style" teachers, but who in the 1910s wrote love stories. Ch'en Hsiao-tieh, while working at *Shen pao,* was also a regular contributor to *Saturday.*

Another group, small but distinct, with which the "Saturday School" and the *Shen pao* group shared some overlap, was the "Elements of People's Rights" group. The strange name for this group was, like the others, taken from its major publishing organ, in this case a magazine called *Elements of People's Rights (Min-ch'üan su).* The magazine was an outgrowth of a political newspaper called *People's Rights (Min-ch'üan pao),* founded in 1912, edited by Tai Chi-t'ao and managed by Chou Shao-heng. It was an organ of the revolutionary Liberty Party *(Tzu-yu tang).* Yet, in the tradition of the *Su pao,* it balanced its very serious political fare with an amusement section on the back page. Some of the most famous love story writers in the 1910s got their start with it as editors of its entertainment section, in which both Hsu Chen-ya's *Jade Pear Spirit* and Li Ting-i's *A Beauty's Blessings (Mei-jen fu)* were first serialized.[27]

In 1914 *People's Rights Journal* incurred the wrath of Yuan Shih-k'ai and was severely limited in all departments except its love stories. The trouble began with a pictorial supplement to *People's Rights Journal* in which cartoonist Ch'ien Ping-ho (who was also a popular author) did a series of sketches portraying Yuan Shih-k'ai as an ape and making use of the pun on *yuan* ("ape"). Later, when Sung Chiao-jen was assas-

25. YYHTP, pp. 399, 453 and 479–480; interview with Ch'en Ting-shan (Ch'en Hsiao-tieh), July 25, 1973; Ch'en Ching-chih, "Li-pai-liu p'ai ti hsing-ch'i ho shuai-lo," *Ch'ang-liu* 42.10 (January 1, 1971): 16.

26. YYHTP, pp. 476–477.

27. Ch'en Tieh-i, "Hsu Chen-ya yü *Yü-li hun*" (1), *Hsing-tao jih-pao,* October 29, 1973, p. 6; Fan Tzu, "Yuan-yang hu-tieh p'ai hsiao-shuo-chia ch'ün hsiang," *Hsing-tao chou pao,* July 14, 1972, p. 10.

sinated and many people suspected it had been done at Yuan's behest, *People's Rights Journal* began a special column called "Recalling the Soul" *(chao hun chi)* in which Sung was eulogized and Yuan further impugned. At this point Yuan issued an order forbidding that *People's Rights Journal* be sold or passed through the Chinese postal facilities. The newspaper was thus effectively limited to the foreign concessions of Shanghai, and soon thereafter it closed down.[28]

But the monthly magazine *Elements of People's Rights* survived under the close supervision—and probably the approval—of Yuan Shih-k'ai's censors. It began by republishing works from the fiction columns of past issues of *People's Rights Journal,* and later had new works by the same group of authors. Yuan apparently calculated that classical-style love stories would have the effect of dampening the public's tendency to protest. If so, his view on this point coincided exactly with that of May Fourth writers in the 1920s, who singled out the "Elements of People's Rights" group of authors for particular scorn: their endless diversion into saccharine sentimentality would get China nowhere. The standard bearer of the "Elements" group was Hsu Chen-ya, author of *Jade Pear Spirit.* Other leaders in the group were Hsu's older brother, Hsu T'ien-hsiao; Wu Shuang-je, a friend of the Hsu brothers from their childhood in Ch'ang-shu, whose pen name "Double Hotness" signified a wish for warmth of both heart and blood; and Li Ting-i, originally a top student at the Nan-yang Kung-hsueh and author of *A Beauty's Blessings* and other romantic stories, whose acclaim stood second in this group only to those of Hsu Chen-ya.[29]

Perhaps because demand for entertainment fiction remained safely in excess of what the writers of these several groups could supply, rivalry among them was relaxed. Magazines proliferated, and most authors published freely here and there. The "schools" described above had no formal rules or membership criteria.

There were a few more formal affiliations among popular writers in the form of writers' societies. The original model for these was the Southern Society (Nan she), which began soon after 1900 in Shanghai as a small group of revolutionary and reformist writers who would meet informally for an occasional meal and exchange of company. The Southern Society grew in size year by year, until "membership"— which required the unanimous support of current members—became necessary, as did a post of "secretary" to handle red tape. Each year

28. Ch'en Tieh-i, "Hsu Chen-ya yü *Yü-li hun*" (2), *Hsing-tao jih-pao,* October 30, 1973; Fan Tzu, "Yuan-yang hu-tieh p'ai ch'ün hsiang."

29. Yao Min-ai, in YYHTP, p. 148; YYHTP, pp. 287–288, 407–408, 478, 491–493, and 510–511; interview with Yeh Ling-feng, April 28, 1973.

there was a general convocation, which usually met at a Shanghai restaurant but occasionally in Soochow, at Tiger Hill or on the flower boats. Reflecting the trend of late Ch'ing fiction generally, the Southern Society gradually drifted away from its political convictions and towards entertainment writing. Pao T'ien-hsiao had been an early member of the group, and by the late 1910s other leading popular writers, including Fan Yen-ch'iao, Yeh Hsiao-feng, Hu Chi-ch'en and Yao Yuan-ch'u, had also joined. By the late 1910s, the Society's publications were filled with love stories indistinguishable from those of the straight entertainment magazines. Su Man-shu, a long-standing Southern Society member, was an important link between the Society and the entertainment writers. He became acquainted with Pao T'ien-hsiao, Pi I-hung, Yao Yuan-ch'u and Hu Chi-ch'en, and occasionally joined them in drink and revelry. But to most of the writers he remained a shadowy figure, the strange image of a half-Japanese, Western-suit-wearing, shaven-headed romantic author-cum-monk who inspired one from a distance.[30]

The arrival of the May Fourth literary movement, with its Association for Literary Studies (Wen-hsueh yen-chiu hui), Creation Society (Ch'uang-tsao she) and many other formally constituted groups, was further impetus for popular writers to create their own associations. In 1922 two groups were formed. The Green Society (Ch'ing she) was founded in Shanghai on the general pattern of the Southern Society. Its members numbered over twenty and included Pao T'ien-hsiao, Wang Tun-ken, Chou Shou-chüan, Li Han-ch'iu, Pi I-hung, Ho Hai-ming, Hu Chi-ch'en, Chiang Hung-chiao, Hsu Cho-tai and Fan Yen-ch'iao—all of whom have been identified in this chapter—plus Yen Tu-ho, editor of *Hsin-wen pao*'s fiction column in the 1920s, and Ch'eng Hsiao-ch'ing, China's leading detective story writer. Activities of the group consisted of meeting once a week for a banquet and publishing a weekly bulletin called *Evergreen (Ch'ang-ch'ing)*. Membership required a sponsor, a published full-length novel, and the approval of the other members. After meeting only twice, however, the Green Society began to fall apart. One of the reasons for its failure was that certain members objected to the restrictive entrance requirements. Another reason concerned group solidarity. When a leading fiction magazine called *Happiness (K'uai-huo)* began a policy of remunerating member authors at differing rates of pay, some in the Green Society called for a united stand against the magazine. Others declined, and dissension ensued.[31]

30. CYLHIL, pp. 352–354; CYLHIL:HP, pp. 47–48; YYHTP, p. 399; YYHTP, pp. 95–97; Fan Yen-ch'iao, in YYHTP, p. 178.
    31. Fan Yen-ch'iao, in YYHTP, p. 265; YYHTP, p. 424.

Greater longevity and success were achieved by the Star Society (Hsing she), founded in July 1922, one month after the Green Society. Composed primarily of writers from Soochow, it was organized by love story artist Chao Mien-yun, and its early leaders included Fan Yen-ch'iao, Ch'eng Hsiao-ch'ing, Yao Su-feng and Cheng I-mei. Like the Green Society, they saw themselves as following the pattern of the Southern Society, but, unlike the Green Society, had no charter or membership rules. Most members were from Soochow, but others were welcome. They met once a month to enjoy the culinary and conversational arts, to play games and so on, electing each year two of their number to handle the Society's business. Their numbers grew year by year, and in 1937, the year of their last formal meeting, totaled around a hundred. After 1937 the urgencies of the Japanese war directed attention elsewhere and the group gradually dissolved. A number of Star Society publications appeared over the years under such names as *Star Journal (Hsing pao), Starlight (Hsing kuang), Star (Hsing)* and *Sea of Constellations (Hsing-hsiu hai)*.[32]

Finally, account must be taken of a group of popular writers in Tientsin and Peking known as the "Northern School" (Pei p'ai). Developing a few years later than the literary groups in Shanghai, but following their patterns in almost every way, the Northern School was very small in the 1910s and grew slowly in the 1920s. It grew more quickly in the 1930s and—unlike its Shanghai counterpart—flourished in the late thirties and forties as the Japanese-sponsored government encouraged popular fiction for reasons of political control. Leaders of the Northern School in the twenties, both gifted writers, were Ch'en Shen-yen and Chang Hen-shui. Ch'en was a Fukienese returned-student from France who gave up naval science to write scandal novels in the Peking *Ch'en pao*. His most famous work was entitled *Unspeakable (Shuo pu te)*. Chang's reputation, made during the twenties on *Unofficial History of Ch'un-ming (Ch'un-ming wai-shih)* had spread to Shanghai and elsewhere by the 1930s, when he was thought of more as a national figure than as one of the Northern School. Other Northern School figures in the thirties and forties included Wang Tu-lu and Liu Yün-jo, both of whom wrote dozens of vernacular-style love stories. But the main fare of the Northern School turned out to be knight-errant novels. In this line they produced three masters whose skill and popularity were matched in the Shanghai group only by Hsiang K'ai-jan, i.e., Chao Huan-t'ing, author of *Chronicle of the Strange Knights of Unflinching Loyalty (Ch'i-hsia ching-chung chuan)* and known as "the Hsiang K'ai-jan of the North"; Cheng

---

32. Fan Yen-ch'iao, in YYHTP, pp. 265–266; Pao T'ien-hsiao, in YYHTP, pp. 126–127; Ho Ta (pseud. Ning Yuan), in YYHTP, pp. 124–126.

Cheng-yin, whose tales of just retribution numbered at least in the eighties; and Li Shou-min, whose *Swordsmen of the Szechwan Hills (Shu-shan chien-hsia)*, written under the pen-name Huan-chu lou-chu, was probably the best seller of the half-century in the Peking-Tientsin area.[33]

3. Outlook

In the 1930s and forties, when the Northern School reached its highpoint, popular writing had become a highly commercialized endeavor. Authors thought of their stories as market products, and large circulation was an object. But in the 1910s and early twenties, the spirit of group participation in various formal and informal associations was at least as important an incentive as the commercial one. Writers imitated, praised and advised one another. The publication of a substantial work from a major author could be prefaced by as many as ten or twenty introductions or poems by other authors. Some works were coauthored. Of the many literary games the authors played, one was called the "crazy quilt novel" *(chi-chin hsiao-shuo)* in which each chapter was written by a different member of a certain group. The popular "officers' roll call" *(tien chiang)* method of playing the game allowed each participant to determine who would write the next chapter by using that author's pen name in the last line of his own contribution. For example, chapter three of the love story *Moon on the Sea (Hai-shang yueh)*, which was published serially in the "Forest of Lightheartedness" column of *Hsin-wen pao,* concludes with the following lines in description of its youthful protagonist: " . . . the early morning breeze brushed across his face as he watched the last few stars twinkling in the east. The roar of thunder could still be heard, but the violent wind was now nothing but a distant, angry roar."[34] Here the two characters "east" *(tung)* and "thunder" *(lei)* are juxtaposed—in separate phrases, which was the custom—thereby obliging Ch'en Tung-lei ("Eastern thunder") to write chapter four of the story.

It is noteworthy that the "officers' roll call" game was as popular with readers as with the authors themselves. For many authors, in fact, the author-reader relationship became as gratifying as author-author relationships. Readers were asked to join essay contests, to help judge them, or to send in letters with suggestions, appraisals, or questions about particular works. Authors and editors prided themselves on the strength of their hold on readers, and in their fashioning of public

33. Fan Yen-ch'iao, in YYHTP, p. 272; interview with Ma Meng, April 19, 1973; interview with Chao Ts'ung, June 13, 1973.
34. As quoted in Fan Yen-ch'iao, in YYHTP, p. 262.

images liked to claim a personal magnetism strong enough to prevent any reader, once he had joined their following, from ever leaving it. This kind of wish, though expressed in almost every issue of every popular fiction magazine in the 1910s, was perhaps most concisely phrased in an advertising slogan of *Saturday* which read, with a catchy seven-character-per-line gait, "I would rather not take a concubine/ Than miss out once on *Saturday* (*ning-yuan pu ch'ü hsiao lao-p'o, pu-neng pu tu* Li-pai-liu).

The penchant for joking among the authors' groups of the 1910s also could apply to the author-reader relationship. Some cases of trickery with readers became famous, and helped fuel interest by giving readers a sense of participation. One such case involved Ch'en Tieh-hsien, who used to evaluate the quality of manuscripts submitted to his *Shen pao* column using grades of "A," "B" and "C." One day he received a piece which a reader claimed was his own but in reality was a little-known essay by the great T'ang master Liu Tsung-yuan. Not recognizing the piece, and finding it rather dull, Ch'en assigned it a "C" grade, only to have his mischievous reader advertise the mistake by writing to the *Shen pao* letter column. Who is an A, the reader enquired, if Liu Tsung-yuan is a C?[35]

Very few women ventured into the writing or editing of fiction in the 1910s. The only significant exception was Kao Chien-hua, wife of popular writer Hsu Hsiao-t'ien and editor of the monthly magazine *Eyebrow Signals (Mei yü)* between 1914 and 1916. Kao Chien-hua was a *pro forma* editor, however, whose real purpose was to attract attention to the idea of the new-style woman in a magazine written mostly for men. The magazine also included stories ostensibly written by women but in fact, because women writers were so few (or not known), written by men under feminine pseudonyms. One such contributor was Ku Ming-tao, whose novel of the early thirties *Female Knight of the Wild Rivers (Huang-chiang nü-hsia)* was to become a best-seller. Ku Ming-tao's stories in *Eyebrow Signals* elicited a great number of readers' letters, mostly from men addressing him as a woman. Ku, whose habit it was to respond to letters according to the sex in which he was addressed, exchanged enough letters with a certain reader that the reader finally proposed marriage. Only then did Ku divulge the truth, and the anecdote became public testimony to the power and versatility of his pen.[36]

Playfulness was only one symptom of a basic attitude of detachment many writers shared. The attitude is remarkable, considering the context of strife, national emergency, rapid social change, and cultural

35. YYHTP, pp. 399–400.
36. YYHTP, p. 290.

heterogeneity from which it came. But it certainly was not due to a failure to notice the environment. The close ties between the modern press and writers' groups prevented them from losing touch with the news. Some of them were in fact frustrated politicians whose greatest pleasure was to write "scandal novels" satirizing those who had rejected them. (It was thanks to these writers that the "mosquito" press could thrive without paying much for manuscripts.)[37] But even authors with no axe to grind in the public arena were well aware of their environment. They clearly enjoyed displaying in their writing, and in conversation, too, a detailed knowledge of contemporary life at all levels and stations of society. They sought, it seems, to stay acquainted with everything, but detached from anything in particular. For them "leisure *(hsien)*" was more than just left-over time; it was relaxed equilibrium at all times, a total life ideal. They liked to compare themselves with the similarly detached attitudes of poets and thinkers of the past. Hu Chi-ch'en was an admirer of Chuang-tzu, and T'ao Yuanming was one of Chou Shou-chüan's idols.[38]

Yet it is all-important to remember that calm detachment was an ideal, perhaps especially valued precisely because of its difficulty of attainment. One must, to a certain extent, view the popular writers' detachment as a contrivance, at once the expression of an ideal and an escape from harsh reality. Most of the authors, after all, were traditionally-educated but deprived of traditional honors, migrant to the modern foreign-ruled city, and tainted in the view of their families. Some were fatherless, and many were financially insecure though obliged to live in plain sight of ostentatious wealth. They had, in short, very understandable worries and frustrations beneath their placid facades. And there can be little doubt that their readership shared their anxieties. We shall argue in chapter six that stories about tragic lovers or the unmasking of corruption were part of a general quest for comfort in an uncomfortable time.

It may be clearer that the detached attitude of writers had complex origins when one considers another common feature of their personalities — their pervasive sentimentalism. The authors loved to express romantic feelings about poetry, nature, and women; the connection between these feelings and playful detachment was, as they conceived it (or liked to say they conceived it), a kind of ideal cause and effect. One's detachment from mundane affairs cleared one's head, as it were, for a full appreciation of mountains and clouds; of flowers and goldfish (Soochow was a center for flower and goldfish ex-

---

37. Interview with Ch'en Ting-shan, July 25, 1973; YYHTP, p. 414.
38. Chou Shou-chüan, *Hua-ch'ien so-chi,* p. 68.

hibitions in which many writers participated); and the joys and sorrows—mostly sorrows—of the emotion-laden *(to-ch'ing)* beauties and geniuses of the world. Writers used poetry, in real life as well as in fiction, to capture the singular, bittersweet beauty of an occasion. During the Anti-Japanese War Chou Shou-chüan was obliged to flee to southern Anhwei, where he frequently was struck with nostalgia for his native Soochow; once, upon suddenly recalling his goldfish there, he sat down and wrote out ten stanzas of regulated verse.[39]

Often, however, such things as poetry and goldfish were insufficiently comforting, and writers relied upon prostitutes as well. Beyond providing comfort and emotional release, brothels were important to 1910s writers in several concrete ways. First of all, along with restaurants and teahouses, brothels were one of the authors' meeting grounds for general conviviality. (Brotheling did not have to involve sex, nor did it carry a strong social stigma, especially for someone who had already started on the dubious road of fiction writing. As a young child in Soochow, for example, Pao T'ien-hsiao's father introduced him to the "flower boats" of Soochow—and to an opium den as well—but during the same years forbade him to read *Dream of the Red Chamber.*)[40]

Second, the beauties of the pleasure quarter who became companions of individual writers were important in the writers' fashioning of Bohemian or "moody genius" personal images. They served as foils to the genius nature as well as being the only people who truly understood it. Some writers were loyal to the same ladies for years, and many love stories were written "with a certain person in mind."

Third, the authors took an almost sociological interest in the brothel scene, surveying conditions and classifying results, as part of their general claim to be familiar with all aspects of society. The brothels of the lower Yangtze region, one learns, were serviced by two major groups, the Soochow group *(Su pang),* which covered the eastern region including Shanghai, and the Yangchow group *(Yang pang),* which covered the western portion including Nanking. All the cities naturally had one or more distinctive colloquialism to refer to the brothel scene. In Soochow "nine-tailed turtle" *(chiu-wei kuei)* followed the usage of the late Ch'ing novel by the same name; in Peking "the eight great alleyways" *(pa ta hu-t'ung)* was standard; in Shanghai, the Soochow group masqueraded as the "story telling apartments" *(shuo-shu yü).* The various roles of entertainers were differentiated using elaborate terminology based on the distinction of "flowers" *(hua)* for prostitutes

39. Ibid., p. 55.
40. CYLHIL, pp. 47, 50 and 59.

and "leaves" *(yeh)* for the younger girls who assisted by serving tea and smiling.[41] One of the most comprehensive attempts to account for the whole picture was Yao Yuan-ch'u's *Lonely Vessel on a Sea of Woe (Hen-hai ku chou chi)*, a rambling description of emotional attachments and partings among litterateurs and beauties in Shanghai, Nanking, Peking, Harbin and several other cities. It would be too much to argue that the brothel scene determined which types of fiction were popular in the 1910s. But it is true, perhaps fortunately for the authors, that love stories, scandal stories, detective stories, humor, and social portraits could all be made up with the brothel scene as background.

In writing social novels in the tradition of the "castigatory novels" of the late Ch'ing, authors were able to claim a formal shell of respectability for brothel literature. Throughout the 1910s, and even into the twenties and thirties, authors pointed to the theoretical need to reveal the sick side of society in order to heal it. As late as the fifties, Chou Shou-chüan recalled that *Saturday* opposed "the wanton violence of warlords, the tyranny of the family system, and the lack of freedom of marriage."[42] And certain works were indeed worthy of the "castigatory" tradition. Chou Shou-chüan's own *Diary of a Subjugated People* is a patriotic attack on Japan's Twenty-one Demands which was widely reprinted both in 1915 and in 1919, after the May Fourth incident. Yün T'ieh-ch'iao's "The Story of a Laborer" *(Kung-jen hsiao-shih)* exposes the cruel usage of a peasant-turned-worker by capitalists in Shanghai. The justification for brothel stories in particular was sometimes that they exposed the famous or powerful among the clientele of prostitutes. But more commonly the argument rested on sympathy for the prostitutes themselves, who were forced to solicit business every day, who were mistreated by the brothel owners, whose family life suffered in every conceivable way, and so on. In most cases these "progressive" elements were a travesty of progressivism, so thoroughly were they combined with interest in romance and sex. A few stories resembled Ch'ing sex manuals. The true functions of their progressive veneer were two: first, like garnish for the main feast, to lend a twinge of contemporary stylishness to a basic age-old appeal; and second, as far as was possible, to salvage a semblance of respectability.

This two-sided attitude towards prostitution—horrible yet fun—is well exemplified in the novels of Pi I-hung, who, comparatively speaking, took quite seriously the need to expose the condition of brothels. In real life Pi enjoyed a long and loyal romance with a young entertainment lady, who had been introduced to him by Su Man-shu, and

41. CYLHIL, pp. 216 and 367; interviews with Soong Ch'i, April 13, 1973, and with Pao T'ien-hsiao, December 6, 1972.

42. Chou Shou-chüan, "Hua-ch'ien hsin-chi," in YYHTP, pp. 129–130.

he had good access to actual stories. To these he added more or less of his own sense for soap opera, as in the following passage from *Infant in the Entertainment Quarter (Pei li ying-erh)*. In the story, the prostitute Hui-chüan, having given birth to a baby boy, has no choice but to entrust him to the home of the procuress for whom she works. She can go see him there only once or twice a week:

> One day around dusk . . . Hui-chüan was regarding herself in the [dressing-room] mirror, arranging her hair in preparation for her nightly work in the saloons and song parlors. Suddenly the Mama despatched a young maidservant who came hurrying in, shouting for Hui-chüan to come with her.
>
> "And what big emergency could be worth all this clatter and fuss?" exclaimed Hui-chüan. "Come back after I've done a couple of rounds of business, all right?"
>
> "Mama ordered it!" gasped the maid, "She wants you right back! . . . Something's happened to Little Brother."
>
> The words struck Hui-chüan like a bolt of lightning, leaving her speechless with panic. Hurrying back with the young maid, they arrived at the Mama's residence to find the Mama there alone, reclining on the opium couch, smoking. Grief lined her face. Seeing that Hui-chüan had arrived, she turned towards her, and, pointing to the inner room, said in a heavy voice, "He's dead. I called you back to take one last look at him. Then we'll have to send him away."
>
> Hui-chüan rushed inside, her head spinning. There she saw her own son, whom everyone called "Little Brother," lying straight as a board on the floor. He was still wearing the little red polka-dot trousers Hui-chüan had made for him two days earlier, but his little eyes were already shut tight. A wet nurse sat weeping on a low stool which faced the miniature corpse. Raising her head at the sound of Hui-chüan's entrance, she rubbed the tears from her eyes and exclaimed, "Mistress Four! This is awful. Last night he was still jumping around, and this morning he was still giggling. In the afternoon he suddenly took ill and . . . the deathly smallpox . . . how can it be as cruel as this?"
>
> Hui-chüan fell uncontrollably into loud sobbing. Observing her tears, one might not have been able to say exactly what their cause was. Was she mourning the fatherless orphan boy? Was she wailing against the consummately evil Mama? Or against Huang Wu-i, the cowardly father of the child? Or was she bemoaning her own wretched lot? If a single one of her teardrops were analyzed with care, it is most probable that all these factors would be present.
>
> As Hui-chüan continued her unbridled sobbing, she suddenly felt a tug at her elbow. Looking up, she saw the young maidservant. "Mama wants you to stop crying now. There are some

people arriving in the courtyard, and you have to hurry up and
go. Ten or fifteen orders have come in, and they're waiting for
you to come and join the drinking. Better hurry! Here, I brought
you your mandolin. . . ."[43]

Passages such as the foregoing were so common in the late 1910s that
the Great Eastern Book Co. began selecting those which reflected family relations and publishing them under the title "Collected Fiction on
the Brothels" *(Ch'ang-men hsiao-shuo chi).* The collection had ten sections, "The Fathers of Prostitutes," "The Mothers of Prostitutes,"
"The Sons . . . ," "The Daughters . . ." and so on, showing how almost every family relationship was destroyed by prostitution.

The writers' fascination with forlorn courtesans—who had liaisons
with unappreciated geniuses—does much to explain the wide use of
the "Mandarin Duck and Butterfly" label. In its origins this term was
not pejorative. Mandarin ducks and butterflies had long been used in
both classical and popular tradition to refer to pairs of lovers, and love
story writers in the 1910s used the symbols often and quite sincerely.[44]
The *locus classicus* of the association of mandarin ducks and butterflies
in modern popular fiction appears in chapter 15 of *Jade Pear Spirit.*
Meng-hsia, having learned of Li Niang's resolve to die, falls seriously
ill himself and writes her sixty-four lines of regulated verse. The fifth
and sixth lines read:

Where is the butterfly who appears in my dreams?
How senseless if mandarin ducks with linked souls should die.[45]

The reason why these particular lines developed into a tag for love
story writers as a whole was, in the first instance, primarily a matter of
the writers' own preference. As they used it, "Mandarin Duck and
Butterfly" applied, non-satirically, only to Hsu Chen-ya and others in
the "Elements of People's Rights" group who imitated Hsu's style.
Then, partly because these stories were so popular, and partly because
the "mandarin duck" and "butterfly" terms were so handy in advertising a writer's orientation, a welter of novels appeared under such
names as *Lonely Mandarin Duck Talk (Ku yuan-yang yü), Mandarin
Duck Blood (Yuan-yang hsueh), Wild Mandarin Ducks (Yeh yuan-yang)*
and many, many others. A favorite meeting place of the writers in
Soochow, inside the Cho-cheng Gardens *(cho-cheng yuan),* was known

43. Quoted in Fan Yen-ch'iao, in YYHTP, pp. 252–253.
44. See P'ing Chin-ya, " 'Yuan-yang hu-tieh p'ai' ming-ming ti ku-shih" in
YYHTP, pp. 127–129, for some examples. The most familiar allusion in vernacular
tradition is to the story of Liang Shan-po and Chu Ying-t'ai, at whose end the two
lovers become butterflies.
45. YLH, p. 81.

as the "Mandarin Duck Pavilion" *(yuan-yang t'ing)*. Other names of
birds were drawn into the popularity wave as well, producing such
names as "Lone Crane" *(tu ho)*, "Slim Cuckoo" *(shou chüan)* and many
others.

The butterfly symbol spread even faster, due in considerable measure to the example of Ch'en Tieh-hsien, the "Butterfly Immortal"
who called his sons "Little Butterfly" and "Next Butterfly," filled his
novels with butterflies, and made a pair of butterflies the trademark
of his Peerless Facial and Tooth Powder.[46] Over the years writers appeared under such names as Ch'en Tieh-i ("Butterfly Clothing"), Pai
Tieh-hun ("Butterfly Spirit"), Chiang Tieh-lu ("Butterfly Hut"), Li
Tieh-chuang ("Butterfly Farm") and Wang Tsui-tieh ("Intoxicated
Butterfly"). The screen star of the 1930s "Butterfly Wu" (Hu Tieh)
must also be seen in this tradition.[47]

"Mandarin Duck and Butterfly" was first used in a satirical sense in
New Youth magazine before the May Fourth incident. In the early
1920s, the young cadre of May Fourth used the label in scathing attacks
on the 1910s writers. The latter, who were willing to call the May
Fourth writers the "new school" *(hsin p'ai)*, began to prefer the term
"old school" *(chiu p'ai)* in reference to themselves. Twenty years earlier this abdication of newness to someone else would have been
unthinkable by writers who came out of the late Ch'ing reform
movement holding aloft the banner of "new fiction." But by the early
1920s, their tradition had indeed aged enough that it was fitting to call
them "old style" in comparison with May Fourth.

In cultural terms, the "new" versus "old" distinction correlated
with a "Westernized" versus "traditional" distinction. May Fourth
leaders had studied abroad; for the "old school" writers, any kind of
overseas study or serious study of Western literature was extremely
rare. Those who did study abroad, such as Hsiang K'ai-jan and Ch'en
Shen-yen, later abandoned and even satirized their overseas study. Far
from wishing to "Knock Down the Establishment of Confucius and
Sons," as the May Fourth slogan put it, their stories reinforced traditional morality, making only stylish bows in the direction of change
from the West. Like Lin Shu, Wu Wo-yao and their other late Ch'ing
predecessors, they were skeptical about the West and maintained a considerable distance from it. They probably would not have known how
to defend Western morality even if they had so wished.

46. P'ing Chin-ya, in YYHTP, p. 129.
47. Hu Tieh, "Butterfly" Wu, was long a family friend of the Ch'en Tieh-hsien
family (interview, July 24, 1973). For examples of pen names using "tieh" and related
characters, see YYHTP, pp. 520–553.

Their basic life-styles and attitudes were changed very little by the tides of May Fourth. They continued for the rest of their lives to produce stories which upheld pre-Western norms and stayed within the traditional literary styles. (They did increase their use of vernacular after May Fourth—but only traditional vernacular.) They preferred to dress in long gowns, aimed to live five-generations-under-one-roof, and would write only with brushes. By the early 1970s Cheng I-mei, still living in Shanghai, had gone over to wearing "people's dress" *(jen-min chuang)*. But Pao T'ien-hsiao in Hong Kong and Ch'en Ting-shan in Taichung continued to wear gowns and to write fiction, as late as the 1950s and 1960s, in the old style. Ch'en's four-volume *The Fifties (Wu-shih nien-tai)* published in 1973 sold only a few hundred copies in its first six months, but that did not seem to matter. "The linked chapter style," he said, "is our tradition; we cannot give it up."[48] The vestiges of interest in female companionship were also still in evidence. Ch'en lived in the early 1970s with two wives, and had many glamorous photographs on his study wall. And Pao, who died in Hong Kong in November 1973, at age 97, summoned his concubine (who was in her fifties) from Shanghai to be with him at the end.

On the whole, "new versus old" and "Westernized versus traditional" are more useful than "high versus low" to describe the distinction between "Butterfly" writers and May Fourth writers—at least in referring to the 1910s. It was not until the 1930s that urban fiction in China took on the "pulp fiction" quality of cheap literature in the West. Yet the terms "new" and "old" are themselves excessively simple, whether viewed in the context of the early 1900s, when Pao T'ien-hsiao was very "new," or of the early 1920s, when he was already "old." Aside from the simple observation that standards change over time, one can analyze the mixture of "new" and "old" during the 1910s decade by distinguishing the cultural orientation of popular fiction (mostly old) from the technical and social processes in its growth (mostly new).

Sociologically speaking, the techniques of large-scale printing and distribution, the role of the professional writer, the appearance of new readership groups, and the phenomenon of volatile popularity of "hits" were all elements of the modern social revolution of Chinese cities. But, since cultural attitudes do not change as fast as printing technologies, both the consumers and producers of fiction in the 1910s felt more comfortable filling their modern bottles with traditional brew. And this combination proved to be more than a fleeting transition. The "old school" novelists continued through the 1920s to lead

48. Interview with Ch'en Ting-shan, July 25, 1973.

the "new school" in circulation; and they used another modern gadget—the movie camera—in doing so. But their tendency to guard traditional morality from excessive Western influences continued, insofar as this was possible under the circumstances; in fact one might, with Mary Wright's approval, view the old school writers as "the last stand of Chinese conservatism" in fiction.

4. Art

Among the many charges which the new writers of the early 1920s brought against the old school writers was the claim that they were artistically poor. Since the new writers' view eventually emerged as the standard one in modern literary histories, the question of quality among the old school writers has received little serious attention. Even within the old school, the question of artistic standards was not examined seriously. They had no professional critics, and their comments on one another's writing, where it appeared in prefaces or advertisements, consisted mostly of critically useless praise.

Yet the question of quality ought to be taken seriously. Hsu Chen-ya, as we have argued in chapter two, undeniably had a gift with words and an unusual psychological sensitivity, which together allowed him to create passages of exceptional intensity. He also had a lyrical ability, as shown, for example, in his description of Meng-hsia's return by boat along the inland waterways between his home in Soochow and the town near Wusih where he taught school. It was a small boat, guided by a single boatman, and Meng-hsia was the only passenger. After a day of bucking a heavy wind and rain storm, evening arrived and the boatman looked for a place to tie up for the night:

> They entered a mooring. A lonely broken bridge was resting there, and aged trees touched one another in rows. The fishermen's houses along the bank huddled close together, and here and there smoke from cooking fires sifted upward. One could hear the soft murmur of human voices. Three or four little boats were tied at the water's edge. Their lanterns shone out upon the surface of the water, creating a phosphorescent flickering.
>
> "This is a fine spot to tie up for the night," said Meng-hsia's boatman. Having secured the boat against the bank, he set about preparing the evening meal.
>
> The rain had stopped and the boat's sails lay still. The moon had risen, and the river rippled like white silk. It was a beautiful evening.
>
> When they had finished eating, the boatman went straight to sleep. He always wore his coat, even to bed, and soon he was in a deep slumber. Meng-hsia could not fall right to sleep, so went outside to sit quietly on the deck and admire the nighttime scenery

of the autumn river. By now the shining moon completely illu-
minated the riverbanks. The gentle air which arrives after a rain-
storm clears was twice as pure and fresh as before. From the
opposite shore came the sounds of a fisherman's flute, starting and
stopping in an uneven pattern. It was a lonely, melancholy sound,
and it produced sadness in its listener. The twinkle of fireflies
mingled among the shadows around the waterplants, seeming to
compete with the lights from the fishermen's boats.

 Meng-hsia, taking in this touching picture of the night, found
his thoughts turning to Li Niang. . . .[49]

Hsu's liberal use of four-six parallel prose in this passage is an artistic
element which the translation completely misses. The fact that this
kind of passage in this kind of style, from the brushes of Hsu's many
imitators, was typically cliché-ridden and awkward has indirectly
hurt Hsu's reputation; in fact it should enhance it.

 The vernacular novels of the 1910s—"social novels," "scandal
novels" and the others—were of course a very different genre. String-
ing together loosely linked episodes in the traditional vernacular style,
their authors did not even attempt the kind of sustained intensity of
mood which the better love story writers achieved. And the new
commercialization of fiction only served to aggravate the tendency
toward disjointed writing in the vernacular. Newspaper serialization
obliged writers to produce small climaxes or dramatic lines on almost
every page. The advent of fiction as a market commodity subject to
supply and demand led to hasty work and subservience to public
tastes.

 Pao T'ien-hsiao tells several times in his reminiscences how he discovered in the 1910s that fiction "has a time-quality about it."[50] The
styles of the day, the mood of the day, even the news of the day affected fiction. Keng Hsiao-ti, a writer in the "Northern School,"
serialized fiction which incorporated the previous day's news into its
story line.[51] The volume of writing needed to fill the pages of the
ever-increasing numbers of newspapers and magazines, and the fact
that writers were paid on a word-count basis induced them to write
quickly and without revisions. A well-planned story like *Fate in Tears
and Laughter* was rare indeed: most authors seemed unaware of what
would come next until they had written it. Characters who had served
their purpose were summarily dropped. Ch'en Ching-han once tired
of his own serialization of a story he was translating from the Japanese

49. YLH, p. 85.
50. CYLHIL, pp. 220 and 328.
51. Fan Yen-ch'iao, in YYHTP, p. 272.

and rid himself of it by having a dog run out and bite the protagonist to death. In Feng Yü-ch'i's voluminous writings not even dogs are provided to explain the sudden disappearance of important characters.[52]

But in fairness to the popular writers in the 1910s, one must recognize that they did not conceive themselves as high-level intellectuals and were not attempting "high art"—especially not "high art" as defined by the Western version of the novel. When Pao T'ien-hsiao was once accused of being a literary "jack of all trades", he graciously admitted the truth of the claim. He tells us he could not tolerate the atmosphere inside the editorial offices of the Commercial Press because it was "too scholarly." And he once refused a position at Peking Women's Normal College, protesting that he was unqualified, only to receive the public scorn of Lu Hsun for doing so.[53] His refusal reflects feelings he and other "old school" writers had of a growing remoteness from the Westernized elite of May Fourth, and corresponding closeness to the less articulate but "still Chinese" majority of the urban populace.

It is not quite true, either, that the "old school" writers had nothing that might be called a literary standard. Many of them sought to give their writing a distinctive "character" *(ch'i)* or "flavor" *(feng-wei)*. In the 1910s an author's distinctive "flavor" was supposed to be reliably in evidence on every page of his writing, wherever a reader might turn. Overall plot or characterization were largely beside the point. An author's "flavor" was supposed to exist not only in his writing but in his own particular life-style as well. Hsu Chen-ya's flavor was "mournful and captivating" *(ai yen)*, Hu Chi-ch'en's "pure and simple *(chen su)*, Ho Hai-ming's "rash and reckless" *(fang tan)*, Ch'en Hsiao-tieh's "bright and clear" *(ming hui)*, Hsiang K'ai-jan's "spirited and chivalrous" *(hsia lieh)*, Li Ting-i's "warm and tender" *(wen jou)*, Liu Huo-kung's "handsome and exalted" *(chün i)* and so on.[54] The better writers usually succeeded in conveying the aura they sought. One does indeed feel "mournful and captivated" reading Hsu Chen-ya.

Among vernacular writers, Pao T'ien-hsiao, Chang Hen-shui and Ch'en Shen-yen might be singled out for the unusual gift of being able to describe ordinary events in daily life and make them seem lively and interesting. When Pao passed the examination for the *sheng-yuan* degree in Soochow in 1894, the examiner's comment on his scroll was,

52. CYLHIL:HP, p. 100; for discussion of the point, including comment on Feng Yü-ch'i, see Fan Chi-p'ing (pseud. Ssu-ma Hsiao), "'Wo ti t'ung-shih' Chang Hen-shui" in *Ta Jen,* no. 16 (August 1971), pp. 60–62.

53. CYLHIL, pp. 392–393; CYLHIL:HP, p. 93; cf. also CYLHIL:HP, p. 83.

54. Cf. Cheng I-mei, "Pai-p'in," in YYHTP, p. 143.

"your writing has an easy-going air" *(wen yu i-ch'i).* [55] From that time on Pao cultivated fluency, ease, and clarity in his writing, combining it with a keen eye for vivid detail. The following piece is typical of the pleasant, life-like quality which resulted, and which does much to explain Pao's popularity. Here translated from his *Reminiscences,* the same story was woven into his education novel *Little Hsing Goes to School (Hsing-erh chiu hsueh chi).* It describes a trip Pao and his wife Chen-su made to Soochow in 1908 for the purpose of sweeping his parents' grave:

> When the day came, my wife and I set out taking our three-year-old daughter K'o-fen with us. Our old family home was on a little lane in a district known as the Western Island, which was in front of the Ch'eng-t'ien Temple inside the Ch'ang-men Gate. There was an ancient well in front of our house, the same well where Cheng So-nan, as I described earlier, hid his "Heartfelt History" in an iron casket. We of course were going to stay at our old home on this trip; in fact I'd already written to notify my sister, so that she could tidy up the upstairs and all would go smoothly.
>
> It was that time of year just between spring and summer, and the weather was beautifully clear, just the occasion for a springtime outing. However, I had asked for only a few days' leave in Shanghai, so we still had to rush along our way.
>
> The first thing we did upon arriving was to go hire a boat, seeking out the particular one which our family had always employed and knew well. It was a little packet with six glass windows, and it moored itself in front of the old residence of the Ch'ung-chen *chuang-yuan* Ch'iao T'u-lu (Lu Feng-shih's old home). There were no men on the boat — a mother and daughter made it their home, and also depended on it for a living. The old boat lady was a widow, and the daughter, who was called "Little Dragon" and was about 18 or 19 years old, had grown to be smart-looking indeed, a pleasure to behold. Since we were old customers of theirs, there was no need to waste time bargaining for a price. Their boat was free the next day, and we simply reserved it.
>
> In the past, when people from Soochow went to sweep their ancestor's gravesites, women and children seldom made the trip. The women had bound feet, making it difficult to move along the mountain paths; and because the women didn't go, the children didn't go either. But we no longer felt bound by these conventions, and since we were going to ride in sedan chairs anyway, we spent the evening cooking the sacrificial foods, and preparing the sacrificial offerings, and the next day, bright and early, set out.

55. CYLHIL, p. 137.

Our boat headed briskly out the Ch'ang-men Gate, and passing the Iron Ridge Pass, entered the outlying districts. It had been a long time since I'd travelled in the countryside, especially in such fine weather. The peach blossoms had not yet entirely departed, and sprang to view in a cluster here, a cluster there, without anyone's tending to them, blooming just as they pleased. The rapeseed blossoms along the way were also yellow enough to dazzle one's eyes.

When the boat reached the Huan-lung Bridge, there were already quite a few sedan-chair carriers, both men and women, milling and crowding around it. One middle-aged country woman saw us and shouted out, "It's the young master of the Pao family! I've carried him before!"

"He never came last year to sweep the graves!" shouted another, older woman.

All of their memories were very good. Once you'd had any contact with them, they remembered absolutely everything.

We climbed ashore amidst great bustle and commotion. It was still quite a distance to the gravesites, and we had to ride in the mountain sedan chairs. We needed two of them, one for me, and one for my wife and daughter. The sedan chair people decided among themselves how to handle us, and, oddly enough, assigned two women to carry me and two men to carry my wife and daughter. I asked why they arranged things this way and they said, "You by yourself are light (at the time I was extremely thin, scarcely one hundred pounds), but your young madam has a little miss with her." I thought it over and saw that they were right: why should men have to carry men and women carry women? I asked my wife and she had no objections. We added to the party a boy of fifteen or sixteen years to carry the sacrificial items, and together took to the path.

When we reached the gravesite, our tomb retainer (that's what Soochow people called a grave keeper) came promptly out to meet us. She was a middle-aged widow, and we called her the Cloak Queen. We went straight to the gravesite and offered our sacrifices, checked that the gravesite trees were in good shape, swept everything clean, and felt much comforted. Then, as was the custom, we gave the food which the ancestors had not eaten to the tomb retainers. We also distributed "earth-replenishing money." ("Earth-replenishing money" was a custom whereby all the young children from homes neighboring the gravesite would come and look on, and you would give them a few coppers as inducement not to trample the gravesite.) When this was over, our tomb retainer invited us to her house to rest a while, preparing tea and offering it to us. Normally her household did not drink tea, since they could afford only hot water.

They were busy raising silkworms at the time, and also had their own little strip of mulberry bushes. Chen-su and I had already seen silkworms being raised, but for our daughter K'o-fen it was the first time. When she saw all those snow-white silkworms, sleeping on the emerald-green mulberry leaves, she was all set to grab some for herself and take them home to Shanghai. But her mother scolded her and put a stop to it.

Throughout the area of White Horse Stream village, where this gravesite of ours was located, the womenfolk were blessed with an extraordinary range of talents. Besides raising silkworms, they could embroider. Soochow at the time had a special kind of industry which produced "spirit robes and theatre costumes." There were at least ten or a dozen shops in the city which dealt in these "spirit robes and theatre costumes." The so-called "spirit robes" were the gowns worn on the bodies of the various idols, and they had to be covered with embroidery of all kinds of splendid and beautiful things. This was all the more true for theatre costumes: whether it was Peking opera or K'un-shan drama, whether the part of the young man, the old woman, the painted face, or the clown—all had to wear embroidered upper garments. So these shops which sold "spirit robes and theatre costumes" did not do badly at all, as people would come to Soochow from all around to place their orders. The embroidery was all done with thick thread and didn't need to be terribly refined, so the shops sent all the orders out to the countryside for village women to do. It was this kind of "life" which the women in this region "made." (The village women called embroidery "making life.") But remarkably, they could always put aside their painstaking embroidery and go join the rough and tumble of carrying mountain sedan chairs. This was more than versatility—it was an actual combination of the martial and the fine arts.

When we returned to the boat it was already approaching two o'clock in the afternoon. We started back immediately, having our mid-day meal on board. The dishes were prepared by the mother and daughter who ran the boat: red-roasted shark, shepherd's purse with fried pork shreds, shrimp and egg-white soup—two dishes and one soup prepared in true Soochow style. What's more, by this time we were extremely hungry, so the meal seemed all the more appetizing and savory. Afterwards, we sat and watched as the farmland scenery passed before us along the riverbank, the little bridges and running water, the tranquil grass and leisurely flowers. Although it was the busy season for farmers, they set about their work appearing completely carefree and at ease. We reentered the city in the shadows of the setting sun, and by the time we reached home dusk had fallen. We chatted for a few minutes with my sister and brother-in-law, then peacefully retired.[56]

56. CYLHIL, pp. 363–366.

If this writing has an "easy-going" quality, other passages might illustrate the "chivalric" tone of Hsiang K'ai-jan's writing, or the "amiable" nature of Chou Shou-chüan's.

In the 1920s, as commercial influences grew stronger and the distinction between popular and elite (May Fourth) writers became clearer, popular fiction in China grew increasingly to resemble popular fiction in the West. This development makes it more possible to search for standards which characterize modern popular fiction generally, across cultures. Some may wish to speak of mere "characteristics" instead of standards, but in any case there are certain things that make some works more popular than others. Let us try to identify a few of them.

One key feature of popular fiction is that it presents itself in *readily understandable form*. The use of traditional vernacular style by Shanghai writers ensured that even when a story presented new-style content readers could absorb it relatively easily. May Fourth literary style, with its Western forms and Western-influenced language, seemed by contrast alien and dissonant, a fact which May Fourth theorists, notably Ch'ü Ch'iu-pai, pointed out with vehemence beginning in the early 1930s.[57] Another key to popular fiction seems to be *predominance of action* and a corresponding de-emphasis of description. Popular writers both Eastern and Western have remarked upon this feature of their own style, which does not exclude description but only limits it. Where description exists, it must be concrete, lively, and "personal," that is, directly linked to leading characters in a story. Good characterization can still be achieved, as the skillful touch of a writer like Chang Hen-shui attests. But Chang does this through dialogue and action rather than psychological description.

The emphasis on action seems related to a basic purpose of stimulating and holding the attention of readers who perhaps suffer elsewhere in life from boredom or exhaustion. An English popular author in the late nineteenth century frankly states that "the first duty of a story is to keep him who reads it awake."[58] Accordingly popular fiction exhibits what we might call the *immediate pursuit of interest*. When a man sends an amorous letter to a lady, the very next lines on the page may leap across time, space, and formality to report the enquiry's outcome.[59] The reader's fresh-born curiosity cannot be kept waiting.

57. See *Ch'ü Ch'iu-pai wen chi*, 2:853–916; and Paul Pickowicz, "Qu Qiubai's Critique of the May Fourth Generation: Early Chinese Marxist Literary Criticism," in Goldman, ed., *Modern Chinese Literature in the May Fourth Era*, pp. 351–384.

58. H. Rider Haggard, *The Days of My Life*, ed. C. J. Longman (London, 1926), 2:92 (quoted in Leo Ou-fan Lee, "Lin Shu and His Translations," p. 177).

59. See YLH, pp. 14–16, or *T'i-hsiao yin-yuan hsu-chi* (1948), p. 390.

A further source of stimulation might be called the *predilection for the weird or unexpected*. Popular fiction in Shanghai often advertised itself as "marvelous" *(li-ch'i)*, which was a promise of either or both of two things. One was that the reader would learn of shocking events (as in scandal novels) or fantastic ones (as in knight-errant novels), without being bored with ordinary life. Richard Altick, in writing of English popular audiences, observes that "the masses never read, and evidently never cared to read, about people in their own walk of life."[60] (The observation has interesting implications for China's program for worker-peasant-soldier literature in recent decades.) The second part of the promise was that events in a popular story would be connected in surprising ways. This often involved misleading the reader's expectations (someone departs for Tientsin by boat), then shifting grounds (the person shows up in Shanghai). On the very first page of Hsiang K'ai-jan's supremely popular knight-errant story *Chronicle of the Strange Roving Knights* (1924), the trick is pulled three times. An extraordinarily beautiful young couple (1) produce a monstrously ugly son, who is frail and constantly sick, yet who (2) possesses wizardly powers of concentration, can memorize texts instantly and perfectly, and promises to be the most extraordinary of scholars, except that (3) he loathes books and will not study.[61]

The stimulation afforded by sudden turns and strange events is made all the zestier by the *pretense of truth*. In both China and the West, such pretense may have originated from a desire for respectability before orthodox tradition; yet it certainly served also to enliven storytelling. The Western reader is familiar with the ghost story which claims: ". . . these events I saw with my very own eyes." The same spice is standard in Chinese tradition, as in the beginning of *Dream of the Red Chamber*, where the author says he wishes "to record the lives of the several maidens whom I have seen with my own eyes and have listened to with my own ears."[62] In the popular fiction of Shanghai in the 1910s and 1920s we are told countless times about the motivation of authors like Li Han-ch'iu who, in writing his best-selling *Tides of Yangchow*, "for the sake of warning posterity, had to record the behavior of even so vile a person as Yang Ching."[63]

The plot of a popular novel twists, turns, and—in the Chinese case—rambles on for volumes in loosely linked chapters. Its unity, if it has any, usually comes from its characters. Certain main figures

60. Altick, *Common Reader*, p. 360.

61. Hsiang K'ai-jan, *Chiang-hu ch'i-hsia chuan*, 1:1.

62. Ts'ao Hsueh-ch'in, *Dream of the Red Chamber*, tr. Chi-chen Wang (New York: Twayne Publishers, 1958), p. 5.

63. Li Han-ch'iu, *Kuang-ling ch'ao*, 2:130.

emerge from the thick and thin of episode after episode to be familiar persons with whom the reader begins to feel a personal acquaintance. A strong interest, almost like that of gossip, feeds on the details of these persons' experience. Found in Western popular fiction as well, this phenomenon might be called the *primacy of character* in popular fiction.[64] The importance of main characters, moreover, can seldom be separated from their *division into sympathetic and unsympathetic types*. By such division, the confusing world can be simplified and an author's guidance through it made clear. In stories about new-style romance, a reader can be led to the relatively easy positions of viewing it as either stylish or garish, depending upon whether a good or bad character is doing it. There need be no honest confrontation with pros and cons. In hero stories the division of good and bad characters clearly has to do with wish fulfillment through vicarious justice. One English popular author confesses that he deliberately fashioned stories after his private fantasies, in which he himself played a heroic part, and that he guessed his readers were attracted because they imagined themselves in the same roles.[65]

Partly because they are surrogates for real life, stories are more popular when they *deal with emotions which are familiar* in the daily life of readers. The relevant feelings are sometimes transient (and a novel "timely"), as when anti-warlord stories coincide with news about the Northern Expedition; or they may be ever-present concerns like those related to love and death.[66] In a moment of unusual candor Chang Hen-shui once wrote that "new fiction" (i.e., May Fourth work) did not adequately exploit the theme of love between the sexes; even Einstein's theory of relativity could be made popular if one wove it into a love story.[67]

What tends to distinguish popular writers from great writers perhaps more definitively than anything else is a general failure to probe moral questions in any depth. Q. D. Leavis notes this failure in English popular fiction and calls it the *"absence of the disquieting."*[68]

---

64. Cf. Leavis, *Fiction*, p. 58, and Hoggart, *Uses of Literacy*, pp. 88–89. Hoggart is probably not far from the mark when he states that: "If we want to capture something of the essence of working-class life . . . we must say that it is the 'dense and concrete life,' a life whose main stress is on the intimate, the sensory, the detailed, and the personal. This would no doubt be true of working-class groups anywhere in the world" (p. 88).

65. Leavis, p. 53.

66. The point is made for the case of popular drum-singing in Zdeněk Hrdlicka, "Old Chinese Ballads to the Accompaniment of the Big Drum," *Archiv Orientální* 25, p. 129.

67. Chang Hen-shui, *T'i-hsiao yin-yuan hsu chi*, pp. 376–377.

68. Leavis, pp. 60, 62.

China's "new school" fiction artists of the May Fourth tradition can also be found wanting by such standards, but they did, after all, include a Lu Hsun, and also authors like Shen Ts'ung-wen, Lao She, Yü Ta-fu, and Wu Tsu-hsiang, whose moral insights could be profound. The deftness and liveliness of Pao T'ien-hsiao's and Chang Hen-shui's descriptions rival the best in May Fourth, including Lu Hsun's brilliant creations of characters like K'ung I-chi or Hsiang-lin Sao. But Pao's and Chang's writing falls far short of the incisive vision and moral presence which infuses Lu Hsun's. To make the acquaintance, for example, of Pao's "Cloak Queen" (in the passage quoted above)—a poor, middle-aged, village widow—fascinates and delights the reader, and arouses a kind of affectionate respect. But when one is introduced by Lu Hsun to Hsiang-lin Sao, also a poor village widow, nothing so morally easy as fascination or delight is possible. The reader is pressed inexorably through compassion, frustration, despair and outrage, to emerge with a much deeper insight into a country woman and with a respect for her which is not conditioned by the benevolent condescension in Pao's appreciation of the "Cloak Queen."

It is also true, as Communist critics often point out, that despite all their stories about suffering and tragedy, the popular writers stay far from the troubling question of solutions. Occasionally they produce a story, such as Yun T'ieh-ch'iao's "The Story of a Laborer" (K'ung-jen hsiao-shih, 1913), which would almost seem at home in a May Fourth journal. It tells of a young family forced by bankruptcy in the countryside to migrate to Shanghai. After running out of money, the despondent husband attempts to drown himself but is saved by his only friend, a laborer, who proceeds to find him a job in a foreign-owned factory. After many humiliations and a beating at the hands of the foreigners and their lackey Chinese foreman, the young husband is injured in a machine accident and left unable to work. He sends his children to be raised by others, and his wife leaves to be a servant in the International Settlement. That, he reflects in the end, "was all for the best," since he could not support her anyway.[69] But nowhere does the author hint of what should be done about a society where such things happen; he doesn't even suggest that any fate other than the one depicted should be possible for laborers. In fact it is precisely the mournfulness of the story that apparently constituted its appeal. We are supposed to "savor" the tragedy. If we compare this moral stance with Lao She's in writing *Camel Hsiang-tzu* (*Lo-t'o hsiang-tzu*, 1938)—a similar story in its depiction of the harsh degradation of an honest young man—the feelings of indignation and anger which Lao She arouses are remarkable. There is nothing to savor in Hsiang-tzu's ruin, but much to worry about. Lao She's hasty prescription of

69. Yun T'ieh-ch'iao, "K'ung-jen hsiao-shih" in *Hsiao-shuo yüeh-pao*, 4.7 (1913): 1–7.

socialism at the end is simplistic, to be sure, but his evocation of urgency about the condition of society is vastly superior to that of stories like "The Story of a Laborer."

5. Readership

The readership of popular fiction in early twentieth century China is frequently referred to in modern literary histories under the blanket term "petty urbanites" *(hsiao shih-min)*. Nowhere, though, has it been adequately analyzed, and statistics for the purpose are nowhere to be found. The most anyone says is that the term includes clerks, primary school students, small merchants, and others of the so-called "petty bourgeoisie."[70] However vague, these routine references do serve to underscore the correct notion that the early popular readership arose in a Western-influenced commercial environment in the treaty ports. Available figures show that Shanghai's rapid population growth correlates well with both its economic expansion and its boom in popular fiction.[71]

Yet a somewhat more detailed picture—in qualitative terms, at any rate—is available from interviews of authors, publishers and readers from the period.[72] It is clear, for example, that readership extended higher on the social scale than most of the formulaic references indicate. Wealthy and powerful men, not just their employees, read popular fiction, and so did respectable intellectuals. Students in the "new-style schools" were a most important sector of the readership.

Fiction magazines and books were not cheap during the 1910s. Cost, in fact, seems to have been an even greater barrier to circulation than

70. YYHTP, pp. iii, 25, and *passim;* also Hsu P'ei-chün, "T'an yuan-yang hu-tieh p'ai" in *Kuang-ming jih-pao,* January 12, 1954, p. 4.

71. The first major upswing in population, according to Rhoads Murphey, followed 1895 when the Treaty of Shimonoseki legalized foreign manufacturing in Shanghai. Textiles, flour, cigarettes, and other industries were quick to develop and soon were given a second impetus as World War I curtailed Western competition in Chinese and Southeast Asian markets. By conservative estimate, population increased from 0.8 million around 1900 to 1.1 million in 1910 and 1.6 million in 1920 (Murphey, *Shanghai,* pp. 20–22, 167–168). Over the same intervals circulation of best-selling novels jumped from the hundreds to the ten thousands to the hundred thousands (Hu Shih, "Introduction," *Chung-kuo hsin wen-hsueh ta-hsi,* 1:4; Ho Ta, *Hsiao-shuo hsin hua,* p. 63; Ch'en Shou-yi, *Chinese Literature* [Taipei, 1971], p. 620; YYHTP, p. 462).

72. These interviews were with popular authors Pao T'ien-hsiao, Cheng I-mei, and Ch'en Ting-shan; with semi- or non-popular authors Hsu Yü, Yeh Ling-feng, Chang Ai-ling, and Li Hui-ying; with publishers and newspapermen Ch'eng She-wo, Kao Chen-pai, Tseng Hsü-pai, and Chao Ch'ao-kou. Interviews with the drum-singer Chang Ts'ui-feng and screen actress Hu Tieh were also very helpful. Though no informants had readership statistics, and most wisely declined to guess on that question, the considerable unanimity of their basic impressions about the nature of the readership gives one reasonable confidence that the qualitative descriptions of the current section are accurate.

illiteracy. Magazines typically cost ten or twenty cents, sometimes as much as sixty to eighty cents in an economy where, for example, a servant's monthly spending money was one or two yuan, a copyist's pay about four or five, and thirty cents would buy a day's room and board at a traditional-style inn.[73] Working people in Shanghai in the 1920s spent an average of only one yuan per family per year on all entertainment.[74] One of the most convenient ways to analyze the 1910s readership is to note who could afford books with relative ease and who could not. Those who could pay included well-to-do merchants, landlords, bankers, industrialists and their families; a portion of the reform-generation intellectuals of the 1910s, many now government officials, who had followed fiction down its primrose path to entertainment; a group of what might be called "full-time amusement-seekers," wealthy degenerates who were attracted to Shanghai for opium, adventure, and night life; and finally, a considerable number of rural gentry who, though choosing not to live in the city, were fascinated by what issued from it and ordered fiction magazines by mail.[75]

An important aspect of popular fiction's appeal to this group was the fact that it could be consumed in private. For centures, scorn for over-indulgence in *hsiao-hsien* activities of any kind made fiction, by its invisibility, preferable to theater, teahouses, and other public entertainment. This was especially true for women. The new spate of fiction turned out in twentieth century Shanghai made it possible to indulge in diversion of whatever duration and intensity one wished without needing to adjust to society's timetables or to fear exhausting one's supply.

The second—and soon much larger—category of readers were those who could not easily afford fiction. These were students, shop clerks, and office workers who sacrificed the luxury of fiction-in-private for the economy of openly sharing their resources. Used newspapers carrying serialized fiction could often be picked up for no cost, and sometimes were posted in public places. Books and magazines were passed around in offices, shops, and schools, and word-of-mouth previews were exchanged. Clerks and shop assistants would read during meal breaks or idle periods on the job; students would

73. CYLHIL, pp. 123 and 177; interview with Ch'en Ting-shan, July 25, 1973; interview with Hu Tieh, July 24, 1973; Chūzō Ichiko has estimated the Chinese yuan to be "roughly equivalent" to the U.S. dollar in 1909 (in Wright, *China in Revolution*, p. 301).

74. L. K. Tao, *The Standard of Living Among Chinese Workers*, p. 25; see also Sung-ho Lin, *Factory Workers in Tungku*, pp. 64 and 83.

75. From interviews listed in note 72 above; also Kao Chen-pai (pseud. Po-yü), "Chi Pao T'ien-hsiao hsien-sheng" in Pao T'ien-hsiao, *I-shih-chu-hsing ti pai-nien pien-ch'ien*.

hide fiction in their desks and steal glances whenever they could. It was this kind of activity, public but informal, which led to the first of the great booms in modern Chinese popular fiction, the one which centered on Hsu Chen-ya's *Jade Pear Spirit* and its train of imitations.

To a certain extent, the readership may also be divided according to the type of fiction they preferred. The love stories of the 1910s were read mostly by young people, especially students; the social and scandal novels, with their more overtly cynical attitudes, were preferred by an older readership whose optimism about society had peaked in the late Ch'ing years. Knight-errant stories, with their offer of fanciful glory, seem to have been read by all ages.

The strength of the attraction which readers, especially young ones, felt for their favorite authors was probably something new in the history of Chinese fiction. We shall have more to say about the reasons for it in chapter six, but here it is worth noting the extremes which infatuation could reach. A dramatic illustration of the point is an incident which occurred in the late 1920s involving Yen Tu-ho, editor of *Hsin-wen pao*'s fiction column called "Forest of Lightheartedness." Each day Yen contributed a few paragraphs of his own writing to this column, and his keen wit attracted a devoted following. It is said that one day, as he prepared to enter the elevator at *Hsin-wen pao,* one of his faithful readers leapt at his throat with a knife. In court the would-be assassin explained:

> I always liked Tu-ho's commentaries. I read them every day, until they became a regular habit. After a while I came to feel that Tu-ho's commentaries possessed a wizardly power of attraction. If you didn't read them you were all right, but once you did your mind fell under his control, and you were no longer master of yourself in anything you did. It was clear to me that Tu-ho had phantom powers. In order to pacify my own mind, I could only try to assassinate him.[76]

The judge ruled this to be the testimony of an insane man, but probably only because of its conclusion. Talk of "wizardly powers of attraction" was not unusual on the popular fiction scene.

If fiction readership reached the hundred thousands and there were popular crazes of a modern type, should we speak of a "mass" audience? For the 1910s, at least, we still should not. Modern urban fiction in this period was still a middle- and upper-class phenomenon. Only part of the readership we place in the hundreds of thousands lived in Shanghai, after all, since the circulation of leading novels extended to provincial centers and to coastal cities from Tientsin to Hong Kong,

76. YYHTP, p. 402.

even to overseas Chinese communities in Southeast Asia.[77] The bulk of Shanghai's population (and Tientsin's, Hong Kong's, and so on) were migrant peasants turned urban laborers.[78] Mostly illiterate, if they were able to read at all they were unlikely to have read novels like *Jade Pear Spirit* which were written in a rather difficult classical style. In the 1920s and thirties their second generation did become involved in the culture of modern popular fiction, as vernacular works became more numerous, primary education spread, and comic books and cinema made illiteracy less a barrier.

A key to understanding the rapid growth of the younger sectors of the readership is without doubt the "new-style schools" *(hsin hsueh-t'ang)*, also called "foreign schools" *(yang hsueh-t'ang)*. These schools not only provided many with the necessary literacy for reading fiction but also, as with *Jade Pear Spirit*, were major centers in the spread of fads. Statistics on the new schools are problematic in several ways, yet available sources, whose basic validity seems beyond doubt, reveal an overall trend of rapid growth. For all of China, the student population of the new-style schools appears to have risen from around one hundred thousand in 1905 to around five million by the early twenties.[79]

In Shanghai the earliest of the "foreign schools"—which may be defined as schools open to Chinese with a Western curriculum—was opened by missionaries in 1850.[80] Missionaries went on to establish dozens of schools and several post-secondary institutions in the International Settlement before the end of the century. These and a few Chinese schools in the modern style served as examples when the imperial court ordered in 1900–1901 that each county in China establish a new government primary school and each prefecture a middle school. Though the orders came from Peking, real administrative power in the Shanghai region was held by a group of reformist educators called the Central Committee for Education in Kiangsu (Chiang-su chiao-yü tsung-hui) and, in many local areas, by reform-minded gentry acting on their own initiative.[81] By the end of the late Ch'ing decade there were four kinds of new-style schools functioning in the lower Yangtze region: (1) the government schools, known as those "run by officials" *(kuan-pan)*, using revenues which had previously supported the examination system; (2) the "public" *(kung-li)* schools run by local gentry

77. YYHTP, p. 462.

78. Murphey, *Shanghai*, p. 21.

79. Several sources have been assembled, with appropriate caution, by Chow, *May Fourth Movement*, p. 379.

80. Pott, *Short History*, p. 123.

81. CYLHIL, pp. 251 and 351; Evelyn Rawski, "Primary Education in Modern China" (paper presented to Columbia University workshop on Publics and Media in Modern China), p. 4.

on taxes and donations, sometimes built on the base of the "charitable schools" *(i hsüeh)* of the past; (3) the "private" schools which were often based on "family schools" *(ssu-shu)* but now accepted larger numbers of tuition-paying students; and (4) the missionary schools.[82] Within the International Settlement of Shanghai, the Municipal Council in 1899 dropped its policy of not educating Chinese children, and during 1900–1920 established a number of its own government schools for Chinese youth.[83]

Dynamic though it may seem, the spread of the "new-style" schools can be misleading. Most of them were established using the resources of older schools which were part of a well-entrenched system, and the change to the "new-style" was seldom as thoroughgoing as the change in format suggested. Although curricula might be cast in the mold of "history, geography, mathematics. . . ," as established by foreign schools in Shanghai, most schools in fact would continue to stress the Chinese classics and histories.[84] Such conservatism was due in part to difficulty in obtaining new textbooks and to the extreme shortage of qualified teachers. Thousands (merely thousands) had studied in Japan. Many returned with only one-year degrees from schools of doubtful quality, or with no degrees at all, to become instructors in the "new learning." They were joined by members of the reform generation in Shanghai, whose treaty port experience was also accepted in the provinces as adequate qualification to interpret the West.[85]

But the generally superficial "newness" of most new schools was more than a matter of logistics. It was also a result of unwillingness to accept the ideas of the schools, whose foreign origins and strange new regime generated a cultural distance between school and local setting. Graduates of the new primary schools were popularly called "foreign licentiates" *(yang sheng-yuan)*, of the middle schools "foreign provincial graduates" *(yang chü-jen)*, and so on.[86] Students in the provinces were sometimes reluctant to show up at a "foreign" school, even when offered full scholarship plus spending money. Townspeople and peasants in many areas protested and resisted, feeling the schools to be a wasteful drain on their taxes.[87]

Those who registered in the new-style schools frequently felt awkward about their new studies. Some were themselves seasoned teachers of the traditional learning who, when the imperial civil ser-

82. CYLHIL, pp. 253 and 369; Rawski, p. 4.
83. Pott, *Short History,* p. 122.
84. CYLHIL, pp. 288 and 293; Rawski, p. 9.
85. CYLHIL, pp. 252 and 283–286; Rawski, pp. 5, 6 and 7.
86. Wang P'ing-ling, *San-shih nien wen-t'an ts'ang-sang lu,* p. 4.
87. CYLHIL, p. 285; Paul Reinsch, "The New Education in China," *Atlantic Monthly* (April 1909): 520; Wright, *China in Revolution,* p. 25; Rawski, pp. 13–14.

vice examinations ended after 1905, found they needed to acquire some "new learning" in order to continue their careers. Already middle-aged or beyond, these scholars would attend school to learn from a teacher half their age, and many an anomalous situation resulted. Roll call had to be effected by addressing the "students" as "teacher so-and-so"; and students would wear either black or red bands for their queues to indicate clearly which of them were already married.[88]

Younger students, inspired by a well-publicized strike at the Nanyang Kung-hsueh in Shanghai, instigated numerous strikes and protests. A wave of student uprisings spread across the coastal provinces in the middle of the 1900–1910 decade. The protest activity centered on such issues as food in dining halls, or even such tangential matters as the possible omission by a Shanghai publisher of two chapters of the early Ch'ing autobiographical novel *Six Chapters on the Floating Life (Fu-sheng liu chi)*. Yet it was clear even to some observers at the time that the real causes of the protest were not these superficial matters but an uneasiness with the ideology and administration of the schools themselves.[89] The spread of popular fiction in the new schools might be seen both as a part of the general rebellion against the schools' demands, and as a crutch which students used to help them come to terms with the "new style."

One variety of the new–style schools which deserves separate note were the women's schools *(nü hsueh-t'ang)*. Since coeducation was not practiced, these schools were responsible for the entirety of "new-style" education for women. Though there had been missionary precedents, the "Patriotic Women's Study Society" (Ai-kuo nü hsueh-she) founded in Shanghai by Ts'ai Yuan-p'ei served as an example through the late Ch'ing years and into the 1910s for the establishment of women's schools across the lower Yangtze region. Combining a basic "new" curriculum with instruction in needlework and child care, women's schools were set up at the lower primary, primary, and "normal school" level.[90]

Though women's education attracted considerable public attention during the reform-and-revolution years, the number of schools remained small. During the last years of the dynasty, the total student population of new-style women's schools was probably around fifty thousand, or only three percent of the national total.[91]

This fact of course has important implications for estimating the proportions by sex of the popular fiction readership. By analogy to

88. CYLHIL, pp. 252 and 286.
89. CYLHIL, pp. 258 and 289.
90. *China Year Book*, 1912, p. 319; CYLHIL, p. 268.
91. *China Year Book*, 1912, pp. 322–324.

emergent "bourgeois" readerships in the West, one would expect a significant portion of the readership of Butterfly fiction in the 1910s to be women. Yet the indications seem to deny this. First, we know that students in the new-style schools were a major part of the readership but that only about three percent of them were women. Second, popular authors from the 1910s (Pao T'ien-hsiao and Ch'en Ting-shan) say in interviews that they doubt many of their readers were women.[92] Even the popular "women's magazines" they edited were, they feel, actually read by men who were interested in the *idea* of the "new-style" woman. Third, a reason I find convincing despite its subjective basis, is that the most popular stories of the 1910s invite identification with male much more than with female protagonists. If there had existed a growing female readership like that in Richardson's England, one would expect some kind of Pamela or Clarissa to appear. But instead we are continually introduced to a young man's corner of a triangular love story. It is true that things might have been different if there had been some women writers. But with very minor exceptions, there were none; there were only men who played the game (for other men) of writing under female pseudonyms. It appears the only reasonable estimate of the female readership one can make is the sum of a modern component (i.e., the three percent known female constituency of the new-style schools) plus a traditional component, which was probably larger, consisting of the leisured women of wealthy households who had, as a group, read fiction for centuries in China. This traditional group, of whom there were proportionally more in Shanghai than elsewhere in the early twentieth century, may not have looked to fiction for an exploration of new-style roles as much as the female readership of eighteenth century England did, but there can be little doubt that they read popular fiction anyway, and that gradually talk of the "new style" in the fiction had an effect on them.

A thorough understanding of fiction in its social context must account for authors, readers, and literary works, and for the worlds which authors and readers inhabit and which literary works describe. In these terms, the readership of our fiction is, in our present knowledge, the least clear part of the overall picture. The important texts from the 1910s are available in their original forms; information on the authors, and their relations to their texts, is considerable when totaled up, as is general knowledge of the social environment. But the readers? It may seem strange that we have a less detailed picture of who they were than we have, by examining popular texts, of what they thought.

92. Pao T'ien-hsiao, response to question 17 of written interview, May 1973; interviews with Pao T'ien-hsiao, December 6, 1972, and with Ch'en Ting-shan, July 25, 1973.

CHAPTER 6

Fiction for Comfort

> If 50,000 people buy a novel whose shortcomings
> render it tenth-rate, we may be sure that they have
> not conspired to do so, and also that their strange
> unanimity is not due to chance. There must be
> another explanation of the phenomenon. . .
> —Arnold Bennett[1]

It turns out that some of the firmest bases for statements about the modern popular readership are the texts which we know to have been popular. To be sure, the relation between text and reader psychology can be immensely complex. But in the case of a popular text one hard fact is reliable, namely that we can be sure large numbers of readers, for whatever reasons, *liked* to read it. To that extent, at least, we clearly have access to "the popular mind."

Some observers, most importantly May Fourth youth and Marxist literary historians after them, have questioned or denied the value of popular fiction as an access to reader attitudes. Their view has been that the 1910s popular fiction not only served to support ruling class thought—which it did in many cases—but also that the ruling class consciously fashioned the appeal of the fiction in order to control popular ideas.[2] There is, in fact, some evidence that this was tried, both by Chinese warlords and by Japanese invaders, who sometimes subsidized authors, handed out prizes, and so on.[3] But the suggestion

---

1. E. Arnold Bennett, *Fame and Fiction: An Enquiry into Certain Popularities,* p. 5.

2. YYHTP, pp. 25, 109. The main effect of such control, according to the theory, has been one of lulling the masses into lethargy and contentedness. This notion may originally have been taken *en bloc* from the Marxist critique in the West, since in China it was stated as if it were established doctrine. Specific examples were seldom given. Amidst the drama of the times, the listing of evidence considered to be obvious was probably also felt to be unnecessary.

3. In the mid-1910s the pei-yang military clique gave prizes to Li Ting-i for his stories in celebration of chastity (YYHTP, p. 109). Li Ting-i published in the magazine *Elements of People's Rights* which, as we have seen (chapter 5) was itself a result of political maneuvers by Yuan Shih-k'ai. When the Japanese occupied Shanghai after 1937 they pursued a policy of encouraging public entertainments and fostering the appearance of cooperation between themselves and popular figures in many fields. In Shanghai newspapers, for example, the Japanese were quick to install their own editors at the better-known popular fiction columns. Yet it is doubtful that such measures changed the public's feelings about the invasion.

that these efforts could have created a widespread appeal where none already existed is far-fetched. For one thing, prescribed messages seldom even reached the masses because most leading authors resisted them vigorously.[4] And even when access was possible, one ascribes far too much cleverness to the ruling class in supposing they could have analyzed and effectively fabricated the many-sided and often subtle nature of popular fiction's appeal.

This appeal existed at several levels. Perhaps most obvious is the appeal of technique. The clever surprises in the plot of a good knight-errant story, the lively descriptions of unusual characters in a social novel, the syntactic, phonetic, and rhythmical aspects of parallelism in the contrasting of opposites in the love stories—one or more of these kinds of technical appeal were certainly necessary to make a novel a best seller. But clearly there was more. The reading of popular fiction had a place within the life patterns of readers, where it filled psychological needs its readers regularly felt. To understand these needs we must look beyond technique and view the reading of a story as an act in its social context.

In literary histories in China, both Marxist and non-Marxist, a common cliché used to explain the act of fiction reading—for almost all popular fiction in almost all ages — is *hsiao-hsien*. Readers seek to "pass the time." Though it obviously begs many questions, the *hsiao-hsien* notion took somewhat clearer shape in twentieth-century Shanghai because of the new periodicity of on-hours and off-hours which marked modern living and almost seemed to schedule time for such things as fiction reading. Besides off-hours in a day there were off-days in a week. Modern banks and schools took weekends off, and factories and textile mills gave about a half-day off per week on the average.

But if modern work routines created time for fiction reading, they also appear to have created part of the need for it. About the same time

4. Instances of stubborn non-cooperation by China's popular figures are legion. In October 1936 many popular writers participated in a broad coalition, which included Lu Hsun, Pa Chin, and others from the May Fourth tradition, to sign a Declaration of Colleagues in the Realm of Literature and Art for Unity in the Resistance of National Insult and for Freedom of Speech. Pao T'ien-hsiao, one of the signers, has written to me that during eight years of the War of Resistance, while he was in Shanghai, he defied the "literary catastrophe" by refusing to set pen to paper (written interview, May 1973, question 9). Chang Hen-shui's sequel to *Fate in Tears and Laughter* and his famous *Deep in the Dark Night (Yeh Shen-ch'en)* are clear evidence of that author's turn against the Japanese. Prominent actress Hu Tieh enjoys relating the story of her escape from Hong Kong after the Japanese occupied that city and did all they could to cajole her into a collaborative role. Mei Lan-fang, who was in Hong Kong at the same time, grew a moustache as a protest against Japanese efforts to make him cooperate. (The moustache ruled out his singing any of the female parts for which he was famous.)

that Shanghai began undergoing modern social change, the psychological consequences of such change were being given classic formulation in Germany by Georg Simmel: the overwhelming onrush of stimuli in modern urban living leads to an inability of the individual to relate deeply to others; increased isolation gives rise to a stronger need for a sense of personal security; this sense can be achieved through greater self-assertion and self-expression; and one outlet for the urge toward self-expression is vicarious involvement novels.[5] Simmel's powerful theory applies to any modern city; but for the people of Shanghai, like other colonial or semi-colonial cities, there was a complex additional burden. Severe psychological pressures also arose from the city's cultural and historical crisis vis-à-vis the West. In theory, of course, the problem of the West is distinguishable from the problem of "modern" social change. And if modernization could somehow have arrived in Shanghai without the West, everyone's adjustments would certainly have been easier. But the two things did come together, and in fact were so thoroughly part of one another that most people could not sense the distinction between them in any significant way. The West was a symbol for all the problems that came with it.

The pressures of both modernization and westernization created needs to know that, whatever else happened, certain values—such as honesty, frugality, respect for age, respect for nature and the supernatural, and so on—could still be relied on in their traditional forms. This does not mean such values were always to be preferred—only that they should "be there," as a kind of anchor for one's life in case experiments with the new style failed.

Not surprisingly, old people were a common symbol of the old values. They not only exemplified these values more than the impressionable young, but also, as parents and family heads, were important people to those who revered the traditional filial virtues. In popular fiction, the lovableness and goodness of old people is often accentuated by some kind of tragedy which leaves them lonely or dejected in their waning years. Old Mrs. Shen (Shen ta-niang), the mother of Feng-hsi in *Fate in Tears and Laughter,* is such an example. When Feng-hsi is driven to madness:

> Mrs. Shen lived at home and did some needlework now and
> then. When it occurred to her that she was almost half a century
> old, and had no support whatsoever, she wondered what would
> become of her in the future. Her daughter was mad and away in

5. Georg Simmel, "The Metropolis and Mental Life" in Paul K. Hatt and Albert J. Reiss, Jr., *Reader in Urban Sociology* (Glencoe, Ill., 1951), pp. 563–574. See also Louis Wirth, "Urbanism as a Way of Life," ibid., pp. 32–49.

an asylum. Could it be this daughter would go on being mad her whole life?

When she reached this point in her thoughts, tears gushed from Mrs. Shen's eyes. In this way she passed her days, stricken by grief as well as by poverty.[6]

The last line of the excerpt summarizes the twin perils of the aged: the material threat of growing old without support, and the spiritual threat of seeing one's family—whose continuing well-being is one's mission in life—turn out badly. In *Jade Pear Spirit* the reader is led to sympathize with Patriarch Ts'ui right from his first appearance in chapter two. After comforting Meng-hsia over the death of his father, Patriarch Ts'ui speaks of his own case:

The really insufferable fate is my own. I was middle-aged before I ever had a son—then last year he suddenly died of the plague. Cruel indeed was Heaven, stealing my beloved son. And a barren fate it is indeed which lands one in such a sorry state during the twilight of life. . . . What kind of a man am I supposed to be, that I could forget such pain? That I could bear to see a young wife begin the hopeless vigil of a widow? Or see a baby son grow up without a father? It is really painful for me, oh so painful![7]

The manifest goodness of an old person like Patriarch Ts'ui can be contrasted to the moral ambiguity of the "new style", as represented, for example, by his daughter Yun-ch'ien. Though the patriarch is always patient and gentle with Yun-ch'ien, she, fresh from training at a modern girls' school, repeatedly rebuffs him on the question of her marriage. When Meng-hsia asks Patriarch Ts'ui for Yun-ch'ien's hand in marriage, the poor old man must admit his ineffectiveness with his daughter. He can only ask for Li Niang's intervention:

"There's something I must talk over with you," he said. "I am getting old now, about as old as they come. But there's one remaining wish I must see fulfilled. Yun-ch'ien is quite grown up now, yet her marriage has still not been settled. She's already shown several times that she won't listen to me. Can it be she wants to stay unmarried her whole life?

"I've now found her a really fine match. The go-between was just here a moment ago, and I gave my approval. Could you go for me to tell Yun-ch'ien about it? Ask her not to be so contrary. It so hurts this old man's feelings!"[8]

Although old people are never new-style, young people can be old-style, can indeed be exemplars of traditional morality. The *to-*

6. Chang Hen-shui, *T'i-hsiao yin-yuan hsu-pien* (1948), 2:408.
7. YLH, p. 11.
8. YLH, p. 108.

ch'ing lovers of the Romantic Route (see chapter 2) do more than obey Confucian social rules—they are in tune with the immanent ways of nature. Their closeness to nature gives them a purity which sharply contrasts with the confusion and complexity of modern urban life. In this way they are like children, who are also important representatives of the purity of premodern life. In fiction children are always lively and cute. Their sweetness is a "given" the reader may rely upon, and they remind the reader that the new style is acquired and the old style natural. One tiny girl in *Tides of Yangchow* watches some older children sitting down to read their books. She then grabs her own piece of paper—a blank sheet—frowns at it, and begins intoning *"tzu yueh . . . tzu yueh . . ."* with the others.[9] Children are lovable even when they misbehave. P'eng-lang, the little boy in *Jade Pear Spirit*, at one point comes bounding into the quarters of his tutor Meng-hsia in his normally delightful manner, except in this case Meng-hsia has company and P'eng-lang's unguarded words nearly reveal the secret love between Meng-hsia and Li Niang, P'eng-lang's mother:

> "Teacher!" he shouted, holding what appeared to be a letter in his hand, "Mama. . . ."
>
> Meng-hsia was terrified. He coughed to interrupt the boy. P'eng-lang quickly looked around, saw Li [the guest], and fell silent.
>
> Meng-hsia assumed a stern look and addressed P'eng-lang. "As old as you are by now, and still as ill-mannered as this? This is Mr. Li, a good friend of mine. Aren't you afraid, if you go screaming and jumping around as if crazy in front of your elders, that you will make people laugh and call you a badly behaved boy?"
>
> P'eng-lang listened to his scolding without a word, his eyes steady and clear.[10]

More than merely obedient and respectful to his elders, P'eng-lang has good and correct moral impulses of his own. He is closer than most adults to the good, original nature of human beings which only the *to-ch'ing* carry with them throughout life. When his mother is lying seriously ill, for example:

> . . . suddenly there was the sound of someone speaking with the sick one, and it was P'eng-lang who had entered his mother's room. If the boy knew nothing else, he did know he loved his parent. Realizing his mother was too ill even to rise, he abruptly suppressed the frolicking and giggling which was normal in his attitude. Instead he cuddled close to her bed.

9. Li Han-ch'iu, *Kuang-ling ch'ao*, 2:14.
10. YLH, p. 90.

"Mama! Mama is sick," he said, rubbing Li Niang with his little hand. "Do you want some medicine? I should tell Grandpa. He can send somebody to get the doctor."[11]

To be sure, there are many stories about children less sweet than P'eng-lang, including even very naughty boys—who call their classics teacher "old windbag" behind his back, and so on. But even these are merely "naughty", mischievous in a basically lovable way. In real life, children could not have been so consistently sweet; in fiction, the whole range of normal behavior is idealized to represent simplicity and purity.

In a more general sense children and old people, the living end points of traditional family lines, symbolize family values as a whole. A truly good person cherishes these values, obeys all the specific responsibilities of Confucian family relationships, and cares deeply about the survival of the family line. Consider the way Li Niang approaches Yun-ch'ien with the family's engagement plan for her:

> Father loves you, his only beloved offspring in this world, beyond all else. . . . If you keep on being so stubborn, you're sure to hurt him deeply. Think of all the terrible problems he's had over the years . . . and now that he's found a worthy match for his cherished daughter, you could bring a bit of happiness to his heart. What's more, this little boy P'eng-lang has no one to support him. With your marriage, an orphan and a widow would have the much needed support that you and your husband could give them. Think of it from the viewpoint of your aging father, or from the viewpoint of your older brother who has died.[12]

Li Niang weeps as she ends her speech, and Yun-ch'ien, in spite of her new-style ideas, is also moved to tears. When all is said and done, the family still comes first. Patriarch Ts'ui at the same time is eagerly waiting to accomplish his own familial duties, and the news that Yun-ch'ien has finally agreed to a marriage brings him great relief: "When daughter Yun-ch'ien has a husband, my work will be finished."[13]

Amidst the chorus of everyone paying proper familial respects to everyone else at the end of *Jade Pear Spirit,* there is an interesting twist—what initially appears to be a gross exception to the general ethic—in the case of Li Niang's death. Though certainly aware of her duties to her father-in-law, her son, and her sister-in-law, Li Niang nevertheless decides to leave the world for the sake of her love for Meng-hsia. In the superidealistic terms of Li Niang, this is a relatively

11. YLH, p. 61.   12. YLH, p. 120.   13. YLH, p. 121.

selfish act, and she allows herself to do it only after all her Confucian duties have been properly delegated to others. She has seen to Yun-ch'ien's engagement, and fully expects that this marriage will ensure lasting good treatment for her father-in-law and son. Even so, she apologizes to Patriarch Ts'ui as she passes away: "I have no life, and cannot carry my filial responsibilities to an end."[14]

All of the values which were part of the fictional ideal of "old style" life—including simplicity, tranquility, honesty, respect for elders and observance of family duties—were, from the perspective of Shanghai, primarily "countryside" values. The excerpts from Pao T'ien-hsiao and Hsu Chen-ya in the last chapter are examples of this kind of idyllic view. And in fact nearly all the most popular novels of the 1910s and 1920s, although written, published, and for the most part read in the culturally heterogeneous cities, took as their background the countryside and the inland towns which were still relatively free from Western influences.[15] The idea of the countryside's purity and simplicity leads naturally in these works to the notion of the frugality and honesty of country people. Peasants are very *lao-shih*. If you ask a peasant a question, he will not manipulate you with his answer. If you buy something in a little town, you get your money's worth. At a deeper level there was a notion of the countryside as *prior*. It existed before the modern city did, and still in a sense lay beneath it—almost ontologically prior. A person could rise and fall and be hurtled about in the city, and the city itself might entirely collapse, but the countryside would always be there. One could count on it.

Shanghai residents often had personal ties to the countryside, where their families were based, and these ties help explain concretely why both old people and children were important symbols for traditional values. Old people, of course, were the living representatives of those values in their most developed forms. Children suggested the old values in two ways. Not only was their natural purity akin to the *a priori* correctness of traditional values, but a special connection to the past existed through the memories which urban readers, migrants to the city, had of their own childhoods. At one point in *Jade Pear Spirit* an ill and depressed Li Niang ". . . recalled her early years as an untutored maiden, frolicking in the fields with her several sisters, sticking flowers

14. YLH, p. 145.

15. On the basis of estimates of circulation, we take the five best-selling Shanghai novels of the 1910s and 1920s to be: (1) Hsu Chen-ya, *Jade Pear Spirit*, (2) Hsu Chen-ya, *Chronicle of the Great Tears of Bygone Days*, (3) Li Han-ch'iu, *Tides of Yang-chow*, (4) Hsiang K'ai-jan, *Chronicle of the Strange Roving Knights*, (5) Chang Hen-shui, *Fate in Tears and Laughter*. The novels are set, respectively, in a little town near Wusih (the first two), Yangchow, the hills of Hunan, and Peking.

to what extent ↄ fiction index of popular culture/ mentalité?

in her hair and running to look in the mirror. The joy of those years seemed a world apart from her present situation."[16] Readers could join Li Niang in peering back toward a vision of untrammeled life before they, in many cases, had fallen victim to the irritations and dilemmas of the modern city.

There can be little doubt that the idealized view of the countryside arose more from psychological needs in the city than from reflection of the countryside's reality. We must, therefore, look closer at problems of the urban "new style." In the last Ch'ing decade, when Western-inspired ideas first made a significant appearance in Shanghai fiction, the unfamiliar aspects of those ideas were, in a sense, too new to be either accepted or rejected by the reading public. More than anything else, it was merely *interesting* that one would suggest building a boat that flies or a school for women. But when it became clear that leaders in society were pushing Western ideas in earnest, as Liang Ch'i-ch'ao did in fiction, the newness wore off and Western ideas took on positive associations which lasted many years, and even to the present. One of the most important of these was precisely the sense of going along with modern elite opinion.[17] Without necessarily accepting a new-style idea completely, one could pretend one did, or say so to others, or read a novel which—at least on the surface—proclaimed the new style, and in doing such things enjoy the comfort which comes from seeming to support goals which are lauded in public. Following from this association, new-style things took on a character which, for its superficiality and its transience, can only be called stylishness. Concrete symbols of Westernization such as cars, watches, glasses, or doorbells all came to acquire an air of stylishness, as did a few reformist ideas taken from the West, such as women's education, anti-superstitionism, and children's independence from parents. Popular fiction came to be a purveyor to the urban middle class of elite concerns in stylish form. When anti-Manchu ideas were taken very seriously in revolutionary circles before 1911, popular knight-errant novels clothed their accounts of heroism in anti-Manchu rubrics. That these rubrics were merely stylish is clear from the fact that they survived right through the 1920s and 1930s—when they no longer had contemporary relevance.

16. YLH, pp. 59–60; for other nostalgic recollections of childhood, see pp. 77 (Meng-hsia) and 124 (Yun-ch'ien).

17. "Elite opinion" is not intended necessarily to include government leaders. Warlord governments were often as far behind modern trends as any reader of popular fiction. Even the Kuomintang, as late as the 1930s, tried to ban ballroom dancing because it was immoral. See A. C. Scott, *Literature and the Arts in Twentieth Century China* (London, 1965), p. 53.

One of the most prominent test cases of the whole question of the new style was that of new-style young women. Why this was the case is a fascinating question we will largely pass over here, and turn directly to examine the case itself.[18] Starting with the example of Yunch'ien in *Jade Pear Spirit*, we can see how the idea of the new-style young woman was associated with the modern elite, and how it appears to have gained therefrom a certain stylishness among the nonelite. Fresh from training at a "new-style" school in the provincial capital, Yun-ch'ien returns home exuberantly proclaiming that in modern times no woman should accept a traditional-style marriage:

> In the old days, one had to obey the wishes of one's parents . . . but now the tides of the West have surged across Eastern Asia and every single one of the new-style experts regards freedom of marriage as the most important thing in one's life.[19]

The reader of this speech, which occurs about halfway through the story, is already well accustomed to the distinction between young women of the new and old styles. As we have seen in chapter two, Yun-ch'ien and Li Niang, the magnolia and pear, represent two horns of a dilemma which pervaded modern urban life: whether to be modern, foreign-influenced, stylish, and aggressive or old-style, purely Chinese, plain, and retiring. The general distinction, perhaps best captured by the Chinese terms *t'u* (earth, and hence "local, native") and *yang* (ocean — from across the ocean, foreign), dates in Shanghai from the late nineteenth century. According to Pao T'ien-hsiao's memory, people in the lower Yangtze region generally knew in the 1890s that "girls born and raised in Shanghai of course are a bit more boisterous and shrewd than those in the interior."[20]

Since the distinction was clear, readers could take Yun-ch'ien's speech in two ways. She is either striking a blow for progress in China or losing touch with well established values. In her various actions she illustrates both these interpretations. Her Westernisms are subtly associated throughout the novel with the shining but superficial aspects of her beauty. When she is introduced into the story line, the reader is

18. John Weakland has made the interesting argument, based on films about the War of Resistance, that young women are frequently symbols for China, especially in matters of opposition to foreign incursions. They serve as spies, guards, messengers, guerillas, temptresses and much more, yet are always physically attractive, subordinate to males, and generally "feminine." Weakland points to the underlying simile of invasion to rape in such war films, and to the consequent identification of young women with China. See *China Quarterly* 47 (July–September 1971): 439–470.

19. YLH, pp. 70–71.

20. CYLHIL, p. 179.

told that there are crass women in this world, who smear makeup, flirt, and are frivolous, but that Yun-ch'ien is not necessarily like them.[21] Yet the implicit comparison of the over-glamorous magnolia tree and the naturally beautiful pear tree hovers in the background, and Yun-ch'ien is immediately somewhat suspect. Mixed with her beauty are hints of a harshness: she sometimes has a "hard and haughty" *(wu ao)* attitude, and a somewhat cold, unapproachable manner.[22] When Meng-hsia first sees her, he is struck by her seductive beauty as well as by the keen and forbidding element in her bearing, which is powerful enough to keep one from looking directly at her. But then he notices—and here the superficiality of the young woman's sharp side is foreshadowed for the reader—that as soon as she disappears from view, the impression of her brilliance vanishes. "Like wisps of clouds crossing through the sky, her image floats from one's mind."[23]

The reader is not left waiting long for confirmation that the sharp element in Yun-ch'ien's character comes from the "new-style" women's movement. We are told immediately that she attends the O-hu Girls' School, where she comes in contact with all the great ladies of the area. Every time she comes home she informs her family of how "in the present day we are beginning to cast rays of light into the darkness of women's lives." In particular she expresses concern for her sister-in-law, the widow Li Niang, who still "is deeply buried in living hell" where the new rays of light have not reached.[24]

Just as Yun-ch'ien's peppery character is clearly linked to the "new style," so the "new style" is unmistakably associated with the West. Any reader who misses this point when Yun-ch'ien is introduced can hardly miss it three pages later when the *enfant terrible* kneels to pray to the Christian God—something she apparently has also learned at school.[25] And the point that her Westernisms are merely superficial becomes perfectly clear when she herself abruptly abandons them. She performs true to her "new style" identity only until the point in the story when Patriarch Ts'ui, Li Niang, and Meng-hsia conspire to arrange her traditional-style marriage. Then, put to the true test, the new style dramatically collapses. Within a few pages we are given, first, Yun-ch'ien's strongest speech in favor of the new style and then unmistakable indications that she has abandoned it. The strong speech comes immediately after Li Niang tells her of the plan to marry her:

> "Has father lost his senses?! He *knows* what kind of person I am! We've had run-ins over this question more than once in the past,

21. YLH, p. 66.   22. YLH, p. 66.   23. YLH, p. 67.   24. YLH, p. 66.
25. YLH, p. 69.

and he agreed to let me always do the deciding for myself, without any interference from him. This shows that he loves me and
respects my opinions. So how can he suddenly be so muddle-
headed again? Is he trying to deprive me of my right of liberty?
Put me back in the primitive darkness?"

At this point the reader sees the first crack in the disintegration of
Yun-ch'ien's new-style facade. She is sensitive to others' criticisms:

"Sister, listen! Don't think I'm just caught up in the crazes of the
new-style learning, casting off my proper duties as a daughter and
opposing my father's will just because I like to babble about 'liberty'. No, I do what I do because this really is a terribly important
question. There's no telling how many of our sisters are buried
within the hades of the tyrannical family system. Ever since I
went to school I have felt an immense ambition: to promote freedom of marriage, abolish the tyrannical family system, and so to
rescue our countless, pitiable women compatriots who are still
inside that hades!"

Finally there is a hint that Yun-ch'ien is about to change sides:

"Never have I thought only of myself. I wanted to be an example
for others, to be a pioneer in the reform of society. And now I
myself join the stricken ones! Of all the painful things in the
world, what could be worse than this! It's not just that I myself
cannot escape. What am I going to say to all my classmates?"
    As she spoke her eyes glistened, filling with hot tears which
seemed ready to pour down her cheeks.[26]

Part of the reader's interest in the collapse of Yun-ch'ien's new style
lies in knowing about the secret love between Li Niang and Meng-
hsia. Yun-ch'ien, who never suspects such a thing, arrogates to herself
the role of Li Niang's teacher and liberator. The superficiality of the
"new learning" in Yun-ch'ien's head is thus underscored by the
superficial way in which it applies to real life: actually it is Li Niang,
and not Yun-ch'ien, who has much the deeper grasp of what is going
on. Most ironic is the fact that their roles of "liberated" and "unliber-
ated" are in reality the opposite of what Yun-ch'ien assumes them to
be. In real life it is Li Niang, the one supposedly "still living in hades,"
who has freely chosen Meng-hsia as her lover; Yun-ch'ien, the one
"casting rays of light into the darkness," has been assigned to him by
her family.
    It is not only implicitly that Yun-ch'ien's "new learning" is shown
to be superficial, clear though the indications at that level are. Two
pages after her impassioned speech, Yun-ch'ien overtly renounces her

26. YLH, p. 119.

pursuit of the new style. "From this point on," she says, "my will to study is forever dead."[27] Though she has been one of the best students in her school, and is only a few weeks from graduating, she refuses to go back and finish. Li Niang, ironically, tries to change her mind, but cannot.[28]

And what is it that replaces new-style thought in the mind of this lively teenager? It is a deeply emotional and well-grounded respect for Confucian norms, a respect which the reader is given to feel *really* was there all along. The day after the "collapse" of the modern-style Yun-ch'ien, she sits alone in her own room playing the lute and singing a gentle song of her own composition. Without a thought of social revolution, she expresses appropriate Confucian regard for all in her immediate family:

> When I was young I worried not,
> But frolicked away my carefree hours;
> I hated embroidery but loved to read
> And to sit in the shade and look at flowers.
>
> Oh, to sing once, as the sounds do their blending,
> Oh pleasures of ease, where are you now?
>
> I've a father, a father, with hair turning white;
> Who serves him breakfast when morning is nigh?
> Alone at the table a silhouette sits
> Of a lonely old man with a long lonely sigh.
>
> Oh, to sing twice, as the song becomes halting,
> When I sing of my father, my tears are like rain.
>
> I've a mother, a mother, who lies underground;
> Her bones are grown cold and my heart fills with pain;
> She's seven years lost in the vastness beyond—
> When will she enter my dreams once again?
>
> Oh, to sing thrice, as the singing grows muddled,
> The wind whistles bare and the poplar trees sigh.
>
> I've a brother, a brother, oh why did he leave,
> At a mere twenty years, suddenly to die?
> I wanted to follow, but what could I do?
> No message could reach his soul in the sky.
>
> To sing a fourth time, as the song flickers on,
> A lone wild goose calls cold through the air.[29]

Yun-ch'ien becomes increasingly confirmed in her rejection of new-style thought from this time on. Near the end of the story, when Li

27. YLH, p. 121.   28. YLH, pp. 127–128.   29. YLH, pp. 124–125.

Niang grows so gravely ill that everyone in the story, her doctor included, believes that she will die, Yun-ch'ien stands as the only defender of unscientific sentimentalism in refusing to accept this conclusion. She will not believe the doctor. Perhaps the ancestors, she imagines, will see that Li Niang's old father and little son still need her, and yet spare her life.[30] Just before her own death Yun-ch'ien gives a *pro forma* last hurrah for the new style, quoting from Patrick Henry: "Give me liberty or give me death." That this is mere stylishness is now obvious, and casts all that she had said before in the same light. She goes on to point out that really death is her only alternative, and recalls as "extravagant talk" the new-style ideas which she and her classmates held a year earlier.[31]

Portrayals of new-style young women in other works varied in how much sympathy the new style is allowed, but there was remarkable agreement, at any rate, on what the issues were. The old and new, or *t'u* and *yang,* styles were set forth time and again for readers' consideration, usually with at least some room for the imposition of the reader's own preferences. It is hard to escape the conclusion that the appeal of the fiction rested on the possibility of having it both ways: at one level, usually more superficial, a reader could take the new-style woman at face value, and thereby enjoy the stylishness and sense of security which comes from association with the modern elite; but at another, perhaps more visceral level, the same reader could turn from the new style if necessary and enjoy the comfort of knowing that premodern values are still there, waiting in the wings.

It is practically impossible to assign this balance between new and old any relative proportions, either sociologically or psychologically. It is tempting to estimate that about twenty percent of readers in the 1910s favored the new style and about eighty percent favored the old. But it is just as significant that each reader, in his or her own mind, felt a twenty/eighty or some other balance, and that such a balance would vary from story to story, day to day, mood to mood, and so on. It is this kind of changeable relationship between reader and text that makes certain statements by May Fourth critics of popular urban fiction neither true nor false. To characterize that fiction as "reactionary" or "feudal"[32] is to draw attention to only one side of a two-edged sword.

Yet the May Fourth critics are correct to claim that popular authors were not mere observers of the question of the new versus old styles. Their stories often encourage the reader in one or the other direction;

30. YLH, p. 145.
31. YLH, p. 161.
32. YYHTP, pp. 23–28 and *passim*.

and it is probably true that more total *encouraging* is done in the old-style direction, whatever the actual results may have been. It is worthwhile looking closer at how and why an author's rhetoric was important.

On the side of promoting the new style, the origins of modern popular fiction in the progressivism of the late Ch'ing reform movement again prove to be crucial. It was then that advocacy of new-style values was solidly identified with the modern elite. In the beginning this advocacy, in both fiction and real life, was explicit and sincere, although limited to a very few. On the question of the new-style woman, a few publications appeared which were edited by and intended for women, and which helped to make the ideal, if not the reality, of the new-style woman a celebrated cause in progressive circles.[33] In addition, a small number of women actually took the revolutionary plunge into new-style roles. The famous revolutionary Ch'iu Chin, the outspoken Cantonese teenager Hsueh Chin-ch'in, and Ch'en Hsieh-fen, editor of the "women's report" in the *Su pao,* for example, all stood as "liberated women" and reached the attention of ever-increasing numbers of people.[34]

Fiction played an important role in the spread of the idea. In chapter 9 of his *History of Late Ch'ing Fiction (Wan-Ch'ing hsiao-shuo shih),* Ch'ien Hsing-ts'un reviews some leading examples of fiction on "the question of women's liberation." Two works written in the *t'an-tz'u* storytelling style, called *T'an-tz'u on a French Heroine (Fa-kuo nü ying-hsiung t'an-tz'u),* about the life of Mme. Romain Rolland, and *T'an-tz'u on the Torch of Civilization in 20th Century Women's Affairs (Erh-shih shih-chi nü-chieh wen-ming teng t'an-tz'u)* called for "freedom and equality" for women and for women's education in particular, while opposing specific bad customs such as footbinding, the giving of child brides, and confinement of women to the inner chambers. Among a large number of other works on these themes, Ch'ien singles out I-so's *Huang Hsiu-ch'iu,* which was serialized in Liang Ch'i-ch'ao's *New Fiction* beginning in 1905, as the best.[35] "Huang Hsiu-ch'iu" is the name of the story as well as its energetic heroine, whose activities would have seemed a model of progressivism even twenty years later, after the May Fourth movement. Huang Hsiu-ch'iu unbinds her feet, calls for equality between the sexes, and organizes neighborhood women;

33. See chapter 3 and appendix for details on women's magazines.
34. CYLHIL, p. 225; Britton, *Periodical Press,* p. 116; Ch'ien Hsing-ts'un, *Wan-Ch'ing hsiao-shuo shih* (Hong Kong), pp. 112–115; Mary B. Rankin, *Early Chinese Revolutionaries,* pp. 40–46 and 176–179.
35. Ch'ien Hsing-ts'un, *Wan-Ch'ing hsiao-shuo shih* (Hong Kong), pp. 105–106 and 109–112.

she is accused of insanity, arrested, bailed out by her husband (himself an enlightened person) and goes on to establish a girls' school. She calls for freedom of marriage and extends the doctrine even to nuns, whom she involves in the reform movement.

Popular authors in the 1910s and twenties could never quite separate themselves from the precedent of such examples, however suspicious they and their readership might have become of them. At an explicit level they continued to declare themselves opposed to superstition and in favor of "spreading enlightenment" *(k'ai feng-ch'i),* i.e., adopting the new style. Deploring arranged marriage became one of the most common ways of waving the new-style banner. In Li Han-ch'iu's best-selling *Tides of Yangchow,* a young woman who was the daughter of a family's deceased relatives is adopted into their household. There she is allowed to study for a year with a tutor, and then, with all kinds of ceremony and fanfare, is engaged as a second wife to a hoary, buck-toothed opium sot old enough to be her father. When the young woman throws a tantrum against the idea, the family summons her tutor, who is in his seventies, to chastise her. The tutor proceeds to intimidate the bride with his prestige and with a wooden ruler, all the time bemoaning the disappearance of the Three Obediences and the Four Virtues. Finally she is forced to submit to performing the rites with the old opium sot, after which the tutor laughs loudly and goes together with the new husband to recline on the *k'ang.* [36]

There is no question in this and passages like it that readers' sympathies are drawn toward the young woman. Aside from the patent unfairness of the situation, it doubtlessly reminded readers of real life, where the years of a young woman immediately following marriage were some of the most stressful ones for either sex at any time of life. Marriage meant that a young woman would have to leave the security of her own family, adjust to new sexual and maternal roles, and often submit to the domination of unfamiliar parents-in-law as well as her new husband. But this was merely normal. In cases where a match was forced because of a family's interest rather than a girl's own interest, the ordeal could be even more difficult. In fictional accounts, part of the sympathy with a young bride depends upon the fact that she must face her trials alone, with no one (but the reader) as a companion.

Even a story like *Jade Pear Spirit* could be labeled, as it was by its author and its movie producer, a "protest" novel. Though the ideal of chaste widowhood is for the most part upheld as a beautiful thing, the reader is also offered the chance to view it as a cruel "shackle" which can cause a good person like Li Niang to suffer greatly. Insofar as

36. Li Han-ch'iu, *Kuang-ling ch'ao,* 1:106–122.

readers viewed it this way, the late Ch'ing reform movement was still alive in the mid-1910s.

The sense in which a novel like *Jade Pear Spirit* can be read as "protest" is actually very complex. One must, first of all, place the question within the tradition of earlier popular fiction in China. Many of the "reform" issues introduced to the Chinese literary scene in the last Ch'ing decade echoed feelings which had long been part of Chinese cultural and literary history. If, for analytical purposes, we separate modern or Western-inspired protest from the premodern or traditional kind, then we must note that when modern protest appeared in Shanghai fiction it superimposed itself on an already-complex premodern pattern. There was more coincidence between the two "levels" on some issues than on others. The scandal stories which boomed in the late 1910s, for example, exposed official corruption in much the same spirit as the eighteenth-century novel *The Scholars (Ju lin wai-shih)*. Neither the style nor the substance of their protest was changed importantly by placing it under the banner of new-style reforms. What did matter was that authors and readers could claim a new-style affiliation without having to change their attitude. The more a modern protest issue coincided with a premodern one, the easier was its acceptance in the modern century. In fact, given the conflicting pressures at the popular level to associate with elite opinion but at the same time to avoid anything too outlandish, there may have been a tendency among popular authors and readers to exaggerate their enthusiasm for those aspects of modern protest which were familiar in traditional terms precisely in order to cover their skepticism in other areas.

Our example of the new-style young woman itself had a rich premodern background. Pao T'ien-hsiao, who in the 1910s viewed himself as a proponent of the "new style," recalls that at the time of his own marriage in 1894 he *already knew* about the unfairness of the arranged marriage system because he had read about it in old novels.[37] For Pao and other social novelists the matter of writing a "new style" story about arranged marriage was therefore simple: take any of several familiar themes, sharpen their "problem" aspect a bit, call them "new style," and publish. Traditional stories sympathetic to young women who for various reasons are either separated from the man they love, or forced upon one they don't, are too abundant to need listing. It is true that chastity and obedience were widely accepted in Chinese society *as ideals*, at least since Sung times. But the difficulty of living up to the ideals at the same time provided cause to sympathize

37. CYLHIL, p. 131.

with those who were obliged to do so. The plight of young widows like Li Niang, for example, is at least as old in Chinese literature as the stories about Cho Wen-chün, the lovely widow from the second century B.C., who was enticed to elope by the zither playing of Ssu-ma Hsiang-ju.[38] Cho Wen-chün has been a basically sympathetic character for centuries despite her defiance of family authority; more than two thousand years later Li Niang, who would never have dared elope, is far less radical. Thus the ready acceptance in the 1910s of the notion that one should sympathize with Li Niang and, at least in a *prima facie* sense, accept the "modern" issue of widow remarriage, seems attributable at least in part to premodern attitudes.

One can argue much more generally that many stories in the popular tradition, while stopping short of support for female rebellion, provided female points of view with an avenue of expression which male-dominated orthodoxy did not allow. (*Dream of the Red Chamber*'s sensitively differentiated presentations of female psychology are a fine example, and an important influence on later works.) There is a sense in which fiction could give young women a certain "scope" within which various kinds of behavior, even protest, were permissible and even enjoyable to observe. A good illustration of such "scope" is a well-known story called "Record of the Sharp-Tongued Li Ts'ui-lien" (K'uai-tsui Li Ts'ui-lien chi), written probably between 1400–1575.[39] In it a young bride protests her marriage by talking loudly, railing at her parents, intimidating her groom, being rude to the groom's parents, cursing her matchmaker, and so on and on, mostly in rhymed verse. Two things are noteworthy in the story about what we are calling the "scope" allowed to the young woman for her protest. First, it seems quite large. One gets the sense of a storyteller and audience who knew that the event of marriage could be very difficult for a young woman and therefore, in spite of Li Ts'ui-lien's defiance of social proprieties, indulged her. (One gets this sense because it is impossible to enjoy the story without adopting something near to this attitude: Li Ts'ui-lien is not a villain.) Second, the scope has definite limits. Indeed, the entertainment value of the story depends crucially upon the assumption of such limits. Li Ts'ui-lien is amusing because she violates norms which are well-established and because she does not *really*

38. *Shih chi* (Shanghai, 1959) 9:2999–3074 (chüan 117).

39. The story is collected in *Ch'ing p'ing shan t'ang hua-pen* and for many years was assumed to date from Sung or Yuan times: see *Hua-pen hsuan chu* (Chung-hua shu-chü, 1974), p. 21; and H. C. Chang, ed., *Chinese Literature: Popular Fiction and Drama* (Edinburgh, 1973), pp. vii, 29–30. Patrick Hanan has shown that the story was probably created between 1400 and 1575: See Patrick Hanan, *The Chinese Short Story: Studies in Dating, Authorship, and Composition* (Cambridge, 1973), pp. 8, 140–141.

threaten them. If she did, she would be not funny but either villainous or heroic, depending on one's point of view. In fact, her buffeting of the norms indirectly reaffirms their correctness. Viewing the story this way we can see its socially therapeutic side. It points to a chronic irritation in traditional society—the movement of a bride from one family to another—and, by gently laughing at the protests of a young woman in this position, acknowledges the legitimacy of letting off steam even while funneling the steam in a harmless direction. It acknowledges the threat a dissatisfied young woman can pose to the patriarchal family system, and at the same time blunts that threat. It prepares everyone for outbursts by showing, in the relative comfort of a fictional context, that there really is no cause for worry, that outbursts can happen without threatening basic rules. The effect on young girls to be conditioned to accept this view must not be discounted.

Other examples may not be as clear as Li Ts'ui-lien's, but they exist in abundance. A young woman steps out of the normal woman's role, *ipso facto* becomes interesting, but actually serves, in the moral rhetoric of a story, to reinforce by negative example the norms which she opposes. A related kind of example arises in the many stories about female knights-errant *(nü hsia)* or girl soldiers *(niang-tzu chün)* in which the interest in the heroines depends in large part on their assumption of radically non-traditional roles. What they assume, in fact, are paradigm men's roles, yet the reader is not allowed to forget that *nü hsia* are women. Along with their strength and martial skills, female knights-errant possess the good looks and gentle femininity of the ideal woman. It is precisely the *combination* that is interesting, that is part of the "heaven-rending, cloud-startling, ocean-uplifting strangeness" which knight-errant stories always attempt.[40]

In some cases it is obvious that the female knight-errant upholds the traditional order even while being such a dramatic exception to it. The people she fights are those who violate Confucian virtues. As a woman she is physically attractive and "well bred": she defers to males (if they are virtuous), is capable of blushing, and approves of marriage in the Confucian style. Hu Shih and other modern critics have pointed out the incongruous conservatism of the heroine Shih-san mei of the nineteenth century *A Tale of Heroic Young Lovers (Erh-nü ying-hsiung chuan)*.[41] Having illustrated on page after page the unorthodox notion that a young woman can perform great and public acts, Shih-san mei in the end returns docilely to the fold of Confucian propriety. When

40. The phrase is from Cheng I-mei, *"Huang-chiang nü hsia* hsu," in Ku Ming-tao, *Huang-chiang nü-hsia,* 5:5.
41. *Hu Shih wen ts'un,* 3:503–504.

she decides to become the second wife of the young gentleman whose family she has rescued from plunderers, she does so on grounds that it is her filial duty to produce offspring. Besides, having been so close to the young man during the various rescues, she fears it might appear improper if they do not marry. But even when the female knight-errant does not so obviously return to propriety, her adventures in a masculine role are not subversive to the traditional order. This is because she is so clearly exceptional. Her exceptional nature accounts for her entertainment value, and at the same time implies to the reader that she is not a practical role model. Her exception clarifies the rule.

The important fact about the new-style woman in the early twentieth century, when viewed in terms of this background, is that she became viewed as another in the general type of woman who exceeded the accepted limits of a woman's role. This made her, like the others, both inherently interesting and inherently abnormal.[42] In real life, of course, new-style women represented a genuine threat to the traditional order, and a much greater threat than the one Li Ts'ui-lien posed, because of the many other aspects of the challenge from the West associated with it. There could therefore be great additional comfort for readers in finding the new-style woman to be nothing more than an entertaining diversion from proper standards. Her demands were initially interesting but in the last analysis incongruous. Reading about her served the dual purpose of paying respects to the new style while preventing it from subverting the old. And—perhaps most significantly—one could distance oneself from a threat. One could divert to a level of frivolity an issue which in daily life was all-too-worrisome. The diverting of the threat was, if anything, more important to men than to women; and this fact helps to explain why so many readers of stories *about* the new-style woman were men. Thus, having begun a few pages ago with some examples of how popular

42. There were, of course, many differing emphases among less-than-continent women of the old and new styles. On the question of arranged marriage, for example, the sense of unfairness in traditional fiction usually came from a marriage which elders wanted and young people did not. In the last Ch'ing decade and in the 1910s, protest against parental authority occurred increasingly, at least in fiction, for the converse reason: young people did desire a marriage, but one of their own choosing, while parents forbade it. Even the find-your-own theme was not exclusively "modern", of course. Pao-yü and Tai-yü in *Dream of the Red Chamber* had "found" each other. But they found each other among a very limited circle and were at least a possible match in their elders' view. In 1910s and 1920s fiction, a respectable boy or girl could hunt for him- or herself outside the household, and plausibly — sympathetically, in the reader's view — come up with almost anyone. A stranger to the family is possible, and even one of a different social class. (Consider the case of Shen Feng-hsi and Fan Chia-shu in *Fate in Tears and Laughter.*) Even a foreigner is not unthinkable. (See Chou Shou-chüan, "Hsing tz'u hsiang chien," *Li-pai-liu,* no. 3, June 20, 1914.)

fiction could serve to advocate new-style roles for women, we are now ready to look at how it could also push the other way.

It is instructive to begin with some examples which do not confront the new-style woman squarely, but which do show how literature still was used to prescribe a proper scope for women. Li Han-ch'iu's ten-volume social novel *Tides of Yangchow* presents itself in the tradition of progressive "new fiction", yet one of its constant sources of humor is the female who does not keep to proper roles. A little girl stands up before her playmates who are playing school and announces that she, a girl, is going to be *hsien-sheng*. "Impossible," one of the surprised little boys observes.[43] A middle-aged mother fearlessly attacks two men, her husband and her child's tutor, when the two have decided to discipline her child:

> Teacher Lei [the tutor] was just about to raise the bamboo rod when he suddenly heard, streaming across from the other side of the flower well, the shrill cry of a woman's voice.
>
> "You old good-for-nothing! I see you're all decked out in your scary ghost-face again! Dare strike my child and I'll dock you one year's salary and your holiday gifts to boot! Beat him to death and you're a beggar for sure, and with no place to beg! My child, fear not! Hurry inside and have some ice-swallow soup with your mother."
>
> Now, all this talk of course didn't amount to anything, but it was easily enough to scare old Sire Ho [the father] entirely out of his wits. Teacher Lei frantically hid the bamboo rod under his desk, and the two of them sat there in utter silence, scarcely daring to exhale.[44]

The men here are as funny as the woman, and partly because they, too, fail to maintain customary roles.

We might consider in a bit more detail why such behavior should appear comic. In one of his more reasonable little books, *Jokes and their Relation to the Unconscious,* Freud argues that we laugh at actions which appear to turn back the progress of civilization, by which he means actions in which physical effort is wasted for a lack of mental effort: "A person appears comic to us if, in comparison with ourselves, he makes too great an expenditure on his bodily functions and too little on his mental ones."[45] At the crudest level of this theory, slipping on a banana peel is funny because one neglects the simple mental effort

43. Li Han-ch'iu, *Kuang-ling ch'ao*, 2:13.
44. Ibid., 1:136.
45. Sigmund Freud, *Jokes and their Relation to the Unconscious*, tr. James Strachey (New York, 1963), p. 195.

of avoiding the peel, and then must recoup one's loss with physical effort. At a more complex level, the theory suggests that men and women who do not use their brains to stay within social patterns appear funny (to the majority who do) because their deviance is, in the final analysis, wasted effort. And why should someone's wasted effort be funny? Freud adds that: "It cannot be denied that in both cases [of too great an expenditure of physical effort and too little of mental] our laughter expresses a pleasurable sense of the superiority which we feel."[46] In the case of a woman who moves beyond her proper scope, the reader's "pleasurable sense of superiority" assumes that her efforts are futile or otherwise misplaced. It is for this reason that humor is useful in blunting the implicit threats which such a woman poses. The diminution of the threat in turn bolsters the reader's feeling of superiority and brings added confidence that any threat can be contained. The stronger a perceived threat, naturally, the greater the sense of pleasure at release from it. (It is worth noting that, in current theory, the physiological function of laughter is to relieve tension when the cause of the tension disappears.)[47]

When first proposed, the idea of the "new-style" woman in Shanghai was less threatening than it was simply interesting. Western roles in general were new and strange—the "new-style" student, the lawyer, the Western medical doctor, the "revolutionist", and so on. It was all the stranger and more interesting to see women stand in these new roles, and there were stories galore in the late Ch'ing magazines about "girl students" *(nü hsueh-sheng),* "women doctors" *(nü tai-fu),* "women revolutionists" *(nü ko-ming-chia),* "women spreaders of enlightenment," and even "women detectives", "women pilots", et cetera. (The prefix *nü-* was used well into the 1920s and 1930s to designate the fascinating female version of all kinds of new roles. Even among May Fourth writers, who were much more aware of modern notions of women's equality, women writers were consistently referred to not as *tso-chia* but as *nü tso-chia.)*

When novelty turned to satire, passages like the following became common. This one is taken from Yen Tu-ho's *Dreams on the Ocean of Humanity (Jen-hai meng,* late 1910s?), and is a typical satire of the new-style "girl student." (It also seems to be a satire in particular of the famous late Ch'ing revolutionary Ch'iu Chin. Ch'iu Chin was known

46. Ibid., p. 195.
47. Arthur Koestler, "Humor and Wit," *Encyclopaedia Britannica,* 15th ed. (1974), 9:7. See also Koestler's *Insight and Outlook: An Enquiry into the Common Foundations of Science, Art and Social Ethics* (New York, 1949), pp. 3–110; and *The Act of Creation* (London, 1964) pp. 27–97.

to carry a sword and practice public speaking.)[48] In the story an elderly father, Shou-ch'ing, is lecturing to his son Kuo-hsiung about the outrageous behavior of the son's sister Chih-fen, the "girl student":

> Shou-ch'ing suddenly frowned towards Kuo-hsiung and said, "This sister of yours Chih-fen has gotten very caught up in the bad habits of 'civilization' recently. Every word and every gesture just has to be different from the manners of the old-style household. Last year she kicked up a great fuss with me demanding to go to an academy. I refused time and again, but couldn't stand it any more when your aunt joined in on her side. They badgered me to distraction, until finally I sent her off to study at that Yü-hsiu Girl's School nearby.
>
> "Once she'd been to school there was no changing her. A first-class young lady had turned entirely into the likes of one of these 'girl students.' At times she even carried on about stuff like singing songs and doing calisthenics. I heard that during the year-end vacation they ran some kind of a carnival or something and that she was right there in the midst of it making a speech. Making a speech is still all right—but then she starts playing with swords. Now I ask you: what kind of behavior is *that*?!
>
> "When she came home she got a good talking to from me. 'What do you mean by this?' I said, '—messing around with swords and staffs! You want to play the *wu-tan* or something?' And then—of all things!—she retorted with the idea that *I* was being ridiculous. She said that from time immemorial there had always been women who practiced warfare: Liang Hung-yü beating her drums, Hua Mu-lan replacing her father to lead the troops—weren't these good enough examples?"[49]

The daughter's rebuttal sends the father to higher levels of animated expression. It is important to note here that the girl student is not the only object of satire. Her narrow-minded father is also laughable, and hence the reader can to some extent choose which side to blame (to feel superior to, to diminish the threat of, etc.). Or, perhaps most comfortably, the reader can stand above the fray and feel superior to both sides.

But the usual way in which the new-style woman was presented in fiction had definitely changed in a negative direction from ten or fifteen years before. The attention was now less on the outlandishness of what the new-style woman stood for than on the fear that such ideas might actually be implemented. Gradually and quite subtly, the bold-

---

48. Mary Rankin, in Margery Wolf and Roxane Witke, eds., *Women in Chinese Society*, pp. 39–66.

49. Yen Tu-ho, *Jen hai meng*, excerpt in YYHTP, pp. 191–92. "Civilization" is a euphemism for Westernization. *Wu-tan* refers to the lady warrior part in classical opera.

ness of the new-style woman turned to quaintness, and respect for her to a condescending indulgence. Saying so in fiction, and indirectly at that, avoided the unpleasantness of openly contradicting the progressive elite.

The stages in this shift can be illustrated in a magazine like *Women's Times,* which was founded in 1912 as an offshoot of the progressive *Eastern Times (Shih pao)* and was edited by Pao T'ien-hsiao and Ch'en Ching-han. (See also Appendix.) In the "Opening Statement" *(fa-k'an tz'u)* of its first issue, *Women's Times* explains its purpose as one of liberating women both for their own sake and for the sake of the national effort which their liberated energies can serve. Ever since the "new tides" from the West began arriving on China's shores, "our sisters" in the "women's realm" *(nü-chieh)* have been frightened by the increasing urgency of the national situation. These sisters have their special contribution to make, and the purpose of the present magazine is to collect and distribute all of this brilliant *(kuang-mang)* material.

The Opening Statement goes on in this vein at some length. It sounds for the most part like a progressive manifesto of which Liang Ch'i-ch'ao would have approved. Yet it also implicitly introduces the basis for the condescension to women upon which the magazine's amusement value, its most substantial appeal, came to be based. We are told that the ways of the world are getting subtler and trickier, and that this magazine (edited and primarily written by men) will cast a beam of light into the obscurity which holds women back. One problem, though, is that when the barriers come down people often react too fast, abandoning morality as if it were a pair of worn-out old shoes. When this happens the women's movement is hurt, because old conservatives, such as Buddhist moralists, then have a basis to attack the movement, and even ardent reformers will beat their breasts and sigh (over the decline in morals).

The reader is gradually induced to stand back from participation in the women's movement, and, more than that, to stand above it and be its judge. From this vantage point the lively idea of the new-style woman begins to appear quaint and amusing. Much of the magazine's content reads ambiguously. Articles about the new methods of the modern-style housewife, or photos of the graduating classes of various new women's schools, can be taken as either serious or quaint as the reader prefers. There is somewhat less ambiguity in a pictorial survey of women around the world, or an investigation into the headgear of European women: these were primarily for amusement.

The subversion of the new-style woman's cause is more obvious when one considers that the magazine's actual readership was overwhelmingly male.[50] There should be no need to expatiate upon the difference, in general, between magazines which are about women and for women, and magazines about women but for men. Though the element of sexual appeal was never crass in *Women's Times,* it was seldom absent either, and increased with time. The magazine's cover featured a picture of one or two beauties, quite in the fashion of later magazines which made no excuses for their appeal to men. The same opening statement which appears to speak for modern feminism with such gusto also uses all sorts of ornate traditional clichés for female beauty. The final paragraph tells us that the editors are busily searching the country for delicate women contributors:

> The sylph-like hands *(ch'ien hsien shou)* of the land will join together, and our country will rest on an assemblage of comely shoulders *(hsiang chien),* each bearing an equal share of the world's affairs. In searching for patriots from the boudoir *(chin kuei),* be not hesitant or fearful, or concerned for the safety of an unblemished body *(yü t'i).* All the sisters in our generation of compatriots will join in igniting the resplendent fireworks of the national citizenry among the living tapestry of our lands and lakes.[51]

The revolutionary call had a way of quickly becoming very aesthetic.

But although the combination of a call for modern feminism with some very traditional phrases for female beauty may seem highly incongruous, it is not necessary to postulate great hypocrisy on the part of authors or readers in order to explain it. First of all, the phrases were clichés, and though assuredly incongruous, were not as much so at the time as they may seem now. Secondly, the incongruity which does remain is probably explained less well as hypocrisy than as ambivalence toward the new-style woman. In fact acceptance, support, curiosity, delight, skepticism, satire, and rejection were all at work in ways obvious and not so obvious; and there is every reason to suspect that the same readers were subject to varying viewpoints at different or even the same times. The following list of the contents of issue number 5 of *Women's Times* (December, 1912) gives some idea of the strange mixture in the magazine's appeal:

1. The Model of an Ideal Household
2. On the Multifarious Harm and Lack of Any Good in Prostitution
3. A Woman Should Base her Character on Self-Restraint

---

50. See chapter 5, section 5 above.
51. "Fa-k'an tz'u," *Fu-nü shih-pao* 1.1 (1912):1.

4. On the Need for Women's Suffrage
5. The Close Relation between Universal Education and the Education of Women
6. Report on a Survey of the Life of Women in Shanghai
7. The Travels of Hai Yü (Fiction)
8. The Theory of Treating Disease without Medicine
9. Your Virgin Years (Fiction)
10. The Heroic Deportment of the Mother of [George] Washington

The topic of the "girl student", which is raised in the excerpt from *Dreams on the Ocean of Humanity* above, was also a recurrent topic in *Women's Times,* and presumably a recurrent worry among readers. The Opening Statement of *Women's Times* declares with rhetorical indignation that "our country has long professed the nurturance of education, but in women's education has been laggard and gone nowhere." In fact, however, there is much evidence that the idea of the girl student was one of the most difficult ideas for popular authors and readers to accept. The girl student did more than go beyond proper women's roles. What she sought to assume was a male role, and a very key male role at that, one which traditionally had related to the most basic functions of society. She could not be discounted as an oddity (as the woman detective or lion tamer might) because there were ever-increasing numbers of her. Being young she suggested that the future was with her. The force of the West represented by missionary educators and by much elite opinion in China seemed to be on her side. The question of whether the modern girl student was a viable idea was, for all these reasons, singled out as an important test case for the new style as a whole.

The new-style girl student was frequently portrayed as a very special thing—a category unto herself. This was partly an inability to comprehend what she implied and partly the wishful thinking of those who knew only too well. She was always referred to not as a "student" but as a "girl student", a term which carried within it the interest of a paradox. When author Pao T'ien-hsiao and a group of his friends decided to found a girls' school in Soochow, they dispatched Pao to Shanghai expressly to investigate the means and methods employed by girls' schools already in operation. It apparently did not occur to them to model their school on any of the boys' schools in Soochow.[52] A girls' school was an entirely different matter. A few years later, when Pao turned to writing "social" novels, he decided to teach in several girls' schools in order to gather experience for his fic-

52. CYLHIL, p. 267.

tion. What could be more strange and fascinating than to enter a class-room before a roomful of girls? Pao reports that it was his nature to want to experience everything at least once.[53]

The fruits of his investigation were the discovery that girl students in Shanghai were lively, unruly, unpredictable and, in short, cute. In popular parlance they were "thirteen o'clock",[54] a phrase one might translate as "nutty" or "silly" but whose basic meaning derives from the hands of a clock going too far (viz., exceeding their proper role). Similar phrases in English are "too much", or "beyond the fringe." One must, of course, doubt that girl students in Shanghai were any more lively or unruly than boy students. Pao's own examples confirm as much. Girls chatter in class, play mischievous tricks like quoting the classics to rebut a teacher, and are polite in front of foreign missionary teachers but make up outrageous nicknames behind their backs.[55] The girls seem, in other words, to have been healthy and normal. They were considered "thirteen o'clock" only because they were girls.

Boys and young men were seldom such clear-cut symbols as new-style young women, yet they, too, were inevitably touched by the same dilemma and viewed through lenses of various shades because of it. The student Shih-ch'ih in *Jade Pear Spirit,* for example, expends his energies in "the world of new studies" *(hsin hsueh chieh);* and because this is supposed to benefit the nation's future, it is presented as a pass-ing good thing. Yet with his "new studies" there seems to come an insensitivity to inter-personal feelings and proprieties. When Meng-hsia confides to him that Li Niang has suggested he (Meng-hsia) marry Yun-ch'ien—a most delicate situation to say the least—Shih-ch'ih exuberantly seizes the initiative and drags Meng-hsia with him to break the news to Patriarch Ts'ui, Yun-ch'ien's father. Such cavalier insensitivity grieves Meng-hsia and irritates the reader; this new-style person is happy to treat a complex sentimental problem as if it were a simple, mechanical one.[56] While Shih-ch'ih causes mild irritation, the only really evil person in *Jade Pear Spirit* is the school teacher So-and-so Li. Though we know very little about him, we are told that he is arrogant, selfish, and "quite involved with the new styles of the times."[57]

A less Westernized and more sympathetic young man, like Meng-hsia, keeps himself a safe distance from "the realm of new studies" even while acknowledging its usefulness for China. Early in the *Jade*

53. CYLHIL, p. 335.
54. CYLHIL, p. 337.
55. CYLHIL, pp. 335–336.
56. YLH, pp. 121–122.
57. YLH, p. 49.

Pear Spirit story, Li Niang expresses a fear that Meng-hsia will some day sail off in pursuit of new studies and leave her behind. Meng-hsia promises that he will not. He writes her the following in a letter:

> You say that I've had experience in the realm of new studies, but this view is mistaken. I've seen nothing but rough times for the last ten years, and by now all thought of fame and fortune has long since died away. Everything in the world is changing so rapidly these days, as new banners unfold in the world of learning; how can I get involved in pursuing all those currents, in joining all those youth who compete with one another in the arts and letters of the day?[58]

Meng-hsia's feelings illustrate two important components of the general doubt in popular fiction about "new-style" behavior. Most important, as shown in several examples above, is the suggestion of unpleasantness; but equally apparent is the suggestion of insubstantiality. The Western "new learning" appears as a great dither and cry — new banners unfolding, youth frantically competing—which in the final analysis fails to engage reality. A steady person like Meng-hsia eschews it. The latest "new learning" may serve as a style for the times, but what use has it beyond that?

Certain "new style" ideas came in for more scorn than others for their unpleasantness and insubstantiality. The girl student was one of these, and an even clearer example was new-style divorce. We have seen (chapter 4) how the arguments of Western-style lawyers could appear highly suspect; new-style divorce epitomized the same dubiousness. People would do it on a whim, shuffle some papers with a new-style lawyer, and falsely pretend to believe that nothing serious had happened.

The issue arose in the last Ch'ing decade as soon as new-style people began to experiment with divorce. Prominent examples such as Ch'iu Chin shocked most people as much as they pleased a tiny vanguard. Divorce became a recognized category of scandal. In 1910, a work in the "castigatory novel" tradition called *Divorce Cases in Officialdom (Kuan-ch'ang li-hun an)* appeared under the name of T'ien Meng. Leading writers in the 1910s frequently returned to the subject, and in the early 1920s interest seems to have reached a peak. Writers of the Star Society (chapter 5) paid much attention to new-style divorce, partly because one of their number, Pi I-hung, tried it out.[59] Major fiction magazines came out with special issues on divorce.

58. YLH, p. 54.
59. CYLHIL:HP, pp. 58–59.

Stories about new-style divorce almost always show that the act is superficial and its results tragic. It never has a good reason. Friends and neighbors (and the reader) are puzzled when it happens, and seek an explanation. Why *really* would anyone do such a thing? What happiness could one possibly expect from it? Those who undertake Western-style divorce also appear to be acting on the impulse of a moment, or to be carried away by the silly styles of the times, deluded that their behavior is glamorous. In his story "A Divorce After Seventeen Years" (Shih-ch'i nien hou ti li-hun), Wang Hsi-shen comments on the nature and origins of new-style divorce:

> As a matter of fact, the word "divorce" has been quite a fad in society for some time now. And if one asks where in the world divorce is easiest and most common, one must, first and foremost, mention America. Although most politicians like to drone on about China and America clasping hands—these two great Republics, one in the East, one in the West—reflecting one another at a distance, actually there's no way to speak of them in the same breath—except for this matter of divorce. It's almost as if China has caught a contagious disease from America. For no good reason at all we're allowing the big lawyers who hang out their gold-lettered signs to bring in another special item of income. On one day there will be a report that Sir So-and-so and Lady Such-and-such are proceeding with their plan to live together, or that beginning on a certain month and day they will organize a new household. Everything is all spelled out in new-style terminology and sounds extremely nice. Then before long there comes another public announcement saying that the two sides have agreed to seek a divorce.[60]

The real evil of divorce lay not just in the flippant attitude with which it was undertaken but in the tragic consequences. Another story employs a phrase of the traditional storyteller to explain how a single step casually taken (a divorce) could, after a chain reaction of consequence and coincidence, lead to a horrible end. Called "The Coward" *(No-jen)* and written by Chiang Hung-chiao, the story tells of a man who suddenly decides he wants to divorce one woman for another. The first woman, the divorcée, has no relatives and so goes with an American missionary to the United States, where she studies medicine. Later she returns to China to practice. One day a woman comes to her for a fertility operation, and the woman doctor performs the operation, never suspecting that her patient is the same woman for

60. Wang Hsi-shen, "Shih-ch'i nien hou ti li-hun," *Hsing kuang,* vol. 1, item 3, pp. 3–4.

whom her husband had left her. The operation is a success and within a year the second wife gives birth to a daughter. The husband, who by this time feels deeply regretful about his divorce, decides to name the child after his first wife. Later the child falls ill, and the woman-doctor-cum-former-wife is summoned to treat her. When the doctor hears the name of the child everything dawns on her and she faints. When she recovers she prescribes a drug to kill the child, then leaves and completely disappears from the region. In the end the various cruelties of the story are laid at the doorstep of the evil of new-style divorce.[61]

The fact that divorce, unlike some other new-style capers, could be condemned without ambiguity was surely related to its violation of the core family values which were such an important emotional anchor for the modern urban readership. Its false promise of happy freedom turned quickly to the misery of a broken family, solitary living, and unfortunate effects on children. What's more, women could do it to men. Pi I-hung's story "Children After Divorce" (Li-hun hou ti erh-nü) includes an exchange among five children—three sons and two daughters—whose mother has recently left home. The father is eavesdropping and listens in pain to the following:

> "Brother, how come Mother hasn't come home for so many days?" His older daughter was interrogating her brother, who was oldest.
>
> The eldest brother had yet to reply when the youngest brother broke in: "Always before when she went out she took us with her. Why's she gone all by herself this time? She even left Fifth Little Sister behind!"
>
> "What are you talking about!" said the big brother. "Haven't you heard? Mother and Daddy have been divorced."
>
> "What does 'divorced' mean?" asked the middle son and older daughter, almost in unison.
>
> The youngest son and daughter were even more puzzled. Their eyes opened wide as they listened for their oldest brother's answer.
>
> "'Divorced' means," said the oldest brother, "that Daddy and Mother are not man and wife any more."
>
> Again the older daughter and middle son asked together, "If they're not man and wife then what are they?"

At this point in the children's talk, the author introduces a pun on the word *jen-shih* ("recognize") using it first in the Western-influenced legal sense of recognizing a person in the formal status of spouse, then in the ordinary sense of recognizing who a person is.

61. Chiang Hung-chiao, "No jen," *Hsing kuang,* vol. 2, item 1, pp. 1–5.

"From this point on," explained the oldest son, "Daddy will not recognize Mother. And Mother will not recognize Daddy."

The middle brother laughed. "Don't play tricks with us. How can Daddy not recognize Mother? Or Mother not recognize Daddy? Nobody knows each other better than those two. How could they not recognize each other?"

"I don't believe elder brother either," said the older sister.

"But I'm telling the truth!" said the eldest brother. "I'm not joking at all!"

The middle brother chimed in. "You say that from now on Mother will not recognize Daddy, and Daddy will not recognize Mother. You mean if tomorrow or the next day Mother comes back, Daddy wouldn't speak to her? He would pretend he didn't recognize her?"

"You still think Mother's going to come back?" asked the oldest brother. "From now on and forever, Mother's *not* coming back!"

The oldest sister and middle brother heard this sentence as if it were a peal of thunder from the blue sky. They were so terrified they couldn't speak.

The youngest brother and sister could not restrain themselves. With a cry of "Wa!" they both burst into tears.

When the older sister and middle brother had seen the young ones begin to cry, they also broke out with a "Wa!"

"Hey, don't cry!" said the older brother. "If Daddy hears, he'll come give spankings!"

"Mother's—never coming back," stammered the older sister. "How can we keep from crying—"[62]

It is important to note that divorce per se was not the issue, but only new-style divorce. Old-style divorce, which was supposed to allow a husband to be rid of a wife for any of seven reasons, including failure to respect his parents or to produce a male heir, was seldom even mentioned as the same issue. It was also satirized, but separately and less earnestly. New-style divorce was viewed as something unnatural, something extraneous to any responsible social system.

In fact much of what went on in the modern city was felt to be counter to common sense, to judge from some stories. Pointing out the modern city's absurdities nicely complemented the idealization of the countryside (but still was not enough to induce readers actually to return to the countryside). Typical of many pieces is Pao T'ien-hsiao's "The Countryman Revisits Shanghai" (Hsiang-hsia-jen yu tao Shang-hai) which was serialized beginning October 30, 1931, in *Shen pao*. It is a string of vignettes on a story line about a likeable and

62. Pi I-hung, "Li-hun hou ti erh-nü," *Hsing kuang,* vol. 1, item 6, pp. 5–7.

straightforward old peasant who has difficulties getting around the modern city.

He finds Shanghai expensive, foreign, irrational, petty-minded, impersonal, depraved, and chaotic. Things baffle him right from the start. At the railway station he misunderstands a "platform ticket" *(yueh-t'ai p'iao,* literally "moon deck ticket") to be a ticket for a special garden car where one can sit and gaze at the moon. A group of people have congregated to meet a dignitary identified only as a "central committee member" *(chung-yang wei-yüan).* This he understands as "sprout planting committee member," a near homonym, and is profoundly surprised. He goes to buy some five-fragrances tea-leaf eggs and finds they sell for a preposterous price. When he informs the vendor of this fact, the vendor shrugs him off and doesn't seem to care.

Outside the train station, the old man sets about finding the home of a relative. After asking around for a few minutes, he realizes that nobody in the city knows anybody else. The only kind word he hears from anyone is a warning to beware of pickpockets. Finally he learns that the way to get places in the city is by streetcar, and that the streetcar has a first and a third class. Why there should be a first and third class but no second class, is only the beginning of the nonsense associated with streetcars. He learns that they run on hopelessly complicated routes, and that every time they turn a corner it is at an avenue with another crazy-sounding foreign name. It is all the old man can do to remember how to get where he wants to go. When he goes to buy a ticket, the ticket seller takes one look at him and sells him a third class ticket. But when the streetcar comes, third class is so crowded that the old man is disgusted and goes back for a first class ticket. "Why not pay a bit more," he reasons, "and be a first class individual?"

When he gets off the streetcar and walks along the street, he continues to take note of a variety of irrational things. He sees, for example, whole rows of little shops lined up selling the same thing. He takes it upon himself to approach two sweets shops which are next to each other and to suggest that they get together. The shop owners ask if he is crazy. He walks away.

He sees a man reading an illustrated magazine which has pictures of bathing beauties on the cover. Irate, he walks over and snorts: "So this is beauty! Well, I never knew you had to take your pants off to be beautiful!" Later he learns about flesh-colored silk stockings and sex appeal in the movies. It is clear to him that the city has lost its moral bearings. A group of prostitutes accosts him, and he assures himself that no country girl would ever act so shamelessly.

Before the old man left for the city, people in the countryside had been saying bad things about it. They did not know what it was like, but they did know it was a mysterious and evil place. Large, dark forces were at work in it, and one challenged them at one's own peril. Parents tried to keep their children away from the city. One girl who went anyway never returned. The city had gobbled her up and made her a prostitute.[63] In his reminiscences, Pao T'ien-hsiao records that people in Soochow as early as the 1890s thought of Shanghai as "big dye jar" *(ta jan kang);* once a young person was tainted with the dye, he or she could never be washed clean.[64] But while the "dye" might stain a person permanently, its cause, the styles from the West, were still superficial. Like motor oil on a millpond, Western ideas lay on top of basic Chinese values in a film as shiny and colorful as it was thin, breakable, and suggestive of pollution.

Such views emerge so frequently from popular fiction in the 1910s that one might be drawn to conclude that the fiction was strongly conservative, with only a thin disguise of progressivism in deference to the new-style elite. Such was the conclusion of May Fourth critics, except that they discounted even the facade as no more than a trick. But it is difficult to conclude that the popular urban readership was a solid block of conservatism, even considering examples like the girl student, new-style divorce, and the crazy modern city. Something like "anxious ambivalence" is still a better description of the popular mentality.

On the question of city versus countryside, for example, popular fiction's frequent suggestion that life was better in the countryside was false, and readers knew it. That they knew it is demonstrated by their choice in overwhelming proportion to remain in the city even while enjoying stories which extolled the hinterland. In chapters four and five we have touched upon several aspects of the lure of the city: the new occupations which the city offered as a substitute for the old ladder of success; the idealistic attraction of building a new China; the fascination of a complex new environment; the glamor of association with the new style; and so on. There are a few hints of this side of things even in a story like "The Countryman Revisits Shanghai." While all the people in the countryside are bemoaning the loss of a country girl to prostitution in the city, the old man himself points out that great money can be made in the city. Did not even this poor lost daughter send enough money back to the countryside to build a fine cement house for her parents?[65]

There was, moreover, a definite element of condescension in the idealized view of country life, just as in the idealized view of children.

63. Pao T'ien-hsiao, "Hsiang-hsia-jen yu tao Shanghai," *Shen pao,* October 30, 1931 *et. seq.,* installments 1–22.
64. CYLHIL, p. 180.
65. Pao T'ien-hsiao, "Hsiang-hsia-jen yu tao Shanghai," *Shen pao,* October 30, 1931.

The jokes about the old countryman in Shanghai are ironic jabs at the modern city, to be sure; but they are also made at the old man's expense. They are based on his misunderstanding of things which the reader understands, and therefore allow the reader the comfort of feeling superior. Notice the affectionate condescension in an excursion to the countryside by Meng-hsia in *Jade Pear Spirit:*

> Meng-hsia walked straight [towards the school], passing once more through the familiar setting of the town. He noticed that the usually drab market streets were now bustling with activity in a way they had never been before. There were colorful awnings everywhere, and lanterns hanging all over the place. Men and women dressed in all kinds of gaudy outfits decorated the scene. Sounds of the Pan pipe could be heard amidst a commotion which reached to the heavens. What was going on?
>
> Meng-hsia enquired of an aged rustic along the way, and the old man told him it all was a custom. Every year at the beginning of autumn, with everyone looking forward to a bountiful harvest, the people of the town would get together and organize a thanksgiving. They hung lanterns and paid their respects to the gods, celebrating the rich harvest of the five grains. As a rule they spent three days paying these sincere respects, "offering thanks in the fall for what had been prayed for in the spring." And today was the first day!
>
> As Meng-hsia listened to the old man, he had to laugh silently at the country people's superstitions. But at the same time it was truly heartwarming to see them thus: so pure and simple, not forgetting to be thankful for what they had, and finding such joy in the fruits of their labors—like a mother hen delighted with her hatch! I am lucky indeed, thought Meng-hsia, that my return to school should have fallen, not a bit too soon nor too late, upon the day of this fine festival.[66]

If Meng-hsia's visit had not fallen on the fine festival day, would he have found the village boring? Could the pure and simple life be attractive all year round? What is heartwarming—superstitions, or being able to chuckle at them?

Strictly speaking, praise of the countryside and disparagement of the city in a popular novel does not tell us that these were widespread views; it tells us only that many city dwellers enjoyed fiction which expressed such views. The psychological point of extolling the countryside clearly was not to recommend living there but to give other satisfactions to the urban reader. For one thing, the condescending element in the view of the countryside could bring the enjoyment of

66. YLH, p. 86.

feeling superior. (In the harshly competitive city any way to feel superior could be welcome.) At the same time the idyllic element in the view of the countryside could provide the comfort of knowing about a reliable fallback position from the uncertainties of urban life. In this sense the idealized countryside was "sweet grapes": not the denigration of an alternative denied to one, but the romanticizing of an alternative one knew was secure.

In a larger sense both praise of the countryside and satire of the city served not to reject urban living but to make it tolerable. Ironically, perhaps, the anti-urban release offered in fiction may actually be viewed as functionally supportive of the new urban mode of living. The Romantic Route outlined in chapter two, for example, might be viewed as a supply of antidotes for the stings of the modern city, available for more or less use as the individual might require. The strong personal attachment which is exalted in the Route could counter the anonymity and loneliness of the city. A story's delicacy could balance its businesslike brusqueness. And the Route's strong connection with the natural order—inborn talents, supersensitivity to landscapes, the immutability of fate, and so on—could remind the reader of the roots of life. One can observe basically the same functions of fiction operating some twenty years later, among a more modern and Westernized urban readership, in the popularity of Shen Ts'ung-wen's stories about West Hunan. In both cases the need for an idyllic view of the hinterland arose from anxieties about modern life in the city. People in the hinterland itself certainly had no such need.

If urban readers had mixed feelings about the city, it may seem strange that expressions in popular fiction were so one-sided. Why must one hunt for a good word about the city or a bad one about the countryside? The reason seems to be that the good side of city living was comprehended in a reader's daily life, and attested by his or her presence in Shanghai; it therefore needed no expression in fiction. The need for fiction came from the irritating side of life.

We have said much about how fiction handled new-style irritations through satire, through the deflection of threats to the traditional order, through confining the new style to a superficial level, and so on. There can be no doubt that putting the West in its place was a vital factor in popular fiction's appeal, in fact very likely the greatest factor. But other things were happening at the same time. Simply by mentioning the new style, even if it were satirized, a text could serve to accustom its readers to changes that were coming. For example, all the stories about women students, women doctors, women revolutionists, et cetera, while subtly delivering the message that these roles are appropriate only to a bizarre few, nevertheless greatly expanded the audience for the *idea* of such things. People who had never dreamed of a woman pilot now knew that one's daughter should avoid becoming one. Ironically, the notion to try something as a new-style woman might be planted in a girl's mind by a story whose appeal to most people depended on putting down the very same notion. The ability of popular fiction to serve as midwife for new ideas could be quite independent of whether people felt they liked the new ideas, in fact quite independent of their reasons for reading a story.

In addition to the simple phenomenon of new ideas having their strangeness wear off for many people, there was a clear incentive to adjust to change. This incentive, whose pull seemed as steady as a magnet's while many other things were in flux, was the continuing association of the new style with the modern elite. One function of the bourgeois novel in England is supposed by many to have been the teaching of the upwardly mobile how to behave in the circles they aspired to move into. A similar function became increasingly important in Shanghai fiction as it became increasingly clear that the new style came from the upper class. Some fascinating illustrations of upward socialization at work may be found in a "Dear Abby" type of advice column which appeared in the early 1930s in the Tientsin *Ta kung pao.* The column was titled "Modern" (mo-teng) because the editor always gives advice from the "modern" point of view. He favors new-style education, systematic job-hunting, choice of one's own spouse, and then setting up a nuclear family—to be done in that order. Widow remarriage is completely all right (*pace* Li Niang). One should always choose scientific solutions for problems, especially in medicine.[67] The editor's pen name, by the way, was "Mr. Coldheart" *(hsin leng hsien-sheng),* an intended or unintended comment on modern urban life which sociologists since Simmel and Parsons might find satisfying.

Yet the very authoritativeness of Mr. Coldheart's tone bespeaks a continuing ambivalence among his readers. The real question was not whether to choose the new style or old style *in toto,* but how to strike an appropriate balance. Most youth wanted some say in the selec-

67. All the examples listed are taken from 1931, when the column usually appeared around page nine of the *Ta kung pao.* Not every piece of the editor's advice was entirely modern, however, as in the following example which really had no modern solution. A railway worker who had lost his legs in an accident could not afford the several hundred yuan which a modern doctor demanded for artificial legs. The worker's choices, as he saw them, were to ask for contributions, which he felt to be dishonorable, or to give up and go to jail. He asked the *mo-teng* editor's advice. The answer was to buy a board, which will cost only a few yuan, and learn to walk around on your two good hands ("Mo-teng," *Ta kung pao,* Tientsin, January 18, 1931).

tion of their mates and also wanted parental participation.[68] While Mr. Coldheart was urging his readers to use Western medicines exclusively, the *Ta kung pao* elsewhere was running a four-by-six inch advertisement for Bayer aspirin, the appeal of which can only be called "eclectic." The company's name is written in a stylish horizontal-and-vertical cross, in both English and Chinese, in the middle of two circles. A scientific pitch is made in pictures of two pairs of lungs, before and after the ravages of pulmonary consumption. A skull is sketched in to drive home this point. The ad also includes a relatively large sketch of a sage-like old man apparently representing the authority of the herbalist. There are pictures of both the bottle and the box of Bayer. The signature of the artist (of the whole ad?) appears in one corner.[69]

What the advertisement presented to readers was, in a simple form, what many novels offered in regard to the new and old styles. Given the evidence we have seen in this chapter for the considerable tendency, especially when in doubt, to stick with the old style, the task of deliberation became one of vicariously testing different aspects of the new style to see what they were like. Such testing could not extricate itself from anxiety. Not only was the problem frighteningly large and complex, but there might be little tolerance for mistakes. To be too old-style could seem stupid or unstylish; to be too new-style, arrogant or gaudy. The delicate problem of finding a middle path was in several ways shielded by the act of reading fiction. First, thanks to Liang Ch'i-ch'ao on the one hand and to May Fourth leaders on the other, one could always claim that reading a novel was adequately patriotic and progressive, even if the content of the novel was ambivalent about progressive goals. Secondly, the *Gedanken* experiments with the new style which fiction made possible were vastly preferable to experimentation with real life. Reading *Jade Pear Spirit,* for example, a young reader who encounters Yun-ch'ien's exciting ideas on women's liberation might experience a complete change of mind before and after reading about the collapse of Yun-ch'ien's new-style facade. In real life an about-face like this could be extremely costly. But in fiction one could give the new style as much weight as one wished without running risks in matters one did not fully understand. It is, furthermore, of obvious importance that this kind of vicarious testing could, at least sometimes, proceed in private, between one reader and one book. The fact that many people in Shanghai had this chance is another indirect

68. See Marion J. Levy, Jr., *The Family Revolution in Modern China* (Cambridge, 1949), p. 315.
69. *Ta kung pao,* Tientsin, March 1, 1930.

benefit of the rapid growth of the printing industry we have described in chapter three.

Amid all the evidence of ambivalence in the rhetoric of China's modern popular fiction, one element whose constant recurrence might seem surprising is the sad—in fact the positively mournful—ending. (We speak here of the love stories and most of the short stories and short novels—not of the lengthy social novels, or the knight-errant or detective stories.) There are several ways to explain these sad endings. In literary terms one can easily trace precedents in Ch'ing fiction, especially in *Dream of the Red Chamber;* and Chinese Marxists make the general historical argument that, the early twentieth century being a comparatively mournful time for China, mournful stories are to be expected. But in more precise terms sad endings still present an interesting question: what was the appeal of a sad ending to the insecure, ambitious, ambivalent, comfort-seeking average reader of the 1910s?

Part of the appeal of a sad ending would seem to be that it allowed the reader to think himself a talented and good person *even though* he was not doing too well out in the world. This was especially possible in the modern "talent meets beauty" *(ts'ai-tzu chia-jen)* stories we have characterized as the Romantic Route. If Shanghai readers were typically young, separated from family, unemployed, and disease-stricken, it is significant that the *ts'ai-tzu* (talented one) is typically young, separated from family, unemployed, disease-stricken, *and a genius.* The reader feels that the new-style city does not properly appreciate him, and countless stories show that the depressed *ts'ai-tzu* is indeed underrated. He is underrated by everyone—everyone, that is, except the *chia-jen* (the beauty), for whom the reader probably did not have a counterpart, no matter how much he deserved one. This left the reader quite ready to enjoy the *chia-jen* vicariously supplied to him in stories.

But this way of reading a story, often called "identifying" with a protagonist, cannot explain the whole appeal of sad stories. It especially cannot explain finales, where *ts'ai-tzu* usually die and "identification" becomes difficult. Endings in which *chia-jen* die are even more noteworthy because a great many pages of expansive emotionalism are devoted to pitying these beauties. Not only love stories but also social fiction (like "The Story of a Laborer," see chapter five above), often took aim at the reader's feelings of pity. There clearly was an appeal in all this, and it came other than by "identification."

What a reader decides to identify with, he or she can also decide to abandon, just as a jacket which is worn may also be shed. The jacket can then be hung up, brushed off, and regarded from outside. To contrast with "identification," it is useful to think of the "observation" of protagonists in modern popular fiction. Observing could be just as comforting as identifying, depending on the circumstances. At a minimum it moved the reader one step away from the pain and suffering which afflicted fictional characters. Beyond that it let the reader enjoy the feeling of pity which comes when one does not experience pain but sees it inflicted upon someone else. Though it may be a sad comment on human nature, there can be little doubt that "enjoy" is the correct word here. In the love stories of the 1910s such enjoyment is the sweeter and more intense because the typical sufferer is a fragile, helpless, "good" creature, and a female. An element of sexual appeal was often involved, but the essential ingredient was defenselessness in the face of oppression.

We are told that Li Niang's hands are delicate and small (she is a soft creature) but that they must manage the affairs of the entire Ts'ui household (she is a soft creature under duress);[70] and for the good Li Niang, of course, that is only the beginning of suffering.

For most readers the "observation" of sufferers was probably more self-delusive than "identification" with them. In identifying, the reader is prepared to accept at least some of the unpleasant truth about him- or herself. But in standing back and pitying others, the reader implicitly raises him- or herself above them. How far above is not specified, although the ones pitied are known to be beautiful and talented people. This pose, however illusory, comforts the reader. There is ample evidence that this kind of enjoyment exists in all cultures and many contexts. Arthur Koestler and other modern psychologists have referred to the principle of "mock attack",[71] according to which a reader (or television viewer, et cetera) who is presented with the image of a threat can enjoy the release of tension which comes from knowing that the threat is unreal. Essentially the same principle, according to Koestler, underlies horror comics, many jokes, and even tickling. In these terms the mournful-ending story in Shanghai may be seen as a presentation before the reader of dangers he himself fears, and at the same time as a double shield against those dangers. First, the reader knows that fiction is fiction, and this knowledge brings pleasure for the same reason that seeing a Dracula movie is enjoyable while actually meeting Dracula would not be. Second, to the extent that a threatening idea lingers, the reader is offered the reassurance, as it were, that tragedy is something which befalls others.

Tragic figures were usually old-style characters, the ones who stood for purity, honesty, pre-modern life, and so on. Hence it is also worth noting that insofar as a reader opts for observation of, rather than iden-

70. YLH, p. 105.
71. Arthur Koestler, sources cited in note 47 above.

tification with, a suffering genius or beauty, he or she takes a step away from old-style values. The beautiful young person who suffers and dies for Confucian virtues simultaneously suggests to the reader: (1) that, ideally speaking, it would be thrilling indeed to do such a thing; and (2) that, realistically speaking, one should not be expected to do it. Thus, a distinction between actual and ideal behavior is tolerated, and standards at the two levels are assumed to differ. The fictional character can demonstrate pure, self-destructive dedication to virtue while the reader is reinforced in the position of admiring but not imitating such behavior. May Fourth critics who saw pro-Confucian works as "textbooks for feudalism" apparently overlooked this and other ways in which they could be read.

The step away from old-style values in the "observation" mode of story reading was simultaneously a step toward the contrasting pole of modernism. When the reader takes such a step, traditional values move "from life to museum," in J. R. Levenson's phrase, assuming the once-removed quality of nostalgia.[72] This shift helps to explain why the fictional view of traditional life could become so highly idealized. It is probably significant, too, that the shift is most apparent near the ends of stories, where the external view of beauties and geniuses is most natural. This suggests that when all is said and done the reader's modern identity is tentatively vindicated. It is a result which a reader who has tentatively committed himself to living in the city would naturally hope for—in spite of all the difficulties.

The rhetoric of stories can show us how an author invited his readers to respond, and the fact that certain stories were popular is evidence that such responses were common. But it is certainly just as futile to try pinning down how most readers took a text ("identifying," "observing," "experimenting," et cetera) as it is to try to capture "the" popular view of the great question of the old versus new styles. It is most likely, in fact, that precisely the multiplicity of uses for popular texts explains their broad appeal. Not only could ambiguity accommodate differing views; it allowed readers to enjoy the advantages of all views at once, unencumbered by the impossibilities of the real world. A Romantic Route story could assure readers that the pure, pre-modern life was still there *and* that they could consider themselves — potentially, at any rate — superior to it. Reading one could be like taking a therapeutic trip out to the countryside and back, "identifying" on the way out, "observing" on the return, escaping the modern city while feeling sorry for people "trapped" in the traditional setting.

72. Joseph R. Levenson, *Confucian China and Its Modern Fate: A Trilogy* (Berkeley and Los Angeles, 1972), 3:76–82.

The unity in this contradictory pose—that both its aspects served to bolster the reader's sense of security—is the basis of a useful generalization. Many of the important ways in which popular fiction appealed to readers appear essentially to have been ways of aiding and comforting people who faced a heterogeneous and rapidly changing environment. The "new style" was a pervasive problem, one which obliged all modern urban residents to assume a position. In fiction one could learn about it, test it, counter threats from it, balance its summons to stylishness with one's own preference for familiar ways, and so on. If one grew despondent before the very vastness of the problem, or fell victim to feelings of personal inadequacy, popular fiction again could help, in several ways allowing one to feel superior to other people of both the old and new styles. (It is important to note one point upon which the satire of a new-style character like the girl student and the pitying of an old-style character like the withering beauty are congruent: in both the reader is made to feel superior to someone who has certain outward marks of success.) We can call these various aspects of appeal "comfort" because they eased anxieties which were already in readers' minds. One generally looks in vain in modern popular fiction for a writer like Lu Hsun whose strength lies in raising disturbing questions which readers had failed to notice.

I do not claim that the pursuit of comfort tells everything about the appeal of China's modern popular fiction. There was, certainly, appeal in the craft of good storytelling and in the clever or aesthetically pleasing use of words, some of which we have treated in chapters two and five. And there undoubtedly are aspects of popular fiction's appeal I have overlooked. Yet it seems reasonably clear that the greatest service of this fiction was, in several ways, to make people feel better.

Popular Fiction in China in 1979

After the Communist revolution in 1949 popular fiction in the Butterfly tradition suddenly had to stop publication, though it continued to thrive in Hong Kong, Taiwan, and overseas communities. Butterfly books from before 1949 could be found at Shanghai's used-book stores as late as spring 1966, on the eve of the Great Proletarian Cultural Revolution. In the following years every sign of the tradition disappeared from public view.[1]

The need for entertainment did not disappear, however; indeed the need for "comforting" fiction probably grew under the severe social and psychological pressures of the Cultural Revolution. It is not surprising that during the relaxation of social and literary controls after "the smashing of the Gang of Four" in October, 1976, a number of popular novels which had been circulating underground came to light. Some were foreign works in translation. They were hand-copied or mimeographed, and circulated secretly but in some cases very widely. In both content and social function they invite comparison with Butterfly fiction.

The Second Handshake (Ti-erh-tz'u wo-shou) by Chang Yang became the first well-known example of this fiction, both because it circulated underground almost everywhere in China during 1968–76, and because in 1979 it was chosen for official publication by the China Youth Publishing House. Like Chang Hen-shui's *Fate in Tears and Laughter* fifty years earlier, Chang Yang's novel blends a number of well-tried popular themes, including the love triangle, the martial arts hero, and anti-spy detective work. It also reflects elements of the May Fourth tradition, such as science-to-save-the-nation and the glamor—and sometimes humiliation—of going overseas to study.

A handsome young man falls in love with a beautiful young woman after saving her from drowning. Like the protagonists of Romantic

---

1. In spring 1966 Cheng I-mei, a popular writer in the 1910s and 1920s, could still purchase Butterfly books at used-book stores in Shanghai. In 1973 Chang Hen-shui's *Fate in Tears and Laughter* was in the closed stacks at Peking University, but it had not been checked out since the 1950s.

Route stories from the 1910s, this couple is ardent, high-minded, and as brilliant mentally as they are beautiful physically. Both want to devote themselves to science for China. The young man is also superb at the martial arts, but, like the heroes of *Strange Roving Knights* in the 1920s, does not parade his abilities. He remains utterly casual in the presence of a band of armed thugs. When they threaten his girlfriend and resistance becomes quite necessary, he coolly thrashes the lot of them single-handedly.

The two lovers must part when the young woman goes to the United States to study atomic physics. The young man wants to go, too, but his father, reminiscent of the narrow-minded parents often satirized in the social novels of the 1910s, is set against it. He has arranged for his son to marry the daughter of an old friend. The young man is at first defiant, but gives in when this fiancée, also a scientist, proves to be a sensitive, sincere, and courageous person. (Her courage is demonstrated when she is badly injured in a fight with enemy spies who are trying to steal research data.) Meanwhile the first girlfriend becomes an outstanding scientist and, after thirty years' celibacy, returns to China to work and to look for her lost lover. Broken-hearted to learn that he has married, she is saved from further self-banishment only by the intervention of Premier Chou En-lai. (Chou plays *deus ex machina* in this and many other stories and plays of the late 1970s.)

The story's sidelight about struggle with enemy spies owes less to pre-revolutionary detective fiction than to anti-spy stories from the Soviet Union. In the 1950s, cooperation between the Soviet Union and China brought a Soviet influence even to popular fiction; Russian spy stories in translation (*The Secret of the Firing Range* was a leading example) were published in great numbers. Chinese writers also imitated the style extensively. The Masses Publishing House, administered by the Ministry of Public Security, devoted itself almost exclusively to publishing detective and spy stories, presumably on the theory that the more such fiction was read by Chinese agents, and by the Chinese people at large, the more effective would be China's vigilance against spies. Be that as it may, spy stories did become very popular. During the Cultural Revolution they were banned, like almost everything else; but after 1976 they resurfaced. In Peking and Canton in 1979 the commonest answer I had (from non-intellectuals, at any rate) to the question "What fiction do you like?" was *"fan-t'e"* (anti-spy).

The published version of *The Second Handshake* was the seventh the author wrote. The first he did in 1963 at age twenty. It was about five thousand characters in length, the equivalent of about eight printed pages. He re-wrote it in 1964, 1966, 1970, and 1973 at lengths steadily increasing from fifteen thousand to eighty thousand characters (twenty-five to a hundred and thirty printed pages). This diligence was only incidentally for improving the story; actually Chang was replacing manuscripts as they disappeared.[2]

It was in the nature of so-called "hand-copied volumes" *(shou ch'ao pen)* that once lent out they were passed from hand to hand and often became irrecoverable. Readers themselves would re-copy a text, typically using flashlights under blankets. A story could spread rather quickly throughout the country, though with many versions due to the embellishments of copiers along the way. *The Second Handshake* was originally named "Sea Spray" (Lang hua) by its author;[3] the second version he called "How Red the Luscious Mountains" (Hsiang shan yeh cheng hung), and the third "Homecoming" (Kuei lai). Somewhere along the way a reader-copier changed "Homecoming" to "The Second Handshake," and this fourth name stuck, though its fashioner is still unknown.[4]

Chang's fifth manuscript unfortunately found its way into the hands of the authorities. Yao Wen-yuan condemned it as a revisionist poisonous weed which "opposed Chairman Mao's revolutionary line"; which sought the "homecoming" of capitalism and the "reversal of the verdict on Liu Shao-ch'i and Lin Piao"; which "extolled the wasted ghosts of landlords, the bourgeoisie, and all manner of demons and monsters"; and so on.[5] The manuscript was traced to Chang. When he was arrested he was found in possession of a sixth version of two hundred thousand characters. This went into his file as he went to prison on January 7, 1975. Four years later he was exonerated and released, but went straight to the hospital for the rest of the year to recover from tuberculosis and pleurisy he had contracted in prison.

Meanwhile editors at the China Youth Publishing House recovered

2. Wang Wei-ling, "Tsai chien-k'u-chung mo-lien, tsai tou-cheng-chung ch'eng-chang: chi 'ti-erh-tz'u wo-shou' ti hsieh-tso ho tsao-yü" ("Tempered by hardships, raised in struggle: notes on the writing and the fate of *The Second Handshake*") *Wen-i pao* (Peking) no. 357 (September 1979): 47–48; and interview at the China Youth Publishing House, October 8, 1979.
3. "Lang hua" has another sense which might be translated "the vagabond beauty."
4. Wang Wei-ling, *Wen-i pao* 357:47–48. In Canton in early 1980 I found a hand-copied version of "Woman in the Tower" ("T'a-li nü-jen") by the famous pre-revolutionary Bohemian writer called Wu-ming-shih ("Anonymous"). The volume was 142 thin pages copied during the Cultural Revolution on stationery bearing the imprint "Revolutionary Committee of the Second People's Hospital of K'ai-feng City." Judging from the handwriting, eight people took turns doing the copying. It is crudely bound with string between two unmarked covers of thick paper.
5. Wang Wei-ling, *Wen-i pao* 357:48.

the sixth manuscript from Chang's file. Adding a few ideas of their own, they helped prepare the version which is now in print.[6] In its first three months (July to September, 1979) it was printed in 2,830,000 copies at presses in eleven cities. Before the end of 1979 it had also appeared in comic strip form, as a radio play, and in many local dramatic and operatic productions. In 1980 the Beijing Film Studio was preparing a film version.[7]

The book was very hard to buy in late 1979. Most local bookstores were sold out and waiting lists were long. News of its publication had been carried in newspapers and on radio, but according to the publishers word-of-mouth was probably the most important medium of announcement. The reading public had had no chance to buy a book like this openly for at least thirteen years. In October 1979 the publishers were getting several hundred letters a day asking for copies, even though this was not an approved method of buying books. Readers would send in money and postage stamps, which was not only risky but in violation of a law against sending cash through the mails.

The market situation of *The Second Handshake* was not too unusual in 1979. Demand was exceeding supply for almost all the fiction then being published or republished. Prices were relatively low (*The Second Handshake* cost eighty-four Chinese cents, or fifty-six cents U.S.) and were fixed throughout the country according to a uniform but very complex formula.[8] The price of books was not the crucial barrier to circulation it had been in the 1910s, nor was literacy. The biggest problem was *access* to purchasing opportunities.

Books were distributed through the New China Bookstore, a state monopoly, according to an elaborate quota system which allowed branch stores different numbers of books depending on their size, lo-

6. The material which was added by the editors, including a few whole new incidents, was aimed to promote the current policies of emphasizing science, praising Chou En-lai, and fostering friendship between China and America.

7. Interview at the China Youth Publishing House, October 8, 1979; Ku Chih-ch'eng, "The Second Handshake, a New Bestseller," *Chinese Literature* (Peking) no. 1, 1980, p. 104.

8. The formula was based on the quality of paper, the amount of paper, the number of illustrations, the number of colors in the illustrations, the type of cover, the projected circulation, and the nature of the material. The last of these factors varied according to how much the government wished to encourage circulation. Thus political reports and propaganda were assigned lower rates than literature, which in turn had lower rates than technical materials for limited audiences. Even within literature there were variations. Contemporary Chinese literature costs less per page than May Fourth era literature or foreign works in translation. Interview at Peking People's Publishing House, October 20, 1979; interview at Kwangtung People's Publishing House, March 4, 1980.

cation, and proximity to specific publishers. Within the quota system, *ad hoc* adjustment was possible for branches with special needs, or among branches who wished to trade with one another. Fiction magazines, like all periodicals, were distributed by the General Post Office, which administered a similar massive system of quotas.[9]

As in the 1910s, fiction reading in the late 1970s was still predominantly an urban phenomenon. The lower demand for books in the countryside was matched by lower quotas assigned to its bookstores and post offices. Among cities, some were more favored—sometimes much more—than others. For example, in 1978 a systematic program was undertaken to reprint thirty-five classics of Chinese and world literature. After the Cultural Revolution the thirst for such books among the reading public was immense and the decision to publish them in numbers ranging from only three to eight hundred thousand per title meant that many readers would still have to do without.[10] Yet it was decided that one-fourth of the entire country's allocation should go to the city of Peking. According to officials at the New China Bookstore, this was because of "the concentration of high-level intellectuals and high cadres" in the city.[11]

After reaching a local bookstore or post office, books and magazines were sold according to established priorities. Work units took precedence over individuals; units or individuals whose work required certain materials outweighed those whose did not; special people like high officials or foreigners had special privileges. For many books and periodicals, especially those with technical, scholarly, or politically restricted uses, all copies were channeled exclusively to approved subscribers. In late 1979 the post office handled about eleven hundred periodicals nationwide, of which about seven hundred were of this type that went only to subscribers. But literary magazines, about fifty of them, were all in the freest category, that is, the one that allowed subscriptions to people in all occupations as well as retail sales in certain post offices. Conscious efforts were made to reserve an adequate proportion for retail (forty percent for the leading *People's Literature*) in order to insure that all readers have a chance to buy their own.

This meant that would-be subscribers were diverted to the retail market, where the competition to purchase popular books and maga-

9. Interview at the New China Bookstore, Wang-fu-ching branch, Peking, October 30, 1979; interview at the Ssu-tao-k'ou post office, Peking, October 16, 1979.

10. Three to eight hundred thousand may seem ample numbers, especially when compared with the 1910s. The reason the numbers were insufficient is that *only* thirty-five titles were reprinted *for the whole country*. This followed twelve years when no foreign literature of any kind was openly circulated.

11. Interview at the New China Bookstore, Wang-fu-ching branch.

zines was intense. Word spread astonishingly whenever a local bookstore or post office received a shipment of something attractive. Long lines usually formed. But when the prize was especially desirable a jostling, clamorous crowd would press itself from all sides upon one or two harried clerks. Somehow the clerks would choose among dozens of outstretched, money-clenching fists. (Every exchange was an exact-change transaction, since anyone requiring change would have no chance.) Many people, rather than contend with such frays, sought so-called "back-door" private connections through friends, or friends of friends, who worked in post offices or bookstores. Such connections were publicly scorned, but nonetheless very common. People with relatives or income sources overseas could get preferential access to books by handing in foreign-currency coupons. (These coupons were designed to encourage remittance of foreign currency; Chinese citizens could receive them, in addition to the equivalent in Chinese currency, when money came to them from overseas.) To buy *The Count of Monte Cristo* in Shanghai in 1975 one needed sixty coupons, representing a bonus on the remittance of about U.S. $170. By 1979 the coupon requirement had been reduced to twenty.[12]

Readers who failed to buy their own copy of something were not necessarily lost, however. First they could try to borrow from others. The People's Literature Publishing House estimated in 1979 at least ten readers per copy for its books.[13] For literary magazines this ratio must have been, if anything, higher. Second, almost every work unit (factory, school, whatever) had its own small library where one could borrow books and periodicals. Popular items were hard to find, however. In Peking a book or magazine was called a *fei-shu* ("flying book") when one borrower passed it on to another, and he to another, and so on — each recognizing that it was a library book but none returning it to the library. (The lending period at a Communist Youth League reading room at a commune in Nan-hai county in Kwangtung was a whole month, and seldom observed at that.) The major public libraries in Chinese cities were used for research purposes and very seldom served readers of entertainment fiction.[14]

Third, one could try to rent. In the fall of 1979 the Peking post office was beginning to experiment with renting literary magazines. They required a deposit of nearly double the purchase price and charged a rent of three or four cents a day. Their loss rate in the very initial stages

12. *The Count of Monte Cristo,* well known in China for four decades, became especially popular in the declining years of the Cultural Revolution (1973–77). Its renewed favor seems to have been partly due to its theme of revenge.

13. Interview at People's Literature Publishing House, Peking, September 28, 1979.

14. Interview at Peking Library, October 28, 1979.

was twenty-five percent.[15] There was also a private market, somewhat larger, in both the sale and rental of books and magazines. For publications which were both current and open, prices were low and transactions casual; for unofficial publications, old or foreign books, or limited circulation materials including foreign works in translation, prices could be high and transactions shady. Before it was republished in 1979, *The Count of Monte Cristo* could get eight yuan (about five U.S. dollars) for only twenty-four hours' rental in Peking.

During 1978–79 the illicit and the specially privileged markets in fiction declined as the public media became—comparatively speaking—much more open and flexible. Young people were asked to hand over their hand-copied volumes, and many did. The circulation of leading literary magazines grew in great leaps. *Tso-p'in (Literary Works)*, published in Canton and well regarded throughout China for its—comparatively, again—"liberated thought," had a circulation of around fifty thousand in 1975. By mid-1978 this had risen above seventy thousand, and six months later to one hundred and thirty thousand. When the figure rose to two hundred and ten thousand in spring 1979, authorities in Canton set a limit for *Tso-p'in* of three hundred thousand. The stated reason was paper shortage. In early 1980 the limit was raised to five hundred thousand, and actual circulation rapidly attained that level.[16]

Tso-p'in was not unusual in this regard. Throughout China in 1979 the largest single factor which kept supply behind demand was paper shortage. Like most things in short supply, paper was rationed. The State Publication Administration Bureau centrally controlled the allocation of paper (excluding its non-publication uses). Every publisher in the country was assigned a quota of paper. These quotas generally rose from year to year during the late 1970s but were only marginally flexible. Quotas could be increased for short-term special needs, but not by much and only if approved. In some cases paper quotas were traded. Hunan province, for example, decided in 1979 to give fifteen tons of its annual allotment of paper to Kwangtung province in exchange for 12,500 extra copies per month of *Tso-p'in*.[17]

15. Interview at the Ssu-tao-k'ou post office, Peking.

16. Interview at the *Tso-p'in* editorial offices of the Kwangtung Writers' Association, Canton, March 4, 1980. *Tso-p'in* was called *Kuang-tung wen-i (Kwangtung Literature and Art)* from 1972 until July 1978.

17. Interview at China Youth Publishing House, Peking, 1980; interview at *Tso-p'in* editorial offices. Besides paper, printing facilities were a problem in the late 1970s. The proliferation of publications kept China's outmoded presses whirring overtime. In order to insure timely publication, manuscripts for literary periodicals had to be delivered two or three, sometimes more, months in advance.

The popularity "wave" phenomenon was at least as pronounced in the late 1970s as in the 1910s and 1920s, though the genesis of waves invites interesting comparisons. Publishers reported in 1979 that when a certain story attained the limelight, other young authors would send in thousands of manuscripts in the same mold.[18] Very few of these would be published, of course. The challenge for the young writers who realized this became one of trying to find a new pattern, to start a new wave.

But on a political-literary landscape which still contained many "forbidden zones" *(chin ch'ü)*, such probing could be perilous. The failures at the game are unknown to us, though there is no doubt their local Party or Youth League branches attended closely to their reinstruction. But to someone like the young playwright Tsung Fuhsien, both fame and fortune resulted from breaking into a forbidden zone and having the move eventually declared "correct." Viewed in perspective, Tsung's play called "From the Silent Region" ("Yü wu-sheng ch'u," 1978) which extolled the "T'ien An Men incident" before it was officially proper to do so, is undistinguished.[19] It is inferior to many subsequent pieces, both published and unpublished. But Tsung was *first,* and took considerable risk in being so. For this he was rewarded.

Literary works showing how the Gang of Four persecuted old revolutionary cadres like Chou En-lai and Chu Te were a kind of officially sanctioned popularity wave in the late 1970s. (Explicit praise of Teng Hsiao-p'ing and other living leaders was just as much a "forbidden zone" as explicit attack on Mao Tse-tung.) In referring to an "official sanction" I am not suggesting that such works lacked genuine popularity; it is clear that readers relished the opportunity to vent negative feelings about at least some of the top leaders of the Cultural Revolution.

But more popular, understandably, were stories which exposed the pernicious effects of the Cultural Revolution on the average citizen. A pace-setting piece of this type was Lu Hsin-hua's "The Wounded," in which the charge of "renegade" against an elderly woman causes her daughter to abandon her and, because political crimes taint whole

18. Interview at China Youth Publishing House; interview at *Kuang-chou wen-i* editorial offices, March 7, 1980.

19. Tsung Fu-hsien, "Yü Wu-sheng ch'u" *Wen-hui pao* (Shanghai), October 28–29, 1978. The T'ien An Men (Gate of Heavenly Peace) incident was a spontaneous demonstration on April 5, 1976, by hundreds of thousands of people at the martyrs' memorial in Peking's massive T'ien An Men square to honor Chou En-lai. The occasion was the Ch'ing-ming Festival, when Chinese pay respects at the tombs of loved ones. The demonstration was unauthorized and forcibly suppressed.

families, almost causes the daughter's boyfriend to leave the daughter as well.[20] In another very popular story called "What Am I to Do?!," a young woman remarries after her first marriage is destroyed by politics and her first husband, she thinks, is dead.[21] But he is not dead, and after the Cultural Revolution his release from prison leaves her with two spouses. Strange as it may seem, her dilemma did not seem out of the ordinary to Chinese readers in the late 1970s. On the contrary, it reminded millions of their own broken family situations.[22]

These stories about the fate of regular people were less enthusiastically welcomed by the political leadership than the stories pointed straight at the Gang of Four. When stories touched upon readers' own lives directly and powerfully, that distinction so crucial to the leadership—between the scourge of the Gang of Four (until 1976) and the "second liberation" (after 1976)—became blurred. The intrusion of politics into people's lives at any time, before or after, emerged as an issue. The issue took very concrete form when the culprits in stories became middle- and lower-level officials, many of whom, in real life, were the same before and after the Gang of Four.

The public's taste for "exposure literature" grew during 1979 despite officialdom's disapproval. In many ways the pieces which resulted—and which were published thanks to the vision and courage of certain editors—can be seen as a continuation of the "castigatory" tradition in late Ch'ing fiction and the "black curtain" and other muckraking fiction of the 1910s–1940s. These works have never been primarily negative. Their exposure of corruption carries a strong implicit endorsement of the same norms whose violation they record. Their opponents have argued that they "teach corruption"; but it is actually much more common that readers participate in an author's moral indignation.

Such was certainly the case with the play "What If I Were Real?" which rocked the Chinese political-literary scene in late 1979.[23] Based on actual events, this is the story of a young man who impersonates

20. Lu Hsin-hua, "Shang-hen" Wen-hui pao (Shanghai), August 11, 1978; translated by Bennett Lee as "The Wounded" in Geremie Barmé and Bennett Lee, trans., The Wounded: New Stories of the Cultural Revolution, 77–78 (Hongkong, 1979), pp. 9–24.

21. Ch'en Kuo-k'ai, "Wo ying-kai tzen-mo pan?" Tso-p'in, no. 2 (1979): 37–50.

22. The story elicited an unusual number of letters from readers. In Tso-p'in, no. 11 (1979), author Ch'en Kuo-k'ai reviews a real-life case in a piece called "This Is What They Did!" ("T'a-men che-yang pan!").

23. Sha Yeh-hsin, Li Shou-ch'eng, and Yao Ming-te, "Chia-ju wo shih chen-ti". In the fall of 1979 the play was performed in Shanghai, Peking, and other cities for restricted audiences only. For a few days in December it was performed openly in Canton, but then was closed everywhere on instruction from authorities. The script is published in Ch'i-shih nien-tai (Hong Kong) January 1980, pp. 76–96.

the son of a high official in order to get some theater tickets. After his modest goal is achieved, he finds it difficult to divest himself of his false identity. Several levels of officials in turn approach him offering favors in return for their "back door" requests—a better job assignment, a son transferred back from the countryside, membership on a delegation going overseas, and so on. In the end, the young man's fraud is discovered and he is brought to trial. He admits his guilt but demonstrates that—except for his initial act of impersonation—in every instance a corrupt society scrambled to offer him favors without his soliciting them. Was this his fault? Audiences delighted in his punch line: "What if I were real?"

As in the 1910s, the most pervasive theme in the stories of the late 1970s was romantic love. Love stories were officially proscribed during the Cultural Revolution and, perhaps for that reason, appeared in force soon afterwards. Not only were they widespread in 1979, but often needlessly tacked onto a story whose main interest was quite different. ("What If I Were Real?", for example, includes a love story.) The triangular love situation exemplified by *The Second Handshake* was one of the commoner themes. Another was the long separation of faithful lovers who finally meet again—usually by incredible coincidence.[24] Yet another was a latter-day version of the "problem" story, so popular in the early twentieth century, in which some kind of artificial social barrier separates young lovers. In a 1979 movie called "Mental Misery,"[25] a young worker loses his beloved younger sister in a heart operation and is led by an evil Party Secretary to believe that the surgeon was responsible. Actually this false charge is part of the 1975 political campaign to "oppose the rightist tendency to reverse the tide," of which the surgeon is a hapless victim. The young worker is stunned when he learns that the surgeon is his girlfriend's father, and

24. The fanciful twists and turns of coincidence in some stories of the late 1970s would be enough to make a Ming dynasty storyteller slap his table in delight. In "The Other Side of the Stream" ("Tsai hsiao-ho nei-pien") by K'ung Chieh-sheng (*Tso-p'in,* no. 3 [1979]), two young people meet in the countryside and fall in love. Both are originally from the city. Not until they have spent the night together do they learn they are brother and sister, their parents having divorced several years ago in a squabble over Lin Piao's political line. "Calamities never come alone," and the boy also learns that his mother is gravely ill. He rushes back to the city, but too late. She has died. She has left a note, however, which explains why the divorce from his father was necessary and also reveals that his sister (lover) was adopted into the family and therefore not related to him by blood. All's well that ends well. The story was immensely popular in spite of the official criticism it bore for reflecting pre-marital sex. In early 1980 cinema commissar Hsia Yen summed up this kind of objection with reference to "What If I Were Real?" (which includes a pre-marital pregnancy) and two similarly bold filmscripts. Reflection of such things is "un-Chinese," Hsia declared.

25. "K'u-nan ti hsin," Ch'ang-ch'un Film Studio, 1979.

that she is staunchly devoted to this idealistic and hard-working man. The "problem" is resolved when the young man suffers a fall at work and needs a sophisticated operation from the only person who can do it: the same surgeon.

Many of the "problem" love stories of the late 1970s addressed the issue of whether it is acceptable to marry a person from any class background, social station, or occupation. The implied answer was always yes: one must not punish youth because of their parents' high class background, as was done during the Cultural Revolution; nor must one despise "low status" people of any kind. A story called "Skating Love Song" tells about a boy who falls in love with a girl who always wears gloves, both on and off the skating rink where they meet.[26] She wears them because her job is to dress corpses in a funeral parlor and she is afraid other people will not want her to touch them. The boy's friends and relatives urge him to leave her. How can her fingers be clean? Besides, they are unpropitious: that which touches corpses brings death elsewhere. But the boy scientifically rejects their superstitions and sticks with the girl. *Canton Literature and Art,* the magazine that published this story, expected it to stir up some controversy.[27] But they did not foresee the objections of funeral parlor directors who wrote letters complaining that now it would be even harder for their young employees to find mates. The letter writers reasoned—probably correctly—that in this particular regard the story did more harm by dramatizing the issue than good by giving the "right" answer.

Besides reading contemporary stories, youth in the late 1970s spent much time catching up on what they had not been allowed to read during the Cultural Revolution. They especially favored modern Western fiction and the famous vernacular novels of the Ming and Ch'ing dynasties, such as *Romance of the Three Kingdoms* and *Dream of the Red Chamber.* Modern Chinese literature from the late Ch'ing period through the Cultural Revolution was not read as much as the classics or post-1976 literature.[28]

Interest in foreign literature was not merely, or even mostly, literary. It came from a burning desire, especially among youth, to know

26. Huang T'ien-yuan, "Liu-ping lien-ch'ü," *Kuang-chou wen-i,* no. 7 (1979): 8–14; 41.

27. Interview at *Kuang-chou wen-i* editorial offices.

28. An important exception was a collection of stories reprinted from the "hundred flowers" period of 1956 and early 1957, especially those by Wang Meng and Liu Pin-yen (*Ch'ung-fang ti hsien hua,* Shang-hai wen-i ch'u-pan she, 1979). There was also lively interest in a handful of stories from Taiwan by Pai Hsien-yung which were published in several cities during 1979.

the details of life outside China after more than a decade of isolation. The American films "Future Worlds" and "Convoy," and a television serial "Man From Atlantis," drew the attention of tens of millions. Americans living in China found it difficult to explain that in America these were generally considered neither high art nor perfect reflections of reality. Audiences would gasp even at scenes of the interior of an upper-middle class home, let alone more imaginative scenes. One day in 1979 students of English at Sun Yat-sen University in Canton struck classes in order to see the French-Italian movie "Zorro." Though dubbed in Chinese, it could "teach them Western culture." The leadership of the English department did not approve, but the students, led by the daughter of a high cadre (who finally was unafraid to flail and shout before a vice president), were not going to bypass such a marvellous opportunity. It turned out to be the closest thing to a good knight-errant movie they had seen for some time.

This kind of undiscriminating zeal in exploring the West was present in both the late Ch'ing and May Fourth periods. The great appeal of love stories and detective stories also recalls the early part of the century. But some things were very different in the late 1970s. The government's control of literary publication, even during the most relaxed years since 1949, still left literature rather stiffly bound in comparison to the free-wheeling scene in the first half of the century. The great enthusiasm of readers, which certainly was genuine, must be attributed largely to the wasted landscape of the immediately preceding years. Clearly the modest flower garden of the late 1970s still had a fence around it.

Writers were free, according to official pronouncement, to write anything so long as it did not harm the Communist Party, the socialist system, or the dictatorship of the proletariat. Beyond that, no "forbidden zones" were laid down except, as Minister of Propaganda Hu Yao-pang announced in early 1980, that "each writer should impose forbidden zones upon himself." One still did not blame Mao Tse-tung for the Cultural Revolution, obvious as the connection was to all; nor was one supposed to write "exposure literature" about society's problems without telling in the same piece the "correct" way to solve the same problems.

As a consequence of political controls, the literary scene across China was still remarkably unified in comparison to the early part of the century. Popular or controversial pieces would sweep the country whether they first appeared in Harbin or Canton. Writers by no means limited themselves to publishing in their own provinces, a tendency which further homogenized the national scene. It is true that places like Shanghai and Canton worked to maintain distinctive reputations in contemporary literature, but this was due as much to "liberated" editorial policy in general as to reflection of local culture. Some journals developed brief reputations precisely for their political audacity, for example *Poetry (Shih k'an)* in mid-1979 or *Anhwei Literature* in early 1980.

The written language of the 1970s was also much more unified than that of the early part of the century, when writers used several kinds of language both classical and vernacular, and some struggled to forge a new modern vernacular style. For better or worse, just such a standard style, which relied heavily on Western grammar, had been established by the 1970s. Young writers were fluent in this style; most had no knowledge of classical Chinese. They were fascinated by techniques they had noticed briefly in Western literature and film: the manipulation of time, "stream of consciousness," black humor, and so forth.

There had been great changes in popular fiction over sixty years, in form and style, in size and mode of circulation, and in subservience to political authority. The life which stories reflected had changed in significant ways as well. But the basic staples of popular fiction's appeal—romantic love, the thrills of a detective story, the reunion of relatives by coincidence, the unmasking of corruption—had stayed in many ways quite the same.

Magazines of the 1910s

Several of the most important early fiction magazines were conceived and designed at the newspaper offices of *Shih pao (Eastern Times)*. *Hsiao-shuo shih pao (Fiction Times)* was a monthly which began publication in September 1909. It was edited by, and featured the fiction of, Pao T'ien-hsiao and Ch'en Ching-han of the *Shih pao* staff. The founder and manager of *Shih pao*, Ti Ch'u-ch'ing, had wished to implement Liang Ch'i-ch'ao's idea of "fiction to build the nation." He published his own political essays in *Fiction Times*, and made available to it all the resources of *Shih pao*. Advertisements for manuscripts ran daily in *Shih pao*, and *Shih pao*'s printing presses, with lead-type characters and lithograph for illustrations, were used by *Fiction Times*. Distribution services were provided by the affiliate Yu-cheng Book Company. Color illustrations were one of the greatest attractions of the magazine in its early years. Famous Soochow courtesans, heavily adorned in stylish garments, appeared on the covers of the early issues against a background of an appealing light green. Inside there were fifteen pages of illustrations, some to accompany the fiction, some as unrelated attractions (such as photographs of two Westerners, one 595 lbs., one 685 lbs., "the largest in Europe and America").

The table of contents page of the early issues ran two public notices to readers, one calling for manuscripts and explaining payment schedules, the other explaining the features of the magazine which were unequalled by its competition. These were five: (1) *Fiction Times* would never run more than one story in an issue which had to be completed in the following issue; (2) should the magazine cease to exist, the editors promise to notify readers six months in advance, and further promise to leave no story unfinished; (3) all stories will fall into a balanced, half-year plan, thereby avoiding the common fault in other magazines of throwing things together at the last minute; (4) the magazine uses large paper (it was 7¼" by 10¼") and small characters, and has numerous pictures, assuring the reader his money's worth; (5) all photographs and pictures are of famous things, or done by famous people, and are identified as such—not simple and cheap as in other publications.

The first issue of the magazine cost 80 cents, but this was lowered to 60 cents with the second issue and remained at that level until the magazine ceased publication in 1917. It was revived for five months in 1922, under the editorship of Li Han-ch'iu and at a selling price of 30 cents. But, though it briefly brought together a star-studded assemblage of popular writers, it could not survive in the more intensely commercial market of the twenties.[1]

The *Shih pao*'s Ti Ch'u-ch'ing liked the idea of supplement magazines, and after the successful start of *Fiction Times,* he tried several others. His interest in Buddhism led to a *Buddhist Studies Times (Fo-hsueh shih pao),* which quickly died of undercirculation. *Women's Times (Fu-nü shih pao)* was much better received and became the first of several 1910s fiction magazines intended for women. Founded in 1912 and edited by Pao T'ien-hsiao, *Women's Times* appeared in ten issues per year, at 40 cents per issue. It was about the same size as *Fiction Times,* but, like most of the 1910s magazines, was printed in large-sized characters (3/16″ square). On the cover of the first issue was a picture of two women holding, and fondly regarding, a copy of the magazine itself. In all subsequent issues an effort was made to follow the precedent of including stylish pictures, but, since it was a woman's magazine, the usual pictures of entertainment ladies were mostly replaced with photographs from the "new-style" girls' schools and pictures of Western women. The magazine's contents emphasized women's education, the role of women outside the home, and other progressive themes—at least on the surface. In fact, however, its readership was probably less than ten percent female, while the attraction for the more than ninety percent of male readers lay not in progressivism but in the curiosity and interest of "new-style" women.[2]

The idea of women's magazines caught the fancy of Shanghai publishers, and *Women's Times* did not lack for imitators. Two or three of these are worthy of mention. *Woman's World (Nü-tzu shih-chieh),* a monthly which appeared in December 1914, was edited by Ch'en Tieh-hsien and supported by popular writers from his "Unfettered Talk" group. The contents featured photographs of famous Chinese women from all walks of life, plus the paintings and calligraphy of women artists. Besides fiction, poetry and essays, it included sections on "industrial arts" (tailoring methods, information on cosmetics, etc.), "family," and "health." Though well staffed, *Woman's World* closed after seven issues in the face of competition from *Woman's Mag-*

---

1. *Hsiao-shuo shih pao,* no. 1 (September 1909) ff; YYHTP, pp. 280–282; CYLHIL, pp. 358–359.
2. *Fu-nü shih pao,* no. 1 (1912) ff; YYHTP, pp. 283–284; CYLHIL, pp. 361–362; interview with Pao T'ien-hsiao, December 6, 1972.

azine (Fu-nü tsa-chih), a very similar publication which had appeared in January 1915 from the Commercial Press under the editorship of Wang Yun-chang. Wang was a Southern Society member, and drew upon his fellows of the Society for most of his magazine's contributions. During its second year of publication, *Woman's Magazine* was edited by a woman, Hu Pin-hsia, but mostly for appearances. Wang Yun-chang and the men of the Southern Society continued to be its major contributors. During its third year, while under the chief editorship of Chang Hsi-ch'en, the magazine turned away from fiction and other frills towards practical aspects of a woman's life. There appeared sections on household economy, childrearing, and a highly controversial one called "On the New Sexual Morality" (t'an hsin hsing tao-te), for the publication of which the Commercial Press relieved Chang Hsi-ch'en of his editorship. Thereupon Chang, not to be stayed, collected together the loyalties of some friends and opened his own Enlightened Book Company (K'ai-ming shu-chü), publishing a magazine called *New Woman (Hsin nü-hsing)* which stood for a few years in direct competition with *Woman's Magazine*.[3]

After *Fiction Times*, the next major successful fiction magazine to appear, in July 1910, was the *Short Story Monthly (Hsiao-shuo yueh-pao)*. This magazine set standards in commercial fiction. First, it cost only a quarter as much as *Fiction Times*, or 15 cents per issue, and offered one-sixth off for a year's subscription. Second, it clearly indicated and advertised its scale of payment for manuscripts which ran from one to six yuan per thousand characters, and its charges for advertising space, which ran from twelve to thirty yuan per page. The magazine enjoyed unusual success in circulation and longevity, passing through several distinct phases in its lifetime.

In what might be called its "original phase" in the early 1910s, it was edited by Wang Yun-chang and therefore, like *Woman's Magazine*, carried the fiction of the Southern Society. This included both long and short stories, both translations and creations. Lin Shu was a feature contributor. During this stage the magazine carried very much of the flavor of the late Ch'ing period: the spirit of discovery, the sense of a fathomless variety of things in the world, and so on.

In the magazine's second stage, beginning in the mid-1910s, Southern Society members such as Hsu Cho-tai and Hu Chi-ch'en helped spread its range of contributors among other groups of popular writers, especially love story specialists of the original "Mandarin Duck and Butterfly" school. (The magazine's cover had always borne the impression of a pair of mandarin ducks.) The magazine's editor

3. *Nü-tzu shih-chieh,* no. 1 (December 1914) ff; YYHTP, pp. 304–305 and 307–309; interview with Ch'en Ting-shan, July 25, 1973.

beginning in 1913 was Yun T'ieh-ch'iao, who took a very serious and direct attitude towards developing the "literary scene" (before he abandoned it to study medicine) and helped discover important new popular writers, such as the Soochow middle school principal and master of humor, Ch'eng Chan-lu.

In its third stage, the editorship of *Short Story Monthly* was abruptly transferred by the Commercial Press from the entertainment writers of the 1910s to Shen Yen-ping and the May Fourth Movement writers, under whom it flourished until 1932.[4]

(There were at least two other "old-style" magazines with the identical title of *Short Story Monthly,* which bore no direct relation to the famous one. One of these appeared in only two issues in 1907, published by the Shanghai Competition Society (Ching-li she), and the other, which appeared under Japanese auspices during 1940–1944, was published by the United China Publication Company (Lien-hua kuang-kao kung-szu) and edited by Yen Tu-ho.)[5]

After 1912, the Commercial Press and the Chung-hua shu-chü stood as the two major rival leaders in Shanghai book and magazine publishing (see chapter three). The success of *Short Story Monthly* therefore naturally brought a response from Chung-hua shu-chü. Their magazine, a monthly called *The World of Chinese Fiction (Chung-hua hsiao-shuo chieh),* cost 20 cents and was similar to *Short Story Monthly* in format. Its contributors were drawn from an even wider circle, though, including Pao T'ien-hsiao, Ch'en Tieh-hsien and Hsu Chen-ya, as well as writers who were to become famous in the May Fourth era, such as Liu Pan-nung and Chou Tso-jen. The magazine ceased publication after three years. It was later revived, but only for a short time, under the name *The New World of Chinese Fiction (Chung-kuo hsin hsiao-shuo chieh).*[6]

Recreation Magazine (Yu-hsi tsa-chih) began in September 1913 by republishing the contents of *Shen pao*'s fiction column "Unfettered Talk" under the title *The Unfettered Magazine (Tzu-yu tsa-chih).* After the name change, Wang Tun-ken and Ch'en Tieh-hsien, its editors, guided it to independent existence as an important fiction magazine in its own right. In addition to all the usual features in abundant supply

4. *Hsiao-shuo yueh-pao,* no. 1 (July 1910) ff; YYHTP, pp. 282–283; Wang P'ing-lin, p. 12. Chang Ching-lu, *Chin-tai,* 2:432, erroneously lists 1909 as the inaugural year of the *Hsiao-shuo yueh-pao.* His *Pu-pien* lists the year as 1910 (p. 558).

5. *Hsiao-shuo yueh-pao,* Shanghai Competition Society, September and October 1907; YYHTP, pp. 283 and 379–380.

6. *Chung-hua hsiao-shuo chieh,* no. 1 (January 1914) ff; YYHTP, p. 287. Liu Pan-nung changed the "nung" from "I" (Mathews 4769) to "peasant" (Mathews 4768) during the May Fourth Movement.

(usually over two hundred pages for 40 cents), *Recreation Magazine* initiated drama reviews and a column on magic.[7]

Saturday (Li-pai-liu) appeared every week on Saturday mornings for one hundred weeks beginning in June 1914, then halted publication, only to be revived for another hundred weeks beginning in March 1921. It was a small volume (5 in. × 7 in. and about 60 to 70 pages), sold for 10 cents, and was the best-selling magazine of its time. Chou Shou-chüan, *Saturday's* steadiest contributor and its editor for a time, had the following recollections in 1958 on the origins of the magazine:

> In America there was a weekly called the "Saturday" Evening Post, and it had originated from the hand of Franklin. Its history was longest, its circulation widest and it was the most beloved of reading material in the West. Therefore we fixed upon the name *Saturday* for our publication. There weren't many periodicals in early Republican times, and *Saturday* was quite the rage for a while. Every time Saturday came around, early in the morning, there would be quite a few readers waiting outside the door of the China Library Company, which distributed *Saturday*. When the door was opened, they would go bursting in, devil-take-the-hindmost. It was just like the scramble at the breakfast snack shops.[8]

Though figures are unavailable, estimates put the circulation of *Saturday* at twenty to thirty thousand during 1914–16, and about 50,000 during 1921–1923. (By comparison, *Recreation Magazine* and *Women's World*, which were distributed by the same China Library Company (Chung-kuo t'u-shu kuan), reached twenty thousand at most.) *Saturday's* cover featured catchy portraits of coy-looking girls, and sometimes awkward-looking boys, in water colors by Ting Sung. The contents during the magazine's early years were almost entirely tragic love stories and social-portrait fiction, most of it in classical language. A new element was introduced beginning May, 1915, when a special section called "Records of the National Shame" appeared, which recalled and discussed the humiliating loss to Japan in 1895.

Saturday was an immediate stimulus to the magazine market generally. New magazines imitated it in obvious ways, including one which even imitated the name *Li-pai-liu* with its title *Li-pai hua (Weekly Flower)*. Demands on *Saturday's* contributors increased, and the pressures on them to go their separate ways led to the magazine's cessation after

7. *Yu-hsi tsa-chih,* no. 1 (January 1913) ff; YYHTP, pp. 284–286; interview with Ch'en Ting-shan.

8. *Chou Shou-chüan,* "Hua-ch'ien hsin-chi" in YYHTP, p. 130.

one hundred issues. Five years later, when Chou Shou-chüan and Wang Tun-ken revived it, their purpose was to reestablish an outlet, and a commercial opportunity, for their group of "old-style" writers who were now beginning to feel the threat of competition from the May Fourth writers. The second hundred issues drew from a wider range of writers than the original "Saturday School" and included, in addition to fiction, all kinds of anecdotes, jokes, notes from overseas, and other special features. As an incentive to subscribers, full-year subscriptions were accompanied by a set of four pairs of scroll prints of famous paintings, a scroll of Wang Tun-ken's calligraphy, and an opportunity to buy a complete set of the earlier one hundred issues of *Saturday*, with a glass case, at half price.[9]

(In the 1930s, an unrelated magazine by the same name appeared, edited by T'ien Chi-hen and carrying articles on politics, economics, world affairs and society.)

Elements of People's Rights (Min-ch'üan su), an important monthly whose development from the outlawed *People's Rights Journal* we have described above (chapter five), was published by the People's Rights Publishers (Min-ch'üan ch'u-pan pu) from April 1914 through April 1916. Famous for its love stories, among which original compositions outnumbered translations, and classical prose was more common than the vernacular, it attracted some of the best writers, including Hsu Chen-ya and the redoubtable Su Man-shu. At the same time it maintained the pretense of being a political journal by publishing famous essays by people such as T'ang Ts'ai-ch'ang and Chang Ping-lin.[10]

But *Elements of People's Rights* was not the only magazine representing this group of writers. After the *People's Rights Journal* was closed, its contributors moved to establish their own Thicket of Fiction Publishing Company, which put out *Thicket of Fiction* magazine *(Hsiao-shuo ts'ung-pao)*. Appearing from January 1914 to August 1919, *Thicket* developed into the main organ of the "Elements of People's Rights" group. It was edited by Hsu Chen-ya (and briefly by his close associate Wu Shuang-je) and published a number of leading novels including Hsu's *Chronicle of Great Tears of Bygone Days (Hsueh hung lei shih)*. Cheng I-mei made his name with this magazine as the "Great Master of Fillers" *(Pu-pai ta-wang)*, which meant that he could fill the leftover bits of various pages with brief notes of extraordinary interest. With most of its contributors Soochow people, the magazine also initiated

9. *Li-pai-liu,* no. 1 (June 1914) ff; interview with Ch'en Ting-shan; YYHTP, pp. 117–119, 129–130 and 290–293; Wang P'ing-lin, pp. 12–13: Ch'en Ching-chih, "Li-pai-liu p'ai ti hsing-ch'i ho shuai-lo," p. 16.

10. YYHTP, pp. 287–290 and 407–408.

the publication of love stories in the style of Soochow *t'an-tz'u,* which several other magazines later imitated.[11]

In March, 1915, Li Ting-i, a central figure in the "Elements" group, undertook to edit his own magazine in emulation of *Thicket of Fiction,* which he called *New Fiction Journal (Hsiao-shuo hsin pao)* and which survived through 1924. Like other magazines which were offshoots of their prototypes, *New Fiction Journal* turned out to be less factional than its parent organ and accepted manuscripts from a wide variety of contributors. Nevertheless, Li Ting-i's own love stories were its perennial drawing card.[12]

Li's branching away from *Thicket of Fiction* was friendly, but Hsu Chen-ya's, three years later, definitely was not. Hsu had led *Thicket* since its beginnings, but had a falling out with others in the group (whom he declined to name in his public explanation) and left that magazine to found *Fiction Quarterly (Hsiao-shuo chi pao).* First appearing in August, 1918, this magazine offered a good sampling of well-known authors and came out four times a year in a giant deluxe volume (done in imitation of Pao T'ien-hsiao's *Grand Magazine,* see below) which sold for 1.20 yuan. It was distributed by Hsu's own publishing house, the Ch'ing-hua shu-chü. Despite the bonus gift of Hsu's calligraphy offered to subscribers, however, 1.20 yuan was too much for many readers to afford at one time, and the *Quarterly's* circulation suffered sharply. It survived until May, 1920.[13]

The authors of the group which developed around Pao T'ien-hsiao at *Shih pao* came out with three noteworthy magazines in 1915. *Sea of Fiction (Hsiao-shuo hai)* was a little pocket-sized volume whose hallmark was economy of space. Its contents were packed together so tightly that there were no spaces left even between stories, to say nothing of paragraphs. *Double Star (Shuang hsing)* offered remarkably varied contents but survived for only four issues. Most important of the three was *Grand Magazine (Hsiao-shuo ta-kuan)* published by the Wen-ming shu-chü. This was another of Pao T'ien-hsiao's creative innovations in popular fiction. Its cover showed no picture; instead it carried the four characters of the title writ large in red, with white borders, against a light green background. Its principle was popular fiction on a jumbo scale. The first fiction quarterly to appear in China, each of its volumes contained a minimum of three hundred thousand characters or more than three hundred large-sized pages. There were a

11. *Hsiao-shuo ts'ung-pao,* no. 1 (May 1914) ff; interview with Ch'en Ting-shan; YYHTP, pp. 293–298; YLH, advertisement, p. i.

12. *Hsiao-shuo hsin pao,* no. 1 (March 1915) ff; YYHTP, pp. 309–312.

13. YYHTP, pp. 319–321 and 461–462.

dozen or so photographs near the front—three or four times the usual number in magazines—and some of these added the special feature of artificial tinting. By publishing on this scale, the magazine could offer readers the attraction of publishing complete pieces without serialization. Each issue published in their entirety more than ten short stories, and long stories were not broken unless they exceeded one hundred thousand characters. (Three or four in this category appeared in every issue, since a small amount of overlapping serialization was still desirable to ensure continuing readership.) Pao further attempted to raise standards in the quality of fiction in *Grand Magazine.* In the "Introduction" to its first issue, he promised to select works which "are beneficial to society and contribute to morality," by which he meant to stress "social" novels and to deemphasize tragic love stories. Translations, furthermore, were to be "responsible" and to avoid casual "copying from here and plagiarizing from there" as was the practice with other, inferior magazines. *Grand Magazine* cost one yuan—a jumbo price for a jumbo product—but thanks in part to skillful distribution by Shen Chih-fang at the Wen-ming shu-chü, the magazine always sold at least four to five thousand copies, and maintained itself until June, 1921.[14]

The last of Pao T'ien-hsiao's interesting innovations in fiction publication appeared in 1917. The conception of *Fiction Pictorial (Hsiao-shuo hua-pao)* occurred to him, he tells us, one night when he had insomnia. The magazine first appeared in January, 1917 under the following four principles: (1) All stories must be in the vernacular language and none in classical (a rule directed in particular against the ornate love stories of the time). (2) All stories had to be original creations and not translations (to guard against the sloppy translating current at the time). (3) The magazine was printed not with lead type but with stone lithography, which by then was more than a decade out of date. It was, furthermore, issued in a string-bound volume. Though "seemingly backward," according to Pao, this style was actually a source of "fresh interest" (a sentiment shared, we might note, by the Peking Wen-wu ch'u-pan-she with its publication in 1974 of Mao Tse-tung's poetry in a string-bound edition). (4) Every piece of fiction—whether novel or short story—was accompanied by careful and detailed hand-drawn illustrations. (Prior to this time illustrations had been either unrelated to the content of a story or, when related, only cartoon-like sketches.) A dozen of the best illustrators in Shanghai were marshaled into this effort, including Ch'ien Ping-ho, who held the position of co-editor for illustrations. The cover of the magazine featured paintings of

14. *Hsiao-chuo ta-kuan,* no. 1 (August 1915) ff (*The Grand Magazine* was its official English title, not a translation of *Hsiao-shuo ta-kuan);* YYHTP, pp. 306–307 and 312–315; CYLHIL, pp. 376–378.

animals—lions, tigers, elephants, peacocks—until the first issue of 1918, which was the Year of the Horse. Beginning then, each cover illustrated a four-character proverb which mentioned horses. The magazine cost 30 cents and sold adequately, but, because of the ambitious nature of its editorial principles, it soon fell behind its publication schedule and had to close in September, 1919.[15]

In the early 1920s *Pastime Monthly (Hsiao-hsien yueh-k'an)* was edited in Soochow by Chao Mien-yun and Cheng I-mei, who had earlier edited a magazine in Shanghai called *New Recreation Journal (Yu-hsi hsin pao)*. This effort had failed quickly because it lacked its own distribution section and had to rely on other book companies to promote sales, so Chao and Cheng decided to distribute and promote *Pastime Monthly* themselves, right in Soochow (though the printing was still done in Shanghai.) They set up a distribution center at Cheng's house, No. 40 Niu Family Lane, and charged 20 cents for the small-sized (5 in. × 7 in.) volume. Soochow may not have been ready to support this type of fiction magazine on its own, however; circulation did not hold up well and *Pastime Monthly* folded in mid-1922.[16]

In Shanghai, the Great Eastern Book Company turned with new vigor toward the establishment of popular fiction magazines in 1921 and 1922. With the end of Pao T'ien-hsiao's *Grand Magazine* in June, 1921, Pao was ready to turn his talents elsewhere; in February, 1922, with the encouragement of Great Eastern, he commenced editing *Weekly (Hsing-ch'i).Weekly* contained mostly vernacular short stories, appeared every week with the two big characters of its name on its cover, and cost 10 cents. It featured many "special issues," including "The Marriage Special Issue," "The Birth Special Issue" and "The Knight-Errant Special Issue." Editing the magazine alone, however, Pao T'ien-hsiao grew weary after several months of the pressure to produce another volume every seven days. After one full year of publication he explained to Great Eastern his wish to resign, and did so, even though the magazine itself was successful.[17]

Great Eastern had more success with Chou Shou-chüan, whose editing responsibilities in the 1920s grew to the ponderous proportions of Pao T'ien-hsiao's in the 1910s. In April, 1920, Chou assumed the editorship of *Shen pao*'s "Unfettered Talk," and in March, 1921, revived and began editing *Saturday*. To those major undertakings he added a third, equally ambitious: the editorship of *The Semi-Monthly (Pan-yueh)* beginning in September, 1921, for which Great Eastern as-

15. *Hsiao-shuo hua-pao*, no. 1 (January 1917) ff; YYHTP, pp. 316–319; CYLHIL, pp. 379–380.

16. YYHTP, pp. 323–326.

17. CYLHIL, p. 384; YYHTP, pp. 334–336.

sumed distribution responsibilities five issues later. *The Semi-Monthly* was a big success. Chou's widening range of contacts made possible a great variety of contributions and a number of lively special issues. One of the most successful special issues was "The Childhood Issue," in which almost all the best-known names in popular fiction contributed stories of their naughty exploits as children. The magazine was also the first in Shanghai to feature a copperplate color photograph on its front cover.[18]

After four years of publication, Chou sensed that the magazine was losing its leading edge. He decided in December, 1925, to end the magazine and replace it with another called *Violets (Tzu lo-lan)*. Like its predecessor, *Violets* was a semi-monthly and was published by Great Eastern. The magazine's special issues included more than one on romantic love, plus others on "The Frustrations of Youth," "Detective Fiction," "In Commemoration of Pi I-hung," and, significantly for the time, "Cinema" and "Movie Stars." The magazine ceased publication in June, 1930, following which the Great Eastern Book Company published individual volumes of all the works which had appeared therein, including stories by Pao T'ien-hsiao, Chiang Hung-chiao, Ho Hai-ming and a dozen or more leading writers.[19]

As if all this were not enough popular fiction for one editor and one distributor, Chou Shou-chüan and Great Eastern began two other fiction monthlies in the early twenties, namely, *Recreation World (Yu-hsi shih-chieh,* 1921–1923), which Chou edited in cooperation with Chao T'iao-k'uang, and *Fallen Violet Petals (Tzu-lan hua p'ien,* 1922–1924), which bore the remarkable characteristic of carrying nothing but Chou's own works. Chou maintained sufficient energy to fill the magazine for twenty-four issues, then gave it up. But his example served to inspire others, including Hsu Pi-po, who later established the fiction magazine called *Tung-hai* which published only authors with the same Hsu surname.[20]

The fortunes of the World Book Company, Great Eastern's major competitor, rose in 1922 when its founder Shen Chih-fang discovered an energetic editor named Shih Chi-ch'ün. The previous year Shih had demonstrated his seriousness by selling all his property to invest in his first fiction magazine *New Voices (Hsin sheng)*, which he guided to success by attracting a wide range of writers. Shih tried even to include

18. *Pan yueh,* no. 1 (September 1921) ff; YYHTP, pp. 291, 330–333 and 400.

19. *Tzu lo-lan,* no. 1 (December 1925) ff; YYHTP, pp. 343 and 356–359; Ch'en Tieh-i in *Ta-ch'eng,* no. 12 (November 1974) p. 58.

20. *Yu-hsi shih-chieh,* no. 1 (July 1921) ff; YYHTP, pp. 328–329 and 343–344. See also chapter 2 above.

May Fourth writing in a special section called "The Thought Tides" *(Ssu ch'ao)*. but gave up the project when it became clear the "new" and "old" did not mix well.[21]

In 1922, with Shih on their staff, the World Book Company launched a vigorous effort to compete with the Great Eastern Book Company in the area of popular fiction. In March, the first issue of *Hung tsa-chih,* called in English *The Scarlet Magazine,* was published. To counter the prestige of Chou Shou-chüan at Great Eastern, who was also an editor at *Shen pao,* World persuaded Yen Tu-ho, of *Hsin-wen pao,* to serve as chief editor of *The Scarlet Magazine.* Shih Chi-ch'ün remained the *de facto* editor, however, as the magazine appeared weekly for one hundred issues beginning in August, 1922. Although the publishing companies were in fierce competition, most authors were not partisan. Large numbers who wrote for Great Eastern's publications happily contributed to World's as well. *The Scarlet Magazine,* in fact, garnered a larger proportion of the leading names than any other magazine of the 1910s or 1920s. It was also extremely faithful to its readers in arranging well-balanced content and prompt publication. While many magazines fell behind their publication schedules, Shih Chi-ch'ün actually edited *The Scarlet Magazine* four issues in advance. Its pages were divided in a new way to attract attention: the top third of each page carried anecdotes and short interest pieces, while the bottom two-thirds was fiction. The great majority of the stories, but not all, were in vernacular style.[22]

Following its first one hundred issues, the magazine was replaced (in July, 1924) by its successor *Red Roses (Hung mei-kuei).* Yen Tu-ho continued as honorary editor, and practical editing was handled by Chao T'iao-k'uang. *Red Roses* remained successful into the 1930s, serializing, in particular, the original version of Hsiang K'ai-jan's outstanding popular *Chronicle of the Strange Roving Knights (Chiang-hu ch'i-hsia chuan).* *Red Roses* competed closely with Chou Shou-chüan's *Violets.* In 1928 it began publishing every ten days rather than weekly.[23]

The choice of "red" as a symbol for the World Publishing Company (or "scarlet," as they often translated it themselves) was explained for readers by Yen Tu-ho in his opening statement in *The Scarlet Magazine.* Some people, Yen explained, suppose the reason to be patriotism, since red is the main color in the national flag. Others guess it to refer to the lucky opportunity *(hung yun)* to gather supe-

21. YYHTP, pp. 326–328.
22. *Hung tsa-chih,* no. 1 (August 1922) ff; YYHTP, pp. 336–337.
23. *Hung mei-kuei,* no. 1 (July 1924) ff; YYHTP, pp. 338–340.

rior writing of various kinds together in one place. Yet neither of these, said Yen, is the true reason: really "red" represents the crystallized heart-blood of China's best writers, earnestly offered to society by the magazine. However, Yen's preface to *Red Roses* two years later was a bit more candid: "As for the color red, in the minds of our countrymen it subtly suggests 'abundance,' and 'prosperity,' and hence is very well-received by most people."[24] As the term "red" developed in the popular culture of the twenties, it came to exceed the traditional associations Yen refers to and connote stylishness, or special favor, as in a novel, movie or personality.

World's other fiction magazines of the early twenties included *Household Magazine (Chia-t'ing tsa-chih)*, a monthly edited by Chiang Hung-chiao during 1923–1924; and *Happiness (K'uai-huo)*, published every ten days during 1923. *Happiness* was very successfully edited by the famous author of *Tides of Yangchow*, Li Han-ch'iu (see chapter five). But Li, once again true to his Bohemian image, abruptly resigned in an editorial disagreement with Shen Chih-fang and headed back to Yangchow. The magazine collapsed. *World of Detectives (Chen-t'an tsa-chih)*, edited by Shih Chi-ch'ün and others, appeared twice monthly for a year beginning in June 1923. Though more loyally followed by its readers than most magazines, *World of Detectives* had to close after one year because of the difficulty of obtaining adequate manuscripts. Good detective stories seem to have been harder to write than other types of popular fiction, and the two most skillful specialists in Shanghai, Ch'eng Hsiao-ch'ing and Lu T'an-an, though they contributed diligently, could not continuously turn out enough copy to fill the magazine's pages.[25]

24. *Hung tsa-chi*, no. 1 (August 1922); YYHTP, p. 338.
25. *Chen-t'an tsa-chih*, no. 1 (June 1923) ff; YYHTP, pp. 342–345.

Photographs

Hsu Chen–ya in 1923.
Photo from *Hsing-kuang*, no. 2,
1923.

Wu Shuang-je in 1923.
Photo from *Hsing-kuang*, no. 2,
1973.

Li Ting-i in 1914. Photo from *Hsiao-shuo ts'ung-pao,* March 1914.

The core of the *Shen pao* group: Ch'en Tieh-hsien (T'ien-hsu wo sheng), seated, and his sons Tz'u-tieh (left) and Hsiao-tieh, and the latter's wife, in 1938. Photo given me by Ch'en Hsiao-tieh in Taichung, Taiwan, 1973.

Ch'en Hsiao-tieh (Ting-shan) at home in Taichung, Taiwan, 1960s. Personal photo of Ch'en's.

Pao T'ien-hsiao in 1973, aged 97. My photo.

Chou Shou-chüan in 1923. Photo
from *Hsing-kuang*, no. 2, 1923.

Chiang Hung-chiao in 1923. Photo
from *Hsing-kuang*, no. 1, 1923.

Fan Yen-ch'iao (left) and Chao Mien-yun in the editorial office of the *Star
Society* in 1923. Photo from *Hsing-kuang*, no. 1, 1923.

Hsu Cho-tai in 1923. Photo from
Hsing-kuang, no. 1, 1923.

Ho Hai-ming in 1923. Photo from
Hsing-kuang, no. 2, 1923.

Cheng I-mei in 1923. Photo from
Hsing-kuang, no. 1, 1923.

Yen Tu-ho in 1940. Photo from
Ta-jen (Hong Kong), no. 40.

Ch'eng Chan-lu in 1923. Photo
from *Hsing-kuang,* no. 1, 1923.

Li Han-ch'iu in 1923. Photo from
Hsing-kuang, no. 1, 1923.

Hsiang K'ai-jan in the mid-1950s.
Photo from *Ta-kung pao* (Hong
Kong), February 17, 1957.

Ku Ming-tao in 1923. Photo from
Hsing-kuang, no. 2, 1923.

Chang Hen-shui and his wife in
1946.
Photo from *Kung-chiao ching*
(Hong Kong), no. 61 (October
1977).

Glossary

ai-ch'ing	愛情
ai-ch'ing	哀情
Ai-kuo nü-hsueh-she	愛國女學社
ai yen	哀艷
chan-cheng	戰爭
Chang Chien	張謇
Chang Chih-tung	張之洞
Chang Ching-lu	張靜廬
Chang Cho	張鷟
Chang Chü-sheng	張菊生
Chang Ch'un-fan	張春帆
Chang Fei	張飛
Chang Hen-shui	張恨水
Chang Hsi-ch'en	章錫琛
chang-hui	章回
Chang I-han	張毅漢
Chang Ming-fei	張冥飛
Chang Pi-wu	張碧梧
Chang Ping-lin	章炳麟
Chang Tan-fu	張丹斧
Chang Yang	張揚
Chao Feng-ch'ang	趙鳳昌
Chao Huan-t'ing	趙煥亭
chao hun chi	招魂集
Chao Mien-yun	趙眠雲
Chao T'iao-k'uang	趙苕狂
chen su	貞素
Chen-su	震蘇

chen-t'an	偵探
chen-t'an hsiao-shuo	偵探小說
Chen-t'an tsa-chih	偵探雜誌
Chen-ya lang mo	枕亞浪墨
Cheng Chen-to	鄭振鐸
Cheng Cheng-ch'iu	鄭正秋
Cheng Cheng-yin	鄭證因
cheng-chih	政治
Cheng I-mei	鄭逸梅
Cheng So-nan	鄭所南
chi-chin hsiao-shuo	集錦小說
Chi-ch'eng t'u-shu kung-szu	集成圖書公司
Chia Pao-yü	賈寶玉
chia-t'ing	家庭
Chia-t'ing ch'ang-shih	家庭常識
Chia-t'ing tsa-chih	家庭雜誌
Chiang-hu ch'i-hsia chuan	江湖奇俠傳
Chiang Hung-chiao	江紅蕉
Chiang-su chiao-yü tsung-hui	江蘇教育總會
Chiang Tieh-lu	江蝶廬
Chiang Yü-ch'üan	蔣裕泉
chiao-hua ch'uan	脚划船
chiao pien-chi	脚編輯
chiao-yü hsiao-shao	教育小說
Chieh yü hui	劫餘灰
chih ch'ing	至情
Chih-fen	芷芬
chin-chang	錦章
chin ch'ü	禁區
Chin-kang-shih ya-fen	金剛石牙粉
Chin-kang tsuan	金剛鑽
Chinkiang (Chen-chiang)	鎮江
chin kuei	金閨
Ching-li she	競立社
Ching pao	京報
Ching pao	晶報
Chiu ming ch'i yuan	九命奇冤

chiu p'ai	舊派
Chiu-wei kuei	九尾龜
cho-cheng yuan	拙政園
Cho Wen-chün	卓文君
Chou Jung-yao	周榮曜
Chou Shao-heng	周少衡
Chou Shou-chüan	周瘦鵑
Chou Tso-jen	周作人
Chu Shao-p'ing	朱少屏
Chu Shu-jen	朱樹人
Chu Ta-k'o	朱大可
Chuang-tzu	莊子
chuang-yuan	狀元
Chung-hua hsiao-shuo chieh	中華小說界
Chung-hua hsin pao	中華新報
Chung-hua shu-chü	中華書局
Chung-hua t'u-shu-kuan	中華圖書館
ng-kuo Fu-erh-mo-ssu Huo-sang t'an-an	中國福爾摩斯霍桑探案
Chung-kuo hsin hsiao-shuo chieh	中國新小說界
Chung-kuo nü pao	中國女報
Chung-kuo pai-hua pao	中國白話報
Chung-kuo pao-hsueh shih	中國報學史
Chung-kuo t'u-shu-kuan	中國圖書館
Chung-kuo t'u-shu kung-szu	中國圖書公司
Chung-wai jih-pao	中外日報
Chung-yang jih-pao	中央日報
chung-yang wei-yüan	中央委員 ； 種秧委員
Chueh. See Hsu Chueh.	
chueh chü	絕句
Chueh mo lu	嚼墨廬
chün i	俊逸
chün t'an	軍探
Ch'a-hua nü	茶花女
ch'a-yü fan-hou	茶餘飯後
Ch'ang-chou	常州
Ch'ang-ch'ing	長青

ch'ang-ho	塲合
Ch'ang-men	閶門
Ch'ang-men hsiao-shuo chi	倡門小說集
Ch'ang-men sung-chia lu	倡門送嫁錄
Ch'ang-shih	常識
Ch'ang-shu	常熟
Ch'en Ching-han	陳景韓
Ch'en Ch'iu	陳球
Ch'en Hsiao-tieh (Ting-shan)	陳小蝶（定山）
Ch'en Hsieh-fen	陳擷芬
Ch'en Kuo-k'ai	陳國凱
Ch'en Meng-p'o	陳夢坡
Ch'en pao	晨報
Ch'en Shen-yen	陳愼言
Ch'en Tieh-hsien	陳蝶仙
Ch'en Tieh-i	陳蝶衣
Ch'en Ting-shan. See Ch'en Hsiao-tieh.	
Ch'en Tu-hsiu	陳獨秀
Ch'en Tung-lei	陳東雷
Ch'en Tz'u-tieh	陳次蝶
Ch'en Yen-yen	陳燕燕
Ch'eng Chan-lu	程瞻廬
Ch'eng Hsiao-ch'ing	程小青
Ch'eng She-wo	成舍我
Ch'eng-t'ien	承天
Ch'i	妻
ch'i	氣
Ch'i-chu sheng	泣珠生
ch'i-ch'ing	奇情
Ch'i-hsia ching-chung chuan	奇俠精忠傳
Ch'iang hsueh hui	强學會
Ch'iang-hsueh pao	强學報
Ch'iao T'u-lu	橋堍陸
Ch'ien Cheng	錢徵
Ch'ien Chieh-ch'en	錢芥塵
ch'ien hsien shou	倩纖手
Ch'ien Hsing-ts'un	錢杏村

Ch'ien Ping-ho	錢病鶴
ch'ien-pien i-lü	千篇一律
ch'ien-tse hsiao-shuo	譴責小說
ch'ih	癡
ch'ing	情
Ch'ing-chu. See Pao Ch'ing-chu.	
Ch'ing-hua shu-chü	清華書局
Ch'ing-i pao	清議報
Ch'ing-lou pao	青樓報
ch'ing mo	情魔
Ch'ing-p'u	青浦
Ch'ing she	青社
ch'ing wang	情網
Ch'ing-wang chu-ssu	情網蛛絲
Ch'iu Chin	秋瑾
ch'ou	仇
ch'uan-ch'i	傳奇
ch'uan ying lou	釧影樓
Ch'uang-tsao she	創造社
ch'un ch'iu	春秋
Ch'un-ming wai-shih	春明外史
Ch'ung-chen	崇禎
Ch'ün-ch'iang pao	群強報
Ch'ü Ch'iu-pai	瞿秋白
ch'ü-wei	趣味
erh-chieh	二傑
erh-nü	兒女
Erh-nü ying-hsiung chuan	兒女英雄傳
rh-shih nien mu-tu chih kuai hsien-chuang	二十年目睹之怪現狀
Erh-shih shih-chi	二十世紀女界文明燈彈詞
nü-chieh wen-ming teng t'an-tz'u	
Erh-shih tsai fan-hua meng	二十載繁華夢
Fa-hsing shu-chü	法興書局
Fa-kuo nü ying-hsiung t'an-tz'u	法國女英雄彈詞
fa-k'an tz'u	發刊詞
fa-lü hsiao-shuo	法律小說

Fan Chia-shu	樊家樹
fan-t'e	反特
Fan Yen-ch'iao	范烟橋
fang-hsing k'an-wu	方形刊物
fang tan	放誕
fei shu	飛書
fei-t'ing	飛艇
Fei-yun ko	飛雲閣
Feng Che	馮喆
feng-ch'i	風氣
Feng-hsi. See Shen Feng-hsi.	
Feng Meng-chen	馮夢楨
Feng Meng-lung	馮夢龍
feng wei	風味
Feng Yü-ch'i	馮玉奇
Fo-hsueh shih pao	佛學時報
fu-chang	附張
fu-ch'ou	復仇
fu kuei ping	富貴病
fu lu shou	福祿壽
fu lu yuan-yang	福祿鴛鴦
Fu-nü shih pao	婦女時報
Fu-nü tsa-chih	婦女雜誌
Fu-sheng liu chi	浮生六記
fu-wu	服務
Hai-shang fan-hua meng	海上繁華夢
Hai-shang hua	海上花
Hai-shang yueh	海上月
Han-yü tz'u-tien	漢語辭典
Hangchow pai-hua pao	杭州白話報
hei-mu hsiao-shuo	黑幕小說
Hen hai	恨海
Hen-hai ku chou chi	恨海孤舟記
hen tao	恨島
Ho Hai-ming	何海鳴
Ho Li-na	何麗娜

Ho Meng-hsia	何夢霞
Hongkew	虹口
Hsi Hsiang chi	西廂記
Hsi Jung	西戎
hsi lou	息樓
Hsi-ts'ang	西倉
Hsi Yü-fu	席裕福
Hsia hsing she	夏星社
hsia-k'e	俠客
Hsia Jui-fang	夏瑞芳
hsia lieh	俠烈
hsia-tzu a-ping	瞎子阿丙
Hsia Yen	夏衍
hsiang chien	香肩
Hsiang-hsia-jen yu tao Shang-hai	鄉下人又到上海
Hsiang-kang ching pao	香港晶報
Hsiang K'an-jan	向愷然
Hsiang-lin Sao	祥林嫂
Hsiang shan yeh cheng hung	香山葉正紅
hsiang-yen hsiao-p'in	香艷小品
Hsiao chuan tien	小專電
hsiao-hsien	消閒
Hsiao-hsien pao	消閒報
Hsiao-hsien yueh-k'an	消閒月刊
Hsiao hsin-wen	小新聞
Hsiao pao	笑報
hsiao pao	小報
hsiao shih-min	小市民
Hsiao shih pao	小時報
hsiao shu	小書
Hsiao-shuo chi-pao	小說季報
Hsiao-shuo hai	小說海
Hsiao-shuo hsin pao	小說新報
Hsiao-shuo hua-pao	小說畫報
Hsiao-shuo lin	小說林
Hsiao-shuo ming-hua ta-kuan	小說名畫大觀
Hsiao-shuo shih-pao	小說時報

Hsiao-shuo ta-kuan	小說大觀
Hsiao-shuo ts'ung-pao	小說叢報
Hsiao-shuo yueh-pao	小說月報
hsiao-t'i wen-fu	小題文府
hsieh-ch'ing	寫情
hsieh-ch'ing hsiao-shuo	寫情小說
hsieh-shih	寫實
hsien	閒
Hsin chia-t'ing tsa-chih	新家庭雜誌
Hsin Chung-hua hsiao-shuo chieh	新中華小說界
Hsin Chung-kuo wei-lai chi	新中國未來記
hsin chü	信局
Hsin ch'ing-nien	新青年
Hsin ch'un lin	新春林
Hsin hsiao-shuo	新小說
Hsin hsin hsiao-shuo	新新小說
hsin-hsueh chieh	新學界
Hsin-hsueh pao	新學報
hsin hsueh-t'ang	新學堂
hsin-i	辛夷
hsin ku-tung lu	新骨董錄
hsin leng hsien-sheng	心冷先生
hsin min	新民
Hsin-min ts'ung pao	新民叢報
Hsin nü hsing	新女性
Hsin pao	新報
hsin p'ai	新派
Hsin shen pao	新申報
Hsin sheng	新聲
Hsin shih-t'ou chi	新石頭記
hsin-wen chih	新聞紙
Hsin-wen pao	新聞報
Hsing-ch'i	星期
hsing-ch'ü	興趣
Hsing-erh chiu-hsueh chi	馨兒就學記
Hsing-hsiu hai	星宿海
Hsing-kuang	星光

Hsing pao	星報
Hsing she	星社
Hsiu-hsiang hsiao-shuo	繡像小說
hsiu-ts'ai	秀才
Hsiung Fo-hsi	熊佛西
Hsu Chen-ya	徐枕亞
Hsu Cho-tai (Pan-mei)	徐卓呆（半梅）
Hsu Chueh	徐覺
Hsu Hsiao-t'ien	許嘯天
Hsu Pan-mei. See Hsu Cho-tai.	
Hsu Pi-po	徐碧波
Hsu T'ien-hsiao	徐天嘯
Hsueh Chin-ch'in	薛錦琴
Hsueh hung lei shih	雪鴻淚史
Hsueh-mei	雪梅
hsueh ni hung chua	雪泥鴻爪
hsueh-pao	學報
Hsueh Pao-ch'ai	薛寶釵
Hsun-huan jih pao	循環日報
Hu Chang	胡璋
Hu Chi-ch'en	胡寄塵
Hu Fang-lan	胡仿蘭
Hu Pao	滬報
Hu Pin-hsia	胡彬夏
Hu Shih	胡適
Hu Tieh	胡蝶
Hu Yao-pang	胡耀邦
hua-chi	滑稽
hua-chi hsiao-shuo	滑稽小說
Hua-chi yü-t'an	滑稽餘談
Hua-ch'ien hsin-chi	花前新記
Hua-hsien	花仙
Hua Mu-lan	花木蘭
Hua pao	畫報
Huan-chu lou-chu	還珠樓主
an-ch'iu Chung-kuo t'ung-hsueh hui	寰球中國同學會
Huan-hai sheng-ch'en lu	宦海升沈錄

Huan-lung	環龍
Huang-chiang nü-hsia	荒江女俠
Huang Chin-jung	黃金榮
Huang Hsiao-p'ei	黃小配
Huang Hsing	黃興
Huang Hsiu-ch'iu	黃繡球
Huang Po-hui	黃伯惠
Huang Sheng-pai	黃勝白
Huang Shih-chung	黃世仲
Huang T'ien-yuan	黃天源
Huang Yuan-yung	黃遠庸
Hui-chüan	蕙娟
Hung Chün	洪鈞
Hung lou meng	紅樓夢
Hung mei-kuei	紅玫瑰
Hung-ping pi-hsueh kuan	紅冰碧血館
Hung tsa-chih	紅雜誌
Hung wu	紅屋
hung yun	紅運
Huo Sang	霍桑
i chün	義軍
i hsueh	義學
i-shu ch'u	譯書處
I-so	頤瑣
I-tzu i-lei	一字一淚
I-yin cheng-chih hsiao-shuo hsu	譯印政治小說序
Jen-chien ti-yü	人間地獄
Jen-hai meng	人海夢
jen-min chuang	人民裝
jen-shih	認識
jou yü	肉慾
Ju-lin wai-shih	儒林外史
Kajin no kigu	佳人の奇遇
kanji	漢字

Kao Chien-hua	高劍華
Keng Hsiao-ti	耿小的
Ko Kung-chen	戈公振
ku-chi	古籍
Ku Ming-tao	顧明道
ku-wen	古文
Ku yuan-yang yü	孤鴛鴦語
Kuan-ch'ang hsien-hsing chi	官場現形記
Kuan-ch'ang li-hun an	官場離婚案
Kuan Hsiu-ku	關秀姑
Kuan Shou-feng	關壽峯
kuan pan	官辦
kuan wai	關外
Kuan Yü	關羽
Kuang-chih shu-chü	廣智書局
Kuang-i	廣益
Kuang-ling ch'ao	廣陵潮
kuang mang	光芒
Kuei lai	歸來
kun-t'ung	滾筒
kung-an	公案
Kung Chieh	龔傑
Kung-i. See Pao Kung-i.	
Kung-jen hsiao-shih	工人小史
kung li	公立
Kung-shang hsueh pao	工商學報
Kung Tzu-ying	龔子英
Kuomintang	國民黨
Kuo-hsiung	國雄
Kuo-min jih jih pao	國民日日報
Kuo Mo-jo	郭沫若
Kuo-wen pao	國聞報
Kuroiwa Ruikō	黑岩淚香
k'ai feng-ch'i	開風氣
K'ai feng-ch'i ti nü-hsing	開風氣的女性
K'ai-ming shu-chü	開明書局
K'ao-shih hsin hsiao-hua	考試新笑話

k'ang	炕
K'ang-Liang	康梁
K'ang Yu-wei	康有爲
K'o-fen	可芬
k'o-hsueh	科學
k'o-hsueh hsiao-shuo	科學小說
k'u-ch'ing	苦情
K'u she-hui	苦社會
k'uai	快
K'uai-huo	快活
K'uai-huo lin	快活林
K'uai-tsui Li Ts'ui-lien chi	快嘴李翠蓮記
K'uang K'uei-sheng	況夔生
K'un shan	崑山
K'ung Chieh-sheng	孔捷生
K'ung I-chi	孔乙己
K'ung ku lan	空谷蘭
K'ung Ming	孔明
Lan-kuei hen	蘭閨恨
Lang hua	浪花
Lao She	老舍
lao-shih	老實
Lao ch'in-shih	老琴師
Lao-ts'an yu-chi	老殘遊記
lei	雷
Lei chu yuan	淚珠緣
Leng-hsueh	冷血
li-chiao	禮敎
li ch'i	離奇
Li Han-ch'iu	李涵秋
li-hsiang hsiao-shuo	理想小說
Li-hsueh hui	勵學會
Li-hsueh i-pien	勵學譯編
Li-hun hou ti erh-nü	離婚後的兒女
Li Hung-chang	李鴻章
Li Li-hua	李麗華

Li Lieh-wen	黎烈文
Li mou	李某
Li Niang	梨娘
Li-pai hua	禮拜花
Li-pai liu	禮拜六
Li-pai liu p'ai	禮拜六派
Li pao	立報
Li Po-yuan	李伯元
li-shih hsiao-shuo	歷史小說
Li Shou-ch'eng	李守成
Li Shou-min	李壽民
Li Tieh-chuang	李蝶莊
Li Ting-i	李定夷
Liang Ch'i-ch'ao	梁啟超
Liang Hung-yü	梁紅玉
Lieh-jen ou-chi	獵人偶記
lien	戀
Lien-hua kuang-kao kung-szu	聯華廣告公司
Lin K'ang-hou	林康侯
Lin Shu	林紓
Lin Tai-yü	林黛玉
Lin Tsu-chin	林祖潘
Lin Yü-t'ang	林語堂
Liu Ch'i	劉琦
Liu Ch'un-lin	劉春霖
Liu Hsiang-t'ing	劉襄亭
Liu Huo-kung	劉豁公
Liu O	劉鶚
Liu Pan-nung	劉半儂（農）
Liu Pin-yen	劉賓雁
Liu-ping lien-ch'ü	溜冰戀曲
Liu Te-chu	劉德桂
Liu Tsung-yuan	柳宗元
Liu-tung wai-shih	留東外史
Liu T'ieh-leng	劉鐵冷
Liu T'ieh-yun	劉鐵雲
Liu Yuan-ying	劉沅穎

Liu Yun-jo	劉雲若
Lo-t'o hsiang-tzu	駱駝祥子
Lo Wei	羅維
Lu Fei-k'uei	陸費逵
Lu Feng-shih	陸鳳石
Lu Hsin-hua	盧新華
Lu Hsun	魯迅
Lu Shih-o	陸士諤
Lu T'an-an	陸澹安
Lü-shih t'ai-tu chih Hua-sheng-tun	律師態度之華盛頓
Lun hsiao-shuo yü ch'ün-chih chih kuan-hsi	論小說與羣治之關係
Lun pao-kuan yu-i yü kuo-shih	論報館有益於國事
lun-shuo	論說
Lung-feng hua-chu	龍鳳花燭
Lung-t'ang hsiao-shih	弄堂小史
Ma Chih-ch'ien	馬志千
Mao Tun	茅盾
Meiji	明治
Mei-jen chieh	美人劫
Mei-jen fu	美人福
Mei-yü	眉語
Meng-hsia. See Ho Meng-hsia.	
Meng-hsueh k'e-pen	蒙學課本
mi-ssu	密斯
mi-ssu-t'o	密斯脫
Min-chung hsi she	民衆戲社
min chün	民軍
Min-ch'üan ch'u-pan pu	民權出版部
Min-ch'üan pao	民權報
Min-ch'üan su	民權素
Min-hsing she	民興社
Min-hsu pao	民吁報
Min-hu pao	民呼報
Min-kuo jih-pao	民國日報
Min-li pao	民立報
Min pao	民報

Ming-hsing ying-p'ien kung-szu	明星影片公司
ming hui	明慧
ming-shih p'ai	名士派
mo-teng	摩登
Morita Shiken	森田思軒
Nan-hai	南海
Nan she	南社
Nan-yang kung-hsueh	南洋公學
niang-tzu chün	娘子軍
Ni Huan-chih	倪煥之
Nieh hai ch'ing t'ien	孽海情天
Nieh hai hua	孽海花
Nieh pao	孽報
Nieh yuan ching	孽冤鏡
ning-yuan pu-ch'ü hsiao-lao-p'o,	寧願不娶小老婆，不能不讀禮拜六
pu-neng pu-tu Li-pai liu	
Niu-lang chih-nü	牛郎織女
No jen	懦人
No no hana	野の花
nu	怒
Nung-hsueh pao	農學報
nü chieh	女界
nü-hsia	女俠
nü hsueh-sheng	女學生
Nü hsueh-sheng chih mi-mi chi	女學生之秘密記
nü hsueh-t'ang	女學堂
nü ko-ming-chia	女革命家
Nü pao	女報
nü tai-fu	女大夫
nü tso-chia	女作家
Nü-tzu shih-chieh	女子世界
O-hu	鵝湖
Pa Chin	巴金
Pai-hsia	白俠
pai-hua	白話

pai–hua pao	白話報
pan–wen pu–pai	半文不白
Pan yueh	半月
Pao Ch'ing–chu	包清柱
pao–kuan pa–ku	報館八股
Pao Kung–i	包公毅
pao p'i–ku	報屁股
Pao T'ien–hsiao	包天笑
Pao-yü. See Chia Pao-yü.	
pa ta hu–t'ung	八大胡同
Pai Hsien–yung	白先勇
pei	悲
Pei-li ying-erh	北里嬰兒
Pei p'ai	北派
Pen-kuan fu-yin shuo-pu yuan-ch'i	本館附印說部緣起
pen–pu hsin–wen	本埠新聞
Pi I–hung	畢倚虹
ping	病
po ming	薄命
pu–pai ta–wang	補白大王
pu shou–ch'ou	不受酬
P'ang Ching–chou	龐京周
P'eng kung-an	彭公案
P'eng–lang	鵬郎
p'i–p'a	琵琶
p'ien–li	骈驪
P'ing-chiang pu-hsiao sheng	平江不肖生
P'ing Chin–ya	平襟亞
p'ing–hua	平話
p'ing–pan	平版
p'ing–teng ko	平等閣
Sai–chin–hua	賽金花
San chien-k'e	三劍客
San-hsiao yin-yuan	三笑因緣
san–hsien	三絃
san min chu-i	三民主義

San-shih-liu yuan-yang	三十六鴛鴦
San-yu shu-she	三友書社
Sao-mi chou	掃迷帚
Seiji Shōsetsu	政治小說
Sha Yeh-hsin	沙葉新
shan-shu	善書
Shang-hai chin-pu shu-chü	上海進步書局
Shang-hai t'u-shu-kuan	上海圖書館
shao-nien	少年
Shao P'iao-p'ing	邵飄萍
she-hui hsiao-shuo	社會小說
Shen Chih-fang	沈知方（芝芳）
Shen-chou jih-pao	神州日報
Shen En-fu	沈恩孚
Shen Feng-hsi	沈鳳喜
shen-kuai	神怪
Shen Kuo-ying	沈國英
Shen pao	申報
Shen San-hsüan	沈三玄
Shen Ta-niang	沈大娘
Shen Ts'ung-wen	沈從文
Shen Yen-ping	沈雁冰
Sheng Hsüan-huai	盛宣懷
Sheng tien chi	聖殿記
sheng-yuan	生員
Shiba Shirō	柴四郎
Shih Chi-ch'ün	施濟羣
Shih-chieh fan-hua pao	世界繁華報
Shih-chieh shu-chü	世界書局
Shih-ch'i nien hou ti li-hun	十七年後的離婚
Shih-ch'ih	石癡
Shih hsueh pao	實學報
Shih k'an	詩刊
Shih kung-an	施公案
shih-li yang-ch'ang	十里洋塲
Shih Liang-ts'ai	史量才
Shih pao	時報

shih p'ing	時評
Shih-san mei	十三妹
Shih-shih hsin pao	時事新報
Shih-tzu ya-fen	獅子牙粉
Shih-wu pao	時務報
shou-ch'ao pen	手抄本
Shou-chüan	瘦鵑
Shou-ch'ing	壽卿
Shu-shan chien-hsia	蜀山劍俠
shu yuan	書院
Shuang hsing	雙星
Shui-hsin t'ing	水心亭
Shui-hu chuan	水滸傳
Shuo pu-te	說不得
shuo shu yü	說書寓
Ssu ch'ao	思潮
Ssu jen chi	斯人記
Ssu-ma Hsiang-ju	司馬相如
ssu ma-lu	四馬路
ssu-shu	私塾
ssu-wen li	斯文里
Su-chou pai-hua pao	蘇州白話報
Su Man-shu	蘇曼殊
Su pang	蘇幫
Su pao	蘇報
Su pao kuan	蘇報館
sui pi	隨筆
Sui-tsan chi	碎簪記
Sun Tung-wu	孫東吳
Sun Yat-sen	孫逸仙
Sun Chia-chen	孫家振
Sung Chiao-jen	宋教仁
ta-i	打夷
ta jan kang	大染缸
Ta kung pao	大公報
Ta ma pien	大馬扁

Ta shih-chieh pao	大世界報
ta shu	大書
Ta-tung shu-chü	大東書局
ta-t'i wen-fu	大題文府
Tai Chi-t'ao	戴季陶
tao wang tz'u	悼亡詞
Ti Ch'u-ch'ing	狄楚青
Ti-erh-tz'u wo-shou	第二次握手
ti pao	邸報
tien	殿
tien chiang	點將
Tien-shih-chai	點石齋
Tien-shih-chai hua pao	點石齋畫報
Tien shih-chieh	電世界
Ting Sung	丁悚
to-ch'ing	多情
Tōhō tsūshin sha	東方通信社
Tseng Hsu-pai	曾虛白
Tseng P'u (Tseng Meng-p'u)	曾樸（曾孟樸）
tso-chia	作家
Tso-p'in	作品.
Tsou Jung	鄒容
Tsung Fu-hsien	宗福先
ts'ai	才
Ts'ai Jui-chu	蔡蕊珠
ts'ai-tzu	才子
ts'ai-tzu chia-jen	才子佳人
Ts'ai Yüan-p'ei	蔡元培
Ts'ai yün	彩雲
Ts'ao Yü	曹禺
Ts'ui	崔
Ts'ui weng	崔翁
ts'ung shu	叢書
Tuan hung ling yen chi	斷鴻零雁記
tui-lien	對聯
Tung-fang tsa-chih	東方雜誌
Tung-hai	東海

Tung-hai san lang	東海三郎
Tung-ya ping-fu	東亞病夫
tung-yang ch'e	東洋車
tzu lan hsiao chu	紫蘭小築
Tzu-lan hsiao-chu chih chuei-i	紫蘭小築之追憶
Tzu lan hua p'ien	紫蘭花片
Tzu lo-lan	紫羅蘭
Tzu lo-lan an	紫羅蘭盒
Tzu-yeh	子夜
Tzu-yu tsa-chih	自由雜誌
Tzu-yu tang	自由黨
Tzu-yu t'an	自由談
tzu-yueh	子曰
Tz'u Yuan	辭源
T'a-li nü-jen	塔裏女人
T'aip'ing	太平
t'an hsin-hsing tao-te	談新性道德
t'an-tz'u	彈詞
T'ang Chien-wo	湯劍我
T'ang Ts'ai-ch'ang	唐才常
T'ao Po-ho	陶伯和
T'ao Yuan-ming	陶淵明
T'ien Chi-hen	田寄痕
T'ien ch'iao	天橋
t'ien-hsia	天下
t'ien-hsia ts'ai-tzu shu	天下才子書
T'ien-hsiao sheng	天笑生
T'ien hsu wo sheng	天虛我生
T'ien meng	天夢
t'u	土
T'u-hua chou-k'an	圖書週刊
T'u Kuang-ch'i	屠光啓
t'un	臀
T'ung-ch'eng	桐城
T'ung hsueh pao	通學報
T'ung shih	痛史
T'ung-wen shu-chü	同文書局

wai-chiao hsiao-shuo	外交小說
wai-pu hsin-wen	外埠新聞
Wan-kuo kung pao	萬國公報
Wang Shih-chen	王士禎
Wang Hsi-shen	王西神
wang hung lou	望鴻樓
Wang I-nien	汪詒年
Wang Meng	王蒙
Wang Tsui-tieh	王醉蝶
Wang Tu-lu	王度廬
Wang Tun-ken	王鈍根
Wang Tzu-jen	王子仁
Wang T'ao	王韜
Wang Yun-chang	王蘊章
Wang Yun-wu	王雲五
wei-hsin p'ai	維新派
Wen-hsueh hsün-k'an	文學旬刊
Wen-hsueh yen-chiu hui	文學研究會
wen jen	文人
wen jou	溫柔
Wen Kung-ta	文公達
wen-ming	文明
Wen-ming shu-chü	文明書局
wen t'an	文壇
wen yen	文言
wen yu i-ch'i	文有逸氣
Weng-yu yü-t'an	甕牖餘談
wu ao	兀傲
Wu Chih-hui	吳稚暉
Wu Ching-tzu	吳敬梓
Wu Chueh-mi	吳覺迷
Wu-hsi pai-hua pao	無錫白話報
wu-hsia	武俠
Wu Huai-chiu	吳懷疚
Wu Nung-hua	吳農花
wu-shang hsiao-hsien p'in	無上消閒品
Wu-shih nien-tai	五十年代
Wu Shuang-je	吳雙熱

wu-tan	武旦
Wu-ti p'ai ts'a-mien ya-fen	無敵牌擦面牙粉
Wu Tsu-hsiang	吳組緗
Wu Tuan-shu	吳端書
Wu T'ing-fang	伍廷芳
Wu Wo-yao	吳沃堯
Wu yun chi	吳雲記
yang	陽，洋
yang chü-jen	洋舉人
yang ch'ang ts'ai-tzu	洋場才子
yang hang	洋行
yang hsueh-t'ang	洋學堂
Yang Pai-min	楊白民
yang pang	揚幫
yang sheng-yuan	洋生員
yang wei	洋味
Yao Ming-te	姚明德
Yao Su-feng	姚蘇鳳
yao wen	要聞
Yao Wen-yuan	姚文元
Yao Yuan-ch'u	姚鵷雛
Yeh Ch'u-ts'ang	葉楚傖
Yeh Hsiao-feng	葉小鳳
Yeh Shen ch'en	夜深沈
Yeh Sheng-t'ao	葉聖陶
Yeh yuan-yang	野鴛鴦
yen-chiang	演講
yen-ch'ing hsiao-shuo	言情小說；艷情小說
Yen Fu	嚴復
yen-i	演義
Yen-shan wai-shih	燕山外史
Yen Tu-ho	嚴獨鶴
yin-kuo	因果
Yin tu fu	淫毒婦
ying-hsiung	英雄
Yorozu Chōhō	萬朝報

Yu-cheng Shu-chü	有正書局
Yu-hsi hsin-pao	游戲新報
Yu-hsi pao	游戲報
Yu-hsi shih-chieh	游戲世界
Yu-hsi tsa-chih	游戲雜誌
yu-hsien k'u	遊仙窟
Yü chih fu	余之夫
Yü ch'ing-t'ing	玉蜻蜓
Yü hsing	餘興
Yü hsing tsa-chih	餘興雜誌
Yü-li hun	玉梨魂
Yü Ta-fu	郁達夫
Yü Ta-hsiung	余大雄
Yü wu-sheng ch'u	於無聲處
yü t'i	玉體
Yü Yu-jen	于右任
yuan	猿，元
Yuan Han-yun	袁寒雲
Yuan Kuan-lan	袁觀瀾
Yuan Shih-k'ai	袁世凱
Yuan-yang hsueh	鴛鴦血
yuan-yang hu-tieh p'ai	鴛鴦蝴蝶派
Yuan-yang meng	鴛鴦夢
Yuan-yang tan kan	鴛鴦膽肝
Yuan-yang t'ing	鴛鴦亭
yueh ch'in	月琴
yueh-t'ai piao	月台票
Yueh-yueh hsiao-shuo	月月小說
Yun-ch'ien	筠倩
Yun T'ieh-ch'iao	惲鐵樵

Bibliography

A Ying (pseud.). See Ch'ien Hsing-ts'un.

Altick, Richard. *The English Common Reader: A Social History of the Mass Reading Public 1800–1900.* Chicago: University of Chicago Press, 1957.

Barnett, Suzanne W. "Silent Evangelism: Presbyterians and the Mission Press in China, 1807–1860." *Journal of Presbyterian History* 49 (Winter 1971): 287–302.

Bennett, E. Arnold. *Fame and Fiction: An Enquiry into Certain Popularities.* New York: E. P. Dutton and Company, 1901.

Bosanquet, Helen. "Cheap Literature." *Contemporary Review* (London) 79 (May 1901): 671–681.

Britton, Roswell S. *The Chinese Periodical Press, 1800–1912.* Shanghai: Kelly and Walsh, 1933.

Cawelti, John G. *The Six-gun Mystique.* Bowling Green, Ohio: Bowling Green Popular Press, n.d.

Chang Ching-lu 張靜廬 *Tsai ch'u-pan chieh erh-shih nien* 在出版界二十年 [Twenty years in the publishing field]. Shanghai, 1938.

——— . *Chung-kuo chin-tai ch'u-pan shih-liao* 中國近代出版史料 [Historical materials on publishing in China in recent times]. 2 vols. Shanghai: Ch'ün-lien ch'u-pan-she 羣聯出版社 , 1954–1958.

——— . *Chung-kuo ch'u-pan shih-liao pu-pien* 中國出版史料補編 [Supplement to historical materials on publishing in China.] Peking: Chung-hua shu-chü 中華書局 , 1957.

Chang, Hao. *Liang Ch'i-ch'ao and Intellectual Transition in China.* Cambridge: Harvard University Press, 1971.

Chang Hen-shui 張恨水. *T'i-hsiao yin-yuan* 啼笑因緣 [Fate in tears and laughter]. Shanghai: San-yu shu-she 三友書社 , 1930 (3 vols), 1948 (2 vols. including sequel).

——— . "Wo-ti sheng-huo ho ch'uang-tso" 我的生活和創作 ["My

life and works"]. *Ming Pao Monthly* 明報月刊 11.12:74–78 (December 1976) and 12.1:29–34 (January 1977).

Chang Ming-ming 張明明 "Hui-i fu-ch'in Chang Hen-shui" 回憶父親張恨水 [Reminiscences about my father Chang Hen-shui]. *Kuang-chiao ching* 廣角鏡 nos. 61–69 (October 1977–June 1978).

———. "Wo ti fu-ch'in Chang Hen-shui" 我的父親張恨水 ["My father Chang Hen-shui"]. *Ming Pao Monthly* 11.12:69–73.

Chen t'an tsa-chih 偵探雜誌 [The world of detectives]. Shanghai, June 1923 and following.

Cheng I-mei 鄭逸梅. "Hui-i '*Ching pao*'" 回憶「晶報」. *Ta jen* 大人, no. 21 (January 1972), pp. 88–91.

Cheng, Ying-wan. *Postal Communication in China and its Modernization, 1860–1896*. Cambridge: East Asian Research Center, Harvard University, 1970.

Ch'en Ching-chih 陳敬之. "Ch'ing-lou ts'ai-tzu Pi I-hung" 青樓才子畢倚虹 ["The genius of the pleasure quarters Pi I-hung"]. *Chang-ku yueh-k'an* 掌故月刊 no. 3, November 1971.

———. "Li Han-ch'iu i chueh Yang-chou" 李涵秋一覺揚州 ["Li Han-ch'iu tells of Yangchow"]. *Chang-ku yueh-k'an*, no. 4, December 1971.

———. "Li-pai liu p'ai ti hsing-ch'i ho shuai-lo" 禮拜六派的興起和衰落 ["The rise and fall of the Saturday school"]. *Ch'ang liu* 暢流 42.10:15–20.

———. "Yuan-yang hu-tieh p'ai ta shih Hsu Chen-ya" 鴛鴦蝴蝶派大師徐枕亞 ["Maestro of the mandarin duck and butterfly school, Hsu Chen-ya"]. *Chang-ku yüeh-k'an*, no. 2, October 1971.

Ch'en San 陳三 "T'an li-pai-liu p'ai" 談禮拜六派 ["Speaking of the Saturday school"]. *Tang-tai wen-i* 當代文藝, no. 6, April 1976, pp. 117–123.

Ch'en Tieh-i 陳蝶衣 "Chiu-wei-kuei tso-che, Chang Ch'un-fan hsien-sheng" 九尾龜作者張春帆先生 ["Mr. Chang Ch'un-fan, author of *Nine-tailed Turtles*"]. *Wan-hsiang* 萬象, no. 4, October 1975, pp. 21–24.

———. "Hua k'o tsui hsieh" 花窠醉寫 ["Drunken writings in a flower nest"]. *Hsing-tao jih-pao*, September 2–4, October 15–30, November 1–2, December 12, 1973; January 26 and 28, 1974.

——— . "Li-pai-liu p'ai ts'ang sang shih" 禮拜六派滄桑史 ["The
vicissitudes in the story of the Saturday school"].*Ch'ang liu* 暢流
42.10:15–20.

——— . " 'Tzu-lan hsiao chu' chih chui i" 「紫蘭小築」之追憶
["Recalling 'the little house of violets' "]. *Ta ch'eng* 大成 , no. 12,
November 1974, pp. 58–60.

——— . "Yen Tu-ho yü Chou Shou-chüan" 嚴獨鶴與周瘦鵑 ["Yen
Tu-ho and Chou Shou-chuan"]. *Ta jen,* no. 38, June 1973, pp.
86–92.

Ch'en Ting-shan 陳定山.*Ch'un-shen chiu wen* 春申舊聞 [Old stories
from early Shanghai] Taipei, 1967.

Ch'en Ts'un-jen 陳存仁 ."Ch'in Shou-ou ti liang pu Ch'ing-kung
hsiao-shuo" 秦瘦鷗的兩部清宮小說 ["Two novels about the
Ch'ing court by Ch'in Shou-ou"]. *Ta ch'eng,* no. 18, May 1975,
pp. 19–27.

Ch'eng Chi-hua 程季華.*Chung-kuo tien-ying fa-chan shih.*
中國電影發展史 ["A history of the development of film in
China"]. 2 vols. Peking, 1963.

Chesneaux, Jean. *Le Mouvement Ouvrier de 1919 à 1927.* Paris-La Haye:
Mouton, 1962. Translated by H. M. Wright as *The Chinese Labor
Movement, 1919–1927.* Stanford: Stanford University Press, 1968.

Chieh k'e 傑克.(pseud.). "Chuang-yuan nü-hsu Hsu Chen-ya"
狀元女婿徐枕亞 ["The *chuang-yuan*'s son-in-law Hsu Chen-ya"].
Wan hsiang 萬象, no. 1, July 1975, pp. 42–48.

Ch'ien Hsing-ts'un 錢杏村,pseud. A Ying 阿英.Hsien-tai Chung-kuo
wen-hsueh lun 現代中國文學論 [On modern Chinese literature].
Shanghai, n.d.

——— . *Wan-Ch'ing wen-i pao-k'an shu-lueh* 晚清文藝報刊述略 [An
account of late Ch'ing literary periodicals]. Shanghai, 1959.

——— . *Wan-Ch'ing Hsiao-shuo shih* 晚清小說史 ["A history of late
Ch'ing fiction"]. Taipei, Jen-jen wen-k'u 人人文庫,1968.

——— . *Wan-Ch'ing hsiao-shuo shih.* Hong Kong, 1973.

Chih Hsi 志希 (pseud.). "Chin-jih Chung-kuo chih hsiao-shuo
chieh" 今日中國之小說界 ["The realm of fiction in present-day
China"]. *Hsin ch'ao* 新潮,1.1 (January 1919).

Chin ching 金晶 (pseud.). "Chang Hen-shui chuan" 張恨水傳 ["The
life of Chang Hen-shui"]. *Nan pei chi* 南北極 no. 77 (October
1976), pp. 69–72; no. 78 (November 1976), pp. 77–81; no. 79
(December 1976), pp. 99–103.

Chou Shou-chüan 周瘦鵑. *Hua-ch'ien so chi* 花前瑣記 [Trifling notes before flowers]. Peking, 1955.

Chou Shu-jen 周樹人, pseud. Lu Hsun 魯迅. "Shanghai wen-i chih i-p'ieh" 上海文藝一瞥 ["A glimpse of Shanghai literary art"]. *Erh hsin chi* 二心集 [Two hearts collection]. Hong Kong, 1965.

Chou Tso-jen 周作人 *T'an lung chi* 談龍集 ["Speaking of dragons"]. Shanghai: K'ai ming shu tien 開明書店, 1927.

Chow Tse-tsung. *The May Fourth Movement: Intellectual Revolution in Modern China.* Stanford, Ca.: Stanford University Press, 1967.

Chung-hua hsiao-shuo chieh 中華小説界 ["The world of Chinese fiction"]. Shanghai, January 1914 and following.

CYLHIL. See Pao T'ien-hsiao, *Ch'uan-ying lou hui-i lu.*

CYLHIL:HP. See Pao T'ien-hsiao, *Ch'uan-ying lou hui-i lu hsu-pien.*

Drège, Jean-Pierre. "L'entreprise Privée d'Edition en Chine dans la Première Moitié du XXᵉ Siècle: la Commercial Press de Shanghai (1897–1949)." Ph.D. dissertation, University of Paris, 1976.

Fan Chi-p'ing 范基平, pseud. Ssu-ma Hsiao 司馬小. " 'Wo ti t'ung-shih' Chang Hen-shui" 「我的同事」張恨水 [" 'My colleague' Chang Hen-shui"]. *Ta-jen,* no. 16, (August 1971) pp. 60–62.

Fan Tzu 范子 (pseud.). "Yuan-yang hu-tieh p'ai hsiao-shuo-chia ch'ün hsiang" 鴛鴦蝴蝶派小説家羣像 ["A general view of mandarin duck and butterfly school authors"]. *Hsing-tao chou-pao* 星島週報, July 14 1972, p. 10.

Fan Yen-ch'iao 范烟橋. *Chung-kuo hsiao-shuo shih* 中國小説史 [History of Chinese fiction]. Hua-hsia ch'u-pan she 華夏出版社, n.p., n.d.

Fu-nü shih-pao 婦女時報 [The women's times]. Shanghai, 1912 and following.

Gans, Herbert. *Popular Culture and High Culture.* New York: Basic Books, 1974.

Ho Ta 何達, pseud. Ning Yuan 寧遠. *Hsiao-shuo hsin-hua* 小説新話 [New talk about fiction]. Hong Kong: Shang-hai shu-chü 上海書局, 1972.

Hoggart, Richard. *The Uses of Literacy.* London: Chatto and Windus, 1957.

Hsia Chih-ch'ing 夏志清 [C. T. Hsia]. *Ai-ch'ing, she-hui, hsiao-shuo* 愛情, 社會, 小説 [Love, society, and the novel]. Taipei: Ch'un wen-hsueh ch'u-pan she 純文學出版社, 1970.

———. "Yen Fu and Liang Ch'i-ch'ao as Advocates of New Fiction." *Journal of Oriental Studies* 14.2 (July 1976): 133–149.

Hsiang K'ai-jan 向愷然. *Chiang-hu ch'i-hsia chuan* 江湖奇俠傳 [Chronicle of the strange roving knights]. Shanghai: Shen Tung-hai 沈東海, 1947.

Hsiao-shuo hsin pao 小說新報 [New fiction journal]. Shanghai, March 1915 and following.

Hsiao-shuo hua pao 小說畫報 [The fiction pictorial]. Shanghai, January 1917 and following.

Hsiao-shuo shih-chieh 小說世界 [The fiction world] Shanghai, March 30 1923 and following.

Hsiao-shuo shih pao 小說時報 [The fiction times]. Shanghai, September 1909 and following.

Hsiao-shuo ta-kuan 小說大觀 [The grand magazine]. Shanghai, August 1915 and following.

Hsiao-shuo ts'ung-pao 小說叢報 [Thicket of fiction]. Shanghai, May 1914 and following.

Hsiao-shuo yueh pao 小說月報 [The short story monthly]. Shanghai, September–October 1907.

Hsiao-shuo yueh-pao. Shanghai, July 1910 and following.

Hsing I 醒嚘. (pseud.). "Li Han-ch'iu i-shih" 李涵秋軼事 ["Anecdotes on Li Han-ch'iu"]. in *Chang-ku yueh-k'an* 掌故月刊, no. 29 (January 1974), pp. 45–48.

Hsing-kuang 星光 [Starlight]. No. 1, two volumes, Summer 1923. No further issues.

Hsu Chen-ya 徐枕亞. *Yü-li hun* 玉梨魂 [Jade pear spirit]. Shanghai: Min-ch'üan ch'u-pan-pu 民權出版部, 1914. (Cited as YLH.)

——— . *Hsueh hung lei shih* 雪鴻淚史 [Chronicle of the great tears of bygone days]. Shanghai: Hsiao-shuo ts'ung-pao she 小說叢報社, 1934.

Hsu P'ei-chün 徐佩珺. "T'an yuan-yang hu-tieh p'ai hsiao-shuo" 談鴛鴦蝴蝶派小說 ["On the fiction of the mandarin duck and butterfly school"]. *Kuang-ming jih pao* 光明日報, January 12, 1964.

Hsun Ching 洵錚. (pseud.). "Ch'ien-ch'en hui-shou i 'san Chang' " 前程回首憶三張 ["Peering into the past to recall the 'three Changs' "]. *Chang ku yueh-k'an* 掌故月刊, (Hong Kong) 25:62–63 (September, 1973).

Hu Han-chu 胡憨珠. "Shen pao yü Shih Liang-ts'ai" 申報與史量才 ["*Shen pao* and Shih Liang-ts'ai"]. *Ta jen* nos. 1–30 (May 1970–October 1972).

Hu Shih 胡適. "Chien-she ti wen-hsueh ko-ming lun" 建設的文學革命論 ["On a constructive literary revolution"], reprinted in Chao Chia-pi 趙家璧,ed. *Chung-kuo hsin wen-hsueh ta-hsi* 中國新文學大系 [A compendium of the new literature in China], Shanghai, 1935– 36, 1:127– 140.

———. "Shih-ch'i nien ti hui-ku" 十七年的回顧 ["A look back after seventeen years"]. *Shih pao* October 13, 1921.

———. "Tao-yen" 導言 ["Introduction"] to Chao Chia-pi 趙家璧, ed., *Chung-kuo hsin wen-hsueh ta-hsi.* Shanghai, 1935– 36, 1:1– 32.

Hu Tun-yuan 胡遯園. "Yü Hsiang K'ai-jan t'an chiang-hu ch'i hsia" 與向愷然談江湖奇俠 ["A talk with Hsiang K'ai-jan about strange roving knights"] in *I-wen chih* 藝文誌 no. 95 (August 1973), pp. 29– 31.

Huang Mao-an 黃猫庵. "Su-chou ti i ke wen-i t'uan-t'i, hsing she" 蘇州的一個文藝團體, 星社 ["A literary group in Soochow, the star society"]. *Wan hsiang* 萬象 no. 2 (August 1975), pp. 30– 32.

Huang, Philip C. *Liang Ch'i-ch'ao and Modern Chinese Liberalism.* Seattle: University of Washington Press, 1972.

Hung mei-kuei 紅玫瑰 [The red rose]. Shanghai, July 1924 and following.

Hung Shen 洪深. "Wang T'ao k'ao-cheng" 王韜考證 [A critical research of Wang T'ao]. *Wen-hsueh* 2.6 (1934).

Kao Chen-pai 高貞白, pseud. Po-yü 佰雨. "Chi tsui-lao ti tso-chia Pao T'ien-hsiao hsien-sheng" 記最老的作家包天笑先生 ["On the oldest of authors Mr. Pao T'ien-hsiao"]. *Ta-ch'eng,* no. 2 (January 1974), pp. 32– 39.

———, pseud. Lin Hsi 林熙 "P'ing-chiang pu hsiao sheng Hsiang K'ai-jan" 平江不肖生向愷然 ["The unworthy son of P'ing-chiang, Hsiang K'ai-jan"]. *Wan hsiang,* no. 2 (August 1975), pp. 40– 43.

———, pseud. Lin Hsi 林熙. "Wu-shih-wu nien ch'ien ti 'hsing kuang' " 五十五年前的星光 ["The 'starlight' of fifty-five years ago"]. *Ta ch'eng,* no. 56 (July 1978), pp. 34– 38.

Kindai bungaku kenkyū sōsho 近代文學研究叢書 47 vols. Tokyo, 1956– 1978.

Kinmonth, Earl. "The Self-Made Man in Meiji Japanese Thought." Ph.D. dissertation, University of Wisconsin, 1974.

Ko Kung-chen 戈公振. *Chung-kuo pao-hsueh shih* 中國報學史 [History of the press in China]. Peking: San-lien shu-tien 三聯書店, 1955.

Ku Ming-tao 顧明道. *Huang-chiang nü-hsia* 荒江女俠 [Female knight of the wild rivers]. Shanghai, Wen-yeh shu-chü 文業書局, 1937.

Lam Sai-chun 林世濬. "Shang-hai yuan-yang hu-tieh p'ai hsiao-shuo hsing-ch'i yü mo-lo" 上海鴛鴦蝴蝶派興起與末落 ["The rise and fall of the Shanghai mandarin duck and butterfly school"], M. A. dissertation, University of Hong Kong, 1973.

Leavis, Queenie D. *Fiction and the Reading Public.* London: Chatto and Windus, 1932.

Lee, Leo O. F. "Lin Shu and His Translations: Western Fiction in Chinese Perspective." *Papers on China,* 19:159–193 (December 1965).

——— . *The Romantic Generation of Modern Chinese Writers.* Cambridge: Harvard University Press, 1973.

Levenson, Joseph R. *Liang Ch'i-ch'ao and the Mind of Modern China.* Cambridge: Harvard University Press, 1965.

Li Han-ch'iu 李涵秋. *Kuang-ling ch'ao* 廣陵潮 [Tides of Yangchow]. 10 vols. Shanghai: Chen-ya shu-chü 震亞書局, 1941.

Li Hui-ying 李輝英. *Chung-kuo hsiao-shuo shih* 中國小說史 [A history of Chinese fiction]. Hong Kong: Tung-ya shu-chü 東亞書局, 1970.

——— . "Hsu Pan-mei ti hui-i lu" 徐半梅的回憶錄 ["The reminiscences of Hsu Pan-mei"]. *Hsing-tao wan pao,* July 9 1973, p. 8.

——— . *San yen liang yü* 三言兩語 [Talk about this and that]. Hong Kong: Wen-hsueh yen-chiu-she 文學研究社, 1975.

Li-pai-liu 禮拜六 [Saturday]. Shanghai, June 1914 and following.

Liang Ch'i-ch'ao 梁啟超. *Yin-ping-shih ho chi* 飲冰室合集 [Collected works of the ice-drinker's studio]. Shanghai: Chung-hua shu-chü 中華書局, 1941.

Lin, Sung-ho. *Factory Workers in Tungku.* Peking: China Foundation for the Promotion of Education and Culture, 1928.

Lin Yutang. *A History of the Press and Public Opinion in China.* Chicago: The University of Chicago Press, 1936.

Link, Perry. "Introduction" and two translations in John Berninghausen and Ted Huters, eds., *Revolutionary Literature in China.* White Plains: M. E. Sharpe Company, 1977, pp. 12–19.

——— . "Traditional-style Popular Urban Fiction in the 'Teens and Twenties" in Merle Goldman, ed., *Modern Chinese Literature in the May Fourth Era.* Cambridge: Harvard University Press, 1977, pp. 327–349.

Liu Chia-yu 劉嘉猷. "Tao-nien Yen shih Tu-ho" 悼念嚴師獨鶴 ["In memory of my teacher Yen Tu-ho"]. *Ta jen,* no. 40 (August 1973), pp. 63–65.

Liu Hsin-huang 劉心皇. *Hsien-tai Chung-kuo wen-hsüeh shih hua* 現代中國文學史話 [A history of modern Chinese literature]. Cheng-chung shu-chü 正中書局 (no location given), n.d.

Liu Wen-chao 劉文昭. "Hsü Chen-ya yü chuang-yüan ch'ien chin" 徐枕亞與狀元千金 ["Hsu Chen-ya and the *chuang-yuan*'s daughter"]. *Chung-wen wen-chai* 中文文摘 59:24 (July 1973).

Liu, Wu-chi. *Su Man-shu*. New York: Twayne Publishers, 1972.

Lu Hsun. See Chou Shu-jen.

Ma wu hsien-sheng 馬五先生.(pseud.)."Hsien-tai ti wen-tzu yin-yüan" 現代的文字因緣 ["Trends in modern written language"]. *K'uai pao* 快報, June 5, 1976, p. 6.

Mao Tun. See Shen Yen-ping.

Mei-tzu 眉子.(pseud.). "Lun Huan-chu-lou-chu chi ch'i tso-p'in" 論還珠樓主及其作品 ["On Huan-chu-lou-chu and his works"]. *Ta ch'eng,* 9:33– 35, 10:33– 38, and 11:52– 55 (August– October 1974).

Millar, J. H. "Penny Fiction." *Blackwood's Magazine* (London), (December 1898), pp. 801– 811.

Min Yu 民猶.(pseud.). "P'ing Chang Hen-shui 'T'i-hsiao yin-yuan' " 評張恨水「啼笑因緣」 ["Review of Chang Hen-shui's *Fate in Tears and Laughter*"]. *Ta kung pao wen-hsueh fu-k'an* 大公報文學副刊 January 4, 1932, p. 8.

Mou hsien-sheng 某先生.(pseud.). "Hsu Cho-tai yü Wang Hsiao-i" 徐卓呆與王小逸 ["Hsu Cho-tai and Wang Hsiao-i"]. *Chen pao* 眞報 (Hong Kong), July 15, 1973, p. 3.

Murphey, Rhoads. *Shanghai: Key to Modern China*. Cambridge: Harvard University Press, 1953.

Nakamura Tadayuki 中村忠行."Shinmatsu tantei shōsetsu shi kō" 清末探偵小説史稿 [A history of late-Ch'ing detective fiction] *Shinmatsu shōsetsu kenkyū* 清末小説研究 (Nara) 2:9– 42 (1978) and 3:10– 60. (1979).

Ning Yuan. See Ho Ta.

Nishida Taketoshi西田長寿.*Meiji jidai no shimbun to zasshi* 明治時代の新聞と雑誌 [Newspapers and magazines of the Meiji period]. Tokyo: Shibun dō 至文堂,1961.

Nü-tzu shih-chieh 女子世界 [Woman's world]. Shanghai, December 1914 and following.

Ōtsuka Reizō 大塚令三."Shanhai no Shōhō ni kansuru Ichi Kōsatsu" 上海の小報に関する一考察 ["An examination of the circumstances of the mosquito newspapers of Shanghai"], *Mantetsu Shina Gesshi* 満鉄支那月誌 6.3 (June 1929):63– 73.

Pan yueh 半月 [The semi-monthly]. Shanghai, September 1921 and following.

P'ang Kuan-ch'ing 龐貫清."T'i hsiao yin-yuan tien-ying shuang-pao an" 啼笑因緣電影雙包案 ["The twin cases of the *Fate in Tears and Laughter* movie] in *Ta-jen,* no. 4, pp. 45–47.

Pao T'ien-hsiao 包天笑. *Ch'uan-ying lou hui-i lu* 釧影樓回憶錄 [Reminiscences of the bracelet shadow chamber]. Hong Kong: Ta-hua ch'u-pan-she 大華出版社, 1971. (Cited as CYLHIL.)

——— . *Ch'uan-ying lou hui-i lu hsu-pien* 釧影樓回憶錄續編 [Sequel to reminiscences of the bracelet shadow chamber]. Hong Kong: Ta-hua ch'u-pan-she, 1973. (Cited as CYLHIL:HP.)

——— . "Hsiang-hsia jen yu tao Shanghai" 鄉下人又到上海 ["The countryman visits Shanghai again"]. *Shen Pao,* October 30, 1931, and following.

——— . *I-shih-chu-hsing ti pai-nien pien-ch'ien.* 衣食住行的百年變遷 [Changes in daily life over a hundred years]. Hong Kong: Ta-hua ch'u-pan-she, 1974.

Pei-ching ta-hsueh Chung-wen hsi 1955 nien-chi 北京大學中文系 1955 年級. *Chung-kuo hsiao-shuo shih kao* 中國小說史稿. [A history of Chinese fiction]. Peking: Jen-min wen-hsueh ch'u-pan-she. 人民文學出版社, 1960.

Pott, F. L. Hawks. *A Short History of Shanghai.* Shanghai: Kelly and Walsh, 1928.

Prusek, Jaroslav. "The Beginnings of Popular Chinese Literature: Urban Centers — the Cradle of Popular Fiction." *Archiv Orientalni* 35 (1968).

Rankin, Mary B. *Early Chinese Revolutionaries.* Cambridge: Harvard University Press, 1971.

Reinsch, Paul. "The New Education in China." *Atlantic Monthly,* April 1909.

Saneto Keishū 実藤恵秀. *Chūgokujin nihon ryūgaku shi* 中國人日本留學史 [A history of Chinese studying in Japan] Tokyo, 1960.

Sansom, George Bailey. *The Western World and Japan: A Study in the Interaction of European and Asiatic Cultures.* New York: Alfred A. Knopf, 1951.

Schwartz, Benjamin. *In Search of Wealth and Power: Yen Fu and the West.* Cambridge: Harvard University Press, 1964.

Senuma Shigeki 瀬沼茂樹. *Hon no hyakunen shi* 本の百年史 [A hundred-year history of books]. Tokyo: Shuppan nyūsu sha 出版ニュース社 1965.

Shang kuan tai-fu 上官大夫. (pseud.). "Chang-hui hsiao-shuo-chia

Chang Hen-shui ch'i jen ch'i shih" 章回小說家張恨水其人其事 ["All about the linked-chapter novelist Chang Hen-shui"]. *Ch'un ch'iu* 春秋 (Hong Kong) 284:15–18 (May, 1979).

Shen pao 申報. Shanghai, 1872–1935.

Shen Yen-ping 沈雁冰, pseud. Mao Tun 茅盾. "Tzu-jan chu-i yü Chung-kuo hsien-tai hsiao-shuo" 自然主義與中國現代小說 ["Naturalism and modern Chinese fiction"]. *Hsiao-shuo yueh-pao* 13.7 (July 1922).

Shōji Sensui 庄司浅水. *Nihon no shomotsu* 日本の書物 [Books of Japan]. Tokyo: Sōgensha 創元社, 1954.

Ssu-ma Hsiao 司馬小. See Fan Chi-p'ing 范基平.

Storey, Graham. *Reuters: The Story of a Century of News Gathering.* New York: Crown Publishers, 1951.

Ta kung pao 大公報 Tientsin, 1931–1932.

Tao, L. K. *The Standard of Living Among Chinese Workers.* Shanghai: China Institute of Pacific Relations, 1931.

T'an Pi-an 譚彼岸. *Wan-Ch'ing ti pai-hua wen yun-tung* 晚清白話文運動 ["The late Ch'ing vernacular movement"]. Wuhan: *Hu-pei jen-min ch'u-pan she* 湖北人民出版社, 1956.

Tseng Hsu-pai 曾虛白. *Chung-kuo hsin-wen shih* 中國新聞史 [History of the press in China]. Taipei, Kuo-li cheng-chih ta-hsueh hsin-wen yen-chiu-so 國立政治大學新聞研究所 1966.

Tseng P'u 曾樸 · *Nieh-hai hua* 孽海花 [Flower on a sea of evil]. Hong Kong, 1957.

Tzu lo-lan 紫羅蘭 ["Violets"]. Shanghai, December 1925 and following.

Wang P'ing-ling 王平陵 · *San-shih nien wen-t'an ts'ang-sang lu* 卅年文壇滄桑錄 [Great changes over thirty years on the literary scene]. Taipei, 1965.

Weakland, John. "Chinese Film Images of Invasion and Resistance." *China Quarterly* 47 (July–September 1971):439–470.

Wen-hsueh hsun-k'an 文學旬刊 · [Literary thrice-monthly]. Peking, May 10, 1921, and following.

Wolf, Margery, and Roxane Witke, eds., *Women in Chinese Society.* Stanford: Stanford University Press, 1957.

Wright, Mary C. *China in Revolution: The First Phase, 1900–1913.* New Haven: Yale University Press, 1968.

Wright, Thomas. "On a Possible Popular Culture." *Contemporary Review* (London) 40 (July 1881): pp. 25–44.

Wu, K. T. "The Development of Typography in China during the Nineteenth Century." *The Library Quarterly* 22.3 (July 1952): 288–301.

Wu Wo-yao 吳沃堯 · "Chiu ming ch'i-yuan" 九命奇寃 ["Strange grievances of nine lives"]. *Hsin hsiao-shuo* 新小說, no. 4 (1902).

YLH. See Hsu Chen-ya, *Yü-li hun*.

Yu-hsi shih-chieh 游戲世界 [Recreation world]. Shanghai, July 1921 and following.

Yu-hsi tsa chih 游戲雜誌 [Recreation magazine]. Shanghai, January 1913 and following.

Yuan Ch'ang-ch'ao 袁昶超 · *Chung-kuo pao-yeh hsiao-shih* 中國報業小史 [A brief history of newspapers in China]. Hong Kong: Hsin-wen t'ien-ti-she 新聞天地社, 1957.

"Yuan-yang hu-tieh p'ai tui hsi-chü ti ying-hsiang ho p'ing-lun chieh tui t'a ti p'ing-lun" 鴛鴦蝴蝶派對戲劇的影響和評論界對它的評論 ["The influence of the mandarin duck and butterfly school on drama and the criticism of it from criticism circles"]. *Hsin-hua yueh-pao* 新華月報, January 1964, pp. 269–270. No author listed.

Yuan-yang hu-tieh p'ai yen-chiu tzu-liao 鴛鴦蝴蝶派研究資料 [Research materials on the mandarin duck and butterfly school], ed. Wei Shao-ch'ang 魏紹昌 · Shanghai: Wen-i ch'u-pan she 文藝出版社, 1962. (Cited as YYHTP.)

Yun lang 筠廊 · "Yang-chou ts'ai-tzu Pi I-hung ch'uan ch'i" 揚州才子畢倚虹傳奇 ["The romance of the Yangchow genius Pi I-hung"]. *Ch'un ch'iu* 春秋 (Hong Kong), no. 292 (Aug. 1969), pp. 20–22 and no. 293 (Sept. 1969), pp. 22–24.

YYHTP. See *Yuan-yang hu-tieh p'ai yen-chiu tzu-liao*.

Index

Access to the popular mind, 4, 5–7, 63–64, 196–197
Account of the Future of the New China (Liang Ch'i-ch'ao), 132
Adventures of Sherlock Holmes (C. Conan Doyle), 129, 130, 147, 159; popularity of, 138, 143
Aged, the, role in popular fiction, 198–199
Agricultural Studies, 127
Altick, Richard, 186
American Exclusion Act, 139
Anhwei Literature, 248
Annals of Sorrow (Wu Wo-yao), 132
Arithmetic, 127
Art. *See* Literary style
Association for Literary Studies, 168
Author-reader relationships. *See* Reader-author relations
Authors: attitude of detachment expressed by, 171–172; background of, 10–11, 64, 156–157, 172; commercial relations with publishers, 152–155; cultivated images of, 161–163, 173; groups and societies of, 164–170, 254; impact of commercialized media on, 13–14, 180; life-styles of, 156–163; literary games played by, 170; marriage of, 46–47; payment of, 51–52, 84, 87, 90, 152–155, 161, 162; successful, 157–159
Autobiography, 47–48, 52

Beauty, of ideal literary lovers, 66–67, 76
Beauty's Blessings, A (Li Ting-i), 41, 166, 167
Beijing Film Studio, 239
Bennett, Arnold, 196
Bitter Society, The, 139
Blind storytellers, 22

Bodily desire, 70
Books: costs of, 6, 12, 190, 239; quota distribution system for, 239–240; renting of, 157
Bookstores, payment to publishers by, 84–85
Bourgeois fiction, social background of, 55–58
Boxer affair, 125, 140
British journalism, 141. *See also* English popular fiction
Britton, Roswell, 91, 112
Brothels, in popular fiction, 173–176
Buddhism, 27, 30; and death, 76
Buddhist Studies Times, 250
"Butterfly," 8. *See also* Mandarin Duck and Butterfly School

Camel Hsiang-tzu (Lao She), 188–189
Canton, 242; novels published in, 140; and Western contacts, 88
Canton Literature and Art, 246
Cases Investigated by the Chinese Sherlock Holmes (Ch'eng Hsiao-ch'ing), 22, 147
"Castigatory" fiction, 138–139, 143, 145–146, 174, 222; in the late 1970s, 244; popular attitudes toward, 157
Chang Chien, 88, 113
Chang Chih-tung, 99
Chang Ching-lu, 112
Chang Ch'un-fan, 54
Chang Chü-sheng, 87
Chang Hen-shui, 15, 67n, 124, 169, 181, 187, 188, 266; career of, 157; *Fate in Tears and Laughter* by, 12–13, 22–39, 41, 57 *(see also Fate in Tears and Laughter); Informal History of Ch'un-ming* by, 37; literary style of, 35–39, 185; name of, 35; *This Person's Notes* by, 46

Chang Hsi-ch'en, magazines for women edited by, 251
Chang I-han, 164, 165
Chang Ming-fei, 162
Chang Ping-lin, 254
Chang Tan-fu, 120
Chang Yang, *The Second Handshake* by, 236–239, 245
Chao Feng-ch'ang, 88, 113
Chao Mien-yun, 169, 257, 263
Character portrayal, in popular fiction, 187
Chastity, 54, 56, 57, 210; of ideal literary lovers, 67, 69
Ch'en Ching-han, 105, 106–107, 114, 115, 164, 180–181; magazine edited by, 218; role in *Fiction Times,* 249
Ch'en Ch'iu, *Informal History of Yen Shan* by, 59
Ch'en Hsiao-tieh, 181, 262. *See also* Ch'en Ting-shan
Ch'en Hsieh-fen, 209
Ch'en Shen-yen, 18–19, 169, 177, 181
Ch'en Tieh-hsien, 117, 164, 250, 262; butterfly symbol used by, 177; career of, 158–159, 165–166; manuscripts evaluated by, 171; *Teardrop Destiny* by, 41
Ch'en Ting-shan, 189n, 195; *The Fifties* by, 178; salary of, 154
Ch'en Tu-hsiu, 19
Ch'eng Chan-lu, 252, 265
Cheng Chen-to, 7, 11, 17, 88
Cheng Cheng-yin, 169–170
Ch'eng Hsiao-ch'ing, 22, 147, 168, 169
Cheng I-mei, 169, 178, 189n, 257, 264
Ch'eng She-wo, 124
Chesneaux, Jean, 5–6
Ch'iang-hsueh pao, 100, 126
Chiang Hung-chiao, 164, 168, 263; story on "new-style" divorce by, 223–224
Chi-ch'eng Book Company, 93
Ch'ien Cheng, 96, 97
Ch'ien Hsing-ts'un, *History of Late Ch'ing Fiction* by, 135
Ch'ien Ping-ho, 166, 256
Ch'ih, in love stories, 69–70
"Children After Divorce" (Pi I-hung), 224–225
Children, in popular fiction, 200–201
China Youth Publishing House, 236, 238
Chin-chang Book Co., 93

Ch'ing, in love stories, 50, 70, 72, 74, 77
Ch'ing-hua shu-chü, 52, 53, 93
Ch'ing-i pao, 130
Ching pao, 109, 110, 119–120
Ch'iu Chin, 58, 209
Chou En-lai, 237, 243
Chou Shao-heng, 44
Chou Shou-chüan, 15, 91, 148, 164, 166, 168, 173, 185, 263; career of, 117–118, 257–258, 259; *Diary of a Subjugated People* by, 174; family background of, 157; role at *Saturday,* 253
Chronicle of the Great Tears of Bygone Days (Hsu Chen-ya), 52–53, 254
Chronicle of the Strange Knights of Unflinching Loyalty (Hsiang K'ai-jan), 169
Chronicle of the Strange Roving Knights (Hsiang K'ai-jan), 22, 162, 237, 259
Ch'ü Ch'iu-pai, 18, 19, 185
Chung-hua Library, 93
Chung Hwa Book Company (Chung-hua shu-chü), 45, 88–89, 92, 93, 252
Chung-kuo pai-hua pao, 101–102
Chung-wai hsin pao, 96
Chung-wai jih-pao, 104, 105, 108
Chung-yang jih-pao, 119
Cities, compared to the countryside, 225–229
Civilization Book Company, 152
Civil service examinations, 4, 10, 82, 83, 194
Clarissa (Samuel Richardson), 56–57
Classical literary style, 59–60. *See also* Literary style
Class structure: access to the views in, 3–4, 5–6; in knight-errant stories, 37–38; lower classes in, 5–6, 19–20, 37–38; occupations in, 5. *See also* Middle class
"Coldheart, Mr.," 230–231
"Collected Fiction on the Brothels," 176
Color illustrations, 249
Comfort of readers. *See* Readership of popular fiction, psychological comfort of
Comic books, 12, 17–18
"Comic stories," 158. *See also* Humor
Commercialization: of entertainment fiction, 149–155; impact of, 11–13; of newspapers, 97, 103–104, 116, 150–152; and payment to authors by

Commercialization (cont'd)
    publishers, 152 – 155; of the printing
    industry, 84 – 95; and sale of books, 150
Commercial Press, 11, 89, 92, 93, 108,
    134, 160, 181, 251; influence and history
    of, 85 – 88; payment to authors by, 153,
    154
Communist Youth Leagues, 241, 243
Condescension: in idealized view of
    country life, 227 – 229; toward
    "new-style" women, 218
Confucianism, 56, 57; attitudes of
    fictional lovers toward, 67, 68 – 69; in
    family relationships, 201, 207; and
    female knights-errant, 213; suffering
    and death for, 234
Copyrights, 16, 51, 150
Cosmic order, 68
Count of Monte Cristo, The, 241, 242
Countryside, 2 – 3, 157; idealization of,
    225 – 229; popular attitudes toward,
    202 – 203, 225 – 229 passim
"Coward, The" (Chiang Hung-chiao),
    223 – 224
Creation Society, 168
Crystal, 119 – 123
Cultural Revolution, 236, 237, 240, 245,
    246; literary expression of, 243 – 244
Culture, and nationalism, 3

Dame aux Camélias, La, 54, 59, 136
Dating, modern-style, 24
Death: in love stories, 75 – 77; for
    patriotic love, 76 – 77
Destiny of Three Smiles, 60
Detachment of popular writers, 171 – 172
Detective stories, 22, 44, 140, 158 – 159;
    and degeneration of the "new fiction,"
    147; in magazines of the late 1970s, 260;
    narrators in, 48; translation of Western,
    129
Dialogue, 60, 61
Diamond, The, 123 – 124
Diary of a Subjugated People, 174
Dickens, Charles, 8, 135, 138
Disease, 74 – 75
Divorce Cases in Officialdom (T'ien Meng),
    222
Divorce, new-style, 222 – 225
"Doctor-writer," 158
Double Star, 255
Dream of the Red Chamber, 42, 49, 131, 138,

Dream of the Red Chamber (cont'd)
    164, 173, 186, 212, 232, 246; effect on
    readers, 131; influence of, 64; literary
    style of, 59 – 60
Dreams on the Ocean of Humanity (Yen
    Tu-ho), 216 – 217, 220

Eastern Times. See Shih pao
Editing, costs of, 90 – 91
Editors: female, 107, 171, 209, 251; salaries
    of, 154
Education: discussed in newspapers,
    107 – 108; "foreign schools," 192 – 194;
    "new-style," 126 – 127, 158, 164, 189;
    "new-style" schools, 10, 192 – 194;
    "novels," 153, 160, 182; physical, 158;
    textbooks for, 85 – 86, 88, 153; of
    women, 58, 194, 216 – 217, 220 – 221
Elements of People's Rights, 160, 166, 167;
    publication history of, 254
"Elements of People's Rights" group,
    166, 176
Elite, relations with successful authors,
    159 – 160
"Elite" fiction, 11
Emotions, caused by social change, 56
Emotions of readers: evocation of, 54; in
    fiction and in daily life, 187;
    magnification of, 131
English popular fiction, 8, 55, 129, 187,
    230; compared to Chinese urban
    popular fiction, 56 – 57; in newspapers,
    151
Enlightened Book Company, 251
Entertainment fiction: commercialization
    of, 149 – 155; and the degeneration of
    "new fiction," 146 – 149; demand for,
    167; "new fiction" influenced by,
    140 – 149; relationship with serious
    journalism, 144 – 145, 166; sheets of,
    141 – 142; types in periodicals, 143 – 144
Evergreen, 168
Evil, in love stories, 72
"Exposure literature," 244, 247
Eyebrow Signals, 171

Fallen Violet Petals, 91, 258
Families of authors, 156 – 157
Family values, 201
Fantastic Grievances of Nine Lives (Wu
    Wo-yao), 61, 147
Fan Yen-ch'iao, 148, 164, 168, 169, 263

Fate, in love stories, 72 – 73
Fate in Tears and Laughter (Chang
Hen-shui), 12 – 13, 15, 41, 57, 180, 236;
plot of, 34 – 35; role of old people in,
198 – 199; sequel of, 31 – 34; serialization
of, 31, 34, 117; summary of, 22 – 30
Female Knight of the Wild Rivers (Ku
Ming-tao), 14, 117, 171
Feng Meng-lung, 55
Feng Yü-ch'i, 15, 181
Ferguson, John C., 99
Fiction. *See* Entertainment fiction; "New
fiction"; Popular fiction
Fiction Pictorial, 19; publication history of,
256 – 257
Fiction Quarterly, 45, 255
Fiction Times, 90, 134; publication history
of, 249 – 250; serious satire in, 144 – 145
Fifties, The (Ch'en Ting-shan), 178
Flashback device, 49, 61 – 62
Flower on a Sea of Evil (Tseng P'u), 42, 94,
139, 149, 162
"Foreign schools," 192 – 194. *See also*
Education
Forest of Fiction, 134, 143, 162
"Four-six" style, 59 – 60, 63, 180
Freud, S., 77; theory of humor developed
by, 215 – 216
"From the Silent Region" (Tsung
Fu-hsien), 243

Gamble, William, 81
Gang of Four, 236; in modern popular
fiction, 243, 244
Gedanken experiments, 231
General Post Office, 240
Genius: "country bumpkin" style, 163;
and death, 76 – 77; and fiction for
readers' psychological comfort, 232;
"of the foreign mall," 161 – 162; of ideal
literary lovers, 66 – 67, 72 – 73; popular
attitudes on, 66 – 67, 72 – 73, 76 – 77,
161 – 162, 163, 173; and prostitutes, 173,
174
"Girl students," 216 – 217, 220 – 221, 222
Glamorous Trifles, 149
Grand Magazine, The, 90, 165; publication
history of, 255 – 256, 257
Great Eastern Book Company (Ta-tung
shu-chü), 89, 91, 92, 93, 176, 257,
258 – 259
Green Society, 168 – 169

Haggard, H. Rider, 8, 135, 138, 152
"Hand-copied volumes," 238, 242
Hang-chou pai-hua pao, 101
Hangchow, 157
Happiness, 168, 260
Happy endings, 53; of love stories, 62;
readers' demand for, 31
Hardy, Mary Duffus, 137
Hauser, Arnold, 63
Hell on Earth (Pi I-hung), 164
History of Late Ch'ing Fiction (Ch'ien
Hsing-ts'un), 135, 209
History of the Alleyways (Yeh Hsiao-feng),
161
Hoggart, Richard, 63, 187n
Ho Hai-ming, 168, 181, 264; career of, 160
Holmes, Sherlock. *See Adventures of
Sherlock Holmes*
Household Common Knowledge (Ch'en
Tieh-hsien), 159
Hsia Jui-fang, 86 – 87
Hsia, T. A., 37
Hsiang K'ai-jan, 18 – 19, 169, 177, 181, 185,
265; career of, 162 – 163; *Chronicle of the
Strange Roving Knights* by, 22, 162, 237,
259; pen name of, 162
Hsiao-hsien concept, and modern popular
fiction, 190, 197
Hsiao shih-min, 6, 189; described, 5,
189 – 192
Hsin pao, 98
Hsin shen pao, 114 – 115
Hsin-wen chih, 95 – 96
Hsin-wen pao, 12, 31, 91, 99, 100, 105, 106,
108; changes in, 103 – 104; circulation
of, 117; fiction column of, 118, 168, 170,
191; rivalry with other newspapers,
114 – 115
Hsu Chen-ya, 7, 93, 261; biography of,
44 – 48; career of, 254, 255; *Chronicle of
Great Tears of Bygone Days* by, 52 – 53,
254; group of authors associated with,
167, 176; *Jade Pear Spirit* by, 40 – 54,
56 – 57 (see also *Jade Pear Spirit*); literary
style of, 48 – 51, 179 – 180, 181; pen
names of, 44, 45, 46, 52n; salary of, 154
Hsu Cho-tai, 164, 168, 251, 264; career and
life of, 158, 163
Hsu Hsiao-t'ien, wife of, 171
Hsu Pi-po, 258
Hsu Yü, 189n
Hsun-huan jih-pao, 96

Hu Chi-ch'en, 166, 168, 172, 251; literary style of, 181
Hu Pin-hsia, 251
Hu Shih, 19, 213
Hu Yao-pang, 247
Hua pao, 81
Huan-chu lou-chu, 170. *See also* Li Shou-min
Huang Chin-jung, 121
Huang Po-hui, 116
Huang Shih-chung (Huang Hsiao-p'ei), 140
Huang Yuan-yung, 110, 114
Humor, 170–171; in literature on new social roles of women, 215–217
Huxley, Thomas, 127

Illiteracy, 192
Illness and disease, in love stories, 74–75
Imperial Post Office, 100
Incidental Notes of a Hunter (Hsiang K'ai-jan), 162
Industrial and Commercial Studies, 127
Industrialism, and sentimental fiction, 55
Industrial Revolution, 8; adaptation to, 127–128
Infant in the Entertainment Quarter (Pi I-hung), 175–176
Infatuation, 69
Informal History of Overseas Study in Japan (Hsiang K'ai-jan), 19
Informal History of Yen Shan (Ch'en Ch'iu), 59
International news in Chinese newspapers, 111–112
International popular fiction, 8–9; characteristics of, 185–189
Interviews, 64, 189, 195, 239n–241n
"Invalid of East Asia," 162. *See also* Tseng P'u

Jade Dragonfly, 60
Jade Pear Spirit (Hsu Chen-ya), 40–54, 56–57, 64, 69, 72, 76, 149, 191, 192; autobiographical nature of, 47–48; children and family relationships in, 200–202; compared to *Chronicle of the Great Tears of Bygone Days,* 52–53; compared to Samuel Richardson's *Clarissa,* 56–57; "countryside" in, 202–203, 228; literary style of, 179–180; narrator in, 48, 50;

Jade Pear Spirit (cont'd)
"new-style" education in, 221–222; "new-style" women in, 204–208; as a "protest" novel, 210–211; publication history of, 51–52, 166; role of old people in, 199; structure of, 49; testing of new-style ideas in, 231
Japan, 125; China attacked by, 22, 33; China occupied by, 118, 119; international wire service of, 112; "political novels" in, 130, 132; Shanghai attacked by, 123; "Twenty-one Demands" issued by, 159, 174
Japanese literature: and late Ch'ing fiction, 137; modern popular fiction in, 8–9; and translations of Western fiction, 8, 136–137
Jokes, 145–146, 171
Journalism, risks of, 157

Kao Chien-hua, 171
Keng Hsiao-ti, 22, 180
Knight-errant fiction, 25, 30, 138, 158, 162, 191, 203; authors of, 169–170; characteristics of, 38–39; female heroines of, 213–214; popularity of, 22; psychological comfort provided by, 20; value of, 14; view of the lower classes in, 37–38
Koestler, Arthur, 233
Ko Kung-chen, 115–116
Kuang-chih shu-chü, 88, 89
Kuang-i Book Co., 93
Ku Ming-tao, 124, 266; *Female Knight of the Wild Rivers* by, 14, 117, 171
Kuomintang, newspaper of, 111
Kuo Mo-jo, 17
Kuo-wen pao, 129
Kuroiwa Ruikō, 136–137

Laboring class, 5–6
Lao She, 36; *Camel Hsiang-tzu* by, 188–189
Late Ch'ing fiction: attitudes toward the West in, 137–138; cultivated images of writers of, 161–162; and development of popular fiction, 7, 133–140, 168, 232; role of translations in, 135–137, 138; types of, 138–140
Laughter: function of, 216; need for, 15. *See also* Humor
Lawyers, Western-style, 145, 222

League of Left-Wing Writers, 17
Leavis, Q. D., 187
Lee, Leo, 3, 42, 54, 138
Liang Ch'i-ch'ao, 100, 105, 128, 143, 203;
   modern fiction advocated by, 129 – 133,
   134, 140, 146, 150; payment received
   from publishers, 154; political ideas of,
   1, 129 – 133 *passim*
Libraries, 241
Li Han-ch'iu, 168, 250, 265; career of, 260;
   image of, 163; *Tides of Yangchow* by, 22,
   37, 163, 186, 200, 210, 215, 260
Li-hsueh i-pien, 100
Li Hung-chang, 94
Li Lieh-wen, 117 – 118
Li pao, 124
Li Po-yuan: entertainment sheet edited by,
   141; *Panorama of Officialdom* by, 138, 139,
   143
Li Shou-min, *Swordsmen of the Szechwan
   Hills* by, 16, 170
Li Ting-i, 7, 181, 262; *A Beauty's Blessing's*
   by, 41, 166, 167; fiction magazine edited
   by, 255
Life-styles of authors, 156 – 163
"Lines of sympathy," 63 – 64
Linked chapter style, 152, 178
Lin Pai-shui, 101
Lin Piao, 238
Lin Shu, 54, 59, 101, 152, 251; attitude
   toward the West, 138, 177; income from
   publishers, 153 – 154; translation
   method and style used by, 135 – 136;
   translations used by, 49, 61, 149
Lin Yü-t'ang, 15
Literacy, increase in, 10
Literary games, 170
Literary genius, 66, 161. *See also* Genius
"Literary man," image of, 161 – 162
Literary style, 9, 41; forms of, 59 – 60; of
   international modern popular fiction, 9,
   185 – 189; in the late 1970s fiction, 248;
   linked chapters in, 152, 178; in love
   stories, 48 – 51, 59 – 63; of old-school
   writers, 179 – 189; Western influences
   on, 61 – 62. *See also* "Four-six style";
   Vernacular
Literary Thrice Monthly, The, 17
"Literary wizard of the foreign mall," 134
Lithography, 81 – 83
Little Hsing Goes to School (Pao
   T'ien-hsiao), 182
Liu Huo-kung, 181

Liu O, 134, 138, 139
Liu T'ieh-leng, 45, 60
Liu Tsung-yuan, 171
Liu Yun-jo, 169
London Mission Society Press, 81, 86
London Times, 12
Lonely Mandarin Duck Talk, 176
Lonely Vessel on a Sea of Woe (Yao
   Yuan-ch'u), 174
Lone Swan, The (Su Man-shu), 42
Love, perfect, 70 – 71; symmetry of, 71;
   tragic aspect of, 72
Lovers, fictional: characteristics of,
   65 – 70, 76; purity and secrecy of,
   70 – 71; supersensitivity of, 68 – 70,
   73 – 74
Love stories, 9, 22, 40 – 78, 158, 168, 191;
   autobiography in, 47 – 48; effects of,
   167; endings of, 62, 75 – 77, 232 – 233;
   female readers of, 56 – 57; in late Ch'ing
   fiction, 139 – 140; in late 1970s popular
   fiction, 245 – 246; literary style of,
   48 – 51, 59 – 61, 71; male readership of,
   75; precedents of, 54, 60, 64, 148;
   sentimentalism in, 49 – 50, 51, 54, 55,
   63; summarized example of, 23 – 39
   passim; traditional symbols in, 7, 176;
   tragic, 50; triangular affairs in, 41 – 42;
   truth in, 48 – 49, 51. *See also* Romantic
   Route
Love, trap of, 72, 76
Lu Hsin-hua, Cultural Revolution in
   fiction by, 243 – 244
Lu Hsun, 17, 62, 181, 235; attitude toward
   Butterfly writers, 17; "castigatory
   novels" described by, 138 – 139; moral
   issues probed by, 188
Lu Shih-o, career of, 157 – 158
Lu T'an-an, 124

Machismo, 67
Magazines, 89 – 92, 249 – 260; circulation
   and costs of, 90 – 91, 189 – 190;
   commercialization of, 149, 150; edited
   by women, 171; fiction manuscripts
   solicited by, 153; group of authors
   associated with, 166 – 167; innovations
   in, 255 – 257; number of, 92; pictorial,
   81; public access to, 240; of the reform
   culture, 134; renting of, 241 – 242; types
   of stories in, 90; for and about women,
   58, 107, 146, 171, 218 – 220, 250 – 251
Magnificent Dreams in Shanghai (Sun

Magnificent Dreams (cont'd)
  Chia-chen), 54, 158
Major, Ernest, 96, 97, 101
Male readers of magazines about women,
  219
Manchuria, Japanese occupation of, 32, 33
Mandarin Duck and Butterfly School,
  7–23, 251; compared to Chinese
  popular fiction in 1979, 236–248;
  context in literary history, 7, 8, 9–10,
  134–140, 236–248; decline of, 14–15;
  definition and scope of, 7–8;
  disparagement of, 16–17, 59, 62–63,
  177; influence of commercialized media
  on, 11–14; literary style of, 41, 48–51,
  58–63; origins of term, 7, 176–177;
  quantity of, 15–16; transition from late
  Ch'ing fiction to, 134–140. *See also*
  Popular fiction
Mandarin Duck Blood, 176
Manuscripts: evaluation of, 171; payment
  for, 10, 13, 84, 152–153, 162
Mao Tse-tung, 1, 243, 247
Mao Tun, 7, 11, 15, 17, 62, 88
Marriage: arranged vs. free, 22, 204, 210,
  211, 212; of authors, 46–47; in the late
  1970s fiction, 246
Masses Drama Society, 158
Masses Publishing House, 237
Masses, the 1–2; access to the views of, 4,
  5–6; and readership of modern popular
  fiction, 191
May Fourth Movement, 2, 6, 7, 102,
  117–118, 136; defined, 6n
May Fourth Movement, writers of, 7, 11,
  15, 234; associations and societies of,
  168; attitudes on "new-style" women,
  216; attitudes toward Butterfly
  literature, 7, 17–18, 46, 51, 53–54, 59,
  62–63, 167, 177, 208; distinguished
  from "Butterfly" writers, 11, 178–179;
  literary style of, 19, 185; moral issues in
  fiction by, 187–189; national defense
  promoted by, 32; readership of, 11,
  18–20. *See also* "New fiction"
Medhurst, W. H., 81
Media, impact of new forms of, 11–14
Medicine, 157, 158; Western, 25, 231
Middle class, 5, 6; attitudes toward
  Westernization, 20
Min, developing importance of, 1–2
Min hu pao, 160
Min hsua, 1

Min-kuo jih-pao, 111
Min li pao, 1–2, 160
Min pao, 101
Missionaries, 101, 102; printing methods
  introduced by, 80–81; schools
  established by, 192
Modernization, 55, 57, 73, 79–80, 198;
  introduced by popular fiction, 21, 128;
  need for fiction stimulated by, 197–198
Monthly Fiction, 134, 143, 147
Moon on the Sea, 170
Moral issues in popular fiction, 187–188
Morrison, Robert, 80
"Mosquito press," 142n, 143, 151, 173;
  described, 118–124
Movies, 12, 48, 53–54, 239; American,
  247

Nanyang Academy, 126
Narrators: and flashbacks, 61; in love
  stories, 48–49
Nationalism: and development of Chinese
  modern popular fiction, 125–133;
  popular basis of, 1–3
New China Bookstore, 239, 240
"New fiction," 177, 187; degeneration of,
  147–149; distinguished from "old
  fiction," 132; growth in Shanghai,
  133–134; influence of entertainment
  fiction on, 140–149; moral issues in,
  187–188; and origins of modern
  popular fiction, 134–140, 141, 144–145;
  purpose of, 129–133. *See also* May
  Fourth Movement, writers of
New Fiction, 130, 134, 209; contents of,
  132, 143, 147, 150
New Fiction Journal, 255
New New Fiction, 160
News, incorporated in popular fiction,
  22, 180
Newspapers, 95–124; advertising in, 108;
  anti-Manchu, 160; circulation of,
  97–98, 99, 116–117, 151; competition
  among, 114–116; correspondents and
  reporters for, 106, 108–110;
  entertainment features of, 143–144;
  evening papers, 98–99; fiction
  columns in, 106–107, 117–118,
  150–151; "foreign flavor" of, 99, 103,
  115; foreign reporting in, 111–112;
  gossip columns and "mosquito" press,
  118–124; groups of authors associated
  with, 164–165; innovations and

Newspapers (cont'd)
diversity in, 104–112; *pai-hua,* 101–102, 107, 126, 127; political, 99–104, 113; prices of, 96, 99, 151; "revolutionary," 102–104, 113; role of women in, 107; sale increased by fiction in, 150–151; serialized fiction in, 12, 51, 151–152, 180, 190; transportation of, 98, 100. See also *Hsin-wen pao*; *Shen pao*; *Shih pao*
"Newspaper's rump," 144
Newsprint, 95, 104
"New-style": divorce, 222–225; education, 126–127, 158, 164, 189; schools, 10, 192–194
"New-style" vs. "old-style" behavior: balance and vicarious testing of, 21, 23–25, 230–231, 234; comfort from fiction about, 222–235; correlated with "Westernized" vs. "traditional," 177–179; evaluation of, 63, 73; in traditional morality, 199–200; by women, 23–25, 204–222 *passim,* 229–230
New Voices, 258
New Woman, 251
New Youth, 18, 177
Nieh-hai hua. See *Flower on a Sea of Evil*
North China Herald, 96, 98
Northern School, 169–170, 180
"Notes on the Sage's Palace," 121–123
Novels: "castigatory," 138–139, 143, 145–146, 157, 174, 222, 244; commercialization and sale of, 149–150; costs of, 83–84; "crazy quilt," 170; of ideals, 139; kinds of, 7; political, 130, 132; of "protest," 210–211; reform ethic and entertainment combined in, 146; renting of, 157; "social," 22, 37, 139, 161, 164, 174, 180; vernacular, 180

Occupations, 5
"Officers' roll call" game, 170
Old Lute Player (Ho Hai-ming), 160
Old people in popular fiction, 198–199
Opium, 162

Pa Chin, 15
Pai-hua newspapers, 101–102, 107, 126, 127
Panorama of Officialdom (Li Po-Yuan), 138, 139, 143

Pao T'ien-hsiao, 74, 90, 101, 105, 133, 158, 162, 168, 180, 195, 218, 262; career of, 181; "The Countryman Revisits Shanghai" by, 225–227; death of, 178; entertainment papers viewed by, 142; father of, 173; and *Fiction Times,* 249; group of authors associated with, 164–165, 255; income of, 152–153, 154; innovations in popular fiction by, 255–257; literary journalism of, 106–107, 117; literary style of, 182–184, 188; "mosquito" press interpreted by, 121–123; and "new-style" education, 126, 127; pen names of, 148; publishers viewed by, 150; role in education of women, 220–221; social contacts of, 159; translations by, 136–137
Paper: production of, 94–95; shortage and quotas of, 242
Pastime Monthly, 257
Patriotic heroism, 77, 78n
Patronage, 164–165
Payment: to authors, 51–52, 84, 87, 90, 152–155, 161, 162; to newspaper reporters, 108–109
Peasants, and nationalism, 2–3
Peking, 36; literary group in, 169; news reports from, 105–106, 109–111; Women's Normal College in, 181
Pen names: and literary games, 170; purpose of, 162, 163, 167
People's Journal, The, 1
People's Literature, 240
People's Literature Publishing House, 241
People's Rights Journal (Min-ch'üan pao), 45, 51, 93, 166–167, 254
People's Rights Publishing Section (Min-ch'üan ch'u-pan pu), 51, 93
People, the, importance of, 1–2
Photographs, in periodicals, 143–144, 146
Photogravure, 83, 85
Pickwick Papers, The (Charles Dickens), 12
Pi I-hung, 115, 117, 148, 168, 222; brothel literature by, 174–176; career at *Shih pao,* 164; "Children After Divorce" by, 224–225; father of, 157
Poetry, 173
Political fiction: and entertainment, 141; in the late 1970s, 243–245; role in the reform movement, 129–133
Political newspapers, 99–104, 113, 166
Popular attitudes: access to, 4, 5–7,

Popular attitudes (cont'd)
63 – 64, 196 – 197; on chastity, 57, 67,
69; on children, 200 – 201; on the
Chinese state, 129 – 133 *passim*; on
Confucianism, 68, 201, 207; on the
cosmic order, 68; on the countryside,
202 – 203, 225 – 229; on death, 75 – 76;
on disease, 74 – 75; on duty, 69, 202; on
elders, 198 – 199; on the family,
201 – 202; on fate, 72 – 73; on genius,
66 – 67, 72 – 73, 76 – 77, 161 – 162, 163,
173; on prostitution, 174 – 176; on
romance, 64 – 77; on the secular world,
69; and undermining of political
idealism, 140 – 149 *passim*. *See also* West,
the; Women, new social role of
Popular fiction: compared to elite fiction,
11; circulation of, 53, 64n, 90 – 91;
context in literary history, 7 – 8,
133 – 140; international characteristics
of, 8 – 9, 185 – 188; leaders of, 148;
literary style of, 179 – 189; moral
questions in, 187 – 189; political
function of, 129 – 133; readership of,
189 – 195; sad endings in, 232 – 234;
testing of "new-style" ideas in, 21 – 22,
230 – 231; types of, 9, 20, 22, 37 – 38,
40, 90, 138, 191
Popular fiction, genesis of: in the
degeneration of "new fiction,"
146 – 149; in late Ch'ing fiction,
134 – 140, 141; in the mixture of
entertainment and serious journalism,
144 – 145; in newspapers, 106 – 107,
117 – 118
Popular fiction, in the late 1970s,
236 – 248; access to, 239 – 242;
government restrictions on, 242 – 243,
247; literary style of, 248; love stories
in, 245 – 246; political influence on,
243 – 245; popularity waves in, 243;
renting of, 241 – 242; spy stories in, 237
Post offices, fiction distributed by,
240 – 241
Presbyterian Mission Press, 81
Printing industry, 80 – 95, 178, 232; and
color illustrations, 82, 115 – 116;
commercialization of, 84 – 95,
149 – 155; expansion of, 10, 92 – 93;
lithography, 81 – 83; magazines
published by, 89 – 92; paper for,
94 – 95; paper molds in, 83, 85;

Printing industry (cont'd)
revolving-cylinder printing machines
in, 114; small publishing houses,
93 – 94; technical advances in, 83, 87
Prostitutes, 140, 160; relations with
authors, 173 – 176
"Protest" novels, 210 – 211
Prusek, Jaroslav, 61
Psychological descriptions, 61
Publishers: book distribution by, 84 – 85,
commercial, 150 – 155; paper quotas, of,
242; and payment to authors, 51 – 52,
84, 152 – 155; production levels of,
11 – 12; small, 93 – 94

Reader-author relations, 7; and attitude of
detachment expressed by writers,
171 – 172; in autobiographical fiction,
48; contacts with the social elite,
159 – 161; emotional intensity of, 191; in
literary games and joking, 170 – 171; in
May Fourth fiction, 18 – 20; and
psychological comfort, 20 – 21; and
public images created by authors,
161 – 163, 173; and tragic love stories, 50
Readership of popular fiction, 189 – 195;
age of, 191, 192, 246 – 247; bourgeois
basis of, 55 – 58; economic factors in,
189 – 191; effect of literature on, 131 –
132; female, 56 – 57; literary standards
of, 63; and "new-style" schools,
192 – 194; psychology of, 6 – 7, and
reversal of readers' expectations, 30;
selection of story endings by, 62; sex of,
194 – 195; size of, 16; and social status,
20; urban basis of, 240
Readership of popular fiction, attitudes of:
identification with protagonists, 232,
233; observation of protagonists, 58,
232 – 233, 234
Readership of popular fiction,
psychological comfort of, 20 – 21,
196 – 235; in love stories, 73, 74; about
new-style divorce, 222 – 225; about
new-style women and their social roles,
204 – 210, 214 – 222; quest for, 172; in
sad endings, 232 – 234; in superior
attitudes toward rural life, 228 – 229;
and vicarious testing of new-style ideas,
231
"Record of the Sharp-Tongued Li
T'sui-lien," 212 – 213

Recreation, 141, 143

Recreation Magazine, 165; publication history of, 252–253

Recreation World, 258

Red Roses, 91, 259, 260

Reform movement, publications of, 100–102; fiction magazines, 134; humor and satire in, 144–146; political fiction in, 129–133; translations of Western fiction in, 129, 135–136; Western ideas discussed in, 128. *See also* "New fiction"

Reminiscences (Pao T'ien-hsiao), 182–184

Renting of popular fiction, 157, 241–242

Reporters for newspapers, 108–109

Reuters wire service, 112

"Revolutionary" newspapers, 102–104, 113

Richardson, Samuel, 55, 63, 195; *Clarissa* by, 56, 57

Rickshas: pullers of, 2; in Shanghai, 133–134

Romance of the Three Kingdoms, 60, 246

Romance of the Western Chamber, 60

Romantic Route, 64–78, 200, 232, 234, 236–237; and attitudes toward urban life, 229; characteristics of ideal fictional lovers in, 65–70; destruction and death in, 75–77; "falling in love" stage in, 70–72; fate in, 72–73; worry and illness in, 73–75

Salaries of fiction specialists, 154–155. *See also* Payment

San-yu shu-she, 93

Satire, 216–217, 229

Saturday, 21, 117, 161, 164, 167, 174; advertising slogan of, 171; popularity of, 166; publication history of, 253–254, 257, 258

"Saturday School," 166, 254

"Scandal novels," 20, 22, 37, 160, 169, 172, 180, 211

Scarlet Magazine, The, 91, 259

Scholars, The, 37, 132, 138, 211

Schoolmaster Ni Huan-chih (Yeh Sheng-t'ao), 166

Schools, new-style, 10, 192–194. *See also* Education

Science, 21, 139; in modern popular fiction, 236, 237; "novels" of, 139

Sea of Fiction, 255

Sea of Resentment (Wu Wo-yao), 132, 139–140, 147

Second Handshake, The (Chang Yang), 236–239, 245

Secular world, 69

Semi-Monthly, The, 257–258

Sensitivity of ideal literary lovers, 67, 68–70

Sentimentalism, 147; of authors, 172; in love stories, 49–50, 51, 54, 55, 63

Serialization of popular fiction, 31, 34, 51, 53, 91; literary style influenced by, 180; in newspapers, 12, 51, 151–152, 180, 190

Sex: and characteristics of ideal lovers, 66–67, 76; and patriotic heroism, 78n; of the readership of popular fiction, 57, 75, 194–195, 214, 219

Shanghai: beginnings of the modern newspaper press in, 95–124; compared to the countryside, 225–227; development of "new fiction," in, 133–144; disease in, 75; entertainment fiction from, 9 (*see also* Entertainment fiction); growth of, 4; modernization of, 55, 57, 73, 79–80, 198; printing industry in, 10, 80–95

Shanghai Competition Society, 252

Shanghai Library, 158

Shanghai Progressive Book Company, 147

Shao P'iao-p'ing, 109–110

Shen Chih-fang, 258

Shen-chou jih-pao, 113, 120

Shen pao, 81, 91, 95, 99, 100, 110, 119, 128, 129, 225; changes in, 103–104, 113, 114; circulation of, 97–98, 105, 108, 113, 116; "common knowledge" column of, 159; and development of modern popular fiction, 148; fiction columns of, 117–118; group of authors associated with, 165; and innovations in Chinese journalism, 104, 105, 106; origins and early format of, 96–97, 141; *pai-hua* supplement of, 101; salaries of staff at, 154; "Unfettered Talk" of, 12, 157, 159, 165, 252, 257; Western ideas and literature in, 128, 129

Sheng Hsuan-huai, 99

Shen Ts'ung-wen, 188, 229

Shen Yen-ping, 88, 252. *See also* Mao Tun

Shiba Shirō, *The Strange Encounters of Beauties* by, 130

Shih Chi-ch'ün, 258 – 259

Shih Liang-ts'ai, 114

Shih pao (Eastern Times), 93 – 94, 109, 110, 117, 128, 218; decline of, 114, 115 – 116; fiction columns and supplements in, 107, 117, 148, 150 – 151; fiction magazines initiated by, 249 – 250; group of authors associated with, 164, 165; innovations by, 104 – 108, 141, 148; "monarchist" reputation of, 105, 113; payment to contributors of, 154; "Resting Place" of, 114, 115, 121, 159 – 160; role in the development of popular fiction, 148, 150 – 151; theatre articles in, 158

Shih-shih hsin pao, 113, 115

Shih-wu pao, 100; contents of, 129, 130; detective stories introduced by, 143, 147

Short Story Monthly, 11, 87, 89, 134; publication history of, 251 – 252

Simmel, Georg, 10, 198, 230

Sincerity of ideal lovers, 67

Singing, and love stories, 60 – 61

Six Chapters on the Floating Life, 194

"Skating Love Song," 246

Smiles, Samuel, 128

Social change: adjustment to, 128, 230 – 231, 235; and bourgeois fiction, 55 – 58

Socialization, upward, 230

"Social novels," 22, 37, 139, 161, 164, 174, 180; scope of, 139

Social "problems," in love stories, 42, 62, 71

Soochow, 10, 98, 133, 156; decline of, 4; flower and goldfish exhibitions in, 172 – 173; magazines published in, 100; storytelling style of, 60; writers from, 169

Southern Society, 160; development of, 167 – 168; and *Woman's Magazine*, 251

Soviet Union, Chinese popular fiction influenced by, 237

Spencer, Herbert, 127

Spy stories, 237. *See also* Detective stories

Stage performances, 15, 53

Star Film Company, 53

Star Journal, 169

Star Society, 169, 222

"Story of a Laborer, The," (Yun T'ieh-ch'iao), 188, 189, 232

Storytellers, 152

Storytelling, of "great" and "small" stories, 60

Strange Encounters of Beauties, The (Shiba Shirō), 130

Strange Phenomena Viewed Over Twenty Years (Wu Wo-yao), 132, 138, 139, 147

Students, 125 – 126; female, 216 – 217, 220 – 221; in Japan, 162; in "new-style schools," 189

Su-chou pai-hua pao, 102

Su Man-shu, 42, 168, 174, 254

Summer Star Society, 93

Sun Chia-chen, 161; book company owned by, 158; *Magnificent Dreams in Shanghai* by, 54, 158

Su pao: entertainment features of, 143; legal case of, 102, 157; and "revolutionary" newspapers, 102 – 104

Surplus Chatter from a Tiny Window (Wang T'ao), 141

Swordsmen of the Szechwan Hills (Li Shou-min), 16, 170

Szechwan Study Journal, 125

Ta kung pao, 30, 109, 119; advice column in, 230 – 231

Talent. *See* Genius

Tale of a Broken Hairpin (Su Man-shu), 42

Tale of Heroic Young Lovers, 213

T'ang Ts'ai-ch'ang, 254

T'an-tz'u, 60 – 61, 254

T'ao Yuan-ming, 172

Teardrop Destiny (Ch'en Tieh-hsien), 41, 158

Telegraphic news reports, 110 – 111

"Tension-and-curtain" format, 151

Textbooks, 85 – 86, 88, 153

Thicket of Fiction, 45, 52, 53, 60, 154; publication history of, 254 – 255

This Person's Notes (Chang Hen-shui), 46

Three-day Crystal, 119 – 123

Ti Ch'u-ch'ing, 113, 116, 150; career of, 104 – 105, 249, 250

Tides of Yangchow (Li Han-ch'iu), 22, 37, 163, 186, 200, 210, 215, 260; humor in, 215; purpose of, 186

Tientsin, 10, 169

Ting Sung, 253

To-ch'ing temperament of literary lovers, 68 – 70, 74, 77, 199 – 200

Toothpowder, 159, 177

Tragic literary protagonists, 233 – 234

"Tragic love fiction," psychological comfort provided by, 20–21
Translations, 9, 13, 16, 60; centers for, 135; methods of, 135–137; payment of translators, 84; in reform journals, 129; selection of, 138. *See also* Lin Shu
Travels of Lao Ts'an (Liu O), 134, 138, 139
Treaty port protection, 103
Ts'ai-tzu, concept of, 161, 232. *See also* Genius
Ts'ao, Yü, 15
Tseng P'u (Tseng Meng-p'u), 94, 134; *Flower on a Sea of Evil* by, 41–42, 139, 149, 162; life-style of, 162
Tse-tsung Chow, 3
Tso-p'in (Literary Works), circulation of, 242
Tsou Jung, 103
Tsung Fu-hsien, 243
Tuberculosis, 74–75
Tung-hai, 44
T'ung hsueh pao, 126
Twain, Mark, *The Californian's Tale* by, 62
Tz'u Yuan, 87

United China Publication Company, 252
Unofficial History of Ch'un-ming (Chang Hen-shui), 169
Unofficial History of Overseas Study in Japan (Hsiang K'ai-jan), 162, 163
Unspeakable (Ch'en Shen-yen), 169
Urban: environments, 225–229; readership, 240

Verisimilitude: in love stories, 48–49, 51; in newspaper reporting, 97–98
Vernacular: literary style, 6, 59, 60, 152, 180; in May Fourth fiction, 19; plot of stories in, 31
Verne, Jules, 8
Violets, 91, 258

Wang Hsi-shen, new-style divorce viewed by, 223
Wang T'ao, 96; fiction by, 141
Wang Tu-lu, 169
Wang Tun-ken, 164, 168, 252, 254; career of, 165, 166
Wang Tzu-jen, 135–136
Wang Yun-chang, magazines edited by, 251

Wang Yun-wu, 88
Washington, George, 144–145, 150
Wasted Ink of Chen-ya (Hsu Chen-ya), 45
Water Margin, The, 60, 131, 138
Waves in popular fiction, 22, 40; in the late 1970s, 243; of love stories, 54–64
Weekends, 21
Weekly, 165; publication history of, 257
Weekly Flower, 253
"Weeper of pearls," 46
Wen-ming shu-chü, 88, 89, 92, 93
Wen-yen style in translations, 136
Westerners, Shanghai newspapers started by, 96
Westernization, 19–20, 25; and distinction between "Butterfly" and May Fourth writers, 177–179; humorous approach to understanding of, 144–145; in Shanghai, 133–134; stylishness of, 203; and traditional values, 198; and "testing function" of popular fiction, 21, 23–25, 231
Western literature: compared to Chinese modern popular fiction, 9, 11, 185, 186, 187; female readers and heroines compared to Chinese women, 56–57; readership in the late 1970s, 246–247; stylistic influence on Chinese fiction, 61–62; translations of, 60, 62, 128, 129, 132, 135–137
West, the, 8; and appeal of popular fiction, 229, 247; attitudes of late Ch'ing writers toward, 137–138; bourgeois sentimentalism in, 55, 56; discussed in reform journals, 128; and modernization, 198; and "new learning," 222; "new-style" behavior patterns of, 57; and "new-style" women, 216, 218
"What If I Were Real?," 244–245
Woman's Magazine, 250–251
Woman's World, 250
Women: beauty and genius of literary heroines, 66–67; in early journalism, 107; education of, 58, 194, 216–217, 220–221; fiction by, 171; heroines in knight-errant stories, 213–214; magazines for and about, 58, 107, 146, 171, 218–220, 250–251; magnolia and pear-type, 41–42, 204–205; and patriotic heroism, 78n; as readers and fictional protagonists, 56–57; and

Women (cont'd)
readership of Butterfly fiction, 195;
rights movement of, 195
Women, new social role of, 41 – 42,
57 – 58; contrasts in, 204 – 208; humor
in literature about, 215 – 217; liberation
in, 209 – 210, 218; "scope" of, 212 – 213,
215 – 216, 229 – 230
Women's Times, 218 – 220; publication
history of, 250
Wood-block printing, 80, 82, 85; for
magazines, 100
World Book Company (Shih-chieh
shu-chü), 89, 91, 92, 93; publications of,
258 – 260
World of Chinese Fiction, The, 45, 89, 252
World Detectives, 260
Worry, by fictional lovers, 73 – 74
"Wounded, The" (Lu Hsin-hua),
243 – 244
Wright, Mary, 113, 179
Writers' societies, 167 – 170. *See also*
Authors
"Writing of sentiment," 54, 147. *See also*
Sentimentalism
Wu Ching-tzu, *The Scholars* by, 37. See
also *Scholars, The*
Wu-hsi pai-hua pao, 101
Wu Shuang-je, 7, 44, 167, 261
Wu Tsu-hsiang, 188

Wu Wo-yao, 54, 161, 177; *Fantastic
Grievances of Nine Lives* by, 61, 147;
fiction by, 132, 138, 139 – 140, 147 – 148;
Monthly Fiction edited by, 134, 147; role
in transition from "new fiction" to
entertainment fiction, 147 – 148

Yangchow, social portrait of, 163. See also
Tides of Yangchow
Yao Su-feng, 165, 169
Yao Wen-yuan, 238
Yao Yuan-ch'u, 165, 168; *Lonely Vessel on a
Sea of Woe* by, 174
Yeh Ch'u-ts'ang, 161, 165. *See also* Yeh
Hsiao-feng
Yeh Hsiao-feng, 161, 165, 168
Yeh Ling-feng, 189n
Yeh Sheng-t'ao, 166
Yen Fu, 127; cultivated image of, 161 – 162
Yen Tu-ho, 91, 168, 264; career of, 191;
satire by, 216 – 217
Yu-cheng shu-chü, 93 – 94, 154, 249
Yü Ta-fu, 188
Yü Ta-hsiung, 120 – 121, 122 – 123
Yü Yu-jen, 1, 120
Yuan Shih-k'ai, 22, 110, 112, 140, 160; and
People's Rights Journal, 166 – 167
Yun T'ieh-ch'iao, 174, 252; "The Story of
a Laborer" by, 188, 189

Designer: Randall Goodall
Compositor: Viking Typographics
Printer: Thomson-Shore, Inc.
Binder: John H. Dekker and Sons
Text: VIP Bembo
Display: Phototypositor Arrighi
Paper: 55 lb. P&S Regular Offset, A-50